KANT'S HUMAN BEING

Kant's Human Being

ESSAYS ON HIS THEORY OF HUMAN NATURE

Robert B. Louden

UNIVERSITY PRESS

Oxford University Press is a department of the University of Oxford.
It furthers the University's objective of excellence in research, scholarship,
and education by publishing worldwide.

Oxford   New York
Auckland   Cape Town   Dar es Salaam   Hong Kong   Karachi
Kuala Lumpur   Madrid   Melbourne   Mexico City   Nairobi
New Delhi   Shanghai   Taipei   Toronto

With offices in
Argentina   Austria   Brazil   Chile   Czech Republic   France   Greece
Guatemala   Hungary   Italy   Japan   Poland   Portugal   Singapore
South Korea   Switzerland   Thailand   Turkey   Ukraine   Vietnam

Oxford is a registered trade mark of Oxford University Press
in the UK and certain other countries.

Published in the United States of America by
Oxford University Press
198 Madison Avenue, New York, NY 10016

© Oxford University Press 2011

First issued as an Oxford University Press paperback, 2014.

All rights reserved. No part of this publication may be reproduced, stored in a retrieval system,
or transmitted, in any form or by any means, without the prior permission in writing of
Oxford University Press, or as expressly permitted by law, by license, or under terms agreed
with the appropriate reproduction rights organization. Inquiries concerning reproduction outside
the scope of the above should be sent to the Rights Department, Oxford University Press,
at the address above.

You must not circulate this work in any other form
and you must impose this same condition on any acquirer.

Library of Congress Cataloging-in-Publication Data
Louden, Robert B., 1953–
Kant's human being : essays on his theory of human nature / Robert B. Louden.
 p.   cm.
Includes bibliographical references (p.   ) and index.
ISBN 978-0-19-976871-4 (hardcover); 978-0-19-935414-6 (paperback)
1. Kant, Immanuel, 1724-1804.   2. Human beings.
3. Philosophical anthropology.   I. Title.
B2798.L77 2011
128.092—dc22   2010045102

For my daughters, Elizabeth and Sarah
(who have also taught me about human nature)

Preface and Acknowledgments

THIS BOOK IS a collection of some of my essays on interrelated aspects of Kant's theory of human nature. With one exception, each of the essays was written after the publication my book *Kant's Impure Ethics: From Rational Beings to Human Beings* (Oxford University Press, 2000). In that book, I examined the underexplored second or impure part of his ethics, an empirical part which does not always fit easily with the better-known first or pure part, but one which Kant himself viewed as a necessary and important constituent of his project in practical philosophy. The essays included in the present volume continue and deepen avenues of exploration initiated in *Kant's Impure Ethics*—i.e., they explore different branches of his empirical work on human nature, with special reference to the connections between this body of work and his ethical theory.

This volume also includes one of my earliest Kant essays—"Kant's Virtue Ethics," first published in 1986, long before I started work on the *Kant's Impure Ethics* project. In hindsight, it is clear to me that my early attempts to make sense out of Kant's unorthodox theory of virtue were largely responsible for my later efforts to track his empirical work on human nature, and this is why I have chosen to include the early essay in the present volume. Behind, around, and in Kant's theory of virtue are many assumptions and commitments about the nature of human beings, but it took me longer to locate the latter.

In preparing the essays for republication in the present volume, I have (with two exceptions) made only minor stylistic revisions, partly in order to establish a uniform citation system and ensure consistency in style. (The two exceptions are chapters 3 and 11. In both cases, I have restored some deletions that were made in the first published versions. In chapter 11, I have also adopted a new title.) In rereading these essays, I was occasionally tempted to iron out some youthful indiscretions, but have refrained from doing so. As a result, there are a few inconsistencies in the text, but they are meant to indicate that I have changed my mind on a few issues over the years. There is also some occasional overlap in several of the essays, for which I beg the reader's indulgence.

Many different individuals, organizations, and institutions have helped to bring the following essays into existence—often by way of a generous invitation to contribute a piece on a specific Kantian theme for a conference, book, or special journal issue, but sometimes by way of extended conversation on issues of mutual interest and puzzlement. Heartfelt thanks to each of the following: Warner Wick, Jerry Schneewind, Mary Gregor, Otfried Höffe, Onora O'Neill, Ludwig Siep, Marcia Baron, Johns Hopkins University, the National Endowment for the Humanities, Manfred Kuehn, Heiner Klemme, Dieter Schönecker, Phillips-Universität Marburg, Deutsche Forschungsgemeinschaft, Thomas Pogge, Xu Xiangdong, Peking University, Jeanine Grenberg, Patrick Frierson, American Philosophical Association Pacific Division, Joshua Gert, Victoria Costa, Claudia Schmidt, Nancy Gish, Florida State University, North American Kant Society, Zeljko Loparic, Maria Borges, Brazilian Kant Society, Universidade Estadual de Campinas, Universidade Federal de Santa Catarina, Brian Jacobs, Patrick Kain, Graham Bird, Isabell Ward, United Kingdom Kant Society, University of Hertfordshire, Alix Cohen, University of Cambridge, Marquette University, Jens Timmermann, Andreas Vieth, Norbert Mertens, Alexander von Humboldt Foundation, Universität Münster, Sharon Anderson-Gold, Pablo Muchnik, Aarhus University, Anders Moe Rasmussen, Carsten Nielsen, Eduardo Mendieta, Stuart Elden, Durham University, Werner Stark, Eric Watkins, Joseph S. Wood, Steven M. Cahn; Richard L. Velkley, Susan Meld Shell, University of Leeds, American Philosophical Association Central Division, Peter Ohlin, and the staff at Oxford University Press.

Finally, I am very grateful to the original publishers for permission to reprint the following essays:

Chapter 1: "Kant's Virtue Ethics," *Philosophy* 61 (1986): 473–89. Reprinted by permission of Cambridge University Press.

Chapter 2: "Moral Strength: Virtue as a Duty to Oneself," in Heiner F. Klemme, Manfred Kuehn, and Dieter Schönecker, eds., *Moral Motivation: Kant und die Alternativen* (Hamburg: Felix Meiner, 2006), 79–95. Reprinted by permission of Felix Meiner Verlag. (Originally published in German as "Moralische Stärke: Tugend als eine Pflicht gegen sich selbst.")

Chapter 3: "Kantian Moral Humility: Between Aristotle and Paul," *Philosophy and Phenomenological Research* 75 (2007): 632–39. Reprinted by permission of Wiley-Blackwell.

Chapter 4: "'Firm as a Rock in Her Own Principles' (But Not Necessarily a Kantian)," *Social Theory and Practice* 33 (2007): 667–78. Reprinted by permission.

Chapter 5: "The Second Part of Morals," in Brian Jacobs and Patrick Kain, eds., *Essays on Kant's Anthropology* (Cambridge: Cambridge University Press, 2003), 60–84. Reprinted by permission of Cambridge University Press.

Chapter 6: "Applying Kant's Ethics: The Role of Anthropology," in Graham Bird, ed., *A Companion to Kant* (Malden, MA: Blackwell Publishing, 2006), 350–63. Reprinted by permission of Wiley-Blackwell.

Chapter 7: "Anthropology from a Kantian Point of View: Toward a Cosmopolitan Conception of Human Nature," *Studies in History and Philosophy of Science* 39 (2008): 515–22. Reprinted with permission from Elsevier.

Chapter 8: "Making the Law Visible: The Role of Examples in Kant's Ethics," in Jens Timmermann, ed., *Kant's Groundwork of the Metaphysics of Morals: A Critical Guide* (Cambridge: Cambridge University Press, 2009), 63–81. Reprinted by permission of Cambridge University Press.

Chapter 9: "Evil Everywhere: The Ordinariness of Kantian Radical Evil," in Sharon Anderson-Gold and Pablo Muchnik, eds., *Kant's Anatomy of Evil* (Cambridge: Cambridge University Press, 2010), 93–115. Reprinted by permission of Cambridge University Press.

Chapter 10: "'The Play of Nature': Human Beings in Kant's Geography," in Stuart Elden and Eduardo Mendieta, eds., *Reading Kant's Geography* (Albany: State University of New York Press, 2011). Reprinted by permission of SUNY Press.

Chapter 11: "Becoming Human: Kant and the Philosophy of Education," in Steven M. Cahn, ed., *Philosophy of Education: The Essential Texts* (New York: Routledge, 2009), 281–92. Reprinted by permission of Routledge. (Originally entitled "Afterword.")

Chapter 12: "National Character via the Beautiful and Sublime?" in Susan Meld Shell and Richard L. Velkley, eds., *Kant's "Observations" and "Remarks": A Critical Guide* (Cambridge: Cambridge University Press, 2012). Reprinted by permission of Cambridge University Press.

Contents

Note on Citations and Translations xiii
Introduction xvii

PART ONE | HUMAN VIRTUES
1. Kant's Virtue Ethics 3
2. Moral Strength: Virtue as a Duty to Oneself 16
3. Kantian Moral Humility: Between Aristotle and Paul 25
4. "Firm as a Rock in Her Own Principles": (But Not Necessarily a Kantian) 38

PART TWO | ANTHROPOLOGY AND ETHICS
5. The Second Part of Morals 49
6. Applying Kant's Ethics: The Role of Anthropology 65
7. Anthropology from a Kantian Point of View: Toward a Cosmopolitan Conception of Human Nature 78
8. Making the Law Visible: The Role of Examples in Kant's Ethics 91

PART THREE | EXTENSIONS OF ANTHROPOLOGY
9. Evil Everywhere: The Ordinariness of Kantian Radical Evil 107
10. "The Play of Nature": Human Beings in Kant's Geography 121
11. Becoming Human: Kant and the Philosophy of Education 136
12. National Character via the Beautiful and Sublime? 150

Notes 165
Bibliography 203
Index 217

Note on Citations and Translations

QUOTATIONS FROM KANT'S works are cited in the body of the text by volume and page number in *Kants gesammelte Schriften*, edited by the Royal Prussian (later German, then Berlin-Brandenburg) Academy of Sciences (Berlin: Georg Reimer, later Walter de Gruyter, 1900–), 29 vols., except for quotations from the *Critique of Pure Reason*, which are cited by the customary use of the pagination of its first (A) and second (B) editions. When available, I use—with occasional modifications—the English translations in *The Cambridge Edition of the Works of Immanuel Kant* (general editors Paul Guyer and Allen W. Wood; Cambridge: Cambridge University Press, 1992–), 16 vols. The traditional Academy volume and page numbers (and also the A and B pagination from the *Critique of Pure Reason*) are reprinted in the margins of most recent editions and translations of Kant's writings.

The following German shortened titles and abbreviations are used to refer to specific works of Kant:

Anfang	*Mutmaßlicher Anfang der Menschengeschichte* (*Conjectural Beginning of Human History*), 8: 107–23
Anth	*Anthropologie in pragmatischer Hinsicht* (*Anthropology from a Pragmatic Point of View*), 7: 117–333
Aufklärung	*Beantwortung der Frage: Was ist Aufklärung?* (*An Answer to the Question: What Is Enlightenment?*), 8: 33–42
Beob	*Beobachtungen über das Gefühl des Schönen und Erhabenen* (*Observations on the Feeling of the Beautiful and Sublime*), 2: 205–56
Ende	*Das Ende aller Dinge* (*The End of All Things*), 8: 325–39

Frieden	*Zum ewigen Frieden* (*Toward Perpetual Peace*), 8: 341–86
Gebrauch	*Über den Gebrauch teleologischer Principien in der Philosophie* (*On the Use of Teleological Principles in Philosophy*), 8: 157–84
Gemeinspruch	*Über den Gemeinspruch: Das mag in der Theorie richtig sein, taugt aber nicht für die Praxis* (*On the Common Saying: That May Be Correct in Theory, But It Is of No Use in Practice*), 8: 273–313
Geo	*Physische Geographie* (*Lectures on Physical Geography*), edited by Friedrich Theodor Rink, 9: 151–463
Gr	*Grundlegung zur Metaphysik der Sitten* (*Groundwork of the Metaphysics of Morals*), 4: 385–463
Idee	*Idee zu einer allgemeinen Geschichte in weltbürgerlicher Absicht* (*Idea for a Universal History with a Cosmopolitan Aim*), 8: 15–31
KpV	*Kritik der praktischen Vernunft* (*Critique of Practical Reason*), 5: 1–163
KrV	*Kritik der reinen Vernunft* (*Critique of Pure Reason*), references are to the standard A and B pagination of the first and second editions
KU	*Kritik der Urteilskraft* (*Critique of the Power of Judgment*), 5: 165–485
Logik	*Logik* (*Lectures on Logic*), edited by Gottlob Benjamin Jäsche, 9: 1–150
MAN	*Metaphysische Anfangsgründe der Naturwissenschaft* (*Metaphysical Foundations of Natural Science*), 4: 465–565
MdS	*Metaphysik der Sitten* (*Metaphysics of Morals*), 6: 203–493
Menschenrace	*Bestimmung des Begriffs einer Menschenrace* (*Determination of the Concept of a Human Race*), 8: 89–106
Nachricht	*Nachricht von der Einrichtung seiner Vorlesungen in dem Winterhalbjahre von 1765–1766* (*Immanuel Kant's Announcement of the Program of His Lectures for the Winter Semester of 1765–1766*), 2: 303–13
Naturgeschichte	*Allgemeine Naturgeschichte und Theorie des Himmels* (*Universal Natural History and Theory of the Heavens*), 1: 215–368
Päd	*Pädagogik* (*Lectures on Pedagogy*), edited by Friedrich Theodor Rink, 9: 437–99
Pro	*Prolegomena zu einer jeder künftigen Metaphysik die als Wissenschaft wird auftreten können* (*Prolegomena to Any Future Metaphysics That Will Be Able to Come Forward as Science*), 4: 253–383
Racen	*Von den verschieden Racen der Menschen* (*Of the Different Races of Human Beings*), 2: 427–43
Refl	*Reflexionen* (*Notes and Fragments*), 14–23, references are first to the Academy *Reflexion* number, followed by the Academy volume and page number
Rel	*Die Religion innerhalb der Grenzen der bloßen Vernunft* (*Religion within the Boundaries of Mere Reason*), 6: 1–202
Streit	*Streit der Fakultäten* (*Conflict of the Faculties*), 7: 1–116

Träume	*Träume eines Geistersehers, erläutert durch Träume der Metaphysik* (*Dreams of a Spirit-Seer Elucidated by Dreams of Metaphysics*), 2: 315–73

Other texts cited from the Academy edition—particularly lecture transcriptions—are referred to either by the name of the transcriber (e.g., *Collins*) or the traditional title (e.g., *Menschenkunde*), followed by volume and page number.

Introduction

"WHAT IS THE HUMAN BEING?"

KANT ASSERTS IN three different texts that the question "What is the human being?" is the most fundamental question in philosophy, one that encompasses all others (*Logik* 9: 25; cf. letter to Stäudlin of May 4, 1793, 11: 429; *Pölitz* 28: 533–34).[1] And he adds that the question is "answered by . . . *anthropology*" (9: 25), a subject on which he lectured annually beginning in 1772 and continuing up to his retirement from teaching in 1796. In 1798 he published *Anthropology from a Pragmatic Point of View*, a work that he modestly describes as "the present manual for my anthropology course" in a footnote at the end of the preface (7: 122n). So this particular text is the most obvious place to look for Kant's own answer to the question "What is the human being?" However, Kant's views about anthropology were far from static. Over the years, many different student and auditor transcriptions from his twenty-four-year cycle of classroom lectures on anthropology have also been published. The most substantial and authoritative collection of these lectures is in volume 25 of the German Academy edition of *Kants gesammelte Schriften*, translated excerpts of which are also included in a volume in *The Cambridge Edition of the Works of Immanuel Kant*.[2]

But finding Kant's answer to the question "What is the human being?" is not simply a matter of attending to his numerous lectures on anthropology, for several reasons. For instance, the anthropology lectures themselves are partly an outgrowth of his lectures on physical geography, which date back to 1756 and which Kant also revised regularly until his retirement from teaching in 1796.[3] In the introduction to the best-known version of these lectures, edited and published by his former student Friedrich Theodor

Rink in 1802, Kant describes geography and anthropology as two interconnected parts of a greater whole: "Experiences of *nature* and of the *human being* together make up *knowledge of the world*. We are taught *knowledge of the human being* by *anthropology*; we owe our *knowledge of nature* to *physical geography* or *description of the earth*" (9: 157; see also *Racen* 2: 443).

Kant's essays on the philosophy of history, written in the mid-1780s, comprise yet another important source for his answer to the question "What is the human being?" Kant holds that human beings (like other living creatures, and unlike machines) must be studied teleologically in terms of their natural purposes. In the *Critique of the Power of Judgment* (1790), he writes:

> an organized being is . . . not a mere machine, for that has only a *motive* power, while the organized being possess[es] in itself a *formative* power, and indeed one that it communicates to the matter, which does not have it (it organizes the latter): thus it has a self-propagating formative power, which cannot be explained through the capacity for movement alone (that is, mechanism).
>
> (5: 374, see also 398)

Strictly speaking, in Kant's view this assumption of natural purpose should be understood only as a heuristic device, but it is one that strongly influences his reflections on both history and human beings. A substantial portion of his answer to the question "What is the human being?" is concerned with what he calls the *Bestimmung* (vocation, destiny) of the human species. Our *Bestimmung* differs from that of other terrestrial creatures. And this future orientation or focus on where we as a species are headed is also a prominent feature in his writings on history, all of which seek to "discover an *aim of nature* in this nonsensical course of things human" (*Idee* 8: 18).

Kant's writings on education constitute another principal source for his answer to the question "What is the human being?" "The human being is the only creature that must be educated," he announces in the opening sentence of his *Lectures on Pedagogy* (1803); "the human being can only become human through education" (9: 441, 443).[4] Other creatures are able to use their natural predispositions more or less instinctively; we alone require extensive help from others in order to employ ours effectively.

But while geography, history, education, and above all anthropology are certainly among the most significant Kantian sources for locating his answer to the question "What is the human being?" his remarks in these four groups of texts by no means constitute his complete answer. Reflection on human nature is the most pervasive and persistent theme in all of Kant's writings, and as a result it is no exaggeration to say that *all* of his works are relevant to this question. But as we will see shortly, it is also no exaggeration to say that Kant's answer to the question "What is the human being?" ultimately remains somewhat tentative. He offers no complete or final answer to the question, because he does not think that it is possible to do so.

RUDIMENTS OF KANT'S THEORY OF HUMAN NATURE

Each of the essays in this volume deals with one or another specific aspect of Kant's theory of human nature. Before proceeding, readers may find it helpful to first orient themselves by surveying the broader outlines of his account of human nature, and noting how his account differs from competing views. As Kant puts it, "he who wants to derive benefit from his journey must draw up a plan in advance" (*Geo* 9: 157). Without some preparatory orientation, any knowledge gained from a journey is likely to "yield nothing more than fragmentary groping around and no science" (*Anth* 7: 120).

First, Kant definitely subscribes to the view that there *is* a human nature—a set of common characteristics shared by all normal members of the human species in different times and places. This core commitment puts him in opposition to those who, like Sartre, assert that "there is no human nature. . . . Man is nothing but that which he makes of himself."[5] However, as we will see later, the distance between Kant and Sartre on this particular point is not as great as Sartre implies. In their reflections on human beings, both thinkers place a strong emphasis on our capacity for free choice. On Kant's account as well as Sartre's, man "has a character, which he himself creates [*den er sich selbst schafft*]" (*Anth* 7: 321), and Kant specifically differentiates his own pragmatic anthropology from competing "physiological" ones that view human beings as causally determined entities when he states that pragmatic anthropology concerns the investigation of what the human being "as a free-acting being makes of himself, or can and should make of himself" (7: 119).

Kant's commitment to the existence of a human nature also puts him in opposition to historicists, such as Foucault, who hold that "man is an invention of recent date."[6] On Kant's view, human beings have existed for a very long time. Nevertheless, his theory of human nature is certainly not ahistorical. He acknowledges that human life has changed profoundly over the course of centuries, but he also holds that a correct account of human nature is one that includes the conceptual resources to enable us to understand why change has occurred.

Insofar as Kant subscribes to "a context-independent concept of 'Human Nature,'" he is also at odds with "the relativist bent" that is "in some sense implicit in the field [of post-Kantian anthropology] as such."[7] Anthropology as Kant conceives it should be "general" rather than "local": "In it one comes to know not the state of human beings but rather the nature of humanity, for the local properties of human beings always change, but the nature of humanity does not. . . . Anthropology is not a description of human beings, but of human nature" (*Friedländer* 25: 471).[8]

Humans and Nonterrestrial Rational Beings. While Kant is firmly convinced both that there is a human nature and that it is anthropology's job to inform us about this nature, he also believes—somewhat paradoxically—that it is impossible to state definitively what this nature consists in. His main reason for holding the latter view is that in order to know what (if anything) is unique to our species we would need to compare ourselves with other species of rational beings, and we humans have not (yet) encountered any nonhuman rational beings. As he states toward the end of *Anthropology from a Pragmatic Point of View*:

> It seems therefore that the problem of indicating the character of the human species is absolutely insoluble [*schlecterdings unauflöslich*], because the solution would have to be made through experience by means of the comparison of two *species* of rational being, but experience does not offer us this.
>
> (7: 321)

In the *Critique of Pure Reason*, Kant states confidently that he is "ready to bet everything [*alles*]" (A 825/B 853) he has in defense of the proposition that intelligent life does exist on other planets, and in his early work *Universal Natural History and Theory of the Heavens* (1755) he announces that "most of the planets are certainly inhabited [*gewiß bewohnt*]" (1: 354) and that "human nature . . . occupies exactly the middle rung" on the ladder between "the most sublime classes of rational creatures," who inhabit Jupiter and Saturn, and the less intelligent ones, who live on Venus and Mercury (1: 359). So it is clear that Kant, like "many eminent philosophers—among others Aristotle, Nicolas of Cusa, Giordano Bruno, Gassendi, Locke, Lambert, . . . and William Whewell—believed that there is extraterrestrial life."[9] But in his more empirically sober anthropological writings he acknowledges that we have no reliable evidence for this claim. Nevertheless, the fact that Kant clearly does believe in intelligent extraterrestrial life also indicates that he does not subscribe to "the fantasy of human exceptionalism,"[10] a fantasy allegedly fueled by our own narcissism. Kant is not in humanist despair over giving up "the specialness of being human"[11] because he does not think we humans know for sure that we are special. There may be others out there like us.

At one point Kant briefly compares humans with "the idea of possible rational beings on earth in general," conjecturing that what distinguishes the human species is "that nature has planted in it the seed [*Keim*] of *discord*, and has willed that its own reason bring *concord* out of this, or at least a constant approximation" (*Anth* 7: 322, see also 331). This is an allusion to what he elsewhere refers to as humanity's "unsociable sociability" (*Idee* 8: 20)—our bidirectional propensity both to associate with others (sociability) and to compete and fight against each other (unsociability). Kant seems to think that the implanted seed of discord distinguishes humans from other rational beings, but (again) strictly speaking this is speculation on his part. There may also be other rational beings that relate to each other in a similar manner.

Humans and Terrestrial Beings. A definitive statement concerning what is unique about human nature is not possible, in part because we lack empirical evidence of the specific natures of other rational beings. But we can at least compare humans to other terrestrial beings, noting their similarities and differences. Broadly speaking, Kant's comparison of humans to animals is naturalistic and biologically based. Indeed, I am not sure that he would quarrel with E. O. Wilson's pronouncement (issued as a challenge to traditional humanists and social scientists) that "biology is the key to human nature, and social scientists cannot afford to ignore its rapidly tightening principles"[12]—with the caveat that Kant's biology is fundamentally different from Wilson's. Kantian biology is teleological and (when applied to human beings) carries a strong presumption of free choice, whereas Wilson's is mechanistic and deterministic throughout.[13] Also (in part as a result of the former), while Wilson and other contemporary biology-oriented theorists of human nature tend to see only continuities between humans and other animals,[14] Kant does see some fundamental discontinuities. Kant is primarily interested in what human beings can make of themselves, given their natural predispositions (*Anlagen*). On his view, the nature of each species is explainable by reference to its own unique set of predispositions. As he notes in *On the Use of Teleological Principles in Philosophy* (1788): "I myself derive all organization from *organic beings* (through generation) and all later forms (of this kind of natural things) from laws of the gradual development of *original predispositions* [*ursprüngliche Anlagen*], which were to be found in the organization of its phylum" (8: 179). Kantian *Anlagen* are inheritable tendencies passed on to each individual member of a species through reproduction.

In comparing humans to other animals, Kant sees the following basic differences:

Rationality. Humans, he believes, are the only rational terrestrial beings. But two points about his ascription of rationality to humans are worth noting. First, he puts a slight twist on the traditional definition of man as an *animal rationale*. The human being, on Kant's view, is "an animal endowed with the capacity of reason (*animal rationabile*)," and thus "can make out of himself [*aus sich selbst . . . machen kann*] a *rational animal* (*animal rationale*)" (*Anth* 7: 321). Humans have the ability to become rational animals if they exercise their capacities appropriately, but they are not automatically or necessarily rational. As Allen Wood notes: "Human beings are capable of directing their lives rationally, but it is not especially characteristic of them to exercise this capacity successfully. Rather, rationality must be viewed as a *problem* set for human beings by their nature."[15] In characterizing human beings' relationship to rationality in this more qualified manner, Kant adds a further tentative note to his account of human nature. Humans are not inherently rational, but they have the capacity to become rational. And some of us may succeed more than others. Second, what Kant means by "rationality" in this context is not instrumental rationality (choosing efficient means toward goals or ends that one desires) but substantive rationality (deliberating about and freely determining one's ends). An animal that strategizes about how to satisfy its hunger exhibits instrumental rationality; an animal that reflects on and then renounces its hunger (say, in protest over an injustice) exhibits substantive rationality. Kant grants that animals have instrumental rationality—like humans, "animals also act in accordance with *representations* (and are not, as Descartes would have it, machines)" (*KU* 5: 464n; cf. *Pölitz* 28: 274). Animals have desires, and many of them think about how to realize their desires. But Kant also holds that only humans—at least among the class of terrestrial beings—have substantive rationality: "in order to assign the human being his class in the system of animal nature, nothing remains for us than to say that he has a character, which he himself creates, insofar as he is capable of perfecting himself according to ends that he himself adopts" (*Anth* 7: 321). In emphasizing human beings' capacity to pursue ends of their own choosing (substantive rationality), Kant adds yet another tentative note to his account of human nature. Because humans can freely choose their own ends rather than simply pursue the goals that they instinctively desire, their mode of life is radically indeterminate—open rather than fixed.

Freedom. Closely related to Kant's ascription of substantive rationality to humans is his position on human freedom. On his account, a crucial turning point in human development occurred when our distant ancestors first became aware of their capacity to make free choices. At some point in the distant past, the human being "discovered in himself a faculty of choosing for himself a way of living and not being bound to a single one, as other animals are." At this juncture the human being "stood, as it were, on the brink of an abyss; for instead of the single objects of his desire to which instinct had up to now directed him, there opened up an infinity of them" (*Anfang* 8: 112). Here as well, indeterminacy is injected into his account of human nature. Like the great Renaissance humanist philosopher Giovanni Pico della Mirandola, Kant views human beings as chameleons—creatures with a self-transforming nature who, in virtue of their capacity of free choice, can fashion themselves in whatever shapes they may prefer.[16]

Culture, Civilization, Morality. Human beings' interrelated capacities to determine their own ends and to make free choices among equally compelling alternatives in turn contribute to several additional differences between humans and other animals. In his famous summary of pragmatic anthropology "in respect to the vocation [*Bestimmung*] of the human being and the characteristic of his formation," Kant writes: "The human being is destined by his reason [*durch seine Vernunft bestimmt*] to live in a society with human beings and in it to *cultivate* himself, to *civilize* himself, and to *moralize* himself by means of the arts and sciences" (*Anth* 7: 324). Kant has been repeatedly challenged on two of these claims (viz., culture and morality), but once the competing definitions of "culture" and "morality" employed by each side are factored into the dispute, it is far from clear that he has been refuted.

For instance, in a frequently cited article entitled "Cultures in Chimpanzees" published in *Nature* in 1999, the nine co-authors describe "39 different behavior patterns, including tool usage, grooming, and courtship behaviours [that] are customary or habitual in some [chimpanzee] communities but are absent in others where ecological explanations have been discounted,"[17] all of which in their view provide ample support for the claim that chimpanzees have culture. A few weeks after the article appeared, Stephen Jay Gould published an op-ed column in the *New York Times*, asserting that the study "published in . . . *Nature* proves the existence of complex cultures in chimpanzees," and that one more "favored candidate for a 'golden barrier' to separate humans from animals" had been decisively refuted.[18] Kant, while explicitly acknowledging that the chimpanzee "has many similarities with the human being" (*Geo* 9: 337; cf. *Holstein* 26: 126), also defines "culture" tersely as "the production of the aptitude of a rational being for ends in general (thus those of his freedom)" (*KU* 5: 431). According to this definition, only creatures that have the capacity to set ends for themselves and to freely choose from among these ends can be said to have culture. By contrast, the conception of culture employed by the authors of the article in *Nature* is a minimalist one that makes no reference to substantive rationality or free choice. Rather, "a cultural behaviour is one that is transmitted repeatedly through social or observational learning to become a population-level characteristic."¹⁹ According to the latter definition, any behavior that is not merely instinctual or caused by external environmental factors counts as cultural, while on Kant's view it counts as cultural only if (in addition to not being merely instinctual or ecological) it involves (at least at its inception) both substantive rationality and free choice. One prominent example discussed by both parties in this dispute is dialects in songbirds. Because these phenomena are maintained by "social transmission mechanisms," they count as cultural according to the definition employed in the *Nature* article. Kant readily agrees with the nine co-authors and allows that such birds "do not sing by instinct, but actually learn [*wirklich lernen*]" (*Päd* 9: 443) to do so from their parents. One bird imparts the song to another "through instruction [*durch Belehrung*] (like a tradition)" (*Anth* 7: 323n). Nevertheless, such behavior does not count as cultural according to his definition, since it occurs in the absence of substantive rationality and free choice.²⁰

An additional fundamental disagreement concerning what counts as cultural is that culture on Kant's view is cumulative or progressive, whereas the minimalist definitions of culture favored by primatologists make no reference to this feature. On Kant's view, nature's plan is "to bring about the perfection of the human being through progressive culture" (*Anth* 7: 322). In order to carry out this plan, nature "needs an immense series of generations, each of which transmits its enlightenment to the next, in order finally to propel its germs in our species to that stage of development which is completely suited to its aim" (*Idee* 8: 19). Culture in Kant's sense is not merely behavior that is transmitted via social mechanisms, but substantively rational and freely chosen activity that can be improved upon by later generations. And here he sees another clear difference between humans and other animals:

> [W]ith all other animals left to themselves, each individual reaches its complete destiny [*seine ganze Bestimmung erreicht*]; however, with the human being only the species, at best, reaches it; so that the human race can work its way up to its destiny only through progress in a series of innumerably many generations.
> (*Anth* 7: 324, cf. 329; *Menschenkunde* 25: 1196; *Mrongovius* 25: 1417)

The claim that culture is cumulative is most frequently associated with Michael Tomasello's idea of "the ratchet effect." On Tomasello's view, while we do find some components of culture present among nonhuman animals, the crucial ratchet effect is absent:

> Many nonhuman primate individuals regularly produce intelligent behavioral innovations and novelties, but then their group mates do not engage in the kinds of social learning that would enable, over time, the cultural ratchet to do its work.... The basic fact is thus that human beings are able to pool their cognitive resources in ways that animal species are not.²¹

Insofar as Tomasello sees no evidence of cumulative culture in nonhuman animal social life, his position is quite Kantian. But it should also be noted that his notion of the ratchet effect contains far stronger assumptions than Kant's Enlightenment idea of cultural progress. The internal machinery of a ratchet is designed to allow motion only in an upward direction. When we carry this part of Tomasello's metaphor over to culture, the implication is that human cultural progress is both unilinear and causally determined. But on Kant's view, humans are by no means causally determined to achieve unilinear cultural progress. Rather, we pursue cultural progress as free beings who can and do change our minds. Therefore, both cultural regress and nonlinear cultural change are always possibilities. As he notes in the *Conflict of the Faculties* (1798):

> [N]o one can guarantee that now, this very moment, with regard to the physical disposition of our species, the epoch of its decline would not be liable to occur.... For we are dealing with beings that act freely, to whom, it is true, what they *ought* to do may be *dictated* in advance, but of whom it may not be *predicted* what they *will* do.
>
> (7: 83)

When Kant's strong underlying commitment to human freedom is kept in mind, the resulting picture is that culture on his view is a product of rational agency that is potentially (but not necessarily) cumulative.

Kant's attribution of a predisposition to morality in the human species (and his denial that we find this predisposition in other animal species) has also been repeatedly challenged by Darwinian theorists of human nature. But here as well, once one takes into account the competing definitions of "morality" employed by each side in the debate, the actual extent of the disagreement may be smaller than first assumed.

Those who hold that nonhuman animals have morality typically define "morality" as "a suite of interrelated other-regarding behaviors that cultivate and regulate complex interactions within social groups.... Morality is an essentially social phenomenon."[22] According to this conception, morality is a group-oriented phenomenon born out of mutual dependence that is exclusively other-regarding. As Frans de Waal writes: "A solitary person would have no need for morality, nor would a person who lives with others without mutual dependency."[23] In addition to this exclusively other-regarding focus, a second core assumption in the moral conceptions of those who attribute morality to nonhuman animals is that morality is primarily concerned with instincts and emotions rather than rationality and principles. Morality is "a direct outgrowth of the social instincts that we share with other animals.... [It] is neither unique to us nor a conscious decision taken at a specific point in time: it is the product of social evolution."[24]

Kant would not deny that other-regarding instincts (e.g., helping and caring behavior, empathy, and benevolence) are important building blocks for morality. But when he attributes a moral predisposition to the human being and denies that one is present in other living inhabitants of the earth, he refers not to these phenomena but rather to "a being endowed with the power of practical reason and consciousness of freedom of his power of choice" (*Anth* 7: 324). The realization on our distant ancestors' part that they possessed these specific capacities for "normative self-government"[25] is what marks the real beginning of morality on Kant's view—a beginning that marks a break rather than a continuity between humans and other animals. *When* exactly this happened seems fated to remain a matter of conjecture, but its occurrence marked a decisive turning point in human history (see also *Idee* 8: 112).

In his *Anthropology* and elsewhere, Kant also briefly discusses what he believes are several additional differences between humans and other animal species, which I turn to now. However, I believe the following alleged differences are best viewed as corollaries of the core capacities of rationality and free choice and/or as alternative ways of describing the other human predispositions discussed above.

Preservation, Education, Governance. For instance, after contrasting human beings' capacity to become rational beings with the lack of this capacity in other inhabitants of the earth, Kant distinguishes three tasks of human reason (*Anth* 7: 321–22). The first task, preservation, concerns the art of survival. Other terrestrial animals seem to master this art by instinct, but human beings "must invent their own relationship to nature, and Kant is struck by the wide variety of such relationships human beings have adopted in different climates and situations on the earth's surface."[26] In pursuing the art of survival, human beings also exercise their capacities of reason and freedom. Reason's second task is education. As noted earlier, Kant is convinced that (at least among the living inhabitants of the earth) "the human being is the only creature that must be educated" (*Päd* 9: 441). The radical indeterminacy of our nature entails the necessity of education. In order to develop our predispositions appropriately, we need extensive and prolonged help from others. However, culture (see above) and education for Kant are overlapping tasks. In his *Lectures on Pedagogy* he states: "The human being must be *cultivated*. Culture includes instruction and teaching. It is the procurement of skillfulness. The latter is the possession of a faculty which is sufficient for the carrying out of whatever purpose" (9: 449, see also 441). Third, in virtue of their capacity for reason, humans also have the task of governing themselves "as a systematic whole (arranged according to principles of reason)" (*Anth* 7: 322). Here there is a parallel to Aristotle: "the human being is by nature a political animal," and it is in virtue of his capacity for *logos* that he is a political animal (*Politics* I.2 1253a2–3, 9–10). But for Aristotle the ideal size of a human political entity is a *polis* that is not too small to be self-sufficient but also not too large to be "readily surveyable" (VII.4 1326b24)—perhaps 5,000–10,000 citizens. For "it is difficult—perhaps impossible—for a city that is too populous [*lian poluanthrōpon*] to be well governed" (VII.4 1326a26–27). Kant, on the other hand, like many other Enlightenment intellectuals, supports a version of the *cosmopolis* (in his case, a worldwide federation of sovereign states dedicated to peace). For instance, in the final sentence of the *Anthropology*, he expresses his hope for an eventual "progressive organization of citizens of the earth" into a system that is "cosmopolitically united" (7: 333; cf. *Frieden* 8: 341–86).

Technical, Pragmatic, and Moral Predispositions. Similarly, a bit later in the *Anthropology* Kant declares that human beings are "markedly distinguished [*kenntlich unterschieden*]" from all other inhabitants of the earth by their technical, pragmatic, and moral predispositions (7: 322). By "technical predisposition" Kant refers to our ability to devise appropriate means to achieve our freely chosen ends, and so this predisposition overlaps somewhat with our earlier discussions of rationality and culture. But here

Kant also draws special attention to the remarkable dexterity of human hands and fingers as a concrete expression of our freedom: "by this means nature has made the human being not suited for one way of manipulating things but underdetermined for every way [*unbestimmt für alle*], consequently suited for the use of reason" (7: 323). The pragmatic disposition occupies a special place in Kant's account of human nature, given his own advocacy of an anthropology conducted "from a pragmatic point of view."[27] But in his discussion of this predisposition toward the end of the *Anthropology*, he stresses that it refers to the human being's capacity "to use other human beings skillfully for his purposes" and "to become civilized through culture" (7: 322, 323). And so it overlaps with the human capacities for civilization and culture discussed earlier. The human species' moral predisposition was also discussed earlier.

Humanity, Personality. Finally, in *Religion within the Boundaries of Mere Reason* (1793) Kant briefly discusses two additional predispositions that he believes are present in humans and absent in other terrestrial animal species—humanity and personality. Some commentators argue that the predisposition to humanity described in *Religion* is identical to the pragmatic predisposition discussed in the *Anthropology*; others hold that it encompasses both the pragmatic and technical predispositions.[28] My own view is that the *Religion* and *Anthropology* accounts of the human species' predispositions stand in an ambiguous relationship with one another. In *Religion* Kant describes the predisposition to humanity as a capacity that the human being has "as a living and at the same time *rational* being" (6: 26), and the key reference to "rational" suggests that what he primarily has in mind here is the human being's ability to deliberate about, and to freely choose, his own ends. In describing the predisposition to personality in *Religion* he says that it is a quality the human being has "as a rational and at the same time *responsible* being" (6: 26). So the discussion here presupposes the capacities for rationality, freedom, and morality discussed earlier.

The above list of (what Kant believes to be) distinctive human features is not intended to be exhaustive,[29] but it does include his major commitments and should serve as a useful outline and orientation for approaching the essays in this volume. We can summarize the main points in the above discussion by noting that Kant's theory of human nature is provisional in both its conception and presentation; that his commitment to the possibility of rational life on other planets means that he is not a defender of human exceptionalism; that he believes there is a uniform human nature but that its core feature of free choice means that humanity's nature is marked by radical indeterminacy; that his conception of human nature, while neither historicist nor relativist, also emphasizes historical development and cultural variation; and that he believes a systematic and comparative biological examination of human and other terrestrial animal species reveals both continuities and profound differences.

Virtues, Anthropology, and Beyond

As noted earlier, all of the essays in this volume, with one exception, were written after my book *Kant's Impure Ethics: From Rational Beings to Human Beings* (2000). The exception is chapter 1 ("Kant's Virtue Ethics"), one of my first publications (1986), and still one of my most successful Kant essays. In looking back, I can see now that my early work on the neglected role of virtue in Kant's ethics was largely responsible for leading me into later investigations into Kant's theory of human nature. But this perceived connection between virtue and human nature is not merely a hope on my own part to find "a guiding thread for exhibiting an otherwise planless *aggregate*" (*Idee* 8: 29) of essays as a systematic whole. On Kant's view, "all the moral perfection that a human being can attain is still only virtue" (*KpV* 5: 128, see also 84; *MdS* 6: 383). In other words, his particular theory of virtue is in effect a theory of morality designed to fit (what he believes are) the specific conditions of human beings (as opposed to the conditions of other types of rational beings). Kant arrives at his theory of virtue only after first settling on the parameters of his theory of human nature.

At the suggestion of one of the external readers of this manuscript selected by Oxford University Press, I have added a new prefatory note (marked by an asterisk) to each of the essays, explaining how it arose, what major themes it addresses, and how it fits in with the other essays in the volume. Readers who desire more specific information of this sort are encouraged to consult these new notes.

The essays are organized into three different groups, and in closing I would like to say a few words about the book's tripartite structure.

Human Virtues. Part I consists of four essays, each dealing with different aspects of the nature and role of virtue in Kant's normative ethical theory. For many years I have argued that virtue occupies a greater space within Kant's ethics than is commonly acknowledged. But as I learned more about his theory of human nature, I also began to realize that some of his views about human beings were at variance with other conceptions of human nature (particularly Aristotelian) that more typically influence both classical and contemporary virtue ethics programs. For instance (and this is perhaps the most prominent example), Kant believes there exists a universal propensity to evil within human nature; Aristotelian virtue ethicists clearly do not. The result, or so I argue, is a virtue ethics, but one that differs in certain fundamental ways from the more familiar virtue ethics projects. Viewed as a whole, the essays in part I track my ongoing efforts both to make sense of the very idea of a Kantian virtue ethics as well as to show how it differs from other virtue ethics programs.

Anthropology and Ethics. The essays in part II of this collection represent the core of my work on Kant's theory of human nature. I have always approached his myriad writings on human nature primarily from the perspective of a historically oriented ethical theorist who is concerned with how his account of human nature affects his ethics— rather than, say, that of a biologist, a practicing anthropologist, or a philosopher of science. That all of these approaches (and others) are legitimate, I do not deny. But I continue to believe that the moral dimension dominates all others. At bottom, Kant approaches the study of human nature from the perspective of a moralist (albeit an extremely philosophical moralist). "The sciences are *principia* for the improvement [*Verbesserung*] of morality" (*Collins Moralphilosophie* 27: 462), and this holds in particular for Kantian anthropology.[30] Scholars will continue to disagree about the overall plausibility and coherence of Kant's ethics, the relationship between the pure and impure parts of his ethics, and much more. But that the dominant message in his work on human nature is a moral one is, I believe, beyond dispute.

Extensions of Anthropology. The essays in the final part of the book all deal with aspects of Kant's theory of human nature that he presents and develops outside of his anthropology lectures—viz., in *Religion within the Boundaries of Mere Reason*, the essays and lectures on physical geography, the *Lectures on Pedagogy*, and the *Observations on the Feeling of the Beautiful and Sublime*. As noted earlier, in order to obtain Kant's full answer to the question "What is the human being?" one needs to go beyond his anthropology lectures. At the same time, these specific writings certainly do not exhaust Kant's work on human nature. (As also noted earlier, his writings on the philosophy of history are another important source, and ultimately *all* of Kant's writings have some relevance to the question "What is the human being?") My main reasons for including this third group of essays are that they concern important but often underexamined texts within the Kantian corpus that are beginning to attract increased scholarly attention; that they shed additional light on key issues within Kant's conception of human nature; and, last but not least, that they deal with Kantian texts that I have been continually drawn to over the years.

PART ONE

Human Virtues

Among moral qualities true virtue alone is sublime.
—*Beob* 2: 215

For it is only by means of this idea [of virtue] that any judgment of moral worth or unworth is possible.
—*KrV* B 372

But everything good that is not based on a morally good disposition, is nothing but mere semblance and glittering misery.
—*Idee* 8: 26

1

Kant's Virtue Ethics*

IN THE LATE twentieth century and the early twenty-first, we have heard much about the revival of virtue ethics, of normative theories whose primary focus is on persons rather than on decision making in problematic situations, on agents and the sorts of lives they lead rather than on discrete acts and rules for making choices, on characters and their morally relevant traits rather than on laws of obligation. Contemporary theorists are often motivated by a sense of the impoverishment of modern moral traditions, for in placing primary weight on the agent rather than the act (much less the act's consequences), virtue theorists set themselves off against what are often viewed as *the* two options in modern ethics—utilitarianism and deontologism. The traditional whipping boy in the latter case is Kant, for he is widely regarded as deontology personified, the first moral theorist to place a nonderivative conception of duty at the center of the philosophical stage, the first to establish a nonconsequentialist decision procedure through his universalizability test, etc. In addition, virtue theorists also seem to have historical reasons for disapproving of Kant. For the rise of quandary ethics is often associated with Enlightenment efforts to escape from tradition and the pull of local communities, and a consequent yearning for an ahistorical and universalistic conception of morality. Kant, as spokesman for the Enlightenment, is a natural target of criticism here.

For conceptual as well as historical reasons then, Kantian ethics has suffered badly under the current revival-of-virtue campaign. Alasdair MacIntyre writes: "In Kant's moral writings we have reached a point at which the notion that morality is anything other than obedience to rules has almost, if not quite, disappeared from sight."[1]

Philippa Foot chastises Kant as one of a select group of philosophers whose "tacitly accepted opinion was that a study of the topic [of the virtues and vices] would form no part of the fundamental work of ethics."[2] On her view, Kant should bear a sizable part of the responsibility for analytic philosophy's neglect of virtue. And Bernard Williams is equally critical in his insistent claims that Kantian moral theory treats persons in abstraction from character, and thus stands guilty of misrepresenting not only persons but morality and practical deliberation as well.[3] The underlying message is not simply that Kant is an illustrative representative of the deontological rule ethics perspective, but that his ethics is the worst possible sort of deontological rule ethics, one which is primarily responsible for the eclipse of agent-centered ethics.

Yet some readers of Kant feel that the conceptual shape of his ethical theory has been distorted by defender and critic alike, that his ethics is not rule ethics but virtue ethics. This reading of Kant has had its defenders in the past (he did, after all, write *The Doctrine of Virtue*), but Onora O'Neill has placed it in the context of the contemporary virtue ethics debate. In "Kant after Virtue" (a reply to MacIntyre's book), she states confidently that "what is not in doubt . . . is that Kant offers primarily an ethic of virtue rather than an ethic of rules."[4] So whose Kant is *the* Kant—hers or the more familiar one of MacIntyre & Co.?

The real Kant lies somewhere in between these two extremes. He sought to build an ethical theory which could assess both the life plans of moral agents and their discrete acts. This is to his credit, for an adequate moral theory needs to do both.

THE SHAPE OF VIRTUE ETHICS[5]

What qualifies an ethical theory as virtue ethics rather than rule ethics?

Agents versus Acts

One hallmark of virtue ethics is its strong agent orientation. For virtue theorists, the primary object of moral evaluation is not the intentional act or its consequences, but the agent. Utilitarians begin with a concept of the good—here defined with reference to states of affairs rather than persons. Duty, rights, and even virtue are all treated by utilitarians as derivative categories of secondary importance, definable in terms of utility maximization. Similarly, deontologists take duty as their irreducible starting point, and reject any attempt to define this root notion of being morally bound to do something in terms of good to be achieved. The good is now a derivative category, definable in terms of the right. The good that we are to promote is right action for its own sake—duty for duty's sake. Virtue also is a derivative notion, definable in terms of pro-attitudes toward one's duties. It is important, but only because it helps us to do our duty.

Virtue ethics begins with a notion of the morally good person, which is primitive in the sense that it is not defined in terms of performing obligatory acts ("the person who acts as duty requires") or endstates ("the agent who is disposed to maximize utility through his acts"). On the contrary, right and wrong acts are now construed in terms of what the good agent would or would not do, worthy and unworthy ends in terms of what the good agent would or would not aim at. It is by means of this conceptual shift that "being" rather than "doing" achieves prominence in virtue ethics.

Decision Procedures versus Good Character

Agent ethics and act ethics also diverge in their overall conceptions of practical reasoning. Act theorists, because they focus on discrete acts and moral quandaries, are interested in formulating decision procedures for making practical choices. Because these theorists have derivative and relatively weak conceptions of character to lean on, the agent in a practical choice situation does not appear to them to have many resources upon which to draw. He or she needs a guide—hopefully a decision procedure—for finding a way out of the quandary. Agent ethics, because it focuses on long-term characteristic patterns of action, downplays atomic acts and choice situations in the process. It is not as concerned with portraying practical reason as a rule-governed enterprise which can be applied on a case-by-case basis. Virtue theorists do not view moral choice as unreasoned or irrational; the virtuous agent is also seen as the practically wise agent. But one often finds divergent portraits of practical reason in act and agent ethics.

Motivation

A third general area where we are likely to see differences between agent and act ethics is in their respective views on moral motivation. This complex issue is particularly important in any reading of Kantian ethics as virtue ethics. For the duty-based or deontological theorist, the preferred motive is respect for the idea of duty itself, and the good man is the one who does his duty for duty's sake. This does not entail that the agent who does his duty for duty's sake does so grudgingly, or only in spite of inclinations to the contrary, but simply that the determining ground of the motive is respect for duty. For the goal-based or utilitarian theorist, the preferred motive is a steady disposition to maximize utility.

In virtue ethics the preferred motivation factor is not duty or utility but the virtues themselves. The agent who acts from dispositions of friendship, courage, or integrity is held in higher esteem than the person who performs the same acts from different motives. For instance, a virtue theorist might call a man courageous only if, when in danger, it was clear that the man did not even want to run away (and thus showed signs of being "directly moved" to act courageously), while the duty-based theorist would only call a man courageous if he did not run away out of a sense of duty (but perhaps wanted to anyway—though the "want" is here irrelevant). As the example suggests, matters become troublesome when we bring in reason and inclination. I have not said that one theory asserts we are motivated by reason, another by desire. However, reason and inclination do enter into the motivation issue (particularly in debates over Kant) in the following way. Virtue ethics, with its "virtue for virtue's sake" position on motivation, is also committed to the claim that our natural inclinations play a necessary role in many types of action done from virtue. Acting from the virtue of friendship, for instance, would require that one possess and exhibit certain feelings about friends. Kant, on the other hand, holds (from the *Groundwork* on) that the sole determining ground of the will must be respect (*Achtung*)—a peculiarly non-empirical feeling produced by an intellectual awareness of the moral law. Kant thus appears to deny natural inclinations any positive role in moral motivation, whereas virtue ethics requires it.

VIRTUE AND THE GOOD WILL

Kant begins his ethical investigations with a powerful but cryptic proclamation about the good will: "It is impossible to think of anything at all in the world, or indeed even beyond it, that could be considered good without limitation except a **good will**" (*Gr* 4: 393). From the perspective of virtue ethics, to what extent should Kant's position on the good will be construed as evidence of an agent-centered rather than an act-centered ethics?

As Robert Paul Wolff remarks, it is "noteworthy that the philosopher most completely identified with the doctrine of stern duty should begin, not with a statement about what we ought to do, but rather with a judgment of what is unqualifiedly good."[6] And what is unqualifiedly good, according to Kant, is not an endstate such as pleasure or the performance of certain atomic acts in conformity to rules, but a state of character which becomes the basis for all of one's actions. To answer the question "Is my will good?" (a question which can never be answered with certain knowledge, due to the opacity of our intentions), we must look beyond atomic acts and decisions and inquire into how we have lived. A human being cannot be "morally good in some parts, and at the same time evil in others" (*Rel* 6: 24). Similarly, he cannot, on Kant's view, exhibit a good will one moment and an evil one the next. Steadfastness of character must be demonstrated.

So Kant's opening claim concerning the unqualified goodness of the good will means that what is fundamentally important in his ethics is not acts but agents. But what is the relationship between good will and virtue? Kant defines virtue (*Tugend*) in the *Tugendlehre* as fortitude "with respect to what opposes the moral disposition *within us*" (*MdS* 6: 380). The Kantian virtuous agent is thus one who, because of his "fortitude," is able to resist urges and inclinations that are opposed to moral law. Kantian fortitude is strength (*Stärke*) or force (*Kraft*) of will, not in the sense of being able to accomplish the goals one sets out to achieve, but rather in the sense of mastery over one's inclinations and constancy of purpose.[7]

A good will is a will which steadily acts from the motive of respect for the moral law. But human beings, because they are natural beings, always possess inclinations which may lead them to act against reason. Their wills are thus in a perpetual state of tension. Some wills are better than others, but only a holy will (who has no wants that could run counter to reason, and who can thus do no evil) possesses an absolutely good will. This is why Kant holds that "human morality in its highest stage can still be nothing more than virtue" (*MdS* 6: 383; cf. *KpV* 5: 84–85, *Gr* 4: 414). Virtue is only an approximation of the good will, because of the basic conflict or tension in human wills. Kant's virtuous agent is a human approximation of a good will who through strength of mind continually acts out of respect for the moral law while still feeling the presence of natural inclinations which could tempt him to act from other motives.

Now if virtue is the human approximation of the good will, and if the good will is the only unqualified good, this does imply that moral virtue, for Kant, is foundational, and not (as one would expect in a deontological theory) a concept of derivative or secondary importance. ["But everything good that is not grafted onto a morally good disposition, is nothing but mere semblance and glittering misery" (*Idee* 8: 26).] As Harbison notes: "the essence of [Kant's] moral philosophy is quite different from what it has commonly been supposed to be, for on the basis of this enquiry one must conclude that it is the concept of the good will that lies at its foundation."[8]

But there remains a fundamental problem for this particular argument in favor of a virtue ethics reading of Kant. Both the good will and virtue are defined in terms of obedience to moral law, for they are both wills which are in conformity to moral law and which act out of respect for it. Kant begins with the good will in order to uncover "the supreme principle of morality"—the categorical imperative. Since human virtue is defined in terms of conformity to law and the categorical imperative, it appears now that what is primary in Kantian ethics is not virtue for virtue's sake but obedience to rules. Virtue is the heart of the ethical for Kant, in the sense that it is the basis for all judgments of moral worth. But Kantian virtue is itself defined in terms of the supreme principle of morality. The conceptual commitment to agency and to long-term characteristic behavior rather than atomic acts and decision procedures for moral quandaries is evident here, as one would expect in virtue ethics. But what Kant prizes most about moral agency is its ability to act consistently from respect for law, not in the sense of following specific rules for specific acts, but in the more fundamental sense of guiding one's entire life by respect for rationally legislated and willed law.

Kantian virtue therefore is subordinate to the moral law, and this makes him look like an obedience-to-rules theorist. However, it is obedience to rules not in the narrow-minded pharisaic manner for which rule ethics is usually chastised by virtue theorists, but in the broader, classical sense of living a life according to reason. The two perspectives of agent and rule are thus both clearly present in Kant's account of the good will. The virtuous agent is one who consistently "follows the rules" out of respect for the idea of rationally legislated law. But "the rules," while they do serve as action-guides, are intended most fundamentally as life-guides.

REREADING MAXIMS

A second argument for a virtue ethics interpretation of Kant comes from a rereading of what he means by a "maxim." This strategy is particularly prominent in some of the work of Onora O'Neill and in a piece by Otfried Höffe.[9] Kant defines a "maxim" rather tersely as "the subjective principle of volition" (*Gr* 4: 400n, see also 420n), and from this one can infer that a maxim is (among other things) a policy of action adopted by a particular agent at a particular time and place. Because the principle is subjective rather than objective, it must tie in with the agent's own intentions and interests. So why not simply view Kantian maxims as the agent's specific maxims for his discrete acts? This is a common understanding of maxims, but it is also one that easily lends itself to a rule reading of maxims, since here a maxim becomes, in effect, a rule which prescribes or proscribes a specific act. O'Neill rejects the specific intention reading and argues instead that "it seems most convincing to understand by an agent's maxim the *underlying intention* by which the agent orchestrates his numerous more specific intentions."[10] Suppose I have invited a guest to my house, and that my underlying intention is to make him feel welcome. On most such occasions, I will have numerous specific intentions by means of which I carry out the underlying intention: I may offer him a beer, invite him to put a record on the stereo, show him my vegetable garden, etc.

O'Neill offers two arguments in support of the underlying intention interpretation of maxims. (1) Usually we are aware of our specific intentions for the future, yet Kant frequently asserts that we never know the real morality of our actions. This suggests that maxims and specific intentions are not the same. (2) Sometimes we act without a specific intention (e.g., when we act absent-mindedly), but Kant holds that we always act on some maxim. All actions are open to moral assessment. This again suggests a difference between maxims and specific intentions.[11]

Now if Kantian maxims are best seen as underlying rather than as specific intentions, we do have a strong argument for a virtue reading of Kant's ethics. For our underlying intentions tie in directly with the sorts of persons we are and with the sorts of lives we lead. And the sort of person one is obviously depends upon what virtues and vices one possesses. One's specific intentions, on the other hand, are not always an accurate guide to the sort of person one is "deep down inside." This connection between underlying intentions and being a certain sort of person is stressed by both O'Neill and Höffe.[12] However, two basic problems confront this interpretation. First, O'Neill's use of the phrase "underlying intentions" is ambiguous. At one point, she states that adopting maxims is a matter of "leading a certain sort of life, or being a certain sort of person"; elsewhere, she asserts that maxims (or underlying intentions) "need not be longer-term intentions, for we remain free to change them."[13] This distinction between underlying and longer-term intentions does not sit well with the asserted identification between underlying intentions and being a certain sort of person. For becoming a certain sort of person is a long-term process. One cannot decide at noon on Monday to be courageous and saintly, and then suddenly become so by Tuesday. And in what sense do we "remain free to change" the sort of person we have become? I believe there is a strong sense in which such change can be undertaken, but the effort and time required to carry it out are certainly much greater than are the effort and time required to change one's specific intentions at any given moment. In short, the more that "underlying" intentions are untied from "longer-term" intentions, the less plausible it becomes to assert that maxims (in the sense of underlying intentions) have to do with leading a certain sort of life and with virtue. For the latter are long-term ventures. One does not initiate, abandon, or change them on a daily basis.

One reason for O'Neill's odd insistence on the underlying/long-term intention distinction is perhaps traceable to Kantian texts. In several places, Kant warns that we must not construe virtue "merely as an *aptitude* [*Fertigkeit*] and ... a long-standing *habit* [*Gewohnheit*] of morally good actions" (*MdS* 6: 383, 407; see also *Anth* 7: 147). His point is that human virtue is an extremely precarious achievement of pure practical reason which must constantly be on guard against heteronomy and empirical inclinations. In making this claim he is unfortunately led into some rhetorical skirmishes against Aristotle which reflect a poor understanding of Aristotle's own analysis of virtue.[14] What Kant wants is a moral disposition "armed for all situations" and "adequately secured against the changes that new temptations could bring about" (*MdS* 6: 384). As O'Neill suggests, Kant is aiming at a distinctly modern conception of virtue here, one which is a response to the fragmentation of modern life and the breakdown of communities and institutions. Furthermore, behind his opposition to construing virtues as long-standing habits lies an acute awareness of our powers of rationalization and self-deception in repressing our sense of guilt. Kant might seem to have read his Freud. But nothing in these texts implies that long-term intentions must necessarily turn into mechanical habits, for we have seen already that cultivating a good will is, on Kant's view, an achievement of pure practical reason. So O'Neill's reservations about long-term intentions do not appear to be well-founded.

The second problem with the underlying intentions reading of maxims is that it contradicts several of Kant's own examples of maxims. What he sometimes means by maxims are not life plans or even underlying intentions, but simply specific intentions for discrete acts. Furthermore, the testing of such maxims does not require that they be related to the life plan or the underlying intention of the agent. The maxim of the agent who feels forced to borrow money but knows he can't repay it is very specific, and applies only to restricted dire circumstances which may never even arise. Similarly, the maxim which reveals a perfect duty to refrain from suicide is again a specific intention which is not necessarily related to a life plan.

For these reasons then, the underlying intentions reading of maxims must be taken with a grain of salt. O'Neill's use of "underlying" is ambiguous, vacillating between specific and long-term intentions. Second, Kant's own examples of maxims indicate that what he sometimes means by the term is specific intentions for atomic acts. But because "maxims" for Kant can mean both short- and long-term intentions, we see again that he possesses and employs the conceptual tools to evaluate an agent's discrete acts as well as her course of life. This is to Kant's credit, for both enterprises are essential for an adequate ethical theory.

SELF-PERFECTION AND THE DOCTRINE OF MORALLY NECESSARY ENDS

There is one fundamental use of "maxims" in Kant's texts which unequivocally concerns underlying intentions and the sort of life one leads. This is what Kant calls maxims of ends rather than of dutiful actions—maxims to pursue general, long-term goals (which allow for many different ways of pursuing them), rather than maxims to perform narrowly prescribed acts. The strongest argument for the prominence of virtue in Kantian ethics is to be gleaned from his doctrine of morally necessary ends as presented in the *Tugendlehre*.

Section 3 of the introduction to the *Tugendlehre* is entitled "On the Basis for Thinking of an End That Is at the Same Time a Duty" (*MdS* 6: 384). The core of Kant's argument runs as follows: all acts have ends, for action (by definition) is a goal-directed process. Ends, however, are objects of free choice. We do of course have many desires, wants, and inclinations, which are biologically and/or culturally imposed, and nearly all ends that we do eventually adopt are also objects of desires, wants, and inclinations. But, ultimately, ends are chosen, for we cannot be forced to make anything an end of action; we ourselves must choose to. People can and do renounce even the biological desire for life in extreme circumstances. The adoption of ends is a matter of free choice, and this brings them under the purview of pure practical reason rather than of inclination.

But why assert that ends (which are freely chosen) are also morally necessary? Why claim that there exist ends which agents have a duty to adopt? Isn't this merely a way of implying that all conceptions of the good are not created equal, that reason can discriminate among ends as well as among means? Isn't this dangerously unmodern and illiberal? Perhaps, but Kant's position is clear: we must assume that there are morally necessary ends, for if we don't, "this would do away with any doctrine of morals [*Sittenlehre*]" (*MdS* 6: 385). His reasoning is that if all ends are contingent, then all imperatives become hypothetical. If we are free to accept or reject any goal put before us whenever we are so inclined, then all commands prescribing maxims for action are likewise open to rejection once the goal is dismissed. In other words (by contraposition), if there is a categorical imperative, there must be at least one morally necessary end. We cannot accept the claim that reason categorically requires us to do certain things unless we accept the companion claim that reason categorically requires us to adopt certain ends.

As is well known, Kant goes on to argue in the *Tugendlehre* that there are two ends which agents have a duty to adopt: their own perfection and the happiness of others. The former, for Kant, is the more fundamental of the two, and its connection to moral character is also more direct.

The duty which Kant asserts all agents have to promote their own perfection includes as its most important component the obligation to cultivate one's will "up to the purest virtuous disposition" (*MdS* 6: 387). We saw earlier that the good will is the only unqualified good in the world or beyond it, that it in turn is the condition for the goodness of every other thing. Our highest practical vocation as finite rational intelligences is to produce a will good in itself as an unconditional end, for such a will is the supreme good and ordering principle for all human activities. We saw also that moral virtue, as Kant understands the concept, is a human approximation to the good will. Humans, because of their biological and cultural makeups, always have inclinations which may run counter to the moral law.

The duty to develop an attitude of virtue is obviously a duty to oneself rather than to others. And it is also an ethical rather than a legal duty, that is, a duty in which the motive for action is the thought of the law itself rather than threats of external compulsion. But what is most important to note for our purposes is that the duty to develop one's moral character is the linchpin of Kant's entire system of duties. As he remarks in his discussion of duties to oneself: "For suppose there were no such duties [viz., duties to oneself]: then there would be no duties whatsoever, and so no external duties either. —For I can recognize that I am under obligation to others only insofar as I at the same time put myself under obligation . . . " (*MdS* 6: 417).[15]

Without duties to oneself, no duties whatsoever. Why would Kant make such a claim? His chief contention is that what is basic to all duties—legal, moral, or otherwise—is the concept of binding oneself. Take first the familiar notion of a legal duty to others, say, a loan taken out with a lending institution to help pay for my graduate education. In one sense I am clearly bound to another party (the bank). But Kant's view is that this is so only because I first choose to bind myself to the laws of the government under which I am accountable for the terms of the contract. If I don't first choose to view myself as being obligated to obey my government's laws, it is not likely that I will consider myself to have any duty toward the bank. Similarly, consider a moral duty to others, e.g., the Kantian duty to promote others' welfare. Here I am not even accountable to any specifiable others, as was the case in the previous example, but only to my own conscience. We "owe it to ourselves" to do all we are capable of in fulfilling our moral duties to others.

Once Kant's argument concerning morally necessary ends is considered, it becomes strikingly evident that virtue does indeed have a preeminent position in his ethics. Our overriding practical vocation is to realize a state of virtue in our own character as the basis of all action. Without fulfilling such a duty to ourselves, other duties are not possible. Virtue is not only the heart of the ethical for Kant; it also has priority in morals considered as a whole (that is, in *Recht* and *Tugend* taken together). For if there were no ethical duties to oneself, there would be no duties whatsoever.

But again, virtue itself is posterior to the supreme principle of morality. Virtue remains conceptually subordinate to the moral law. Kant presents us with a virtue ethics in which the "rule of law" nevertheless plays the lead role, and in which the theory is designed to assess not only ways of life but discrete acts as well. However, as noted earlier, the priority of the moral law in Kantian ethics does not entail the pharisaic qualities which virtue critics have usually attributed to it. It does not mean that what dominates Kantian ethics is the attempt to construct a decision procedure for all acts, or even to devise determinate rules for a limited set of specific acts. Yet such attempts are generally conceded to be prominent in rule ethics approaches to practical reasoning. Instead, what we do find in Kant's ethics is the categorical command of reason to cultivate a way of life in which all of one's acts (whatever they may be) are in complete harmony with the idea of lawfulness as such. The moral will is subordinate to law in Kantian ethics and is defined in terms of it. But the result is not a legalistic conformity-to-rules morality, current interpretations to the contrary. It is a conception of a life lived according to reason.

VIRTUE AND EMOTION

While virtue has far greater prominence in Kant's ethics than many of his readers suppose, it is nevertheless overstating matters to assert baldly that Kantian ethics is virtue ethics. Significant aspects of both the agent and act perspectives are present in his ethical theory, though the former does dominate. Kantian ethical theory seeks to assess not only atomic acts but also agents' ways of life. And while the sort of person one becomes (rather than the specific acts one may perform and the short-term intentions one may adopt) is central in Kantian ethics, his conception of moral personhood is defined in terms of obedience to law. The Kantian agent commitment is inextricably fused to a law conception of ethics. Each of the three arguments outlined earlier points to these same conclusions, which is not surprising, since they are closely related to begin with. The later material from the *Tugendlehre* regarding morally necessary ends (of which the duty of moral self-perfection is the most important) restates and deepens the earlier material from the *Grundlegung* concerning the good will. The section on maxims establishes that while not all Kantian maxims refer to underlying intentions and agents' life plans, the most significant ones in ethics (maxims of ends) do.

One notorious roadblock to a virtue interpretation of Kantian ethics remains, and it requires an unconventional but (I believe) Kantian reply. Virtue theorists part ways with their deontological and teleological opponents over the issue of moral motivation. In virtue ethics, agents are expected to act for the sake of virtue; in deontology, for duty's sake; in utilitarianism, for utility's sake. Now at first glance it would seem impossible to argue that Kant espouses a virtue ethics position with respect to motivation, since he holds that only action from duty can have moral worth. However, as my earlier arguments indicate, Kant's notion of action *aus Pflicht* means in the most fundamental sense not that one performs a specific act for the sake of a specific rule which prescribes it (and likewise for other specific acts one performs) but rather that one strives for a way of life in which all of one's acts are a manifestation of a character which is in harmony with moral law. Action *aus Pflicht* is action motivated by virtue, albeit virtue in Kant's sternly rationalist sense.

But it is precisely on the issue of rationalism and moral motivation that Kant has come under such severe criticism. The motivation problem has been a favorite target of Kantian critics from Hegel onward, and to cover all of its dimensions is far beyond the scope of this essay. The following brief remarks focus instead on Kant's position regarding the role of emotion in action from virtue.

It is generally acknowledged that, from a moral perspective, the most praiseworthy acts are often those which agents truly want to perform. As Foot remarks:

> Who shows most courage, the one who wants to run away but does not, or the one who does not even want to run away? Who shows most charity, the one who finds it easy to make the good of others his object, or the one who finds it hard? ... The man who acts charitably out of a sense of duty is not to be undervalued, but it is

the other [i.e., the one who is directly moved and thus wants to act charitably] who shows most virtue and therefore to the other that most moral worth is attributed.[16]

The sense of "wants" here needs to be clarified, and I will attempt to do so in a moment. But first, a restatement of the underlying anti-Kantian argument: acting from virtue is (at least sometimes) action motivated by altruistic emotion or desire. Kant, however, holds that action *aus Pflicht* must be defined independently of all natural emotions and desires. Therefore, there is no place in Kantian ethics for acting from virtue.[17]

Now, back to "wants." Does Foot's agent who "does not even want to run away" act this way by nature or because he knows (in addition, perhaps, to being naturally inclined in this direction) that it is noble to do so? In Aristotelian terminology, does he act courageously out of "natural virtue" or from "virtue in the strict sense," the latter of which involves *phronēsis*, a rational understanding of what one is doing? Aristotle and Kant agree on this fundamental point: acting from virtue in the strict sense means acting rationally. But Aristotle also holds that practical choice is "reason motivated by desire [*orektikos nous*] or desire operating through reason [*orexis dianoētikē*]."[18] Desire and reason are both necessary factors in moral choice, but neither on its own is sufficient. How about Kant? Does acting from virtue, as he understands it, entail acting from desire (in addition to reason)?

Kant has so often been tagged as an enemy of the emotions that it may seem foolish even to ask the question. On most interpretations, Kant allows room for one (and only one) desire in his account of moral choice—respect or reverence (*Achtung*)—a unique "*a priori* feeling," generated by a pure judgment which acknowledges the claim of the moral law, and then in turn acts as the phenomenal spur to action from appreciation of that law. But the role of emotions and natural inclinations in Kant's understanding of moral motivation is trickier than is often assumed. On the one hand, he does assert unequivocally that "what is essential in the moral worth of actions is *that the moral law should determine the will immediately*" (*KpV* 5: 71). This way of talking is often construed as meaning that reason is not only a necessary but also a sufficient ground for moral choice, and that natural emotions (with the sole exception of *Achtung*, which again is an *a priori* feeling and thus not natural) have no positive role to play whatsoever. But while determination of choice through reason is obviously necessary in Kantian ethics, it is not sufficient for the attainment of virtue. There are a host of phenomenal emotions (the most important of which are joy, sympathy, and love) which, while not the direct *Bestimmungsgrund* of the will, must be present in a virtuous disposition. These emotions are phenomenal effects which, as Karl Ameriks puts it, have "noumenal backing" and find their ultimate source in a noumenal acceptance of pure duty.[19] In less Kantian but more Aristotelian terms, these emotions are ones that have been trained *by* reason to work in harmony *with* reason. They are secondary in importance to respect, but they are nevertheless essential components in a morally virtuous life.

Granted, it is difficult to see this if one does not read past the *Grundlegung*. In that work, Kant is engaging in a form of analysis which he compares with a chemical experiment. He discriminates elements in a compound by varying the circumstances, and wants to break the compound into its base elements in the most effective manner. His assumption there is simply that it is easier to determine accurately whether an act was performed from duty if the agent had an inclination to perform the "opposite" act (e.g., feel antipathy rather than sympathy toward the suffering of others) than it would be if the agent were also inclined to perform the same act that duty requires. (Of course, even when natural inclination seems to be ruled out as an incentive, we still can't determine with certainty what ultimately motivates the agent. Kant holds that our moral intentions remain opaque to us.) In a similar vein, Kant states in the second *Critique* that it is "risky" to view altruistic emotions as "co-operating" with the moral law in motivating moral behavior.[20] The reason, again, is that it becomes all the more difficult to ascertain the true motives of action when, in addition to acting out of respect for the law, one has a natural desire to act in the same manner as duty requires. Nevertheless, while it may indeed be risky to enlist the emotions, this does not rule out the possibility that proper cultivation of them may still be necessary for human beings who aspire to a truly virtuous life. And Kant explicitly asserts in his later writings that the emotions have a necessary and positive role to play in moral motivation. In the "Ethical Ascetic" of the *Tugendlehre* (which deals with the cultivation of virtue), he writes: "what is not done with pleasure [*mit Lust*] but merely as compulsory service has no inner worth for one who attends to his duty in this way and such service is not loved [*nicht geliebt*] by him; instead he shirks as much as possible occasions for practicing virtue" (*MdS* 6: 484). Here and elsewhere Kant addresses the need to cultivate a "habitually cheerful heart," in order that the *feeling* of joy accompanies (but does not constitute or determine) our virtue. A parallel passage occurs near the beginning of the *Religion*:

> Now, if we ask, "What is the *aesthetic* constitution, the temperament so to speak, *of virtue*: is it courageous and hence *joyous* [*fröhlich*], or weighed down by fear and dejected?" an answer is hardly necessary. This latter slavish frame of mind can never occur without a hidden *hatred* of the law, whereas a heart *joyous* in the *compliance* with its duty (not just complacency in the recognition of it) is the sign of genuineness in virtuous disposition.
>
> (*Rel* 6: 24n; see also *Anth* 7: 282; *Päd* 9: 499)

These and other related passages state explicitly that the enemy-of-the-emotions reading of Kant favored by so many is a gross misunderstanding. Kant's position is clear: pure practical reason needs to be always "in charge" of the emotions in a truly virtuous life. The *Bestimmungsgrund* of moral choice must be reason, not feeling. But an integral part of moral discipline, or what Kant calls "ethical gymnastics," is training the emotions so that they work with rather than against reason. Acts in which empirical inclinations of any sort are the *Bestimmungsgrund* lack moral worth, but it doesn't follow that a harmonizing sentiment must cancel all moral worth. On the contrary, Kant insists that it is a good thing.

Kant then would agree with Foot's claim that the agent who does not even want to run away shows more courage than the one who wants to run away but does not, provided that the "want" in question is a rational want with which the agent's desires are trained to be in harmony. More generally, acting from virtue, on Kant's view, does entail disciplining the emotions through reason so that one comes to want to perform the same external act that reason commands. But again, as Kant warns, there is a risk, for in training the emotions in such a manner it becomes more difficult to assess one's motives for action. One is perpetually flirting with the possibility that one's conduct is not autonomously willed but merely a product of heteronomy, but cultivation of virtue requires that the risk be taken.

Kant's position on the emotions and their role in action from virtue is not inconsistent with a virtue ethics view. It is remarkably close to Aristotle's view, the major difference being that Kant was much more aware than Aristotle of the dangers of self-deception by emotional enthusiasm pretending to be moral inspiration.[21]

2

Moral Strength

VIRTUE AS A DUTY TO ONESELF*

―――――――――――――――――――――――――――――――

TODAY, MORE THAN two hundred years after Kant's death, discussion of his ethics is more extensive than ever before. While the nations of the earth have unfortunately not yet reached a stage where "a violation of *Recht* on *one* place of the earth is felt in *all*" (*Frieden* 8: 360), and while human individuals have also not made much progress in establishing a worldwide "ethical community" or "universal republic based on laws of virtue" (*Rel* 6: 94, 98), at present the influence of Kant's ethics is nevertheless far stronger and deeper than that of any other single aspect of his wide-ranging philosophical system.

However (as is often the case in philosophy), part of the explanation for the sheer extent of the discussion is that we continue to be confronted with conflicting accounts of the very nature of the subject matter—accounts which, when taken together, seem to cancel each other out and leave no victor standing. For instance, while many scholars continue to point to Kant's ethics as being the archetype of a deontological theory, others have insisted that "Kantian ethics is not a deontology," that Kant "*could* have been a utilitarian," that his ethics either "turns out to be teleological rather than deontological" or at least "undercuts the traditional distinction" between deontology and teleology, and that his "theory of ethical duties is consequentialist in its style of reasoning."[1] To add to the confusion, others maintain that what Kant ultimately aimed at is neither deontology nor teleology but rather "a virtue-based ethics, one in which character plays a central role."[2] Taken together, these remarks would appear to indicate that there is still little consensus as to what exactly Kant's ethics *is*.

In this essay I wish to revisit a fundamental set of questions about Kant's ethics that has long perplexed me:[3] What role does virtue play in his ethics? How does he understand virtue? And to what extent is his ethics best understood as an ethics of virtue or character rather than one of duty or requirement? Although I continue to hold that the concepts of virtue and character are much more central to Kant's ethics than do many of his friends and certainly his foes, I also think it is clear that his understandings of what virtue and good moral character are differ radically from those of nearly all contemporary virtue ethicists—primarily because he does not share their view of human nature. In what follows I will elaborate on and hopefully substantiate these claims.

VIRTUE AND DUTIES TO ONESELF

Kant's commitment to the importance of duties to oneself is a good place to start in analyzing his conception of virtue, in part because one of the commonest objections to the claim that his ethics is a virtue ethics is that he not only fails "to take facts about the virtues to be more basic than facts about duty, he actually *defines* virtue in terms of duty."[4] By examining the role that duties to oneself play within Kant's system of duties, we can better understand his view on the relations between virtue and duty and also assess the charge that he defines virtue in terms of duty.

For many years Kant's endorsement of the legitimacy of duties to oneself was ridiculed as a conceptual confusion. Philosophers as different as Schopenhauer, Mill, Sidgwick, Marcus Singer, and Bernard Williams were all united in the claim that so-called duties to oneself were not real duties but merely prudential oughts masquerading as moral oughts.[5] Real duties, they claimed, are attached to correlative rights, and the party to whom the duty is owed always has the right to release the duty-bearer from her duty. But in the case of an alleged duty to ourselves, we could always choose to release ourselves at will from the obligation, and this means that there could not have been a duty in the first place. Another favorite rejectionist strategy, employed by Kurt Baier among others,[6] was simply to assert that morality by definition is inherently social and other-regarding, the result being that duties to oneself, whatever they are, are not *moral* duties.

I will not examine these criticisms further here, primarily because most of them are simply question begging (*Why* should we assume that all moral duties necessarily involve correlative rights? *Why* need we accept a conception of morality which holds that it is exclusively other-regarding?), but also because philosophical resistance to duties to oneself has definitely waned. However, while several able articulations of Kant's doctrine of duties to oneself have been published,[7] the larger significance of this doctrine for ongoing debates about the nature and shape of his ethics is still underappreciated.

Kant's most extensive discussions of duties to oneself are in the *Metaphysics of Morals* and in several of the *Lectures on Ethics* (particularly *Collins*).[8] On first look, the discussion of duties to oneself in the *Groundwork* is exasperatingly brief, and this itself may partially explain why Anglophone philosophers often pass over the topic. In the *Groundwork*, Kant says merely: "We shall now enumerate a few duties in accordance with the usual division [*nach der gewöhnlichen Eintheilung*] of them into duties to ourselves and to other human beings" (4: 421). However, I believe that many of the

Groundwork's major themes—e.g., autonomy and self-legislation (439–40), the imperative to respect humanity as an end in itself (429), the opening claim that the good will is the only unqualified good in the universe (393), as well as the defense of freedom in section III—can and should be read as providing a background justification for duties to oneself.

In searching for the underlying principle behind duties to oneself (and in criticizing other philosophers for failing to locate it), Kant emphasizes that such duties "have nothing at all to do with well-being and our temporal happiness" (*Collins* 27: 341). This alone should serve as a sufficient warning to critics who dismiss Kantian duties to oneself as mere prudential oughts that they are off-track, but the important point is that on Kant's view such duties are concerned with the intrinsic moral worth of rational agents, with valuing (developing, maintaining, preserving, perfecting) their moral capacities. Duties to oneself, at bottom, are a direct application of the imperative always to respect humanity "whether in your own person or in the person of any other" as an end in itself (*Gr* 4: 429).[9] He who violates duties to oneself, Kant warns, "throws away his humanity, and is no longer in a position to perform duties to others" (*Collins* 27: 341).

As the last citation implies, Kant's most radical claim regarding duties to oneself is that they are the foundation and precondition of all duties. Although he asserts this claim repeatedly, it is not easy to make sense of (in part because we are not given much beyond the bare assertion). For instance, in the *Metaphysics of Morals* he proclaims confidently that if there were no duties to oneself, "then there would be no duties whatsoever" (6: 417). Similarly, in *Collins* we are informed that "duties to oneself are the supreme condition [*die oberste Bedingung*] and *principium* of all morality" (27: 344), the "conditions under which alone the other duties can be performed" (27: 360), and "the most important of all" duties (27: 341; cf. 433).

As others have noted,[10] the sense in which duties to oneself are preconditions of all other duties is not logical or conceptual. For example, in the case of our duty to help others, it would be false to say that it is the value of our own humanity rather than theirs that provides the justification for the duty. Their own moral standing makes a legitimate claim on us. Nor is the kind of priority assumed a temporal one. Kant is not claiming that in the course of human moral development we must first appreciate the importance of duties to ourselves before we are in a position to fulfill duties to others. Finally, he is not implying that duties to oneself are prior in the sense that, in cases of potential conflict with duties to others, the former will override the latter. In other words, he is not endorsing the narcissistic view that we may opt out of our duty to help others by saying, "Sorry, I need to spend more time on what is most important—i.e., developing my own talents."[11]

What then does Kant mean in calling duties to oneself the "most important of all" duties, "the conditions under which alone the other duties can be performed"? Briefly, duties to oneself are prior to and more important than other duties in the sense that in striving to fulfill them we are promoting and realizing fundamental values without which morality itself could not exist. Chief among these values are autonomy or self-legislation, freedom, and respect for human beings as ends in themselves. If we human beings were perfect beings, we would not have any duties to ourselves. Here as elsewhere, "the 'ought' is out of place" (*Gr* 4: 414), though for a different reason than in the case of duties to others. In the latter case, perfect beings as a matter of course always act toward others in ways that the rest of us often have to compel ourselves to try and act (and seldom manage to achieve). They are never tempted to do otherwise. But in the former case, the central capacities of moral agency that (with human beings) are promoted and safeguarded by duties to oneself are already fully present, and they are not in any danger of being corrupted or thwarted. Perfect beings don't have duties to themselves simply because they don't need them (see *MdS* 6: 383).

Nor are we able to directly instill or activate these crucial capacities in other human beings. Parents can, do, and should try to instill them in their children, teachers in their students, religious leaders in members of their congregations, etc. But at most they are able to alter the phenomenal surroundings in ways that might make the necessary noumenal activation a bit more likely to occur. Ultimately, each individual must do it himself (cf. *MdS* 6: 386).[12]

But how does this discussion of the priority of duties to oneself bear on the charge that Kant defines virtue in terms of duty? The crucial concept is that of self-constraint, a gaining control over oneself so that one is "in the state of *health* proper to a human being" (*MdS* 6: 384; see also 405, 409, 419; *Anth* 7: 251). All moral duties—to others as well as to oneself, perfect as well as imperfect—centrally involve self-constraint (*MdS* 6: 380), and Kant also defines virtue itself in terms of self-constraint (*MdS* 6: 394). Thus in a sense he actually defines duty in terms of virtue, rather than vice versa, as critics often allege. And in acknowledging the priority of duties to oneself and the central role that virtue and self-constraint play in defining them we are also able to dispense with another prominent objection to reading Kant's ethics as a virtue ethics, viz., the claim that "worst of all, virtue has at best a partial role to play in [Kant's conception of] morality, dividing the realm with perfect duties which are the archetype of everything the virtue theorist rejects."[13] On the contrary, for Kant, virtue's role is thoroughgoing: human morality cannot get under way without it.

Kant is thus in solid agreement with contemporary virtue ethicists who maintain that "the basic moral facts are facts about the quality of character. Moral facts about action are ancillary to these."[14] At least on this basic point, his ethics is one of virtue or character rather than duty. But as the strong emphasis on self-constraint suggests, and as other related issues to be discussed below reveal even more, Kant's conception of character often differs radically from that assumed by contemporary virtue ethicists.

VIRTUE AND EMOTION

Another site of contention concerns the relation between virtue and emotion. Does virtue necessarily involve emotion in a *positive* sense—feeling emotion, expressing emotion? Most contemporary virtue ethicists are convinced that it does,[15] and most of them are also convinced that Kant denies this allegedly necessary connection between virtue and emotion. On their view, Kant's conception of virtue as strength of will commits him to the view that virtue involves holding down the emotions, "rather like a good cook holds down the lid on a boiling pot."[16]

Here as elsewhere, the point is often made via reference to Aristotle—in this case, to his well-known distinction between continence (*enkrateia*) and genuine virtue. The continent person, through strength of resolve, is able to act as he should, despite the presence of "strong and base appetites" (*Nicomachean Ethics* VII.2 1146a10). But mere continence, on Aristotle's view, "is not a virtue" (IV.9 1128b34), for the fully virtuous person does not battle opposing desires in acting as he should. Here the appetitive part of the soul agrees with reason (III.12 1119b15–16), and the virtuous agent enjoys acting as he should in a way that the merely continent person cannot (I.8 1099a11–24).

Is Kant guilty of hostility toward the emotions[17] in his conception of virtue? On the one hand, as is well known, there are several "pro-emotion" passages that seem to speak in favor of acquittal. For instance, in the *Metaphysics of Morals*, he declares that "what is not done with pleasure [*Lust*] but merely as compulsory service has no inner worth," and that one who acts without pleasure "shirks as much as possible occasions for practicing virtue" (*MdS* 6: 484). Also in *MdS* he asserts that we have "an indirect duty to cultivate the compassionate natural (aesthetic) feelings in us, and to make use of them as so many means to sympathy based on moral principles and the feeling appropriate to them" (6: 457). This strategy of cultivating feelings of compassion is incumbent upon human beings if they are to achieve "what the representation of duty alone might not accomplish" (6: 457). For perfectly rational beings, on the other hand, the mere representation of duty alone always suffices. Similarly, in the *Religion*, Kant emphasizes, in rare opposition to the Stoics, that "natural inclinations, *considered in themselves*, are *good*, i.e., not reprehensible, and to want to wipe them out would not only be futile but harmful and blameworthy as well; we must rather only curb them" (6: 58). And in responding to Schiller he writes,

> Now, if one asks, "What is the *aesthetic* constitution, the *temperament* so to speak *of virtue*: is it courageous and hence *joyous* [*fröhlich*], or weighed down by fear and dejected?" an answer is hardly necessary. The latter slavish frame of mind can never be found without a hidden *hatred* of the law, whereas the heart which is joyous [*das fröhliche Herz*] in *compliance* with its duty (not just complacency in the *recognition* of it) is a sign of genuineness in the virtuous disposition.
>
> (6: 23–24n; cf. *KpV* 5: 83)

On the other hand, there are also several notorious "anti-emotion" passages, belonging to what John Rawls calls "Kant's Manichean strain," "a deeply troubling aspect of . . . [his] thought."[18] In the *Groundwork*, Kant asserts that "inclinations themselves, as sources of needs, are so far from having an absolute worth, so as to make one wish to have them, that it must instead be the universal wish of every rational being to be altogether free from them" (4: 428). A virtually identical passage occurs in the second *Critique*, where he announces that inclinations "are always *burdensome* to a rational being, and though he cannot lay them aside, they nevertheless wrest from him the wish to be rid of them" (5: 118; see also *Collins* 27: 368).

Is there a way to resolve this peculiarly Kantian antinomy regarding the emotions? Regarding the Manichean strain, it is not an appropriate goal for human beings to wipe out their inclinations. For if any human being were to achieve this state she would no longer be a human being but rather "a *holy* (superhuman) being, in whom no hindering impulses would impede the law of its will" and who could thus "never be tempted to violate duty" (*MdS* 6: 405, 383; cf. *KpV* 5: 122). With human beings the appropriate goal is not holiness but virtue, "a self-constraint in accordance with a principle of inner freedom" (*MdS* 6: 394). The Kantian concept of virtue does not even apply to holy beings, but in the case of human beings the highest "moral perfection" attainable "is always only virtue [*immer nur Tugend*]" (*KpV* 5: 128; see also 84, *MdS* 6: 383). This human goal of striving for virtue involves not an extirpation of emotions but controlling and developing them, a special kind of *moral* self-control which, as we saw earlier, also includes the expression of joy and pleasure.

But the antinomy does not disappear this easily. In several of the pro-emotion passages cited earlier, it must be admitted that emotions are still, to an extent, being marginalized. Emotions such as compassion and sympathy, for instance, ultimately have only a derivative or conditional moral value for Kant, for they are valuable only insofar as they enable human beings to accomplish what "the representation of duty alone might not accomplish" (*MdS* 6: 457).[19] If such emotions are present in a human being who somehow still manages not to accomplish what the representation of duty commands (e.g., the famous "sympathetically attuned" benefactor in the *Groundwork* on an unlucky day, when he fails to reflect sufficiently on his conduct; 4: 398), then they lose their value.

Other emotions lauded earlier—particularly the "joyous frame of mind" that is central to the virtuous person's character (*Rel* 6: 24n; see also *MdS* 6: 485) and the pleasure (*Lust*) with which he or she acts (*MdS* 6: 484)—are achieved *as a result of* our ability to successfully constrain ourselves in accordance with a principle of inner freedom. After a human being exercises this constraint, he is able "to feel his own dignity" (*KpV* 5: 152), and this in turn "rouses *a feeling of the sublimity* of our own vocation that enraptures us more than any beauty" (*Rel* 6: 23n; see also *KU* 5: 257, 262; *MdS* 6: 437). The joyous heart and mind that are central to virtuous people's characters are generated by the consciousness of their own freedom,[20] and if and when we reach this state we also "become conscious of being superior to nature within us, and thus also to nature outside of us (insofar as it influences us)" (*KU* 5: 264). All of these emotions are thus effects of moral motivation on feeling. While this is no way implies that Kant's account of them is negative rather than positive (agents must experience these emotions and express them in order to count as virtuous), it does mean that they are basically reason-generated emotions—a conclusion that will not please those contemporary virtue ethicists who reject Kant's commitment to reason's dominant role in ethics. Also, some virtue ethicists will no doubt complain that the pleasure and joy Kant's virtuous agents experience in acting virtuously have an overly abstract look to them, since they stem from an awareness of and awe toward ther freedom as moral agents, not from the particular actions being performed.²¹

Still, Kantian virtue is not mere Aristotelian continence.²² Granted, there is some overlap: both involve the ability to act as one ought in the face of recalcitrant emotions. And Kant's and Aristotle's virtuous agents both take pleasure in doing what is morally required. Aristotle's continent agent, however, does not normally experience pleasure when he is able to act as he should. Similarly, Kant's and Aristotle's virtuous agents both possess an inner peace or tranquility. "The true strength of virtue," Kant notes, "is *the mind at rest [das Gemüth in Ruhe]* with a considered and firm resolution to bring virtue's law into practice" (*MdS* 6: 409). Aristotle's continent agent, on the other hand, because he is continually struggling against opposing inclinations, does not possess a tranquil mind.²³

VIRTUE AS MORAL STRENGTH

The term "strength" predominates in Kant's descriptions of virtue. At one point in *MdS* he asserts baldly that virtue "is the concept of strength" (6: 392), and in the *Collins* lectures he states: "to virtue we attach power, strength, and authority" (27: 465). In the *Vigilantius* lectures Kant explicitly draws attention to the Latin root *vir* (man) of *virtus*: "The very Latin word *virtus* originally signifies nothing else but courage, strength and constancy, and the symbol for it indicates the same: a Hercules, with a lion skin and club, striking down the Hydra, which is the symbol of all vice" (27: 492).²⁴ The German noun *Tugend*, he points out in *MdS*, comes from [the verb] '*taugen*'" (6: 390)—to be fit for—and thus also connotes images of strength and fitness, though perhaps not as bluntly. But of course "strength" in all of these contexts is shorthand for *moral* strength—a strength of will rather than of body. "Virtue signifies a moral strength of the will" (*MdS* 6: 405); it is "moral strength in adherence to one's duty" (*Anth* 7: 147) and "consists precisely in the strength of the resolve to perform our duties" (*Vigilantius* 27: 570).

Human beings need to cultivate moral strength of will, for if they do not, it is highly unlikely that they will be able to follow the moral law at all. Virtue is the strength to resist "constant enticements to do otherwise [than our duty] which sensory feelings [*sinnliche Gefühle*] inspire" (*Vigilantius* 27: 570), i.e., the ability to control those natural inclinations which can and often do come into conflict with our moral resolutions (see *MdS* 6: 394). But this control explicitly does not imply the "total suppression [*völlige Unterdrückung*]" of natural inclinations, "for then virtue would no longer exist at all" (*Vigilantius* 27: 570–71). Virtue's control is rather a form of balance that constitutes "the state of *health* proper to a human being" (*MdS* 6: 384; see also 409, *Anth* 7: 251). And, as we saw earlier in the discussion of duties to oneself, because virtue is a strength of soul rather than of body, it is a state of health that ultimately can be acquired only by self-effort.²⁵

Self-mastery (or what Nietzscheans usually translate as "self-overcoming"; *Selbstüberwindung*)²⁶ is also central to virtue as moral strength (e.g., *Collins* 27: 456; see also *Päd* 9: 492; *Vigilantius* 27: 571, 662—though in the *Vigilantius* passages the term is the more literal *Selbstbeherrschung*). Virtue entails a mastery over that part of us that opposes duty; it is a way "of being able to become master [*Meister werden zu können*] over the greatest obstacles within us" (*Rel* 6: 183; see also *Mrongovius* 29: 603; *Collins* 27: 361–62).

Again though, this mastery over the part of oneself that is tempted to transgress duty is not merely self-constraint, "but a self-constraint in accordance with a principle of inner freedom" (*MdS* 6: 394). Self-constraint in accordance with any other principle, regardless of its impact on conduct, does not count as virtue according to this criterion. What is unique about Kant's conception of virtue is not the emphasis on self-constraint but the stronger emphasis on freedom and autonomy that lies behind the self-constraint.[27] And as we saw earlier, the inner freedom that is the true source of Kantian virtue also brings along its own distinct moral feelings of pleasure, joy, and awe. In attaining control and mastery over those inclinations that stand in the way of duty, human moral agents feel the sublimity of their own vocation. Thus in striving to become virtuous, some feelings are constrained, but others are cultivated and expressed. As Kant writes in *MdS*: "virtue is the product of pure practical reason insofar as it gains ascendancy over such inclinations [viz., those that oppose duty] with consciousness of its supremacy (through freedom)" (6: 477). The inclinations that oppose duty are constrained (though, again, not extirpated), but pleasure, joy, and awe are felt once practical reason becomes conscious of its supremacy through freedom.

HUMAN NATURE: THE DIFFICULTY OF MORALITY

Kant is often accused of being infatuated with a "purist" view of morality which rejects both a "biological perspective" and any "reasonable historical and psychological understanding of morality."[28] But at least in regard to his theory of virtue, this accusation is clearly false. Virtue as Kant understands it applies exclusively to human beings, and it is precisely *because* of our biology, psychology, and history that we need virtue.

In a time when industrious scholars are busy producing competing versions not of only of neo-Aristotelian or eudaimonistic virtue ethics but also of consequentialist virtue ethics, pluralistic virtue ethics, perfectionist virtue ethics, and who knows what else, even those commentators who are confident that they know what virtue ethics is readily admit to the "bewildering variety of claims made by philosophers in the name of virtue ethics."[29] Under these circumstances, perhaps it is not surprising that some have even proposed that "we do away with the category of 'virtue ethics'" on the ground that it "does not demarcate a distinctive approach that can be usefully contrasted with Kantian and Utilitarian ethics."[30]

Although I too in the past often despaired over the elasticity and elusiveness of the concept of virtue ethics,[31] I am not convinced that this category is about to disappear any time soon—if for no other reason than that it does not appear to be substantially more misleading than other central categories in ethics, such as consequentialism or, for that matter, Kantianism. Somewhat like Elizabeth Anscombe's over-the-top proposal to jettison the concepts of obligation and duty, this is a recommendation that may "reach such distinction as . . . to excite a murmur among the zealots,"[32] but most nonpartisans, I predict, will in the end reject it.

So where does this leave us with regard to the puzzling question of Kant and virtue ethics? As I see it, character *is* the central concern of Kant's ethics, and thus, at this basic level, we are entitled to say that he develops not just a *theory* of virtue (which of course nearly all serious moral philosophers have done) but a *virtue-based* ethics. At the same time, as I struggle to keep abreast of the rising tide of contemporary virtue ethics literature, it has also become increasingly evident to me that Kant's understanding of character and virtue differs substantially from that of nearly all of the contributors to this literature who regard themselves as virtue ethicists. Those of us who defend the centrality of character and virtue within Kant's ethics need to be careful not to collapse Kant's position into theirs. At the risk of sounding facile, I believe that at bottom we find a very different picture of human nature in these competing accounts of virtue.

How is Kant's account of human nature different? Basically, on his view, morality is a much more precarious achievement for human beings, one that is always in danger of slipping away and concerning which we are constantly in danger of fooling ourselves. The real issue is not Kant's alleged hostility to the emotions—if the jury is open-minded, he can be acquitted of this charge. Nor is it that Kant's virtuous agents take no pleasure in acting virtuously (as we have seen, they definitely do), nor that they are stuck in a conflict-ridden, pre-virtuous condition of Aristotelian continence (on the contrary: the inner freedom of virtue produces a feeling of peace within the soul).

As Kant explicitly notes, contra Stoicism, the enemy is not the natural inclinations, for they "openly display themselves unconcealed to everyone's consciousness" (*Rel* 6: 57). Rather, it is something far darker and harder to control, viz., "the *malice* (of the human heart) which secretly undermines the disposition with soul-corrupting principles" (6: 57). For Kant, the real enemy is simply the radical evil within the human soul, an opponent whose existence most contemporary virtue ethicists do not even acknowledge. Kantian virtue involves the courage to "look straight in the face of the evil principle within ourselves" (*Frieden* 8: 379).[33] Virtue's true strength, again, shows itself in *das Gemüth in Ruhe* rather than in a state of constant inner turmoil. But this tranquil mind must always be accompanied by "a considered and firm resolution to bring virtue's law into practice" (*MdS* 6: 409), as well as a recognition that at bottom human virtue is a "moral disposition in *conflict*" (*KpV* 5: 84) rather than one of holiness and perfect purity of heart. If either the resolution or the recognition falters, we no longer have virtue in Kant's sense. And the pretense that any human being might somehow be able to be a morally good person without the self-constraint and constant vigilance of virtue's law is "nothing but moral enthusiasm and exaggerated self-conceit" (*KpV* 5: 84).[34]

Unfortunately, when we step back from Kant's texts and reenter the real world, this dark picture of human nature rings true. The multiple acts of "unprovoked cruelty" (*Rel* 6: 33) that human beings inflicted on each other in Kant's day and which he briefly catalogs in part I of his *Religion* pale in comparison with what subsequent generations have witnessed. We are deluding ourselves whenever we believe that virtue can be achieved without moral strength.

Self-denial not the essence of virtue.

—BENJAMIN FRANKLIN, *Pennsylvania Gazette*, February 18, 1734

3

Kantian Moral Humility

BETWEEN ARISTOTLE AND PAUL*

AT FIRST GLANCE, the idea of a Kantian ethics of humility looks like a nonstarter, for at least six reasons. First, Kant does not discuss humility (*Demut*) very much. Other traditional virtues such as courage, beneficence, self-control, and justice receive far more attention.

Second, when he does discuss humility, most of his remarks are reserved for various forms of *false* humility. For instance, in *Religion within the Boundaries of Mere Reason* the term "humility" appears only once, in a footnote where Kant criticizes both Hindus and Christians for their lack of courage and for their self-contempt (*Kleinmüthigkeit und Selbstverachtung*). These religious believers, Kant remarks, "never place any reliance in themselves but constantly look about in constant anxiety for a supernatural assistance." This widespread religious attitude, he notes pointedly, "is not humility" but simply "a sign of a *slavish* cast of mind" (6: 184n). And in the *Metaphysics of Morals* he asserts that "**humility** *in comparing oneself with other human beings* (and indeed, with any finite being, even a seraph) is no duty at all [*gar keine Pflicht*]" (6: 435). Similarly, "belittling one's own moral worth merely as a means of acquiring the favor of another, whoever it may be[1] (hypocrisy and flattery) is false (lying) humility, which is contrary to one's duty to oneself since it degrades one's personality" (435–36). Earlier in this same work, Kant also zeroes in on "false humility (servility)" as one of three vices contrary to oneself as a moral being (6: 420; see also *Collins* 27: 349).

Third, in the *Collins* moral philosophy lecture, which contains Kant's most sustained discussion of humility, his references to humility are submerged in a section entitled "Of Proper Self-Esteem [*Von der geziemenden Selbstschätzung*]." Proper self-esteem,

25

he stresses, "includes, on the one hand, humility; but on the other, true noble pride" (27: 348).[2] In relegating humility to a secondary role as a component of the more important virtue of proper self-esteem, Kant signals his opposition to traditional Christian conceptions of humility.

A fourth reason for wariness regarding a Kantian ethics of humility is that Kant, like Hume, is no friend of the monkish virtues. Hume (in)famously transfers "humility ... and the whole train of monkish virtues" from the column of virtue to the opposite column, placing them "in the catalogue of vices."[3] Kant also explicitly invokes the language of monkish virtue in discussing humility. The false humility of servility, he notes in *Collins*, is merely "a monk's virtue [*eine Mönchstugend*], and this is completely unnatural" (27: 349; see also *Kaehler* 185).[4]

Fifth, as we saw a moment ago, Kant definitely defends pride (*Stolz*) as a necessary part of moral virtue. Pride is *"love of honor [Ehrliebe]"* (*MdS* 6: 465), and "love of honor is the constant companion of virtue" (*Anth* 7: 257). Similarly, in *Collins* Kant asserts that "we approve of love of honor on all occasions in anyone" (27: 409; see also *Kaehler* 274; *MdS* 6: 420). However, traditional Christian defenses of humility always involve steadfast criticisms of pride. Paul, for instance, exhorts his readers: "You must humbly reckon others better than yourselves" (Philippians 2: 3). We should be like Christ, "who made himself nothing, assuming the nature of a slave" (2: 7–8). Similarly, Aquinas argues that "pride is a sin" (*Summa Theologica* 2a2æ. 162, 1) and that "pride is directly contrary to humility" (162, 1 ad3; cf. 162, 6).

Finally, while our nature as sensible rational beings who can only have knowledge of objects by being affected by them provides strong support for the attitude of *epistemic* humility (as Rae Langton puts it, "there is indeed an entire aspect of the world that remains hidden from us"),[5] it by no means follows (contra Jeanine Grenberg) "that the fact of our practical affection and dependence leads to a practical, or moral, humility" (29). The enemy in ethics "is not to be sought in the natural inclinations, which merely lack discipline and openly display themselves unconcealed to everyone's consciousness" (*Rel* 6: 57). Epistemic humility indeed follows from the fact that we are beings who depend upon being affected by the world around us in order to engage in rational activity, but moral humility does not necessarily follow from "the fact of our practical affection and dependence." The fact that we are finite creatures of desire does not, on Kant's view, necessarily imply moral humility.

This list of reasons for wariness concerning a Kantian ethics of humility is by no means exhaustive,[6] and it is certainly not intended as a decisive argument against such a project. But it is intended as a strong cautionary note. Kant is quite critical of Christian accounts of humility, and he also endorses certain aspects of pagan accounts of proper pride. Like Mill, he is convinced that "'pagan self-assertion' is one of the elements of human worth, as well as 'Christian self-denial.'"[7] An accurate account of Kantian moral humility needs to take note of both of these commitments. Kant wants to claim a middle space somewhere between pagan self-assertion and Christian self-denial, a space that is created by bringing together the truths of each tradition.

So while there is certainly much to agree with and to admire in Jeanine Grenberg's book *Kant and the Ethics of Humility: A Story of Dependence, Corruption, and Virtue*, I believe that more caution and qualification are needed at certain crucial junctures in the story that is told about Kantian moral humility. In what follows I will focus on five specific areas of disagreement, arguing in each case that what Grenberg propounds differs from Kant's own position, and that the latter is to be preferred over the former.

VIRTUE, COURAGE, AND HUMILITY

Like Grenberg, I am firmly convinced that "there is a Kantian virtue theory to be explored and appreciated" (7), and that "we need to abandon the assumption that Kantian moral theory is concerned exclusively with action" (70; see also 58).[8] But unlike Grenberg, I am less convinced that the correct Kantian story about virtue is "a story in which humility plays a central role" (7). On this point, I side more with Grenberg's frequent sparring partner, Onora O'Neill, who holds that "for Kant the moral life is a matter of struggle rather than of harmony, and the regulative virtue is neither prudence, nor justice, nor temperance, but courage."[9]

In Kant's own definitions of virtue, the terms "moral strength" and "courage" clearly predominate over "humility."[10] For instance, in the *Metaphysics of Morals* he states: "virtue signifies a moral strength of will," adding that "this moral strength, as *courage (fortitudo moralis)*, also constitutes the greatest and only true military honor of the human being" (6: 405). Here as elsewhere, Kant is intentionally echoing pagan language of courage and military honor, but he is also putting these concepts to new uses. It is not the overcoming of fear on the battlefield with which he is primarily concerned, but rather strength of will in one's commitment and adherence to moral principle—a trait needed by civilian and soldier alike.

Again, this language of strength and courage permeates nearly all of Kant's descriptions of virtue. Elsewhere in the *Metaphysics of Morals*, he asserts that virtue "is the concept of strength" (6: 392). And in *Collins* he states: "To virtue we attach power, strength, and authority. It is a victory over inclination" (27: 465; see also *Kaehler* 356). In the *Vigilantius* lectures, he draws attention to the Latin root *vir* (man) of *virtus*: "The very Latin word *virtus* originally signifies nothing else but courage, strength, and constancy, and the symbol for it indicates the same: a Hercules, with lion skin and club, striking down the Hydra, which is the symbol of all vice" (27: 492). "Virtue consists," he adds later in the same lecture, "precisely, in the strength of the resolve to perform our duties, and to strive against the constant enticements to do otherwise which sensory feelings inspire" (27: 570). Or, as he puts it more concisely in the *Anthropology*: "virtue is moral strength in adherence to one's duty" (7: 147).

It is important to note here that the moral strength entailed by human virtue explicitly does *not* imply a "total repression" of natural inclinations—as Kant himself states in *Vigilantius*, "for then there would no longer be any virtue at all" (27: 570–71). Rather, virtue (a term which for Kant applies only to human beings) applies to a "moral disposition in *conflict"* (*KpV* 5: 84)—both inclination and reason must always be present. In learning how to constrain one's inclination "in accordance with a principle of inner freedom" (*MdS* 6: 394), the human being is "able to feel his own dignity" (*KpV* 5: 152). And this feeling in turn "rouses a *feeling of the sublimity* of our own vocation that enraptures us more than any beauty" (*Rel* 6: 23n; see also *KU* 5: 257, 262; *MdS* 6: 438).

The only passage where Kant directly links virtue with humility occurs in the *Critique of Practical Reason*, in the section entitled "The Existence of God as a Postulate of Pure Practical Reason." In defending the superiority of Christian morals over Stoic, Kant writes:

> [A]ll the moral perfection that a human being can attain is still only virtue, that is, a disposition conformed with the law *from respect* for law, and thus consciousness of a continuing propensity to transgression or at least impurity, that is, an admixture of many spurious (not moral) motives to observe the law, hence a self-esteem combined with humility [*eine mit Demuth verbundene Selbstschätzung*].
>
> (5: 128)

Grenberg makes good use of this passage (she cites it twice, at 178, 190), but I am not convinced that it can support all of the weight that she wants to place on it, for three reasons.

First, and this is another example of a point raised earlier, Kantian humility is described here not as a freestanding attitude but rather as one that must work in conjunction with self-esteem. Even in the midst of a defense of the superiority of Christian morals, Kant signals his rejection of traditional Christian humility. Christian humility, on his view, forfeits the proper self-esteem that is necessary for moral agency. In a footnote, Grenberg does acknowledge that "it is difficult to know what the best word for this attitude toward self is, since it combines traditional notions of both self-respect and humility" (150n15), and in chapter 6 she also argues that humility and self-respect "cannot in fact be understood in isolation from each other" (163). But in most of her discussion, she drops this more cautious approach and simply stresses humility.

Second, the phrase "self-esteem combined with humility" actually refers not to virtue itself, but rather to the consciousness or mental attitude of the person who possesses virtue. In this respect, I think it is more accurate to speak of Kantian moral humility—as Grenberg does at times—as the "meta-attitude" with which the virtuous person approaches the exercise of her agency, rather than as the central virtue itself (150; see also 116, 143, 160, 161). Even here, though, I would stress that humility constitutes only one aspect of this meta-attitude—self-esteem is a necessary second part.

Third, this lone passage where humility is linked to virtue must be weighed against the numerous passages cited earlier where virtue is described as courage and moral strength. At two points in her analysis Grenberg comes close to acknowledging the centrality of courage in Kant's conception of virtue, but she quickly pulls back to the safety of her humility thesis: "the attitude proper to overcoming one's corrupt tendencies is not so much courage as humility (albeit, perhaps, a courageous humility)" (74; see also 91, 93). In my view, Kant's emphasis on moral strength and courage in his definition of virtue must not be forfeited in the attempt to rehabilitate the virtue of humility. If sufficient care is exercised, legitimate places for both attitudes can be found.

RESPECT AND HUMILITY

A second area of disagreement concerns the relationship between respect and humility. Kant's revisionist conception of moral humility is articulated in conjunction with his analysis of the complex feeling of respect (*Achtung*) for the moral law—a feeling that "is produced solely by reason" (*KpV* 5: 76; see also 73; *Gr* 4: 401n). The complexity of respect stems from the fact that it begins with strongly negative feelings of pain and humiliation and then radically shifts over to strongly positive feelings of elation, sublimity, and awe (in a sense, an early theory of bipolar disorder, though of course on Kant's view this violent mood swing is not a disorder to be medicated—rather, it is the only legitimate moral incentive). As other commentators have noted, Kant's analyses of respect and the sublime are very similar: both are complex feelings involving rapid movement from pain to pleasure.[11]

Humility comes in at the beginning, when agents confront the moral law and realize that they have the free choice to make it—rather than their inclinations—the determining ground of their wills. As Kant writes in the second *Critique*: "we can see *a priori* that the moral law, as the determining ground of the will, must by thwarting all our inclinations produce a feeling that can be called pain [*Schmerz*]" (5: 73). Some inclinations—those that can be made to work in agreement with the dictates of the moral law—are merely restricted or infringed upon. But others—those that do not accept the supremacy of the moral law—are demolished, put down completely. These latter inclinations are referred to collectively by Kant as "self-conceit [*Eigendünkel*]," and here, as he famously remarks, "the moral law *strikes down* self-conceit altogether" (5: 73).

When our self-conceit is struck down in this manner, we feel humiliation (*Demütigung*). In Kant's words: "the moral law unavoidably humiliates every human being [*demütigt . . . unvermeidlich jeden Mensch*] when he compares with it the sensible propensity of his nature" (5: 74; see also 73, 79). Simply put, we acquire *proper*[12] moral humility only when we compare ourselves to the moral law. As Kant states in the *Collins* moral philosophy lecture:

> [I]f we compare ourselves with the holy moral law, we discover how remote we are from congruity with it. This low opinion of our person arises, therefore, from comparison with the moral law, and there we have reason enough to humble ourselves [*uns zu demüthigen*]. . . . If moral humility [*moralische Demuth*], then, is the curbing of self-conceit in regard to the moral law, it never implies any comparison with others, but only with the moral law. Humility [*Demuth*] is thus the curbing of any high opinion of our moral worth, by the comparison of our actions with the moral law. Such a comparison makes one humble [*macht demüthig*].
>
> (27: 349–50; see also *Kaehler* 184–86)

Here we see one of Kant's primary criticisms of traditional Christian humility. On his view, we achieve proper moral humility only by comparing ourselves to the moral law. We are not to compare ourselves to other moral agents—whether these moral agents be other human beings, seraphs, Jesus, or even God (see *MdS* 6: 435–36). But Paul, as noted earlier, commands his readers to "humbly reckon others better than yourselves" and to strive to be like Jesus, who "humbled himself" by making "himself nothing, assuming the nature of a slave" (Philippians 2: 4, 7–8).

Again, for Kant these negative feelings of pain and humiliation are merely a first, negative effect of the will's confrontation with the moral law. The second, positive effect comes when the will begins to take an interest in the law, to reflect on its power and majesty, thereby acquiring a feeling of respect for it:

> [T]he lowering of pretensions to moral self-esteem—that is, humiliation [*Demüthigung*] on the sensible side—is an elevation of the moral—that is, practical—esteem for the law itself on the intellectual side; in a word, it is respect for the law, and so also a feeling that is positive in its intellectual cause, which is known a priori.
>
> (*KpV* 5: 79)

However, in the process of acquiring respect for the moral law, we also acquire respect for ourselves and for all other rational beings. For we rational beings collectively are the creators of the very same moral law to which we freely submit ourselves: we give the law to ourselves (see *Gr* 4: 431). As Kant notes in *Religion*:

> The majesty of the law (like the law on Sinai) instills awe [*Ehrfurcht*] (not dread, which repels; and also not fascination, which invites familiarity); and this awe rouses the respect of the subject toward his master, except that in this case, since the master lies in us, it rouses *a feeling of the sublimity* of our own vocation that enraptures us more than any beauty.
>
> (*Rel* 6: 23n; see also *KU* 5: 257, 262)

"True humility [*wahre Demuth*]," on Kant's view, "follows unavoidably from our sincere and exact comparison of ourselves with the moral law" (*MdS* 6: 436). But from the moral agent's realization of his own capacity for internal lawgiving "at the same time there comes *exaltation* [*Erhebung*] and the highest self-esteem, as the feeling of his inner worth (*valor*), according to which he is above any price (*pretium*) and possesses an inalienable dignity (*dignitas interna*), which instills in him respect for himself (*reverentia*)" (6: 436).

I asserted earlier that Kant seeks a middle space between pagan self-assertion and Christian self-denial, a space that unites the truths of each tradition. Briefly, what he retrieves from ancient Greek and Roman ethics is the importance for human beings of proper self-assessment and proper pride regarding their moral capacities. Aristotle, for instance, toward the end of his discussion of magnanimity (*megalopsuchia*, literally, "great-souledness") in the *Nicomachean Ethics*, criticizes the unduly humble person (literally, the small-souled man, the *mikropsuchos*) because he "robs himself of what he deserves . . . and seems also not to know himself" (IV.3 1125a19–20, 22). Kant does not want moral agents to rob themselves of what they deserve, and he does want them to know themselves (indeed, on his view "moral cognition of oneself" is "the beginning of all human wisdom"; *MdS* 6: 441).

Kant sides with Christian ethics in holding that self-conceit must be struck down, but he also parts ways with Christianity over the best strategy for striking it down. His strategy involves a comparison between moral agents and the moral law; Christianity's, a comparison between different moral agents. Kant's own conception of moral humility is thus highly revisionist. However, there is also an important Christian analogue to the bipolar nature of Kantian respect. For in the New Testament we are told that humility is the way of exaltation: "Whoever humbles himself will be exalted" (Luke 14: 11, cf. 18: 14); "Humble yourselves then under God's mighty hand, and he will lift you up in due time" (1 Peter 5: 6–7).

Grenberg discusses most of these matters in some detail, and despite her protest that Kant's analysis of respect is "rather confusing" (152), she does a good job on a difficult topic. However, she reverses Kant's own emphasis. Kant's primary stress is clearly on the positive feelings associated with respect—the awe and exaltation that come with the realization of our own inalienable dignity. The negative feelings of pain and humiliation are only a first step, albeit a necessary one. Grenberg, however, continually accentuates the negative rather than the positive. I would prefer to speak of Kant and the ethics of human dignity and self-respect (with humility playing a strong supporting role), whereas Grenberg opts for Kant and the ethics of humility (with human dignity and self-respect playing supporting roles). However, her choice of language and emphasis come with a price. In reversing Kant's emphasis, she is in danger of reverting back to what Kant sought to overcome: an ethical outlook that places too much weight on self-denial.

Why does Grenberg choose the language of humility over that of dignity and self-respect? To answer this question we must first look at what she says regarding human dependence and corruption, and this is my next topic.

RADICAL EVIL, DEPENDENCE, AND CORRUPTION

In opposition to recent philosophical accounts of humility (108, 128), Grenberg argues at length that if we are to arrive at a satisfactory account of this character trait we "must appeal to some minimal account of human nature as limited" (8); that is, "we must appeal not to idiosyncratic flaws of individual agents, but instead to the limits and failings all humans share in common" (16). But because she also explicitly takes Kant as her guide in offering a redefinition and defense of humility as a virtue (7), this appeal to human nature is likely to raise more than a few eyebrows. For a long and varied line of critics from Hegel to Bernard Williams stand united in their condemnation of Kant's ethics for precisely its alleged failure to take any account of human nature. Kant's ethics is charged with *"empty formalism"* and *"abstract universality,"*[13] an infatuation with a "purist" view of morality which rejects both a "biological perspective" as well as any "reasonable historical and psychological understanding of morality."[14] However, at least as regards Kant's theory of virtue, this accusation is clearly false. Virtue as Kant understands it applies exclusively to human beings, and it is precisely because of our biology, psychology, and history that we need virtue.

While I applaud Grenberg's appeal to human nature in her attempt to rehabilitate the virtue of humility from a Kantian perspective, I will argue in this section that her account of human nature is insufficiently Kantian on two points. First, her heavy emphasis on what she calls the "Dependency Thesis" in explaining the origin of radical evil in human beings is not ultimately tenable. Second, her understanding of human corruption is conceived solely in terms of self-interest, and this is objectionably narrow. Neither dependency nor corruption as construed by Grenberg gives us an adequate account of the radical evil in human nature. At the same time, she is certainly correct to insist that Kant's account of virtue is based very much on his analysis of human nature, that radical evil features prominently in his analysis of human nature, and that most contemporary virtue ethicists do not endorse this stark picture of human nature.

Grenberg's appeal to the limits of human nature focuses exclusively on two key claims about the human condition, which she calls the Dependency Thesis and the Corruption Thesis. Her formal statement of the Dependency Thesis runs as follows: "humans, to engage in the practical activity proper to them, and especially in the practical pursuit of happiness, must admit reliance upon persons and things external to them. The legitimate, and indeed unavoidable, pursuit of one's inclinations is one proper end of dependent rational agency" (26). At bottom, her conception of human dependence corresponds roughly to what other commentators refer to as "finitude." Finite wills, unlike holy wills, have "desires other than those prompted by pure reason."[15] As Kant notes in his discussion of imperatives in the *Groundwork*, "a dependent will [*ein abhängiger Wille*] . . . is not of itself always in conformity with reason" (4: 413n). As a result, dependent beings (*abhängige Wesen*) are also those to whom imperatives apply (see 4: 415), whereas "no imperatives hold for the *divine* will and in general for a *holy* will: the 'ought' is out of place here, because volition is of itself necessarily in accord with the law" (4: 414).

For both Kant and Grenberg, our dependence or finitude is also one of the features of our nature that makes us "limited." For instance, at one point in the second *Critique*, when Kant is discussing concepts that apply only to finite beings, he notes that these concepts

> all presuppose a limitation [*eine Eingeschränktheit*] of the nature of a being, in that the subjective constitution of its choice does not of itself accord with the objective law of a practical reason; they presuppose a need to be impelled to activity [*zur Tätigkeit angetrieben*] by something because an internal obstacle is opposed to it.
>
> (5: 79; cited by Grenberg at 24n29)

Grenberg's second claim about the human condition is the Corruption Thesis, which runs "in its most general formulation" as follows: "humans tend to value the self improperly relative to other objects of moral value" (43). The Corruption Thesis also has strong Kantian roots, and tracks back directly to Kant's thesis concerning "the radical evil in human nature" (*Rel* 6: 18). Indeed, in his discussion of radical evil in *Religion*, Kant employs the term "corruption" at several crucial junctures. For instance, in defining the third and most severe degree of human beings' natural propensity to evil, he writes: "the *corruption* [*Verderbtheit*] (*corruptio*) of the human heart is the propensity of the power of choice to maxims that subordinate the incentives of the moral law to others (not moral ones)" (6: 30). Other corruption passages include the following: the human being's way of thinking (*Denkungsart*) is "corrupted at its root [*in ihrer Wurzel . . . verderbt*]" (6: 30); "the *malice* (of the human heart) . . . secretly undermines the disposition with soul-corrupting principles [*seelenverderbende Grundsätzen*]" (6: 57); and his claim that the Stoic philosophers mistakenly attributed "to the human being an uncorrupted will [*ein unverdorbener Wille*]" (6: 58n).

As we have seen, on Grenberg's account the Corruption Thesis is tied explicitly and solely to self-love: "humans tend to value the self improperly relative to other objects of moral value" (43). However, on Kant's view corruption is much broader than this (though our self-conceit is certainly a major source of evil). All that is necessary for evil to occur is that agents act on "incentives other than the law (e.g., ambition, self-love in general, yes, even a kindly instinct such as sympathy" (6: 30–31). As he remarks in a marginal note in the *Handschrift* on which his published *Anthropology* is based: "The question of whether human nature is good or evil depends on the concept of what one calls evil. It is the propensity to desire what is impermissible, although one knows very well that it is wrong" (7: 412). People are evil for many different reasons, but all of these reasons share a common root: we don't put the moral law first.

Grenberg is clearly correct in holding both that dependence and corruption constitute two major limitations of human nature and that these two limitations provide us with compelling reasons to be humble. However, she diverges from Kant—and in my view also argues implausibly—when she claims that "evil is rooted in the dependent nature of an individual human being" (31) and that evil can be plausibly explained by appeal "to the finite and desiring nature of an individual agent" (32).[16] But Kant states clearly in the *Religion* that our natural inclinations are not the enemy. In suggesting that they are, Grenberg reverts back to the errors of the Stoics, "who mistook their enemy, who is not to be sought in the natural inclinations. . . . *Considered in themselves*, natural inclinations are *good*, i.e., not reprehensible" (6: 57–58). Our sensible nature is not the cause of evil. Radical evil, at least as Kant understands it, has no necessary connection to our natural impulses and inclinations. The ground of evil "cannot lie . . . in any natural impulses" (6: 21).[17] Rather, the source of evil lies simply in our propensity knowingly and consistently to choose maxims contrary to the moral law.

I am sympathetic to Grenberg's desire to demonstrate that Kantian radical evil is not simply "a product of society"[18] and that each individual is culpable for their evil. For in Kant's own attempt to show that "the human being is evil by nature" (6: 32), he emphasizes both that we find horrendous, unprovoked acts of human evil even in the "so-called *state of nature*" where "many a philosopher especially hoped to meet the natural goodness of human nature" (6: 33), and that this evil "is brought upon us by ourselves" (6: 32; i.e., radical evil is something for which each human moral agent is responsible). But in defending these claims, Kant does not embrace the wrongheaded theses that human dependence or finitude is the cause of evil, or that human corruption stems simply from self-love. Neither should we.

MORAL EXEMPLARS AND SELF-OTHER COMPARISONS

A fourth site of disagreement concerns the role of moral exemplars in Kant's ethics. On this issue Grenberg is somewhat inconsistent. At one point (here, she follows Allen Wood),[19] she argues that moral agents must not engage in "comparative-competitive" judgments of each other—must not, that is, compare themselves with each other, and ask who is morally better and who is worse (118). Properly humble moral agents compare themselves only with the moral law, not with other people. But later in her book, when she raises "the question of whether Kantian moral theory can make room for moral exemplars," she suggests that there can indeed be "morally productive self-other comparisons" (200).[20] I agree with Grenberg that Kantian moral theory does make room for moral exemplars.[21] However, as I will try to show, the main role of moral exemplars within his ethics does not really involve self-other comparisons at all.

Kant offers at least four detailed arguments in defense of the claim that moral exemplars are necessary and important in human life. Briefly, these arguments may be summarized as follows:

Moral Education

First, contact with and reflection on moral exemplars is necessary in the moral education of children. Human beings, when young, do not yet have the ability to reason autonomously about moral principles, and this ability can only be fostered effectively through exposure to particular examples. In the *Metaphysics of Morals* Kant writes:

> The experimental (technical) means of the formation of virtue is [a] *good* example on the part of the teacher himself (his exemplary conduct) and [a] *cautionary* example in others, since, for a still undeveloped human being, imitation is the first determination of his will to accept maxims that he afterwards makes for himself.
> (6: 479)

Similarly, in the second *Critique* he argues that in order to bring an uncultivated mind onto the track of the morally good "some preparatory guidance is needed" (5: 152), and he advises educators to search through "biographies of ancient and modern times in order to have at hand examples [*Belege*] of the duties presented" in the students' moral catechism (154). Finally, in his *Lectures on Pedagogy* he recommends that "in order to ground a moral character in children, ... one must teach them the duties they have to fulfill as much as possible by examples [*so viel als möglich durch Beispiele*]" (9: 488).

Limitation of Human Reason

Second, human beings—even when they have reached adulthood—are still equipped only with a "discursive, image-dependent understanding" (*KU* 5: 408; see also *Rel* 64–65n). As a result, "for the human being the invisible needs to be represented through something visible (sensible)" (*Rel* 6: 192)—we need "something that *the senses can hold onto* [*etwas Sinnlich-Haltbares*]" (6: 109; see also *Anth* 7: 254). But the concept of a morally perfect will is an idea of reason, and cannot be derived from experience. Humans therefore need to represent this concept symbolically to themselves by making analogies to tangible, flesh-and-blood examples. As Grenberg rightly notes, "finite minds need images" (208); "we need a person and not just a principle" (206).

Hope and Inspiration

Third, the existence of moral exemplars provides the rest of us with hope and inspiration, for their examples provide us with tangible evidence that what the moral law demands is humanly feasible. Examples "put beyond doubt the practicability [*Tunlichkeit*] of what the law commands" (*Gr* 4: 409), and exemplary conduct "serves as proof of the practicability of acting in conformity with duty [*Beweis der Tunlichkeit des Pflichtmäßigen*]" (*MdS* 6: 480). And the reverse is also true. If there were no moral exemplars, we would then have the excuse that what the moral law commands is humanly impossible. As Kant remarks in the *Collins* lecture: "Human beings like, in general, to have examples, and if none exists they are happy to excuse themselves, on the ground that everybody lives that way" (27: 334; see also *Kaehler* 161).

Emulation

Finally, human beings need moral exemplars in order to have an ideal to emulate. As Kant notes in *Collins*: "examples serve us for encouragement and emulation [*zur Aufmunterung und zur Nachfolge*]. . . . If I see a thing *in concreto*, I recognize it all the more clearly. . . . An example is not for copying, though it is certainly for emulation" (27: 333–34; see also *Kaehler* 159–60).

Granted, all of these arguments in defense of moral exemplars must be interpreted in a way that makes them consistent with Kant's better-known warnings concerning the dangers of examples in ethics. Morality cannot be derived from examples, and "even the Holy One of the Gospel must first be compared with our ideal of moral perfection before he is cognized as such" (*Gr* 4: 408; cf. *Collins* 27: 333). However, the textual evidence makes it abundantly clear that on Kant's view moral exemplars do play a necessary and important role in human life. Here Grenberg actually underestimates Kant's position a bit: she argues only that Kantian moral theory "*can* make room for moral exemplars." But a careful look at Kant's texts shows that he definitely *does* create ample space for moral exemplars.

However, I believe that Grenberg also mischaracterizes Kant's position regarding moral exemplars when she describes it as involving "morally productive self-other comparisons." For on Kant's view, we don't turn to exemplars in order to compare ourselves to them. This sort of comparison game "merely stirs up envy" (*Päd* 9: 491). Rather, we turn to exemplars for epistemological reasons. Exemplars provide young minds who have not yet reached the age of autonomy with illustrations, they provide autonomous adults (who remain saddled with limited discursive intellects) with something tangible, and they provide all of us with concrete evidence that what morality demands is humanly feasible. So even though moral exemplars do play an important role in Kant's ethics, it remains the case that "every comparison between people drops out." When we find an exemplar (even if it be the "Holy One of the Gospel"), Kant's advice is always to make comparisons only with the moral law itself, never with other people (*MdS* 6: 480; *Gr* 4: 408–9; *Collins* 27: 333).

Self-Knowledge, Self-Perfection, and Duties to Oneself

A fifth and final area of disagreement concerns Grenberg's strong emphases on self-knowledge and self-perfection in her account of the virtue of humility. My worries here are two: first, these emphases may result in an overly introspective ethics that lacks sufficient efficacy in a world such as ours where less-than-perfect and less-than-fully-aware moral agents must act; and second, they also mischaracterize the genuine emphasis on the self that is central in Kant's ethics.

Grenberg takes very seriously Kant's remarks about the duties of both self-perfection (89–98; see *MdS* 6: 446) and self-knowledge (217–41; see *MdS* 6: 441), though of course she slants them strongly toward her own humility thesis. For instance, she views humility as the "central attitude to take in pursuit of" self-perfection (91), and she also holds that humility is central to the knowledge of self to which virtuous agents must aspire (226, 228). And I do concur with her basic conviction that Kant's ethics exhibits a strong interiority or focus on the self—which sets it apart from most modern and contemporary ethical theories.[22] This comes out most clearly in Kant's assertions concerning the priority of duties to oneself. If there were no duties to oneself, he proclaims confidently in the *Metaphysics of Morals*, "then there would be no duties whatsoever" (6: 417). Similarly, in *Collins* we are told that "duties to oneself are the supreme condition [*die oberste Bedingung*] and *principium* of all morality" (27: 344), the "conditions under which alone the other duties can be performed" (27: 360; see also *Kaehler* 172), and "the most important of all" duties (27: 341; see also 433, *Kaehler* 171).

Briefly, what Kant means when he calls duties to oneself the precondition of all other duties and the *principium* of all morality is that morality does not exist unless and until moral agents develop and exercise their capacities of agency. But ultimately individuals must do this themselves, for we are unable to directly instill or activate these capacities in others. However, the chief capacity needed is self-constraint. *All moral duties*—to others as well as to oneself, perfect as well as imperfect—presuppose self-constraint. As Kant puts it: "the constraint that the concept of duty contains can only be self-constraint (through the representation of the law alone)" (*MdS* 6: 380). And virtue itself is also defined by Kant in terms of self-constraint. Virtue is "a self-constraint in accordance with a principle of inner freedom" (6: 394). This emphasis on self-constraint (*Selbstzwang*) is a key reason that Kant construes virtue in terms of courage and moral strength rather than humility: moral agents need to cultivate moral strength of will, to become masters over the part of themselves that is tempted to transgress the moral law, in order for morality to exist. As O'Neill remarks (and Grenberg's position here is developed as a response to O'Neill's), Kant's primary emphasis is "on the practical context and the task of learning to live by moral principles,"[23] and this is why courage and moral strength are called for. But the introspective task of self-knowledge is less pressing, and the chances of success here are also less likely. For at least in the case of the human being, "the depths of his own heart (the subjective first ground of his maxims) are inscrutable [*unerforschlich*] to him" (*Rel* 6: 51).

So while Grenberg is certainly right to draw attention to Kant's strong emphasis on the self in his ethics, I think she has mischaracterized this emphasis. Kant's primary focus is not on attaining self-perfection or complete knowledge of one's heart (these are unattainable ideals for humans), but rather simply on acquiring the necessary self-constraint that virtue implies and which acting from duty entails.

I have drawn attention to five specific areas of disagreement concerning Grenberg's analysis of Kant's ethics, but I would like to conclude simply by noting that these are by no means major criticisms of her own project. *Kant and the Ethics of Humility* is a fine book: the author illuminates significant and currently underappreciated areas of Kant's ethics, and she does so in an engaging manner that creates much-needed links between Kant's ethics and current work in virtue ethics, moral psychology, and theological ethics.

4

"Firm as a Rock in Her Own Principles"

(BUT NOT NECESSARILY A KANTIAN)*

KANT AND NOVELS

IN *ANTHROPOLOGY FROM a Pragmatic Point of View* (1798), Kant cautions that "*reading novels, in addition to causing many other mental discords [Verstimmungen des Gemüts]*, also . . . makes distraction habitual" (7: 208), noting further that this habitual distraction leads to a type of forgetfulness "where the head, no matter how often it is filled, still remains empty like a barrel full of holes," and that it "especially seizes women who are accustomed to reading novels" (7: 185). And in his *Lectures on Pedagogy* (1803), after asserting again that "reading novels weakens the memory," Kant goes on to recommend that "all novels should be taken out of the hands of children"—in part because of the possibility that they will "go into raptures [*herumschwärmen*]"[1] while reading them (9: 473).

Given his repeated warnings about the dangers posed by the new genre of the novel, the strategy of appealing to a character in a novel to illustrate Kantian positions in ethics might seem particularly problematic. At the same time, Kant seems not to have heeded his own warnings about the perils of novels. In several versions of his anthropology lectures he points to novels as one of the most important aids (*Hilfsmittel*) for acquiring anthropological knowledge (*Anth* 7: 121; see also *Pillau* 25: 734; *Menschenkunde* 25: 857–58; *Mrongovius* 25: 1213).[2] The main goal of Kant's anthropology is to acquire a reflective understanding of the human condition—a sense of the problems and challenges that all human beings in all times and places share with one another. And Kant is certainly not alone in thinking that we are more likely to acquire this kind of knowledge of human nature from the work of an accomplished novelist than we are from the typical anthropological fieldwork—which by design is focused exclusively on particular groups in particular times and places.[3]

Jane Austen's first novel, *Sense and Sensibility*, was not published until 1811,[4] and *Mansfield Park* did not appear until 1814—ten years after Kant's death. But in his *Anthropology*, Kant repeatedly cites with great approval the earlier canonic English novelists Henry Fielding (1707–1754) and Samuel Richardson (1689–1761).[5] Given Kant's documented interest in English novels, I think the odds are quite good that he would have welcomed Austen's *Mansfield Park* as a valuable source of insight into human nature—even if, in the course of reading it, we are liable to become forgetful or go into raptures.

GRENBERG, HUMILITY, COURAGE

In her book *Kant and the Ethics of Humility* (2005), Jeanine Grenberg argues that there is "a Kantian virtue theory to be explored and appreciated," a virtue theory "in which humility plays a central role."[6] In my critical response to her book (see chapter 3 in this volume), I argued, among other things, that it is not humility that plays the lead role in Kant's theory of virtue but rather courage—courage understood not in the traditional sense of overcoming fear on the battlefield but rather in Kant's sense of strength of will in one's commitment and adherence to moral principle—a trait needed by soldier and civilian alike.[7] Virtue, as he remarks succinctly in the *Anthropology*, "is *moral strength* in adherence to one's duty" (7: 147; see also *MdS* 6: 392, 405; *Collins* 27: 465; *Vigilantius* 27: 492, 570).

In her essay "Courageous Humility in Jane Austen's *Mansfield Park*," Grenberg argues, among other things, that "courage is in fact an aspect of humility."[8] While I welcome this new emphasis[9] on the place of courage in Kant's virtue theory, I wish now to focus on the following two specific sets of questions:[10] (1) Is courage, as understood by Kant, in fact an aspect of humility? What should be made of the hybrid virtue "courageous humility"? (2) Is Fanny Price "a courageously humble person in Kant's sense"?[11] More generally, is Fanny a morally virtuous person according to Kant's ethics?

COURAGEOUS HUMILITY?

Is Kantian courage necessarily connected to Kantian humility? By "courage," again, Kant means not the traditional military virtue of overcoming fear on the battlefield, but "moral strength of will"—a cultivated commitment and demonstrated capacity to live and act according to moral principle, and to consistently withstand temptations against so living and acting. And this capacity of moral strength or courage is also precisely what Kant means by "virtue." For instance, in a section entitled "Of Virtue in General" in the *Metaphysics of Morals*, he states:

> Virtue signifies a moral strength of will. . . . Virtue is . . . the moral strength of a *human being's* will in fulfilling his *duty*, which is moral *constraint* through his own

lawgiving reason.... This moral strength, as courage [*Tapferkeit*] (*fortitudo moralis*), also constitutes the greatest and only true military honor of the human being.

(6: 405; see also 380)

Similarly, in *Religion within the Boundaries of Mere Reason*, he remarks that "*virtue* ... designates bravery and courage [*Mut und Tapferkeit*] (in Greek as well as in Latin)" (6: 57).[12]

Humility, on the other hand, signifies for Kant the proper curbing of self-conceit that occurs when moral agents compare themselves to the moral law. As he notes in the *Metaphysics of Morals*: "True humility must follow unavoidably from our sincere and exact comparison of ourselves with the moral law" (6: 436; see also *Collins* 27: 349–50). False humility, he implies, occurs when we compare ourselves to other moral agents—be they human beings, seraphs, "the Holy One of the Gospel," or even God (6: 436; *Gr* 4: 408–9). At the same time, Kantian moral humility must always be understood in conjunction with dignity and self-respect. When we first compare ourselves to the moral law, our self-conceit is struck down: we are humiliated. But once we realize that as rational beings we are ourselves the co-creators of the very same moral law to which we freely submit ourselves, we are filled with a sense of awe for the dignity of rational agency. As Kant remarks in his famous reply to Schiller in the *Religion*, we become "enraptured [*hinreißt*]"[13] by "*a feeling of the sublimity* of our own vocation" (6: 23n).

However, humility, though a necessary and centrally important attitude for morally virtuous agents as understood by Kant, is not what he means by virtue. For we have seen already that he defines virtue as moral strength of will in fulfilling one's duty. Rather, humility—comparing oneself to the moral law—is, to borrow a phrase from Grenberg's book, the "meta-attitude" with which virtuous people approach the exercise of their agency.[14]

Keeping these Kantian conceptions of courage and humility in mind, let us now return to the question: Is Kantian courage necessarily connected to Kantian humility? Answer: yes. However, since Kant *defines* virtue in general as courage, courage is also connected to *all* of the virtues. The just person, the benevolent person, the charitable person, the honest person—they are courageous too, for they all exhibit strength of will in their commitment to moral principle. Similarly, humility, as the meta-attitude of virtuous agents, is also connected to *all* of the virtues. The just person, the benevolent person, the charitable person, and the honest person all necessarily practice humility in comparing themselves only to the moral law. So in the end, to assert that courage is connected to humility is, at least for Kant, not saying much. The claim is trivially true. And its truth is far from unique, for courage is also part of every other virtue. Likewise, the attitude of humility will also be present in all virtuous agents.

But what then to make of the passage from Kant's *Moralphilosophie Collins* lecture (1785),[15] which Grenberg cites to support her position regarding the need to connect humility with courage? Kant does clearly state here that unless humility is connected to bravery (*Mut*), humble agents, after realizing how remote they are from congruity with the moral law, may succumb to despair (*Mutlosigkeit*) and "venture to do nothing at all" (27: 350).[16] I do not deny that this passage supports the view that Kantian humility must be tied to bravery and courage, though I think it is also clear that in this particular passage Kant is using *Mut* in the traditional sense of "overcoming fear" rather than in his own later, quasi-technical sense of "strength of will in adherence to duty."[17] But regardless of how one interprets *Mut* in this passage, the *Collins* quotation does not negate the claims made earlier. Courage, in the sense of strength of will in fulfilling one's duty, is simply what Kant means by "virtue," and humility—comparing oneself only to the moral law—is the meta-attitude that all virtuous agents must adopt. For Kant, courage and humility are necessarily tied to *all* of the virtues.

FANNY PRICE AND KANT'S ETHICS

> I do not quite know what to make of Miss Fanny. I do not understand her. . . . What is her character?
> —HENRY CRAWFORD, in *Mansfield Park*[18]

Grenberg is by no means the first philosopher to view Jane Austen's novels through the lens of canonical moral philosophy. As she reminds us in her paper, Alasdair MacIntyre, in *After Virtue*, claims that Austen is Aristotelian and anti-Enlightenment in her general approach, and that she "restores a teleological perspective" to the virtues.[19] And MacIntyre, in turn, refers to an essay by Gilbert Ryle, who argues that "Shaftesbury was the direct or indirect source of Jane Austen's moral furniture."[20] Other philosophers have argued that the characters in Austen's novels come closest to "views like those of David Hume rather than those of Kant."[21]

Literary critics also have not been shy in their efforts to tag the moral perspective of Austen and/or various characters in her novels, though their labels of choice are not always drawn from the canon of moral philosophy. Kathryn Sutherland, for example, informs us that "Fanny is a Romantic heroine . . . formed as a contemporary of Wordsworth and Coleridge,"[22] while Marilyn Butler complains that Austen's "morality is preconceived and inflexible; . . . conservative in a sense no longer current."[23] Still other critics, while not quite mustering up a specific ideological label for Fanny Price's moral outlook, make it clear that they find her extremely unattractive. Thus Tony Tanner laments that Fanny "is never, ever wrong. . . . Fanny always thinks, feels, speaks and behaves exactly as she ought."[24] And Lionel Trilling recoils from the "prim, proper, and priggish"[25] Fanny to conclude that "nobody . . . has ever found it possible to like the heroine of *Mansfield Park*."[26]

I am skeptical of the value of arguing whether a character in a novel is or isn't Aristotelian, Shaftesburian, Humean, or Kantian, and thus I approach the challenge of articulating Fanny's moral outlook in the present context warily. For unless we can show that the author was familiar with the philosophical works in question, any connection argued for will be merely coincidental.[27] In saying this, I am by no means endorsing Oscar Wilde's dictum that "[t]here is no such thing as a moral or an immoral book. Books are well written, or badly written. That is all."[28] Novels frequently *do* have moral content, and in such cases readers should struggle to articulate and evaluate it.

But I'm not convinced that describing a novel's moral content by means of labels such as "Aristotle," "Shaftesbury," "Hume," or "Kant" is the way to go. A novel's moral content is a function not of its author's alleged debt to one or another complex system of moral philosophy, but rather of the specific moral dilemmas and challenges faced by its characters.

Keeping these doubts in mind, let me now plunge ahead and address two related questions concerning Fanny Price: (1) Does Fanny display courageous humility in Kant's sense? (2) Is she a morally virtuous person according to Kant's ethics?

FANNY'S "COURAGEOUS HUMILITY"?

Grenberg agrees with the claim of MacIntyre and others that Fanny's refusal of Henry Crawford's marriage proposal "is an act of great courage, an act that is central to the plot of *Mansfield Park*."[29] Or at least she agrees in part. For MacIntyre is using "courage" in a non-Kantian sense. In his view, virtue concepts are "marginal" to Kant, and Kant's ethics exemplifies the unfortunate view that morality is nothing more "than obedience to rules."[30] But Grenberg, as we saw earlier, argues that "there is a Kantian virtue theory to be explored and appreciated,"[31] and she also holds that Fanny "firmly claims the Kantian virtues as her own."[32] Fanny, Grenberg concludes, "is a courageously humble person in the Kantian sense."[33]

The courage in Fanny's refusal stems from her willingness to stand up against the family expectations and social conventions of her time. Every other character in the novel urges her to accept Crawford's proposal. For instance, her uncle Sir Thomas, the owner of Mansfield Park, where Fanny was sent to live at age ten, chastises her:

> Mr. Crawford must not be kept longer waiting. I will, therefore, only add, as thinking it my duty to mark my opinion of your conduct—that you have disappointed every expectation I had formed, and proved yourself of a character the very reverse of what I had supposed. . . . I had thought you peculiarly free from willfulness of temper, self-conceit, and every tendency to that independence of spirit, which prevails so much in modern days, even in young women, and which in young women is offensive and disgusting beyond all common offence. But you have now shewn me that you can be willful and perverse, that you can and will decide for yourself, without any consideration or deference for those who have surely some right to guide you—without even asking their advice.
>
> (*MP*, 293–94)

Lady Bertram, Sir Thomas's wife—a woman, we are informed, for whom "beauty and wealth were all that excited her respect," also urges Fanny to accept the offer of "a man of such good estate as Mr. Crawford," adding pointedly: "You must be aware, Fanny, that it is every young woman's duty to accept such a very unexceptionable offer as this" (*MP*, 307). "This," the narrator informs us, "was almost the only rule of conduct, the only piece of advice, which Fanny had ever received from her aunt in the course of eight years and a half" (*MP*, 308). Even Fanny's cousin Edmund, who is secretly in love with Fanny, and who in the end does win her hand in marriage, urges Fanny to accept Crawford's proposal: "Let him succeed at last, Fanny, let him succeed at last. You have proved yourself upright and disinterested, prove yourself grateful and tender-hearted; and then you will be the perfect model of a woman, which I have always believed you born for" (*MP*, 322).

Fanny's refusal to accept Crawford's proposal is clearly courageous in a traditional sense. She is not afraid to reject the advice of her elders, to spurn social convention, and to risk the definite possibility of a financially insecure future. However, none of this makes her decision courageous in Kant's sense, for we are presented with no textual evidence that Fanny is exercising strength of will in adhering to moral duty. Indeed, from a Kantian perspective, the issues of who to marry and whether to marry at all are not primarily questions of moral duty, but questions of prudence and happiness. To put it in Kant's language, what we are talking about here is "skill in the choice of means to one's own greatest well-being [*Wohlsein*]," a skill that "can be called *prudence* [*Klugheit*] in the narrowest sense" (*Gr* 4: 416).[34] And the imperative in such cases "is still always *hypothetical*; the action is not commanded absolutely but only as means to another purpose" (4: 416)—that is, to one's own well-being. Similarly, Fanny's decision not to marry Crawford does not exemplify humility in Kant's sense, for there is no evidence that in declining his proposal she is comparing herself to the moral law in an effort to strike down self-conceit. Her decision is prudential, not moral.

FANNY'S "KANTIANISM"

Fanny is described in at least three fundamental ways that, at least on the surface, do sound very Kantian. First, consider her response to Henry Crawford, immediately after he says: "'When you give me your opinion, I always know what is right. Your judgment is my rule of right.' 'Oh, no!—do not say so. We all have a better guide in ourselves, if we would attend to it, than any other person can be'" (*MP*, 383). Fanny clearly wants people to follow their own conscience rather than to let other people decide for them. To put it in more Kantian terms, she wants people to "have the courage to make use of their own understanding" (see *Aufklärung* 8: 35), for "the maxim of always thinking for oneself is **enlightenment**" (*Was heißt: Sich im Denken orientiren?* 8: 146n; see also *KU* 5: 294). However, this general commitment to autonomous reasoning is by no means sufficient to mark one as a committed Kantian. Socrates and a good many other philosophers also encourage us to follow the better guide in ourselves.[35]

Second, consider the following trio of remarks, each of which highlights Fanny's firm commitment to principle and to doing the right thing. At one point the narrator says of her: "She must do her duty, and trust that time might make her duty easier than it now was" (*MP*, 306). And Edmund, who eventually wins Fanny's hand, notes on first meeting her that she has "a strong desire of doing right" (*MP*, 17), and—eight years later—that she is "a woman, who firm as a rock in her own principles, has a gentleness of character so well adapted to recommend them" (*MP*, 325). Fanny is clearly a reflective and principled person who is concerned to act appropriately. But of course this is also the way that *most* moralists want people to be. Unless we can show that Fanny is committed to a specifically Kantian conception of moral duty, and moved by a specifically Kantian conception of moral motivation, one that overrides all other motives, this general orientation does not count as uniquely Kantian. And I don't think the text entitles us to make these assumptions.

Third, consider Sir Thomas's remarks on the flawed morals of his two daughters—as opposed to those of the principled Fanny, who clearly has "some touches of the angel" (*MP*, 318) in her: "He feared that principle, active principle, had been wanting, that they never had been properly taught to govern their inclinations and tempers, by that sense of duty which can alone suffice" (*MP*, 430).[36] As every Introduction to Ethics student knows, Kant also urges readers to govern their inclinations by a sense of duty. But (again), so do a good many other moral philosophers. Unless and until we are offered a more detailed story about the precise nature of the sense of duty that is doing the governing, we are not entitled to infer that Fanny is a morally virtuous person in Kant's specific sense.

Finally, there is an additional sense (albeit not one employed by Austen) in which Fanny strikes some readers (particularly those readers who don't like Kant) as being stereotypically Kantian. As we have seen, some critics see her as "prim, proper, and priggish"[37]—as someone who is no fun to be around because she is always struggling to do the right thing in the face of recalcitrant emotions, and who always lets others know about the depth of her struggle. And this particular mindset does recall Schiller's famous dismissal of Kant's ethics:

Conscientious Scruple
Gladly I serve my friends, but alas I do so with pleasure.
    And so often I worry, that I am not virtuous.
    Decision
There is no other remedy: you must try to despise them
    And then do with loathing what duty commands you to do.[38]

However, even if Fanny is accurately labeled as "prim, proper, and priggish" (and there is good reason to reject this description),[39] this would not qualify her as Kantian, for this is not how Kantians act. Kantian virtuous agents do take pleasure in doing what is morally required, as Kant emphasizes in his reply to Schiller:

Now, if we ask, "What is the *aesthetic* constitution, the *temperament* so to speak of virtue: is it courageous and hence *joyous* [*fröhlich*], or weighed down by fear and dejected?" an answer is hardly necessary. The latter slavish frame of mind can never be found without a hidden *hatred* of the law, whereas the heart which is joyous [*das fröhliche Herz*] in *compliance* with its duty (not just complacency in the *recognition* of it) is a sign of genuineness in the virtuous disposition.

(*Rel* 6: 23–24n)

In short, on Kant's view, the truly virtuous person necessarily feels joy in leading a moral life. She must feel and express this emotion in order to count as virtuous. She does not confront duty's demands with loathing, but rather with joy. "Dour moralist" is not an accurate description of the Kantian virtuous agent.

When he asserted that novels are one of the most important aids for acquiring anthropological knowledge and an understanding of human nature, Kant by no means confined his remarks to novels whose authors and/or characters subscribe to his own system of ethics. And this is a very good thing, for it allows us to learn not only from Jane Austen's writings, but from many other novels as well.[40]

PART TWO

Anthropology and Ethics

5

The Second Part of Morals*

THE MISSING LINK?

THERE ARE MANY important reasons for turning to Kant's lectures on anthropology. Anthropology was a new academic discipline in the late eighteenth century, and Kant played a pivotal role in its creation.[1] Kant sometimes claims (and others have followed him on this point) that the fundamental questions of metaphysics, ethics, and religion "could all be reckoned to be anthropology," on the ground that they all refer to the question "What is the human being?" (*Jäsche Logik* 9:25; see also letter to C. F. Stäudlin of May 4, 1793, 11: 414; *KrV* B 833; *Metaphysik-Pölitz* 28: 534). Examining the various versions of the lectures could perhaps help one to see what led Kant to occasionally describe anthropology as a kind of transcendental *Urdisziplin*.[2] Similarly, Kant's anthropology inaugurates the continental tradition of philosophical anthropology, out of which numerous twentieth-century intellectual movements grew (e.g., existentialism) and to which others reacted against (e.g., Foucault's early "archaeological" work). A close look at Kant's lectures might help one better to understand the roots of these and other related philosophical projects. Also, a comparative examination of the various versions of the lectures would enable one to test Benno Erdmann's "senility thesis"—namely, his claim (which others have extended to all of Kant's last publications) that Kant's 1798 *Anthropology from a Pragmatic Point of View* represents only "the laborious compilation of a seventy-four-year-old man as he stood on the threshold of decrepitude."[3] Finally, the wealth of materials provided by the various anthropology lectures enables one to see how Kant's ongoing work in anthropology profoundly affected (and was in turn affected by) many other areas of his philosophical project (e.g., theoretical philosophy, aesthetics, philosophy of history) in ways that are only now coming to be understood.

But for me, the major incentive for exploring Kant's anthropology lectures has always been to get a handle on the mysterious "counterpart of a metaphysics of morals, the other member of the division of practical philosophy as a whole, . . . moral anthropology" (*MdS* 6: 217). Students of Kant know all too well about "the first part of morals," that is, "the metaphysics of morals or *metaphysica pura*." This first, non-empirical or pure part of morals "is built on necessary laws, as a result it cannot be grounded on the particular constitution of a rational being, [such as] the human being" (*Moral Mrongovius II* 29: 599; see also *Gr* 4: 389). But what about "the second part": "*philosophia moralis applicata*, moral anthropology, to which the empirical principles belong" (*Moral Mrongovius II* 29: 599)? "Moral anthropology," as the term suggests, "is morality applied to the human being" (ibid.).

In his writings and lectures on ethics, Kant repeatedly invokes the term "anthropology" when describing this second, empirical part of ethics. Often, as in the previous citations, the favored phrase is "moral anthropology"; sometimes, it is "practical anthropology" (*Gr* 4: 388); and sometimes, it is simply "anthropology" (*Gr* 4: 412; *Moralphil. Collins* 27: 244; *Moral Mrongovius I* 27: 1398). This frequent employment within the practical philosophy texts and lectures of the term "anthropology" as a shorthand means of conveying what "the other member of the division of practical philosophy as a whole" is about gives readers who turn to the anthropology lectures a thoroughly legitimate expectation that the myriad mysteries of Kant's *philosophia moralis applicata* will finally be addressed in some detail. Those who approach these lectures with ethics in mind are inevitably driven by the hope of finally locating a missing link in Kant's system of practical philosophy, a link that will give his ethics the much-needed material content and applicability to human life that critics from Hegel to Max Scheler to contemporary descendants such as Bernard Williams, Alasdair MacIntyre, and many others have claimed are nowhere to be found in Kant.

FOOLED BY HOPE?

However, when one does examine Kant's anthropology lectures with ethics in mind (more specifically, with the aim of tracking the details of the "second part" of morals), it is easy to get frustrated. For nowhere in these lectures does Kant explicitly and straightforwardly say anything like the following: "I shall now discuss in detail what, in my practical philosophy texts, I call 'moral anthropology' or the 'second part of morals'; showing how this second, empirical part relates to the first, non-empirical part of ethics, and why 'anthropology' in my particular sense of the term can properly be said to constitute this second part." Determining why Kant says nothing close to this is fated to remain a guessing game, but I submit that the following three interrelated points provide at least a good part of the answer.

First, the anthropology lectures are primarily an informal, popular project—not a scholarly exercise in technical philosophy. Kant's aim was not to contribute another tome of "science for the school [*Wissenschaft für die Schule*]" but rather to promote "enlightenment for common life [*Aufklärung fürs gemeine Leben*]" (*Menschenkunde* 25: 853). The goal was to produce a "study for the world [*Studium für die Welt*]," and this is explicitly a type of study that "consists not merely in gaining esteem for oneself from guild members of the school but also in extending knowledge beyond the school and trying to expand one's knowledge toward universal benefit [*zum allgemeinen Nutzen*]" (*Menschenkunde* 25: 853; see also *Mrongovius* 25: 1209). As Kant remarks at the end of his 1775 essay, *Of the Different Races of Human Beings*, which also served as an advertisement for his lecture course on physical geography for that year, he wanted to produce a kind of pragmatic "knowledge of the world [*Weltkenntnis*]," a knowledge that would "be useful not merely for school, but rather for life, and through which the accomplished student is introduced to the stage of his destiny, namely, the world" (2: 443; see also *Friedländer* 25: 469; *Pillau* 25: 733–34; *Anth* 7: 120). Partly because of this strong *Weltkenntnis* aim, the anthropology lectures do not involve themselves with technical discussions of ethical theory.

Second (and partly as a result of the first point), the vocabulary of Kant's anthropology lectures also differs strongly from that of his practical philosophy writings. In the anthropology lectures, he seldom employs the technical terminology and jargon of his more formal works. Because of these different vocabularies, the two bodies of work almost seem to be talking past one another—they often don't appear to link up. Reinhard Brandt, for instance, who seems particularly impressed with these lexical differences, points out that "neither in the lecture transcriptions nor in the book version [of Kant's *Anthropology*] are the words 'categorical' or 'imperative' or 'autonomy' cited," which leads him to conclude on the skeptical note that "pragmatic anthropology is not identical in any of its phases of development with the anthropology that Kant repeatedly earmarks as the complementary part [*Komplemenärstück*] of his moral theory after 1770."[4]

Third (and this too is related to the previous points), there is often a formidable conceptual gap between Kant's anthropology lectures and his ethics texts, with the very idea of a *moral* anthropology hovering awkwardly between both fields, at home in neither. For the most part, Kantian anthropology is a descriptive, empirical undertaking; Kantian ethics a prescriptive, normative one founded on a priori principles. The concept of a *moral ought*, on Kant's view,

> expresses a species of necessity and a connection with grounds that does not occur anywhere else in the whole of nature. In nature the understanding can only cognize *what exists*, or has been, or will be. It is impossible that something in it *ought to be* other than what, in all these time relations, it in fact is; indeed, the *ought*, if one has merely the course of nature before one's eyes, has no meaning whatsoever [*ganz und gar keine Bedeutung*].
>
> (*KrV* A 547/B 575; see also *KU* 5: 173)

Given this stern view of ethical norms, how could one legitimately expect to find a moral anthropology anywhere within the Kantian corpus? How can something that claims to be an empirical science also claim to be *moral*—normatively as opposed to merely descriptively *moral*, in Kant's infamous nonnaturalistic sense? Emil Arnoldt, in his 1894 study, describes this awkward "neither here nor there" status of Kantian anthropology:

> As a part of practical philosophy, Kant's anthropology stands under the legislation of reason according to laws of freedom, which prescribe what ought to be; on the other hand, even if it is morally practical, it is part of a comprehensive [empirical] anthropology which stands under the legislation of reason according to the concept of nature, which indicates what is. Kant did not determine this relationship more closely.[5]

The preceding three interrelated points are, I submit, all plausible explanations as to why we do not find a more detailed, explicit discussion of the elusive second part of morals within Kant's anthropology lectures. However, I do not at all believe that the proper conclusion to draw here is that there is no moral anthropology to be found in these lectures. On the contrary, although Kant unfortunately does not lay out a comprehensive, systematic articulation of "the counterpart of a metaphysics of morals" within any of these lectures,[6] it is definitely the case that they reverberate strongly with multiple moral messages and implications. Our task as readers is to bring together, clarify, and (when possible) integrate these moral messages into Kant's overall philosophical project, rather than to continue bemoaning the fact that the anthropology lectures do not provide us with an explicit, systematic, and straightforward account of "the other member of the division of practical philosophy as a whole, . . . moral anthropology." In the remainder of this essay, I propose to begin this necessary work of clarification and integration. Although Kant nowhere (i.e., neither in the anthropology lectures nor anywhere else) hands over to readers a single, complete, tidy package of moral anthropology, I aim to show that a bit of careful detective work nevertheless can lead us to some fulfilled hopes regarding Kant's *philosophia moralis applicata*.

My cautious optimism regarding Kant's moral anthropology project is grounded first and foremost in statements made by Kant himself (albeit, in the case of the anthropology *Nachshriften*, as recorded by students and auditors).[7] However, remarks made by some of Kant's earliest German- and English-language commentators regarding the nature, scope, and divisions of his anthropology also provide an important secondary textual source that gives further support for my interpretation. In 1797, one year before Kant's *Anthropology from a Pragmatic Point of View* appeared, Georg Samuel Albert Mellin published the first volume of his *Enzyclopädisches Wörterbuch der kritischen Philosophie*. In his preface, Mellin states that the "goal of this dictionary is to present the doctrines of the critical philosophy in their entire range, clearly, understandably, and convincingly."[8] At the beginning of his impressive six-page entry "Anthropology," the author notes that Kant's anthropology "divides into two parts, theoretical and practical." "Practical anthropology," Mellin elaborates later, in the wider sense of the term, is the application of morality to the characteristic condition and situation of the human faculty of desire—to the drives, inclinations, appetites, and passions of the human being, and the hindrances to the carrying out of the moral law, and it concerns virtues and vices. It is the empirical part of ethics, which can be called practical anthropology, a true doctrine of virtue [*eigentliche Tugendlehre*], or applied philosophy of ethics or morals [*angewandte Philosophie der Sitten oder Moral*].[9]

Mellin concludes his overview of Kant's practical anthropology by noting:

> The task of practical anthropology is to determine how the human being ought [*soll*] to be determined through the moral law; or what the moral laws are to which human beings under the hindrances of feelings, desires, and passions are subject. . . . No one yet, not even from among the critical philosophers, has produced a practical anthropology from this single, correct point of view.[10]

Similarly, Carl Christian Erhard Schmid, in the fourth edition of his *Wörterbuch zum leichtern Gebrauch der kantischen Schriften* (1798), also subdivides Kantian anthropology into "theoretical" and "practical" parts. "Practical anthropology," he writes, is

> applied and empirical philosophy of morals, a true doctrine of virtue [*eigentliche Tugendlehre*]—it is the consideration of the moral law in relation to the human will, whose desires and drives are hindrances to the practicing of the moral law. Practical anthropology is supported on the one hand by principles of pure ethics [*reine Moral*] or the metaphysics of morals; and on the other hand by doctrines of theoretical psychology.[11]

Finally, English author A. F. M. Willich, in his 1798 book, *Elements of the Critical Philosophy*, based in part on the author's experience as an auditor of Kant's courses "between the years 1778 and 1781 . . . and . . . again in [the] summer of 1792," also subdivides Kant's anthropology into theoretical and practical branches. "Anthropology," Willich writes,

> signifies in general the experimental doctrine of the nature of man; and is divided by Kant, into 1) *theoretical* or empirical doctrine of the mind, which is a branch of Natural Philosophy; 2) *practical*, applied, and empirical Philosophy of Morals; Ethics—the consideration of the moral law in relation to the human will, its inclinations, motives, and to the obstacles in practicing that law.[12]

It is perhaps ironic that we find a more succinct and focused discussion of the nature and aims of Kantian practical anthropology and its relation to the first part of ethical theory in these three early commentaries than we do in Kant's own texts. But each of them does track quite well with remarks Kant makes elsewhere concerning the second part of his ethics. For example, moral theory "needs anthropology for its *application* to human beings" (*Gr* 4: 412). Moral anthropology deals with "the subjective conditions in human nature that hinder people or help them in the carrying out [*Ausführung*] of the laws of a metaphysics of morals" (*MdS* 6: 217). "The reason that morals and sermons . . . have little effect is due to the lack [*Mangel*] of knowledge of the human being. Morals must [*muβ*] be united with [*verbunden . . . mit*] knowledge of humanity" (*Friedländer* 25: 471–2; see also *Moralphil.Collins* 27: 244).

These citations from Kant also suggest that Mellin, Schmid, and Willich were all closer both to the letter and spirit of Kant's moral anthropology than were twentieth-century commentators such as H. J. Paton and Mary J. Gregor, each of whom brashly dismissed the entire enterprise as a Rylean category mistake. According to Paton, for instance:

> "[A]pplied ethics" is used [by Kant] for a special kind of moral or practical psychology (or anthropology as he calls it) concerned with the conditions which favour or hinder the moral life. . . . There is, however, no reason why we should regard such a psychology as practical: it is a theoretical examination of the causes of certain morally desirable effects. Still less is there a reason why we should regard it with Kant as a kind of applied or empirical ethics.[13]

Similarly, his student Gregor writes:

> Moral anthropology is ... not ethics but rather a sort of psychology, a study of the natural causes which can be made to contribute toward the development of moral dispositions and toward making our actions in fulfillment of duty easier and more effective. Why should Kant regard this science as a division of moral philosophy?[14]

Contra Paton and Gregor and in basic agreement with Mellin, Schmid, and Willich, I will argue both that we do find a distinctly *moral* anthropology within Kant's anthropology lectures, and that Kant has compelling reasons for regarding moral anthropology as "the other member of the division of practical philosophy as a whole." At the same time, Mellin's last remark above, though probably not intended as a criticism of the "deeply esteemed professor" (Mellin to Kant, September 6, 1797, 12: 196), also hints at one further reason that we do not find more explicit discussion of *moral* anthropology in Kant's anthropology lectures. Kant did not see it as his task to develop a detailed moral anthropology. Though he states repeatedly that such a moral anthropology is necessary for the proper application of ethical theory to the human situation, and while he gives numerous hints in the anthropology lectures and elsewhere concerning what this moral anthropology should look like and what its aims should be, he does not himself produce a finished version of it. It remains an uncompleted task for others to take "this single, correct point of view" and produce a viable moral anthropology from the exploratory beginnings that he has left us.

MORAL MESSAGES

What then are the main moral messages contained in Kant's anthropology lectures, and how, when taken together, can they legitimately be regarded as constituting the second part of morals? The following list does not claim to be exhaustive, nor are the items in it necessarily ranked in order of importance. But I think that the following fundamental themes, when considered together, do provide very plausible support for the claim (a claim which, as we saw previously, Kant himself gives readers ample grounds to assert) that we find a significant portion of this second part of ethics within the anthropology lectures.

Human Hindrances

In his *Metaphysics of Morals*, Kant states that the "counterpart of a metaphysics of morals" concerns "the subjective conditions in human nature that hinder people or help them in the carrying out of the laws of a metaphysics of morals" (6: 217). In other words, what specific passions and inclinations are human beings subject to that tend to make it relatively difficult (or, as the case may be, easier) for them to adhere to moral principles? What is it about this particular biological species of rational being that makes it hard for them to act morally?[15] Answering these questions is part of the chief task of Kant's anthropology.

Generally speaking, it is in the first part of the anthropology lectures, where Kant discusses the different faculties and powers of soul of the human being (see, e.g., *Friedländer* 25: 624), that his analysis of human hindrances to morality is located.[16] The most obvious example concerns his discussion of egoism. In many versions of the lectures (e.g., *Pillau* 25: 735; *Menschenkunde* 25: 859–61; *Mrongovius* 25: 1215–20; *Busolt* 25: 1438–39; *Anth* 7: 127–30), strong warnings against the human tendency toward multiple varieties of selfishness are sounded very early on. The discussion of egoism in *Anthropology from a Pragmatic Point of View* is the most fully developed account. Here, three forms of egoism are singled out.

> [The *logical* egoist] considers it unnecessary to also test his judgment by the understanding of others, as if he had no need at all for this touchstone (*criterium veritatis externum*). But it is so certain that we cannot dispense with this means of assuring the truth of our judgments that this may be the most important reason why learned people clamor so urgently for *freedom of the press*.
> (7: 128)

In turning his back on this touchstone of truth, the logical egoist is thus in danger of sliding into incoherence, for our capacity to think correctly depends on our thinking "in community with others to whom we *communicate* our thoughts, and who communicate their thoughts to us" (*Was heißt: Sich im Denken orientiren?* 8: 144).[17]

Next is the *aesthetic* egoist, "a man content with his own taste," "who deprives himself of the progress toward improvement when he isolates himself with his own judgment" and who "seeks the touchstone of the beauty of art only in himself" (7: 129–30; see also

Busolt 25: 1438). Because aesthetic judgments on Kant's view are nonconceptual, "there can be no rule by which someone could be compelled to acknowledge that something is beautiful." Still, when we call an object beautiful, we believe ourselves to be speaking "with a universal voice, and lay claim to the agreement of everyone, whereas any private sensation would decide solely for the observer alone and his liking" (*KU* 5: 215–16). The aesthetic egoist remains within the prison of his private sensations, thus forfeiting this opportunity to speak with a universal voice.

Finally, and worst of all, is the *moral* egoist, "who allows himself to be so blinded by his advantages and privileges that he values others little" (*Menschenkunde* 25: 859; see also *Mrongovius* 25: 1215; *Busolt* 25: 1438), and who "locates the supreme determining ground of his will merely in his own happiness and what is useful to him, not in the thought of duty" (*Anth* 7: 130).

Obviously, human beings' widespread tendency toward egoism constitutes a major hindrance to "the carrying out of the laws of a metaphysics of morals." In order to make progress in this area, clearly we "must restrain this emotion of self-love" (*Busolt* 25: 1438). But to return to the questions of whether and why the anthropology lectures can rightfully be regarded as constituting a significant part of "the other member of the division of practical philosophy as a whole," the "human hindrances" part of these lectures is a key part of the story. The overarching goal is to figure out what human nature is like in order more effectively to further moral ends. How, given what we know empirically about human nature, can we make morality more efficacious in human life? In this broader sense, much of Kant's opening analyses of the various faculties and powers of soul of the human being are at least indirectly relevant to the second part of ethics. For the aim is first to learn more about human beings and the world they live in, in order to determine what particular obstacles to the realization of a priori moral principles confront this particular species of rational being, and then to formulate species-specific strategies for dealing with these obstacles. Kantian anthropological knowledge must be objective, empirically accurate knowledge if it is to successfully serve the purpose for which it is intended. (If the information we gather concerning human beings is false, then we will not have succeeded in learning about the subjective conditions in human nature that hinder or help us in carrying out the laws of a metaphysics of morals.) But the motivation behind the desire to acquire such knowledge is clearly a *moral* one: we seek to understand ourselves and the world we live in in order to make morality more efficacious. In this basic respect, Kantian social science is not at all value-free but deeply value-embedded, that is, morally guided.[18]

Weltkenntnis

As noted previously ("Fooled by Hope?"), the anthropology lectures explicitly aim to impart a kind of informal, popular knowledge tagged as *Weltkenntnis*, rather than a formal, scholarly knowledge of the sort that university professors were (and are) usually after. "There are two ways to study, in the school and in the world. In school one learns scholastic cognitions [*Erkenntnisse*] that belong to professional scholars; but in contact

[*Umgang*] with the world one learns popular cognitions that belong to the entire world" (*Mrongovius* 25: 1209). My previous point was simply that the strong *Weltkenntnis* aim of Kant's anthropology lectures is one obvious reason that we don't find more nuanced discussions of technical points about ethical theory and philosophy in these lectures. Now I wish to show how this aim of imparting *Weltkenntnis* to students and auditors of his anthropology lectures also constitutes an important part of a specifically *moral* anthropology.

Weltkenntnis divides into two parts: "the study of nature and of the human being" (*Friedländer* 25: 469; see also *Menschenkunde* 25: 854), or, alternatively, "physical geography and anthropology" (*Collins* 25: 9; see also *Geo* 9: 157). It is not just a *local* knowledge of human behavior "such as merchants have," for this type of street-smart knowledge "is bound to place and time and also provides no rules for acting in common life" (*Pillau* 25: 734). Even a knowledge of the world acquired through firsthand travel (or reading of others' travels) is not yet full-fledged Kantian *Weltkenntnis*, because it "lasts only for a certain time, for when the behavior at the place where he was alters, then his knowledge of it ceases" (*Pillau* 25: 734). Instead, "strong reflection [*starke Reflection*]" concerning "the human beings who are around us" is needed. This more reflective knowledge concerning human beings, Kant notes,

> outdoes by far that which a thoughtless traveler receives. Human beings show the sources of their actions as much in this little space as in the world at large; for this only an attentive eye is required, and a traveler must first be provided with these concepts if he wants utility [*Nutzen*] from his travel.
> (*Pillau* 25: 734)

What is called for is thus "attentiveness to human dispositions, which often show themselves under many shapes." And this attentiveness is to be gleaned not just from firsthand observations of the people around one, but also from "plays, novels, history and especially biographies" (*Pillau* 25: 734; see also *Menschenkunde* 25: 857–58; *Mrongovius* 25: 1213; *Anth* 7: 121).[19]

This rejection of merely local knowledge of human behavior in favor of a reflective, universal understanding means that *Weltkenntnis* ultimately entails a "knowledge of the human being as a *citizen of the world*" (*Anth* 7: 120; see also *Pillau* 25: 734; *Geo* 9: 157; *Racen* 2: 443). It is "a knowledge of the stage [*Schauplatz*] on which we can apply all skill" (*Friedländer* 25: 469; see also *Racen* 2: 443). And on Kant's view, it is precisely due to the lack of *Weltkenntnis* "that so many practical sciences, for example moral philosophy, have remained unfruitful.... Most moral philosophers and clergymen lack this knowledge of human nature" (*Collins* 25: 9). Or, as the *Moralphilosophie Collins* transcription has it:

> People are always preaching about what ought to be done, and nobody thinks about whether it can be done, so that even the admonitions, which are tautological repetitions of rules that everyone knows already, strike us as very tedious, in that nothing

is said beyond what is already known, and the pulpit orations on the subject are very empty, if the preacher does not simultaneously attend to humanity.

(27: 244)

In the *Groundwork*, Kant emphasizes that "morals needs anthropology for its *application* to human beings" (4: 412). "Morals," which here appears to refer exclusively to the rational, non-empirical part of ethical theory (see 4: 388), needs anthropology in part because its a priori laws

> require a judgment sharpened by experience, partly to distinguish in what cases they are applicable and partly to provide them with entry [*Eingang*] to the will of the human being and efficacy for his fulfillment of them [*Nachdruck zur Ausübung*]; for the human being is affected by so many inclinations that, though capable of the idea of a pure practical reason, he is not so easily able to make it effective *in concreto* in the conduct of his life.
>
> (4: 389)

In other words, human beings need *Weltkenntnis* in order to make morality work effectively in their own lives. Human beings cannot simply jump unaided into pure ethics; background knowledge of their own empirical situation is a necessary prerequisite. This necessary empirical background for moral judgment has been well described by Barbara Herman in her discussion of "rules of moral salience." Such rules, she writes, are acquired

> as elements in a moral education, [and] they structure an agent's perception of his situation so that what he perceives is a world with moral features. They enable him to pick out those elements of his circumstances or of his proposed actions that require moral attention. . . . Typically they are acquired in childhood as part of socialization; they provide a practical framework within which people act. . . . The rules of moral salience constitute the structure of moral sensitivity.[20]

An important part of the task of a specifically *moral* anthropology is thus to contribute to human beings' "progress [in] the power of judgment" (see *KpV* 5: 154). This task is carried out in the anthropology lectures through the imparting of *Weltkenntnis* to listeners (and readers).

The Destiny of the Human Species

Finally, a third major way in which the anthropology lectures contribute to a specifically *moral* anthropology lies in their remarks concerning the destiny of the human species. Here Kant is trying to provide his audience with a moral map,[21] a conceptual orientation and delineation of where humanity as a species is headed, along with programmatic hints concerning what needs to be done in order to move us closer to our normative destination. As his friend Moses Mendelssohn remarks in his own essay, "On the Question:

What Does It Mean to Enlighten?" first presented as a lecture before the famous Berlin Mitwochgesellschaft on May 16, 1784, "I posit, at all times, the destiny of the human being [*die Bestimmung des Menschen*] as the measure and goal of all our striving and efforts, as a point on which we must set our eyes, if we do not want to lose our way."[22]

With this third moral message we find considerable overlap between Kant's lectures on anthropology and his philosophy of history (cf. n. 21), as well as with his lectures and essays on education (see, e.g., *Päd* 9: 498–99; *Philanthropinum* 2: 447). However, in my view this overlap does not detract from its importance within the anthropology lectures themselves. Rather, it serves to indicate both the underlying interconnectedness between different areas of Kant's work that tend still to be separated artificially by scholarly predilections and habits, and the central significance of the theme in many areas of Kant's philosophy. The strong teleological thrust of these descriptions of the destiny of the human species in the anthropology lectures also serves as a correction to the view that Kantian anthropology is simply empirical science, however broadly conceived one takes "empirical science" to be. While it remains the case that we do not find in these lectures the ambitious project of a *transcendental* anthropology that makes good on the claim that all philosophical questions at bottom are anthropological questions tracking back to the human subject (see n. 2), so also we are not being presented with a purely descriptive account of human nature and culture. Rather, the underlying vision of a gradually emerging worldwide moral community, extending slowly outward from its all-too-Western, Eurocentric core but aiming ultimately at "a progressive organization of citizens of the earth into and towards the species as a system that is united cosmopolitically [*kosmopolitisch verbunden*]" (*Anth* 7: 333), lies somewhere between transcendental and merely empirical concerns.

Briefly, what according to the anthropology lectures is the destiny of the human species? The "experience of all ages and all peoples" indicates that people "feel destined by nature to develop, through mutual compulsion under laws that proceed from themselves, a coalition in a *cosmopolitan society* (*cosmopolitismus*)—a coalition which, though constantly threatened by dissension, generally makes progress" (*Anth* 7: 331). In other versions of the lectures, three crucial means toward the gradual establishment of this worldwide moral community are stressed: "a perfect civil constitution, good education, and the best concepts in religion" (*Pillau* 25: 847; see also *Menschenkunde* 25: 1198; *Mrongovius* 25: 1427).

Concerning the first means—a better (if not quite perfect, because, as Kant reminds us in his more sober moments, we are talking about an "unattainable idea" that is to serve "merely as a regulative principle"; *Anth* 7: 331) civil constitution—the task is to develop a republican form of government where "each citizen must, so to speak, have his own voice" (*Mrongovius* 25: 1427), that is, where all citizens are involved in the process of making laws, and where the freedom, equality, and independence of all citizens is respected (see also *Gemeinspruch* 8: 290). In *Toward Perpetual Peace*, Kant's "first definite article for perpetual peace" is that "the civil constitution in every state shall be republican" (8: 349). In other words, he believes that republican forms of government are normatively superior to all others, and he predicts that eventually all nations will adopt republican constitutions.

Concerning the second means, improvements in education, the chief goal, as contemporary cosmopolitan Martha Nussbaum remarks, is to teach students to "recognize humanity wherever it occurs, and give its fundamental ingredients, reason and moral capacity, [their] first allegiance."[23] Here, Kant's enthusiasm for the cosmopolitan program of Basedow's Philanthropin Institute comes to the fore, as the following passage from the end of the *Friedländer* lectures indicates: "The present Basedowian institutes are the first that have come about according to the perfect plan of education. This is the greatest phenomenon that has appeared in this century for the improvement of the perfection of humanity; through it all schools in the world will receive another form" (25: 722–23; cf. *Moralphil. Collins* 27: 471). Education in Kant's time was directed largely toward vocational/careerist aims, and so it remains today:

> Parents usually care only that their children get on well in the world, and princes regard their subjects merely as instruments for their own design. Parents care for the home, princes for the state. Neither have as their final purpose the best world [*das Weltbeste*] and the perfection to which humanity is destined, and for which it also has the disposition. But the design for a plan of education must be made in a cosmopolitan manner.
>
> (*Päd* 9: 448; see also *Menschenkunde* 25: 1202)

Concerning the third means to furthering our collective destiny, religious discipline is also needed, "so that what cannot be achieved by *external* constraint can be effected by *internal* constraint (the constraint of conscience)" (*Anth* 7: 333n). Or, as Kant puts it more ambitiously in *Religion within the Boundaries of Mere Reason*, the dominion of good over evil on our planet

> is not otherwise attainable, so far as human beings can work toward it, than through the setting up and spreading [*Ausbreitung*] of a society in accordance with, and for the sake of, laws of virtue—a society which reason makes it a task and a duty of the whole human race to establish in its full scope [*das ganze Menschengeschlecht in ihrem Umfang*].
>
> (6: 94)

Although this trinity of political/legal, educational, and religious means toward the establishment of a cosmopolitan society receives pride of place in the anthropology lectures, on a broader scale Kant stresses that many more fundamental transformations in other areas of human social and cultural life are also necessary. And he also recognizes that we have a very long way to go:

> The majority of human beings are still uncultivated [*noch roh*] and the thorough development of our talents is still lacking. Even the sciences are gratifications [*Befriedigungen*] of the taste of the age, and do not aim at universal benefit [*allgemeiner Nutzen*]. As concerns civilization, with us it is more an effect of taste and

fashion rather than, as it should be, something grounded on maxims for the good of all [*zum allgemeinen besten*]. Up until now we are merely refined and polished, but we do have that which makes a good citizen. As concerns morality, we could say that in this area we have not yet come very far.

(*Mrongovius* 25: 1426–27; see also
Menschenkunde 25: 1198; *Päd* 9: 451; *Idee* 8: 26)[24]

Unfortunately, just as the vast majority of human beings still "consider the step toward maturity to be not only troublesome but also highly dangerous" (*Aufklärung* 8: 35), so too, with respect to the three central means of improving the human condition, "we are, so to speak, in a three-fold immaturity" (*Mrongovius* 25: 1427; see also *Menschenkunde* 25: 1198). The human species has not yet emerged from its self-incurred immaturity, and thus enlightenment is still a long way off (see 8: 35). Nevertheless, even if "millennia are still required" for this emergence from immaturity to come about (*Friedländer* 25: 696; see also *Moralphil. Collins* 27: 471), the moral map provided by the anthropology lectures shows us our destination and helps prevent us from getting lost, in addition to sketching out what we need to do to get there.

MORAL ANTHROPOLOGY AS *PRACTICAL* PHILOSOPHY

I have argued thus far that the various versions of Kant's anthropology lectures, despite their generally informal, nontechnical nature and despite Kant's failure to address systematically and in detail (in these lectures or anywhere else) the vital question of how his projects in anthropology and ethical theory link up with one another, nevertheless do offer us multiple moral messages—messages that, when interpreted sensibly and integrated together, give us a solid sense of what his specifically *moral* (as distinguished from, e.g., *pragmatic*) anthropology is all about. In this final section, I will return to an important question touched on previously ("Fooled by Hope?"): Does Kant have good reasons for regarding his moral anthropology as "the other member of the division of *practical* philosophy as a whole" (*MdS* 6: 217; my emphasis); or, as Paton and Gregor (and, according to them, Kant himself, at least in some places) contend, is moral anthropology merely to be regarded as a part of *theoretical* philosophy? Alternatively stated, is Kant's moral anthropology indeed "the second part of morals" (*Moral Mrongovius II* 29: 599), that is, "the empirical part of ethics" (*Gr* 4: 388)—or is "moral anthropology" simply a misnomer?

Again, both Paton and Gregor hold (see nn. 13–14) that Kant's moral anthropology is a part of theoretical philosophy, on the ground that its primary focus concerns the study of those empirical facts about human nature that favor or hinder the carrying out of a priori moral principles by human beings. In order to qualify as a part of practical philosophy, they argue, moral anthropology would need to consist only of principles grounded "entirely on the concept of freedom [*gänzlich auf dem Freiheitsbegriffe*], to the complete exclusion of grounds taken from nature for the determination of the will" (*KU* 5: 173).

Kant's most detailed defense of this rather austere conception of practical philosophy occurs in the First Introduction to the *Critique of the Power of Judgment*—a text that Kant originally discarded "because of its lengthiness" (Kant to Jacob Sigismund Beck, August 18, 1793, 11: 441), and that was not published in its entirety until 1914, in volume 5 of the Cassirer edition of Kant's works. Paton refers readers to this text in justifying his rejection of Kant's claim (in, e.g., *MdS*, *Gr*, and *Moral Mrongovius II*) that moral anthropology is a part of practical philosophy, though without citing it. However, in order to get a better sense of the problem, it is worth citing at some length from this not terribly well-known text:

> There is a prevailing misconception, which is highly injurious to the way science is to deal with these areas, about what should be considered *practical* in such a sense of the term that it deserves to be included in a *practical philosophy*. It has been deemed proper to include statesmanship and political economy, rules of household management and also of etiquette, precepts for the diet and the health of the body and soul alike (indeed, why not all professions and arts?) in practical philosophy because they all concern practical propositions. But practical propositions are distinguished from theoretical propositions, which comprise the possibility of things and their determinations, not by a difference in their content but by a difference in the way we represent them, and the former alone consider *freedom* under laws. All the rest are just applications of the theory of the nature of things to the way in which we can produce them according to a principle.... In a word: all practical propositions which derive that which nature can contain from the power of choice as a cause [*von der Willkür als Ursache*] belong to theoretical philosophy as knowledge of nature; only those which give freedom its law are specifically differentiated by their content from the former.
>
> (20: 195–97)

According to the preceding way of demarcating practical and theoretical philosophy, moral anthropology would appear to be part of the latter, because it is chiefly concerned with "the subjective conditions in human nature that hinder people or help them in carrying out the laws of a metaphysics of morals" (*MdS* 6: 217). This is the conclusion that both Paton and Gregor reach.

However, one major downside of their reading is that it makes Kant look doubly foolish. First, on their interpretation the very concept of "moral anthropology" (a term which, as we have seen, Kant explicitly uses in a wide variety of texts) becomes a misnomer. Something now counts as "moral" only if it is "practical" in the above stern sense of consisting exclusively of principles that are founded entirely on the concept of freedom. Second, Kant stands guilty of a rather blatant contradiction. For both Paton and Gregor recognize that Kant does assert in several texts that moral anthropology *is* a part of practical philosophy (e.g., *MdS* 6: 217; *Gr* 4: 388)—indeed, it is the existence of such assertions that lead them to criticize the coherency of the very idea of a Kantian moral anthropology.

One possible way out would be to emphasize that Kant unfortunately uses the term "practical" in two different senses. In the wider sense, practical principles "are simply general rules that regulate action. Some practical rules are moral, namely categorical imperatives, and some are nonmoral, for example, subjective maxims and hypothetical imperatives."²⁵ In the narrower sense, "practical" is synonymous with "moral," where both refer strictly to the possibility of categorical imperatives based on freedom. It is this second, narrower sense of "practical" that Kant uses in both of his introductions to the *Critique of the Power of Judgment*. For example, at the beginning of the second introduction (the only version that Kant himself published), he stresses that "philosophy is properly divided into two parts that are quite different in their principles: theoretical, that is to say [als], natural philosophy, and practical, that is to say, *moral philosophy* (for this is what the practical legislation of reason according to the concept of freedom is called)" (*KU* 5: 171; cf. *MdS* 6: 218). Keeping these two senses of "practical" in mind, we could then say that moral anthropology is practical in the broader but not in the narrower sense. And we could also halt our skirmish with Paton and Gregor by noting simply that when they dismiss the claim that moral anthropology is practical, they are relying on the narrower sense of "practical," whereas when we endorse it we are invoking the wider sense.

However, if we adopt this easy truce, Kant still stands doubly convicted—first, for not recognizing that his own use of "moral anthropology" doesn't square with his narrower sense of "practical"; second, for asserting in some places that moral anthropology is part of practical philosophy and in other places that it isn't. Only if we can show that moral anthropology counts as practical in the narrower sense—"practical in accordance with laws of freedom" (*MdS* 6: 217)—is acquittal on these embarrassing charges possible.

How then could a moral anthropology "to which the empirical principles belong" (*Moral Mrongovius II* 29: 599; see also *Gr* 4: 388) qualify as practical in this stern Kantian sense of being in accordance with laws of freedom rather than nature? On my view, it counts as practical in the narrower sense because the use that human beings are to make of empirical precepts is free (determined by pure practical reason) rather than unfree (determined by the interplay of natural causes). We have a moral duty to learn how nature (particularly our own nature) works in order to put into effect "what reason prescribes to us" (*MdS* 6: 218), so that reason can "make room for its own end, the rule of right" (*Frieden* 8: 367). In other words, a moral imperative lies behind the acquisition of this knowledge of our own nature, and because we are regulating our actions (in this case, our anthropological investigations into the nature of our own species) by a moral motive, this regulation counts as practical, even though the resulting knowledge is theoretical—"theoretical" in Kant's special sense of dealing with knowledge of nature. We are to learn about human nature and the world we live in precisely in order to bring about a moral realm, that is, to create the kingdom of ends (see, e.g., *Gr* 4: 439, 437–38). "The concept of freedom," Kant stresses in the *Critique of the Power of Judgment*, "shall [soll] actualize in the sensible world the end proposed by its laws" (5: 176); and this can only happen in the sensible world if human beings use their knowledge of nature to promote moral goals. The moral law itself enjoins this goal of creating a moral world on us, and it enjoins us further "to apply our powers toward the realization [*Bewirkung*] of it" (*KU* 5: 455).

In this larger sense, Kant's moral anthropology is thus a key part of the ambitious *Übergang* project also articulated in the third *Critique*—the project, that is, of establishing a bridge between the seemingly separate worlds of nature and freedom, so that a moral world can be created out of nature (see *KU* 5: 175–76). And this also shows us why the debate over whether moral anthropology should count as practical rather than merely theoretical is much more than an internal terminological quarrel between Kant scholars.[26] Again, at bottom, anthropology and social science generally as envisioned by Kant are not at all Weberian value-free undertakings, but deeply value-embedded and morally guided projects: "The sciences [*Wissenschaften*] are *principia* for the improvement of morality [*die Verbeßerung der Moralität*]" (*Moralphil.Collins* 27: 462). Knowing ourselves and our world stands under the moral imperative of making ourselves and our world morally better. Ultimately, we seek anthropological knowledge in order to further the goal of moralization, that is, to promote "the *Übergang* from civilization to moralization [*Moralisierung*]."[27] Unfortunately, Kant's 1782 estimate of how far humanity had progressed toward this goal would seem to apply equally well to our situation today, over two centuries later: "In progress of culture we have already come very far, in civilization we have come a short way, in moralization we have done almost nothing [*beynahe gar nichts gethan*]" (*Menschenkunde* 25: 1198).

None of this is meant to downplay the obvious fact that Kant provides readers with more than ample opportunities to criticize his moral anthropology. Nowhere is the project carried out systematically or in detail; it is riddled throughout by inaccurate empirical data (i.e., racial, ethnic, religious, and sexist prejudices); etc. But in trying to show both that we really do find a specifically *moral* anthropology within Kant's eclectic anthropology lectures, and that this moral anthropology is at bottom deeply *practical* rather than merely theoretical, I hope I have also convinced readers of the fundamental importance of this neglected part of his philosophical project. Those of us who aspire to construct humanly useful ethical theories ought to consider more carefully Kant's conviction that "the metaphysics of morals, or *metaphysica pura*, is only the first part of morality; the second part is *philosophia moralis applicata*, to which the empirical principles belong" (*Moral Mrongovius II* 29: 599). This is not at all to say that the particular *philosophia moralis applicata* that we find sketched out in his anthropology lectures is a satisfactory one. It clearly is not. Rather, it remains for us today and in the future to develop a more viable moral anthropology from the exploratory and fragmentary beginnings that he has left us.

6

Applying Kant's Ethics

THE ROLE OF ANTHROPOLOGY*

THE SECOND PART OF MORALS

FOR MANY READERS Kant is the moral philosopher least likely to support the claim that anthropology and the empirical study of human nature have necessary and important contributions to make to ethics. As he declares in his most famous work in ethics: "there exists the utmost necessity to work out for once a pure moral philosophy, completely cleansed of everything that may be only empirical and that belongs to anthropology," and "all moral philosophy is based entirely on its pure part; ... when it is applied to the human being it does not borrow the least bit from acquaintance with him (from anthropology)" (*Gr* 4: 389). Indeed, a long and varied line of critics from Hegel to Bernard Williams stand united in their condemnation of Kant's ethics for precisely this reason: it is charged with "empty formalism" and "abstract universality,"[1] an infatuation with a "purist" view of morality which rejects both a "biological perspective" as well as any "reasonable historical and psychological understanding of morality."[2] Even some contemporary commentators on Kant, who generally view themselves as friends rather than foes of the sage of Königsberg, also assert that anthropology has no necessary place in Kant's ethics, and so end up (albeit unintentionally) agreeing with Kant's critics on this point. Thus we are told that "Kant did not believe that anthropological investigations were necessary for moral action,"[3] and that anthropology's "significance for Kant's general ethical theory may be quite limited."[4]

However, Kant's own considered views on the importance of anthropology for ethics are quite different from what these critics and commentators maintain. Moral philosophy, like natural philosophy, does "have its empirical part" (*Gr* 4: 387), a part which

Kant refers to variously as "practical anthropology" (ibid.), "moral anthropology" (*MdS* 6: 217; *Moral Mrongovius II* 29: 599), "anthropology" (*Gr* 4: 412; *Moralphil. Collins* 27: 244; *Moral Mrongovius I* 27: 1398), "the counterpart of a metaphysics of morals" (*MdS* 6: 217), and "the second part" of morals (*Moral Mrongovius II* 29: 599). In a 1785 ethics lecture—transcribed the same year the *Groundwork* was published—Kant states:

> The metaphysics of morals, or *metaphysica pura*, is only the first part of morals; the second part is *philosophia moralis applicata*, moral anthropology, to which the empirical principles belong.... Moral anthropology is morals that are applied to human beings. *Moralia pura* is built on necessary laws, therefore it cannot ground itself on the particular constitution of a rational being, of the human being. The particular constitution of the human being, as well as the laws that are grounded on it, appear in moral anthropology under the name of "ethics."
>
> (*Moral Mrongovius II* 29: 599)

But what exactly is this mysterious second part of morals, a part that has somehow continuously managed to escape the notice of Kant critics and scholars? Where do we find it in the Kantian corpus? What is its relationship to the better-known first part of morals, and what is its overall significance for ethics? These are the questions that I will attempt to answer in the present chapter.

Caution is necessary when discussing the relationship between Kant's ethics and anthropology, for at least two reasons. First and foremost, his views here are not static. Over the years, shifting conceptions of ethics, anthropology, and the relationship between the two are detectable.[5] The most obvious example concerns Kant's pre-critical work in ethics, which often has a marked empiricist tone. For instance, in his *Inquiry Concerning the Distinctness of the Principles of Natural Theology and Morals* (1764), he asserts confidently that "the faculty of experiencing the *good* is *feeling*" (2: 299). The famous pure ethics project is announced as early as 1770: "I have resolved this winter to put in order and complete my investigations of pure moral philosophy, in which no empirical principles are to be found, as it were in the metaphysics of morals" (letter to Lambert, September 2, 1770, 10: 97). But the actual carrying out of this project took nearly thirty years. And by the time the *Metaphysics of Morals* is published in 1797, the term "metaphysics of morals" appears to be used in a way that includes reference to "the particular *nature* of human beings, which is cognized only be experience" (6: 217), whereas in the 1785 *Groundwork* a "metaphysics of morals" was strictly identified with pure, non-empirical ethics.[6]

In what follows, my aim is to articulate and defend Kant's most basic views about the significance of anthropology for ethics, views which I believe hold fairly constant from the time that he first conceptualizes the project of a pure moral philosophy until the end of his life, that is, from 1770 to 1804. The issues to be discussed are not affected by possible changes in Kant's conception of the precise contours of a metaphysics of morals or of anthropology after 1770.

A second reason for caution is that some of Kant's most detailed and compelling remarks about the significance of anthropology for ethics are to be found in student lecture notes from his ethics and anthropology courses, which he taught together each winter semester from 1772 on, but whose accuracy, with respect to both contents and dates, is less than sure.[7] Kant himself, in responding to former student Marcus Herz's request for a serviceable set of lecture notes from one of his metaphysics courses, sounded an appropriate warning against overreliance on them when he remarked that those students "who are most thorough in note-taking are seldom capable of distinguishing the important from the unimportant. They pile a mass of misunderstood stuff under what they possibly have grasped correctly" (10: 242). Kant's lecture notes are important documents, but they should be used conservatively as added support for claims made in his published works—not as stand-alone indications of his position.

DEFINING FEATURES OF PRAGMATIC ANTHROPOLOGY

In his anthropology lectures, Kant repeatedly emphasizes that his approach to anthropology is *pragmatic*. However, he assigns several different meanings to the term "pragmatic," and it is important to familiarize oneself with these different meanings and intended contrasts before turning to the narrower issue of moral or practical anthropology.[8]

Pragmatic versus Physiological

In a letter to Herz (10: 145) written toward the end of 1773, in which he describes his anthropology course, Kant stresses that his approach is "quite different" from the physiological approach advocated by the physician Ernst Platner in his book *Anthropologie für Ärzte und Weltweise* (1772), which Herz had reviewed earlier for the journal *Allgemeine Deutsche Bibliothek*. Twenty-five years later, in the preface to his own published version of the anthropology lectures, Kant continues to contrast his approach to Platner's, noting that physiological anthropology "concerns the investigation of what *nature* makes of the human being; pragmatic, the investigation of what *he* as a free-acting being makes of himself, or can and should make of himself" (*Anth* 7: 119).[9] Essentially, the physiological approach championed by Platner and others is the predecessor of physical anthropology, while Kant's pragmatic anthropology, with its emphasis on free human action, is the progenitor of various philosophical and existentialist anthropologies. Max Scheler, an important voice in this latter tradition, who also influenced Heidegger, notes that the human being is not only an animal being but also "a 'spiritual' being [*ein 'geistiges' Wesen*]" that is "no longer tied to its drives and environments, but rather 'free from the environment' [*umweltfrei*], or, as we shall say, 'open to the world' [*weltoffen*]."[10]

Pragmatic versus Scholastic

In the *Menschenkunde* lectures, probably transcribed in 1781–1782, when the *Critique of Pure Reason* was first published, Kant again criticizes Platner for having merely "written a scholastic anthropology" (25: 856). The scholastics, he adds, produced a "science for the school," but it was of "no use to the human being." Pragmatic anthropology, on the other hand, aims to promote "enlightenment for common life" (25: 853; see also *Mrongovius* 25: 1209). As Kant remarks at the end of his 1775 essay, *Of the Different Races of Human Beings*, which also served as an advertisement for his companion course on physical geography for that year, his aim was "knowledge of the world [*Kenntniß der Welt*]," a type of knowledge which serves "to procure the *pragmatic* element for all otherwise acquired sciences and skills, by means of which they become useful not only for the *school*, but rather for *life* and through which the accomplished apprentice is introduced to the stage of his destiny, namely, the *world*" (2: 443; see also *Friedländer* 25: 469; *Pillau* 25: 733–34). Knowledge of the world, he stresses later in his preface to the 1798 *Anthropology*, "must come after our schooling," and is only properly called pragmatic "when it contains knowledge of the human being as a *citizen of the world*" (7: 120). Accordingly, pragmatic anthropology must also be cosmopolitan in scope. The anthropology that concerns Kant "is not a local, but a general anthropology. In it one comes to know the nature of humanity, not the condition of human beings. . . . Anthropology is not a description of human beings, but of human nature" (*Friedländer* 25: 471; see also *Pillau* 25: 734).

Pragmatic as Involving the Use of Others

As the contrast with scholastic anthropology implies, pragmatic anthropology is useful knowledge. But the main kind of usefulness stressed by Kant in the anthropology lectures involves the skillful use of other human beings. By means of our knowledge of human nature we acquire insight into how to use human beings for our own purposes. "Pragmatic," in this specific sense, refers to the ability "to use other human beings skillfully for one's purposes" (*Anth* 7: 322). In the *Busolt* lectures (1788–1789), Kant is particularly blunt: "We must make an effort to form the way of thinking and the capacities of those with whom we have dealings, so that we do not become too difficult or offensive to them. Now anthropology teaches us this; it shows us how we can use people for our own ends" (25: 1436). Pragmatic anthropology is thus also "a knowledge of the art of how a human being has influence on others and can lead them according to his intention" (*Menschenkunde* 25: 855).

Pragmatic as Prudential

Finally, pragmatic anthropology is also a doctrine of prudence, a *Klugheitslehre*. Kant sometimes uses "prudence" to refer to the skillful use of others (see, e.g., *Menschenkunde* 25: 855; *Gr* 4: 416n, 417n), but his primary use refers to the ability to use one's knowledge of human nature in order to promote the welfare and happiness of oneself as well as others. As he remarks in the *Groundwork*, "skill in the choice of means to one's own greatest well-being can be called *prudence*" (4: 416). And in the *Parow* lectures (1772–1773), he says: "The capacity to choose the best means to happiness is prudence. Happiness consists in the satisfaction of all inclinations, and therefore to be able to choose happiness, one must be free" (25: 413; see also *KrV* A 800/B 828). The *Friedländer* lectures open with a particularly strong emphasis on the prudential nature of pragmatic anthropology: "All pragmatic doctrines are doctrines of prudence, where for all our skills we also have the means to make a proper use of everything, for we study human beings in order to become more prudent" (25: 471).[11]

This is certainly not the whole story behind Kant's anthropology lectures. They comprise an unabashedly eclectic venture, one revealing various origins, competing concerns and aims, and multiple possibilities of application. Kant also strove to make the lectures "entertaining and never dry" (letter to Herz, end of 1773, 10: 146), and held that as a result "they can be read by everyone" (*Menschenkunde* 25: 856–57). Keeping these key features of pragmatic anthropology in mind, let us now turn to the issue of anthropology's significance for ethics.

ANTHROPOLOGY: PRAGMATIC VERSUS MORAL

Kant's anthropology course, from its commencement in 1772 until the last time he taught it in the winter semester of 1795–1796, while often differing on important matters of detail, remained firmly pragmatic in its basic orientation. Nowhere in the lectures for this course does he change direction and offer a comprehensive practical or moral anthropology. To this extent, critics who hold that there is no connection between Kant's ethics and his anthropology are right: "Pragmatic anthropology is . . . not the discipline of practical anthropology, variously described by Kant, that was supposed to function as a complement to pure moral philosophy."[12] But no one, least of all a philosopher who holds that we must treat humanity always as an end, never merely as a means (see. *Gr* 4: 429), has ever seriously maintained that practical or moral anthropology is *identical* to pragmatic anthropology. For the latter, as we have seen, is designed in part to show us how we can effectively use people for our own purposes—whatever these purposes may be. And it is clear that pragmatic anthropology can be put to many different purposes, some of which are blatantly immoral. People can and will choose to do different things with it. For instance, unscrupulous advertisers and businesspeople may use their knowledge of human nature to sell people things that they do not need and cannot afford, and shrewd politicians may exploit their knowledge of human nature to advance their own personal agendas for power and control. Thus any argument about whether pragmatic anthropology is or is not identical to "the counterpart of a metaphysics of morals, the other member of the division of practical philosophy as a whole, . . . moral anthropology" (*MdS* 6: 217) is simply a red herring, a nonstarter.

But we can also choose to use our knowledge of human nature for *moral* purposes, and when we choose to do so, our anthropology becomes a moral anthropology. Moral anthropology is already potentially present within pragmatic anthropology, and we actualize this potential whenever we choose to apply it for moral purposes.[13] It is clear that Kant, throughout his twenty-four years of lecturing on anthropology, explicitly desired that people would choose to make moral use of anthropology. As he notes in the 1775–1776 *Friedländer* anthropology lectures:

> [T]he reason that morals and sermons, which are full of admonitions of which one never tires, have little effect, is lack of knowledge of the human being. Morals must be united with knowledge of humanity. . . . In order that morality and religion obtain their final purpose, knowledge of human beings must be combined with them.
> (25: 471–72; see also *Moralphil. Collins* 27: 244)[14]

One chief advantage that anthropology offers to ethics is practical efficacy—the possibility of providing a priori moral principles with "access to the will of the human being and efficacy for his fulfillment of them" (*Gr* 4: 389). As Kant remarks in several of his moral philosophy lectures, "consideration of the [moral] rule is useless, if one cannot make people prepared to fulfill it" (*Moral Mrongovius I* 27: 1398; see also *Moralphil. Collins* 27: 244).[15]

DEFINING FEATURES OF MORAL ANTHROPOLOGY

Pragmatic anthropology becomes moral anthropology when we choose to make use of our knowledge of human nature for moral purposes. Thus, in principle, *all* aspects of pragmatic anthropology are potentially moral anthropology: all that is needed to turn any aspect of pragmatic anthropology into moral anthropology is the decision to apply it to moral rather than nonmoral ends. But Kant also speaks more specifically about what he believes are the most likely moral applications of pragmatic anthropology, and in the remainder of this essay I will focus on these more specific applications.

Hindrances and Helps

One specific application that is stressed repeatedly in both the ethics and anthropology texts is what Kant calls "hindrances and helps." One of moral anthropology's primary tasks is to point out "the subjective conditions in human nature that hinder or help them in carrying out the laws of a metaphysics of morals" (*MdS* 6: 217; see also *Gr* 4: 387, 389). Similarly, in the *Powalski* ethics lectures, Kant emphasizes that we must study "not merely the object: that is, moral conduct, but also the subject: that is, the human being. This is necessary; one must see what sorts of hindrances to virtue are to be found in the human being" (29: 97). In other words, what is it about the particular species of rational being *Homo sapiens* that makes it difficult for them to act on moral principle, and what sorts of aids for their specific moral development can the informed anthropologist offer?

Throughout his writing career, Kant appears to have held to the conviction that while each and every type of rational being is subject to the same universal moral principle, different types of rational being stand in different relationships to this moral principle (see *Gr* 4: 389). For instance, in his early work *Universal Natural History and Theory of the Heavens* (1755), he notes that the inhabitants of the earth "and perhaps also those of Mars" are "in the dangerous middle position, where temptations of sensible stirrings against the supremacy of spirit have a strong power of seduction," but whose spirit also "cannot deny that it has the capacity to put up resistance" to these temptations (1: 366). Still, things could be far worse for those of us in this dangerous middle position. For instance, our ability to have thoughts that we do not at the same time utter (that is, to deceive one another) at least makes it easy to live in peace with one another. However, those rational beings "on some other planet . . . who could not think in any other way but aloud," would have an entirely different character from the human species, and "unless they were all *pure as angels*, it is inconceivable how they could live in peace together" (*Anth* 7: 332). Those who are concerned to make morality efficacious in human life need to learn more about the distinctive features of human nature.

Among the many hindrances to morality that human beings face and that come under Kant's scrutiny are our affects and passions.[16] These particular types of hindrance are substantial, since "both affect and passion shut out the sovereignty of reason" (*Anth* 7: 251). Affect, however, involves merely a "lack of virtue," whereas passion is "*properly* evil, that is, a true vice" (*MdS* 6: 408). These two kinds of emotion are thus "essentially different from each other, both with regard to the method of prevention and to that of the cure that the physician of souls would have to apply" (*Anth* 7: 251; see also *MdS* 6: 408). Passion "can be conquered only with difficulty or not at all by the subject's reason," while affect refers to a "feeling of pleasure or displeasure in the subject's present state that does not let him rise to *reflection*" (7: 251).

In his anthropology lectures, Kant discusses numerous affects and passions at length, showing both how and why they hinder moral conduct, and offering advice on how to treat and prevent these hindrances. In the case of passions, there often is no treatment—"passion is an *illness* that abhors all medicine," for someone in the grip of passion "does not want to be cured" (7: 266). Here, preventive measures, such as steering clear of them, are the best that can be hoped for. With respect to affects, the prospects for both treatment and prevention are better. Because affects are "rash" and "unpremeditated" as opposed to "sustained and considered," they allow more room for self-treatment, for what an affect "does not accomplish quickly, it does not do at all; and it forgets easily" (*MdS* 6: 407; *KU* 5: 272n; *Anth* 7: 252). Preventive measures also abound. For instance, one should steer clear of "novels, sentimental plays, shallow moral precepts, which make play with (falsely) so-called noble dispositions," and religious sermons that preach "a groveling, base currying of favor and self-ingratiation" (*KU* 5: 273).

As befits a philosopher who often doubts "whether any true virtue is to be found in the world" (*Gr* 4: 407), Kant devotes more attention to human hindrances to morality than he does to helps or aids. Morality is not easy for human beings.[17] But anthropology also teaches us that there are things we can do, given human nature, to promote the development of moral character.

One substantial aid to morality for human beings is politeness.[18] Because of our nature, we are susceptible to influence through politeness, and this influence can and should be used in cultivating moral character. Deception is also part of our nature, since our character "consists in the propensity to lie," but politeness manages to "deceive the deceiver in ourselves," and in order to "lead the human being to virtue, nature has wisely implanted in him the tendency to willingly allow himself to be deceived" (*Anth* 7: 413, 151–52). Politeness helps morality by cultivating self-restraint. The polite person refrains from satisfying illegitimate desires, and this self-restraint itself "betrays a self-mastery and is the beginning of self-overcoming. It is a step toward virtue, or at least a capacity thereto" (*Menschenkunde* 25: 930). In effect, we are fooled into virtue. Politeness itself is only moral *Schein*—an illusion or semblance, rather than true virtue. But it is also a "beautiful *Schein* resembling virtue" (*MdS* 6: 473), which in time will lead to the real thing. For "when people conduct themselves in company in a civilized fashion, they thereby become gentler and more refined, and practice goodness in small matters" (*Moralphil. Collins* 27: 456). The opportunity to practice goodness in small matters through civilized behavior is a mundane feature of daily life, but it has a cumulative effect on character, and eventually we are "won over to actually loving the good" (*Menschenkunde* 25: 931). Here too anthropology shows us how we can be fooled into virtue.

A second, related aid to morality is the civilizing impact that republican regimes—that is, societies where the rule of law is practiced and where all citizens are involved in the practice of making laws—bring to human life.[19] In an important footnote to *Perpetual Peace*, Kant argues that such regimes, by instilling nonviolent behavior patterns, disciplining our emotions, and making us less partial toward our own interests, help to establish a "moral veneer" over human society, and that in doing so, "a great step *toward* morality (although not yet a moral step) is made" (8: 375–76n). Here as elsewhere, the strong influence of Rousseau on Kant's anthropology is detectable. As he remarks in the *Pillau* lectures: "Rousseau shows how a civil constitution must exist in order for the complete end of human beings [*den gantzen Zweck der Menschen*] to be reached" (25: 847).

These are just two examples of the many cultural and institutional practices discussed by Kant in his anthropology lectures that can serve as aids to humanity's moral transformation.

Moral Weltkenntnis

In the *Groundwork*, Kant asserts that while pure moral philosophy "does not borrow the least thing from acquaintance with the human being" in articulating and justifying its basic principles, it does "no doubt still require a judgment sharpened by experience, partly in order to distinguish in what cases they have their application" (4: 389). Here we find a second, fundamental contribution that anthropology makes to ethics.[20] The *Weltkenntnis* aim of anthropology—its goal of imparting a "knowledge of the human being as a *citizen of the world*" (*Anth* 7: 120; see also *Pillau* 25: 734;

Geo 9: 157; *Racen* 2: 443)—provides us with an account of human nature by means of which we can better assess human conduct and character. As we saw earlier, this *Weltkenntnis* has multiple possibilities of application: It can be put to pragmatic, nonmoral uses as well as to moral ones. A businessman who uses his *Weltkenntnis* to expand his company's market share is using it for pragmatic purposes, but people who use *Weltkenntnis* in order more effectively and intelligently to apply pure moral principles to the human situation are using it for moral purposes.

Moral *Weltkenntnis* teaches us how to see a world with moral features: it provides us with the relevant empirical framework to which we are to apply pure moral principles. Human beings cannot simply jump unaided into pure ethics—informed knowledge of the empirical situation to which a priori principles are to be applied is necessary. By contributing to "the progress of the power of judgment," anthropology fills this gap (see *KpV* 5: 154). And it is a gap to which Kant explicitly draws attention in several of his lectures. For instance, in the prolegomena to the *Collins* anthropology lectures, he remarks that it is because of "the lack of *Weltkenntnis* that so many practical sciences, for example moral philosophy, have remained unfruitful. . . . Most moral philosophers and clergymen lack this knowledge of human nature" (25: 9; see also *Moralphil. Collins* 27: 244). The need for moral *Weltkenntnis* is one of the key reasons that pure moral philosophy "needs anthropology for its *application* to human beings" (*Gr* 4: 412).

Moral Education and Character Development

One of Kant's more radical claims concerning human nature is that it is not a given but rather something that must be self-produced by the species. As he notes near the beginning of his *Pedagogy* lectures: "The human being can only become human through education. He is nothing except what education makes of him" (9: 443). In the anthropology lectures, humanity's specific need for *moral* education is stressed repeatedly.[21] The human being needs "to *moralize* himself by means of the arts and sciences" (*Anth* 7: 324); he must "be *educated* to the good" (7: 325). Kant's anthropology and ethics writings also abound in more specific recommendations concerning moral education. For instance, in the doctrine of method in the *Critique of Practical Reason*, which is concerned with finding a way "to provide the laws of pure practical reason with *entrance* [*Eingang*] into the human mind, [and] *influence* [*Einfluß*] on its maxims," Kant encourages educators to search through "the biographies of ancient and modern times with the purpose of having examples at hand of the duties they lay down" (5: 151, 154). By comparing and evaluating similar decisions made under different circumstances, students can thus develop their own capacities for moral judgment. And in the *Metaphysics of Morals*, he discusses at length an elementary method, the moral catechism, which he deems "the first and most essential *doctrinal* instrument of the doctrine of virtue" (6: 478; see also *Päd* 9: 490). Essentially a modified Socratic dialogue, the moral catechism involves an attempt on the teacher's part, in discussing popular cases drawn from ordinary life, to develop the student's judgment about morally right action. However, as the student matures, more emphasis needs to be placed on self-reflection and the development of autonomy. First and foremost, the teacher "must keep students away from imitation" (*Mrongovius* 25: 1386). "The *imitator* (in moral matters) is without character, for character consists precisely in originality in the way of thinking [*Originalität der Denkungsart*]. He who has character derives his conduct from a source that he has opened by himself" (*Anth* 7: 293).

Educational institutions must also be reformed. Above all, teachers must replace the vocational and careerist concerns that politicians and parents typically have for children with a cosmopolitan orientation:

> Parents usually care only that their children get on well in the world, and princes regard their subjects merely as instruments for their own designs. Parents care for the home, princes for the state. Neither have as their final purpose the best world [*das Weltbeste*] and the perfection to which humanity is destined, and for which it has the disposition. But the design for a plan of education must be made in a cosmopolitan manner.
>
> (*Päd* 9: 448)

While Kant discusses moral education in all versions of the anthropology lectures, the *Friedländer* lectures of 1775–1776 contain the most extensive discussion. This particular set of lectures concludes with a six-page section entitled "On Education," and reflects both Kant's strong admiration for Basedow's Philanthropin Institute, founded in Dessau in 1774, as well as his own growing interest in pedagogy. In 1776–1777, Kant taught for the first time a university course on pedagogy, and he also published two short essays in support of Basedow's school (2: 445–52). The Philanthropin Institute, which combined Lockean and Rousseauian concerns with educational methods better suited to children's nature with a strong cosmopolitan orientation, is described by Kant in *Friedländer* as "the greatest phenomenon that has appeared in this century for the improvement of the perfection of humanity" (25: 722–23; see also *Moralphil. Collins* 27: 471).

The central task of moral education is the development of character, and the anthropology and ethics writings also contain extensive discussion of this topic. Moral character is "the distinguishing mark of the human being as a rational being endowed with freedom" (*Anth* 7: 285; see also *Friedländer* 25: 630), and thus the grounding of character must be "the first effort in moral education" (*Päd* 9: 481). At the early stages, "the acquisition of good character with the human being takes place through education" (*Menschenkunde* 25: 1172). Again though, as the student matures, external institutional influences on character recede into the background and self-reflection plays a stronger role. Accordingly, Kantian moral anthropology also contains practical advice on the self-development of character. The basic principles here are

a. not intentionally to say what is false
b. not to dissemble
c. not to break one's (legitimate) promise

d. not to enter into an association of taste with evil-minded human beings
e. not to pay attention to gossip derived from the shallow and malicious judgment of others. (*Anth* 7: 294; see also *Mrongovius* 25: 1387–88, 1392)

Ultimately, we are responsible for our own character, and we are its chief architect. As he notes in *Friedländer*: "We all believe that we are educated in childhood, but we are not really educated. We must still lead ourselves to the result and form our character ourselves" (25: 633).

The Vocation of the Human Species

Kant's anthropological investigations into human nature are also marked by a strong historical and teleological concern. He is keen "to discover an *aim of nature* in this nonsensical course of things human," and wants to trace humanity's "steps from crudity [*Rohigkeit*] toward culture" (*Idee* 8: 18, 21). In the preamble to the *Friedländer* lectures, when Kant is articulating his own specific conception of anthropology, he complains:

> [N]o one has yet written a world history, which was at the same time a history of humanity, but only of the state of affairs and of the change in kingdoms, which as a part is indeed major, but considered in the whole, is a trifle. All histories of wars amount to the same thing, in that they contain nothing more than descriptions of battles. But whether a battle has been more or less won makes no difference in the whole. Henceforth more attention should be given to humanity.
> (25: 472; see also *Idee* 8: 29)

Part of anthropology's task, as Kant conceives it, is thus to contribute to a world history of humanity by articulating the steps in humanity's progress from crudity to culture and by describing our central vocation. In pursuing this task of a world history of humanity, anthropology also makes a fourth important contribution to ethics. For now Kant is also providing his audience with a much-needed moral map, one that describes both the long-term goal of humanity's efforts and the major steps by means of which this goal is to be reached.[22]

The final goal is a worldwide moral community that encompasses "the entire human race in its scope" (*Rel* 6: 94), where all human beings are respected as ends in themselves. And the means? Here, the story is not so pretty. First and foremost, there is our "unsociable sociability," a bidirectional inclination rooted in human nature that leads us both to form associations with others but also constantly to compete and quarrel against each other once we have done so. But as a result of our competitive, self-interested nature, our insatiable desire for status and power, our talents are developed and humanity progresses. Like Adam Smith's famous "invisible hand," social progress for Kant is often the unintended result of the behavior of self-interested individuals.[23] However, in Kant's case the invisible hand is much bigger, for it is held to be the driving force behind the growth of the arts and sciences, political and international legal reform, and even the hoped-for transformation into a cosmopolitan moral whole: "All culture and art that adorn humanity, and the most beautiful social order, are fruits of unsociability, which is compelled by itself to discipline itself, and thus, by an art extorted from it, to develop completely the germs of nature" (*Idee* 8: 22).

Even the destructive power of war is claimed by Kant to be part of "a secret plan of nature" (*Idee* 8: 27), for it too is just "one more incentive for developing in the highest degree all talents that serve culture" (*KU* 6: 433). War is a spur to economic and technological development as well as an incentive for eventually compelling people "to enter into more or less lawful relations" with one another (*Frieden* 8: 363). But unlike other means of progress such as the arts and sciences, war is also programmed by "the great artist nature" (*Frieden* 8: 361) to eventually die out. At some future point,

> after many devastations, reversals, and even thoroughgoing exhaustion of their powers, nature drives human beings to what reason could have told them even without so much sad experience: namely, to go beyond a lawless condition of savages and enter into a federation of nations [*Völkerbund*], where every state, even the smallest, could expect its security and rights.
>
> (*Idee* 8: 24)

Here we also see the strikingly different approaches to war found in a world history of humanity and in standard histories of wars. The latter, again, "contain nothing more than descriptions of battles" (*Friedländer* 25: 472), while the former analyzes the function and purpose of war in human life.

The German word *Bestimmung* can be translated variously as "vocation," "destiny," and "determination," and each of these meanings is present in Kant's use of the term. On the one hand, he is describing what he believes are inherent tendencies and dispositions within human nature. But we also pursue our *Bestimmung* as free human beings and are not irrevocably fated or causally determined to reach it. Whether humanity will actually reach a stage where all human beings are "cosmopolitically united" depends ultimately on what we choose to do (*Anth* 7: 333). Kant's assumption of progress is thus not as rigid as that of other Enlightenment authors. As he notes in the *Conflict of the Faculties*:

> No one can guarantee that now, this very moment, with regard to the physical disposition of our species, the epoch of its decline would not be liable to occur. . . . For we are dealing with beings that act freely, to whom, it is true, what they *ought* to do may be *dictated* in advance, but of whom it may not be *predicted* what they *will* do.
>
> (7: 83)

At the same time, the strong teleological undercurrent in Kant's analysis of humanity's *Bestimmung* is a clear sign that his anthropology, though intended as a science in which "the grounds of knowledge are taken from observation and experience," is not simply an empirical science (*Collins* 25: 7). For the concept of purposiveness itself, as he reminds us in the third *Critique*, while "indispensably necessary" for all investigations of nature, is also "a special *a priori* concept that has its origin solely in the reflecting power of judgment" (5: 398, 181). Still less is Kant's anthropology intended to be a Weberian value-free social science.[24] From the start, it is a deeply value-embedded and morally guided enterprise. As he notes in the *Collins* ethics lectures: "The sciences are *principia* for the improvement of morality" (27: 462; see also Kant's doctrine of the primacy of the practical in *KpV* 5: 121). Theoretical (as well as pragmatic) inquiries ultimately serve the ends of morality.

Finally, yet another distinctive feature of Kant's analysis of humanity's *Bestimmung* is that it focuses exclusively on the species as a whole and across time rather than on individual members at specific times. This broader perspective is one more implication of an anthropology that strives to be "not a *local* but a general anthropology," one concerned "not with the condition of human beings but with the nature of humanity" (*Friedländer* 25: 471; see also *Pillau* 27: 734; *Anth* 7: 120). As Kant writes in his published *Anthropology*:

> First of all, it must be noted that with all other animals left to themselves, each individual reaches its complete *Bestimmung*; however with human beings only the *species*, at best, reaches it; so that the human race can work its way up to its *Bestimmung* only through *progress* in a series of innumerably many generations.
> (7: 324; see also *Menschenkunde* 25: 1196; *Mrongovius* 25: 1417)

ASSESSING KANT'S MORAL ANTHROPOLOGY

Kant's moral anthropology is certainly not problem-free. On the theoretical side, as critics from Schleiermacher onward have pointed out, it is far from obvious how the concept of transcendental freedom that Kant develops in his critical philosophy can make room for the empirical study of human beings as free-acting beings.[25] On the practical side, the project is infected by numerous ethnic, religious, racial, and sexist prejudices that continually threaten to undermine its core progressive principles.

But I hope I have shown both that there exists a distinct moral anthropology within Kant's pragmatic anthropology, and that this moral anthropology has a necessary and important role to play in his moral philosophy. Without moral anthropology, we are travelers without a map who know neither our destination nor our means of reaching it. We do not know how to make moral principles and commitments efficacious, and we lack judgment concerning when, where, how, and why to apply them in daily life. Those of us today who aspire to construct humanly useful ethical theories need to consider more carefully Kant's conviction that "the metaphysics of morals, or *metaphysica pura*, is only the first part of morality; the second part is *philosophia moralis applicata*, to which the empirical principles belong." There are certainly some professors who are keen on "keeping philosophy pure,"[26] but thankfully Kant was not one of them.

7

Anthropology from a Kantian Point of View

TOWARD A COSMOPOLITAN CONCEPTION OF HUMAN NATURE*

A NEW DISCIPLINE

ANTHROPOLOGY WAS A new field of study when Kant first began offering lectures on it at Königsberg University in the winter semester of 1772—a product of the larger Enlightenment effort to emancipate the study of human nature from theologically based inquiries, best captured by Alexander Pope's famous remark:

> *Know then thyself, presume not God to scan:*
> *The proper study of Mankind is Man.*
> —*An Essay on Man*, 1733–1734, Epistle II

Kant was a leader in the development of anthropology as an academic discipline; indeed, he was the first academic to offer regular university lectures on the topic. For instance, in a frequently cited letter to his former student Marcus Herz, written toward the of 1773, he states:

> This winter for the second time I am offering a *collegium privatum* on anthropology, a subject that I now intend to make into a proper academic discipline. But my plan is quite different [*ganz anders*].¹ The intention that I have is to disclose through it the sources of all the sciences that are concerned with ethics, with the skill of social intercourse, of the method of educating and governing human beings, hence of everything that pertains to the practical. I seek then more phenomena and their laws rather than the first grounds of the possibility of modifying human

nature in general. Hence the subtle and in my eyes eternally futile investigation concerning how bodily organs stand in connection with thoughts is left out entirely. I include so many observations of ordinary life that my listeners have constant occasion to compare their ordinary experience with my remarks and thus, from beginning to end, find the lectures always entertaining and never dry. In the meanwhile I am working on a preliminary exercise for students from this (in my opinion) very pleasant empirical study [*Beobachtungslehre*] of skill, prudence, and even wisdom that, along with physical geography[2] and distinct from all other instruction, can be called knowledge of the world [*Kenntnis der Welt*].

(10: 145–46)

Kant's interest in anthropology actually began much earlier than 1772, and can be traced back at least as far as the summer of 1756, when he first began lecturing on physical geography. For example, in his *Sketch and Announcement of a Lecture Course on Physical Geography* (1757), he notes that his lectures will include a discussion "of the inclinations of human beings which flow from the climate in which they live, the variety of their prejudices and ways of thinking, insofar as this can all serve to make the human being more known to himself, [as well as] a short sketch of their arts, business, and science" (2: 9).[3]

A second source for Kant's anthropology was the material on empirical psychology included in his metaphysics lectures, which date from the 1760s. For instance, in the *Announcement of the Organization of His Lectures for the Winter Semester 1765–1766*, Kant states: "after a brief introduction I shall begin with *empirical psychology*, which is actually the metaphysical science of the *human being* based on experience [*metaphysische Erfahrungswissenschaft vom Menschen*]" (2: 30).[4]

However, empirical psychology constitutes only a part of the new experience-based science of man that would eventually be named anthropology. Other important components include the character of the sexes and of the different peoples and nations. In sections 3 and 4 of his 1764 book, *Observations on the Feeling of the Beautiful and Sublime*,[5] Kant offered some reflection on these topics, which he later revised and expanded when he began lecturing on anthropology in 1772.

ANTHROPOLOGY AND THE PHILOSOPHICAL PHYSICIANS

Before turning to Kant's anthropology, it is important to get a sense of one prominent non-Kantian anthropology. As we have already seen from Kant's letter to Herz in 1773, he developed his own approach to anthropology in explicit opposition to the medical or physiological conceptions of human nature that were gaining popularity in the late eighteenth century.[6] His most frequent sparring partner in this regard was the German physician Ernst Platner (1744–1818), whose book *Anthropologie für Ärzte und Weltweise* (Anthropology for Physicians and Philosophers) was published in 1772—the same year that Kant inaugurated his own anthropology course. In his letter to Herz, Kant criticizes what he calls Platner's "eternally futile investigation concerning how bodily organs stand in connection with thoughts," adding that "my plan is quite different" (10: 145).

Twenty-five years later, in the preface to *Anthropology from a Pragmatic Point of View*, Kant again contrasts his own distinct approach to anthropology—which he now calls "pragmatic"—to the physiological approach championed by Platner and others:

> A doctrine of the knowledge of human beings, systematically formulated (anthropology), can exist either in a physiological or in a pragmatic point of view. —Physiological knowledge of the human being concerns the investigation of what *nature* makes of the human being; pragmatic, the investigation of what *he* as a free-acting being makes of himself, or can and should make of himself.
>
> (7: 119)⁷

In the *Menschenkunde* transcription of his anthropology course (1781–1782),⁸ Kant also bluntly criticizes Platner for having merely "written a scholastic anthropology" (25: 856)—an anthropology, that is, that produces "science for the school," but which is of "no utility to the human being" and from which "one could not obtain any enlightenment of common life" (25: 853).

Platner, however, was by no means the only physician championing a physiological approach to the study of human nature, or even the most prominent one. The most famous example from this genre is probably Julien Offray de la Mettrie's book *L'homme machine* (Man a Machine, 1748), in which he declares confidently that in studying human nature we should be

> guided by experience and observation alone. They abound in the annals of physicians who were not philosophers, but not in those of philosophers who were not physicians. Physician-philosophers probe and illuminate the labyrinth that is man. They alone have revealed man's springs hidden under coverings that obscure so many other marvels.⁹

In addition to La Mettrie, other prominent authors associated with a physiological or medical approach to the study of human nature include Charles Bonnet, Albrecht von Haller, and Georges-Louis Leclerc de Buffon.

Kant's interest in these Enlightenment medical approaches to human nature also began early in his career, long before he began teaching his anthropology course in 1772. And he was by no means entirely dismissive of them. For instance, in his *Essay on the Maladies of the Head* (1764),¹⁰ he goes as far as to say that "I see nothing better for me than to imitate the method of the physicians" (2: 260). And in his Review of Moscati's Work *Of the Corporeal Essential Differences between the Structure of Animals and Humans* (1771),¹¹ he congratulates the "astute anatomist" for his insights into early human life—insights that "Rousseau as a philosopher did not succeed" in reaching (2: 423). Other publications of Kant's that are relevant to physiological approaches to the study of human nature include *A Note to Physicians* (1782), *On the Philosophers' Medicine of the Body* (1786), *From Soemmering's On the Organ of the Soul* (1796),¹² and the third essay in the *Conflict of the Faculties*: "The Conflict of the Philosophy Faculty with the Faculty of Medicine" (1796).

Broadly speaking, the physiological anthropology promoted by Platner and other philosophical physicians of the Enlightenment is the predecessor to physical anthropology, whereas Kant's pragmatic anthropology, with its emphasis on free human action, is the progenitor of various philosophical and existentialist anthropologies. For instance, Max Scheler, an important voice in this latter tradition who also influenced Martin Heidegger, holds that the human being is not only an animal being but also "a 'spiritual' being [ein 'geistiges' Wesen]" that is "no longer tied to its drives and environments, but rather 'free from the environment' [umweltfrei], or, as we shall say, 'open to the world' [weltoffen]."[13]

KANT'S PRAGMATIC ANTHROPOLOGY

Kant's most famous marker for his approach to anthropology is of course "pragmatic"—a term that he did not yet stress when he first began teaching his anthropology course in 1772, but which is featured prominently in the title of his 1798 book, *Anthropology from a Pragmatic Point of View*. Described modestly as "the present manual for my anthropology course" in a footnote at the end of the preface, *Anthropology from a Pragmatic Point of View* is essentially Kant's last set of lecture notes for the course that he taught annually for twenty-four years until his retirement from university lecturing in 1796.

But what exactly does he mean in calling his anthropology *pragmatic*? The term "pragmatic," as Kant uses it, is intentionally broad and incorporates a variety of interrelated but different meanings—not all of which fit readily under current mainstream uses of "pragmatic." We have already touched on two of these meanings in the previous section. First, pragmatic anthropology is conceived in opposition to the physiological anthropology of Platner and the philosophical physicians. The latter anthropology concerns "the investigation of what *nature* makes of the human being" while the former involves "the investigation of what *he* as a free-acting being makes of himself, or can and should make of himself" (*Anth.* 7: 119). However, the pragmatic investigation of the human being as a free-acting being is to be conducted empirically, not transcendentally. For Kantian anthropology, as we saw earlier in the letter to Herz, is also conceived of as a *Beobachtungslehre*, an empirical doctrine based on observation. (Whether Kant himself always manages to adhere to this self-imposed constraint is an issue that I will return to later.) As concerns freedom, what this means in effect is that pragmatic anthropology studies the phenomenal effects of human freedom in the empirical world, not their allegedly non-empirical origins.

Second, Kantian pragmatic anthropology is also distinguished from Platner's "scholastic anthropology" (*Menschenkunde* 25: 856). Scholastic anthropology is a "science for the school" that is developed "in accordance with the standards of the school and of the professions," but unfortunately we are unable to "obtain any enlightenment for common life from it"; it is of "no utility to the human being" (*Menschenkunde* 25: 853). Here Kant is invoking a more conventional meaning of "pragmatic," one that had been present in German philosophy at least since 1720, when Christian Wolff employed the term in this manner in one of his works.¹⁴ Pragmatic anthropology is anthropology that is useful and practical for human beings. However, "practical" here is to be understood in opposition to what is merely theoretical or speculative: we are not yet talking about "practical" in Kant's narrower sense of "morally practical." As he remarks in the introduction to the *Critique of the Power of Judgment*, this latter sense of "practical" is restricted to principles "which are grounded entirely on the concept of freedom to complete exclusion of the determining grounds of the will of nature" (5: 173). To call pragmatic anthropology "practical" in this second, narrower sense would entail giving up the requirement that anthropology be a *Beobachtungslehre*. Kantian pragmatic anthropology can certainly be applied to moral purposes, and it is clear that Kant hoped people would choose to make moral use of his pragmatic anthropology.¹⁵ But strictly speaking, the knowledge of human nature that one gains from the study of pragmatic anthropology can be useful for many purposes—moral, nonmoral, and even immoral.

The third core feature of pragmatic anthropology in Kant's sense involves a specific kind of usefulness. Pragmatic anthropology is useful in the sense that the knowledge of human nature we obtain from it enables us more effectively to use others for our own purposes (whatever these purposes may be). As he remarks toward the end of *Anthropology from a Pragmatic Point of View*, pragmatic anthropology teaches a person how "to use other human beings skillfully for one's purposes" (7: 322). In showing us "how we can use people for our own ends" (Busolt 25: 1436),¹⁶ pragmatic anthropology holds out the promise of a kind of usefulness (viz., skill in human relations) not to be found in either physiology or scholastic anthropology. Again though, pragmatic anthropology implicitly contains multiple application possibilities. If people's chosen ends are moral ones, then they can apply anthropology as a means toward this goal. But if their ends are nonmoral, anthropological knowledge of human beings can also be of service.

Finally, a fourth core dimension of Kantian pragmatic anthropology concerns the acquisition of prudence. Pragmatic anthropology is also a *Klugheitslehre*, a doctrine of prudence. Near the beginning of the *Friedländer* anthropology lectures (1775–1776),¹⁷ Kant states: "all pragmatic doctrines are doctrines of prudence, where for all our skills we also have means to make a proper use of everything; for we study human beings in order to become more prudent, which prudence becomes a science" (25: 471). Admittedly, the prudence aspect of pragmatic anthropology overlaps somewhat with the "using others for one's own purposes" aspect discussed above. For instance, at one point in *Anthropology from a Pragmatic Point of View*, Kant glosses the term "prudence" simply as "using other human beings for one's purposes" (7: 201); and later in this same text he refers to "technically practical reason" or "the maxim of prudence," which includes the ability to get "other human beings' inclinations into one's power, so that one can direct and determine them according to one's intentions" (7: 271).

But prudence in Kant's sense also involves more than merely the ability to use other people for one's own purposes, and points ultimately to an understanding of human well-being and happiness. As he writes in the *Groundwork of the Metaphysics of Morals*: "skill in the choice of one's own greatest well-being [*Wohlsein*] can be called *prudence*" (4: 416). And in the earlier *Parow* anthropology lectures from 1772–1773[18] he states: "The capacity to choose the best means to happiness [*Glückseligkeit*] is prudence. Happiness consists in the satisfaction of all inclinations, and therefore to be able to choose happiness, one must be free" (25: 413). In this broader sense of prudence, Kantian pragmatic anthropology holds out a promise, to those who have successfully learned its lessons, that anthropology can show people what they need to learn about human nature in order to achieve a greater level of well-being and happiness. And in making a contribution to greater human well-being and happiness, Kantian pragmatic anthropology also makes good on its claim of obtaining "enlightenment for common life."

TOWARD A COSMOPOLITAN CONCEPTION OF HUMAN NATURE

However, there remains an additional central feature of Kantian anthropology, one that is still underexplored and not at all evident when one focuses on the well-established meanings of his pragmatic anthropology discussed above. In my view this additional component constitutes the single most important dimension of Kant's distinctive approach to anthropology, but it is also one that stands in occasional tension with other core features of his anthropological project.

This additional component concerns the particular conception of human nature that Kant believes a proper anthropological investigation points to, and it is a markedly cosmopolitan conception of human nature. In other words, Kant believes that in studying anthropology in the manner he proposes the student will eventually arrive at a cosmopolitan conception of human nature. Additionally, he holds that the most important reason to study anthropology is to obtain this specific conception of human nature.

Although Kant does not consistently employ a uniform term for this cosmopolitan conception of human nature in his anthropology lectures, he does explicitly articulate it in a number of places. Perhaps the most prominent and direct articulation occurs in the preface to *Anthropology from a Pragmatic Point of View*, where he announces that anthropology is only properly called pragmatic "when it contains knowledge of the human being as a *citizen of the world* [*Erkenntnis des Menschen als Weltbürgers*]" (7: 120). Here, the cosmopolitan conception of human nature is described as a necessary condition for any anthropology's being called pragmatic: the only anthropology that should count as pragmatic is an anthropology that contains knowledge of the human being as a *Weltbürger*. However, there is nothing in either the conventional usage of the term "pragmatic" or in Kant's better-known pronouncements about pragmatic that suggests that this cosmopolitan component needs to be regarded as a necessary part of the definition of pragmatic. The centrality of this wider, normative conception of human nature to Kant's approach to anthropology is further underscored when he adds later on the same page of the preface:

> *General* knowledge always precedes *local* knowledge here, if the latter is to be ordered and directed through philosophy: in the absence of which all acquired knowledge can yield nothing more than fragmentary groping around and no science [*fragmentarisches Herumtappen und keine Wissenschaft*].
>
> (7: 120)

In other words, Kantian anthropology begins with a general conception of human nature (albeit one that is arrived at empirically—more on this later), and then uses this general conception to assess more particular conceptions of particular subgroups of human beings. An anthropology that fails to do this yields nothing more than a fragmentary groping around.

A second key text asserting the centrality of a cosmopolitan conception of human nature occurs in the preamble to the *Friedländer* anthropology lectures, where Kant states:

> Anthropology is not however a local [*locale*] but rather a general [*generale*] anthropology. In it one comes to know not the state of human beings but rather the nature of humanity, for the local properties of human beings always change, but the nature of humanity does not. Anthropology is thus a pragmatic knowledge of what results from our nature, but it is not a physical or geographical knowledge, for that is tied to time and place, and is not constant. . . . Anthropology is not a description of human beings, but of human nature.
>
> (25: 471)

In this text, the term *Weltbürger* does not occur, but the triple emphases on "the nature of humanity," "human nature," and "general anthropology"—each of which is contrasted with a more provincial, transitory, and less global project—clearly point in the same direction. And here also he maintains that anthropology is only properly designated pragmatic when it begins with reflection on a general conception of human nature.

A third key text occurs in the prolegomena to the *Pillau* anthropology lectures (1777–1778),[19] where Kant praises anthropological knowledge above all other kinds of knowledge: "There is no greater important investigation for the human being than knowledge of the human being" (25: 733). When knowledge of the human being "is treated pragmatically," Kant adds, "then it is a knowledge of the world and forms a man of the world [*bildet einen Weltmann*]" (25: 733). However, there are two distinct types of knowledge of the world:

> (1) A local knowledge [*Local Weltkenntniß*] of the world, which merchants [*Kaufleute*] have, which is also called empirical. (2) A general knowledge of the world [*general Weltkenntniß*], which the man of the world has, and which is not empirical but cosmological. Local knowledge of the world is tied to place and time, and also gives no rules to a person to act on in common life. He who becomes acquainted with the world through travel has only this knowledge of it, which,

however, also lasts only for a while, for when the behavior in the place where he has been changes, then his knowledge of it also ceases.

(25: 734)

In each of these three texts Kant explicitly links his use of the term "pragmatic" to a cosmopolitan conception of human nature, a conception that is not tied to time and place. Anthropologies that study only the behavior and characteristics of human beings as they are found in particular times and places are merely "local" anthropologies, but what Kant advocates is a "general" anthropology: an anthropology that is concerned with what human beings in all times and places share with one another.[20] And this wider knowledge of what human beings share in common with one another "is not empirical but cosmological," that is, it is concerned with the totality of human beings as a species throughout space and time, not with features or aspects that only some human beings in some times and places have. As he states in the introduction to his *Physical Geography* lectures, in summarizing the second part of *Weltkenntnis*, knowledge of the human being: "From anthropology one gets to know what is pragmatic in the human being and not speculative. The human being is considered here not *physiologically*, so that one distinguishes the sources of phenomena, but *cosmologically*" (9: 157). The intentionally wide scope of Kantian anthropology results in a knowledge that is pragmatic rather than merely speculative in the straightforward sense of being useful. For once we acquire this knowledge, it never becomes obsolete. On the other hand, the more usual kind of inductively acquired knowledge of particular human beings as they exist in particular times and places becomes obsolete as soon as styles and habits change.

Finally, it is also worth noting that Kant's concern to locate a cosmopolitan conception of human nature not tied to time and place is plainly evident even in some of his pre-critical writings, long before he first began teaching anthropology in 1772. For instance, in the *Announcement of the Organization of His Lectures for the Winter Semester 1765–1766*, he emphasizes the centrality of "the study of man" in his ethics lectures, adding: "And by *man* here I do not only mean *man* as he is distorted by the mutable form which is conferred upon him by the contingencies of his condition. . . . I rather mean the *nature* of man, which always remains [*die immer bleibt*], and his distinctive position within the creation" (2: 311).[21]

AMBIGUITIES AND TENSIONS

Thus far I have tried to achieve two interrelated goals: (1) to articulate what Kant means by a "cosmopolitan conception of human nature," and (2) to establish the central role of this conception within Kant's distinctive approach to anthropology. In the present section, I will address briefly three basic ambiguities and tensions engendered by Kant's cosmopolitan conception of human nature, and do what I can to disambiguate and resolve these problems.

Cosmological/Empirical

Kant's commitment to an anthropology that provides general as opposed to local knowledge of human beings "and which is not empirical [*nicht empirisch*] but cosmological" (*Pillau* 25: 734) appears to contradict his claim that anthropology as he conceives it is a *Beobachtungslehre*—an empirical study or observation-based doctrine (letter to Herz toward the end of 1773, 10: 146). For instance, in *Collins*, one of the earliest surviving anthropology transcriptions (1772–1773),[22] Kant begins by stating that in "the science of man (Anthropologia) . . . the grounds of cognition are taken from observation and experience [*Beobachtung und Erfahrung*]" (25: 7). And the empirical credentials of Kantian anthropology are also touted later, in the preface to the *Groundwork*, when Kant states that "practical anthropology"[23] constitutes "the empirical part [*der empirische Teil*]" of moral philosophy (4: 388, cf. 387). But how can anthropology be both *empirisch* and *nicht empirisch*?

Kant's choice of language here is unfortunate: strictly speaking, he has contradicted himself. However, I believe his considered view is that the knowledge of human nature and of humanity that he emphasizes in his anthropology is a type of empirical knowledge, albeit one that aims at a high degree of generality and stresses reflection on common features and tendencies shared by all individual members of the species rather than on distinguishing marks that set off individuals and/or groups from each other. Kant is certainly not claiming that the kind of knowledge of humanity stressed in his anthropology is an example of what (in the first *Critique*) he calls an "*a priori* cognition"—a cognition that occurs "*absolutely* independently of all experience" (B 3). Rather, knowledge of the nature of humanity is an empirical cognition, which has its source "*a posteriori*, namely in experience" (B 2). But the kind of empirical knowledge he is referring to in his anthropology is one that, while experience-based, emphasizes reflection about the chief tendencies and characteristics of the human species as a whole rather than limited and partial observations about the behavior of particular individuals or groups within the species in particular times and places. This point is evident in the concluding section of *Anthropology from a Pragmatic Point of View*, where Kant discusses the character and vocation of the human species at some length (7: 322–33), and several earlier transcriptions of his anthropology lectures contain similar discussions (see *Friedländer* 25: 675–97; *Menschenkunde* 25: 1194–1203; *Mrongovius* 25: 1415–29).[24] A key statement in this discussion is the following: "The character of the species, as it is known from the experience of all ages and by all peoples [*so wie er aus der Erfahrung aller Zeiten und unter allen Völkern kundbar wird*], is this" (7: 331). Here, the experiential basis of the knowledge is clearly asserted, but so too is its wide temporal and spatial scope.

This emphasis on wide reflection about human nature and humanity is one key reason that Kant repeatedly includes "plays and novels" among the most important aids (*Hilfsmittel*) for acquiring anthropological knowledge (*Anth* 7: 121; see also *Pillau* 25: 734; *Menschenkunde* 25: 857–58; *Mrongovius* 25: 1213). Novelists and playwrights frequently provide us with deeper and more enduring insights into the human condition than do social scientists, for the latter typically are only concerned with specific subgroups within the species as they exist in specific times and places.

Empirical/Normative

A second tension implicit in Kant's cosmopolitan conception of human nature is that between the empirical and the normative. I have discussed the empirical dimension of the concept above, and in the conclusion to this essay I will draw attention to its important moral dimension. Briefly, the primary function that Kant assigns to the cosmopolitan conception of human nature is that of a teleological moral map: a tool by means of which we are to orient ourselves toward the present as well as the future. But here it is the tension between these two dimensions to which I wish to draw attention. How can something be both empirical and morally normative—especially for a non-naturalist such as Kant, who holds that moral oughts are in no way derivable from nature? In the first *Critique*, for instance, he writes:

> *Ought* expresses a kind of necessity and connection with grounds which is not found anywhere else in the whole of nature. In nature the understanding can cognize only *what exists*, or has been, or will be. It is impossible that something in it *ought to be* other than what, in all these time relations, it in fact is; indeed, the *ought*, if one has merely the course of nature before one's eyes, has no meaning whatsoever.
>
> (A 547/B 575)[25]

Is there any viable way to defuse this tension? One possibility might be to argue that the oughts entailed by the cosmopolitan conception of human nature are merely hypothetical rather than categorical—that (for example) when Kant points to a future world in which human beings are "cosmopolitically united" (*Anth* 7: 333), and when he argues that it is humanity's duty to pursue this goal (see, for example, *KpV* 5: 114), he is calling attention merely to a future possibility that is contingent on our own inclinations. But Kant's texts simply do not support such a reading. "We are determined *a priori* by reason to promote with all of our powers the best for the world [*das Weltbeste*]" (*KU* 5: 453; see also *Gemeinspruch* 8: 309–10). The relevant oughts to which he refers are categorical, not hypothetical.

A second strategy, which I have defended in more detail elsewhere,[26] is to argue that a moral (categorical) imperative lies behind the acquisition of knowledge of our own nature. We have a moral duty to learn how nature (particularly our own nature) works in order to put into effect a system of freedom in the world of nature—that is, to bring about a moral world within the natural world in which we live. This strategy, I continue to believe, is viable and coherent. And it enables Kant to hold onto the claim that his anthropology is a *Beobachtungslehre* while still maintaining that there is a distinctly *moral* anthropology within it, which forms the second part of morals (see *Moral Mrongovius II* 29: 599). However, it is unfortunate that Kant's discussion of this strategy is episodic and not systematically developed.

Cosmological/Cosmopolitan

The terms "cosmological" and "cosmopolitan" both feature prominently in Kant's discussions of human nature, and they overlap with each other in virtue of their shared Greek prefix *kosmos* (order, world, universe). Again, however, Kant's use of the term "cosmological" in his discussions of anthropology and physical geography does not signal a non-empirical study of the world or universe, as is often the case, say, in the dialectic of the *Critique of Pure Reason*. When he emphasizes the need for a cosmological approach to the study of humanity in his anthropology, Kant is not dogmatically succumbing to the errors of "an alleged pure (rational) cosmology" (B 435); rather, he is simply stressing the need to focus on the whole rather than the parts. And the relevant whole in this case is the entire human species, conceived teleologically with a view to its long-term political, legal, and moral vocations.

Another key text where this specifically anthropological sense of the term "cosmological" is invoked occurs in an important concluding note to the essay *Of the Different Races of Human Beings* (1775),[27] where Kant in effect advertises his physical geography and anthropology courses for the forthcoming year. Both courses aim "to procure the *pragmatic* element for all otherwise acquired sciences and skills, by means of which they become useful not merely for *school* but rather for *life*, and through which the accomplished student is introduced to the stage of his destiny [*Bestimmung*], namely, the *world*" (2: 443). Additionally, both physical geography and anthropology "must be considered *cosmologically*, namely, not with respect to the noteworthy details that their objects contain (physics and empirical psychology), but with respect to what we can note of the relation as a whole in which they stand and in which everyone takes his place" (ibid.). It is the relation of each individual to the species as a whole, where this whole is conceived both spatially and temporally (the latter in terms of the vocation or destiny of the species, its *Bestimmung*), that ultimately receives pride of place in Kantian anthropology.

The Greek suffix *politēs* (citizen) is crucial to the term "cosmopolitan," and here is where the terms "cosmological" and "cosmopolitan" part ways. There are distinct political, legal, and moral overtones in Kant's anthropological use of the term "cosmopolitan" that are absent in the term "cosmological."

The legal dimension involves a strong commitment to international law and global, as opposed to merely national, jurisdiction; Kant envisions a global civil society where all individuals possess the same basic human rights and are judged by one internationally agreed-upon set of legal principles. In *Idea for a Universal History with a Cosmopolitan Aim* (1784),[28] Kant states that attaining such a society is humanity's most momentous task:

> The greatest problem for the human species, whose solution nature compels it to seek, is the achievement of a **civil society** that administers justice universally. . . . This problem is at the same time the most difficult and the last to be solved by the human species.
>
> (8: 22–23; original italics)

In the conclusion to *Anthropology from a Pragmatic Point of View*, he stresses that while "human beings feel destined [*bestimmt*] by nature to [develop] . . . into a *cosmopolitan* [*weltbürgerliche*] society (*cosmopolitismus*)," we are to regard this goal as "only a regulative principle" (7: 331) rather than a constitutive one. In effect, we are to treat it as an idea that strongly influences our practical orientation toward the world, but not as one that contributes directly to our knowledge of it. We are to regard the present warring nation-states as if they are headed in the direction of a viable, peaceful, cosmopolitan condition, but we have no reliable knowledge that they are in fact doing so. And Kant also holds that all individuals have a moral duty to work toward the achievement of that goal: we are commanded "to pursue this diligently as the vocation [*Bestimmung*] of the human race, not without grounded expectation [*gegründete Vermutung*] of a natural tendency toward it" (7: 331).

However, Kant is exasperatingly vague about the political makeup of this hoped-for cosmopolitan society. At times, he appears to favor the strong universalism of a world state. For instance, in *Toward Perpetual Peace* (1795) he contrasts "the positive idea of a *world republic*" to "the *negative* surrogate of a *league* [*Bund*]" of sovereign states (8: 357); and at the end of the *Theory and Practice* essay (1793) he states that he puts his "trust in theory, which proceeds from the principle of right" and which supports the establishment of "a universal state of peoples [*ein allgemeiner Völkerstaat*]" (8: 313, see also 311). But his considered view appears to favor the initial establishment of a small, voluntary league of nations without coercive powers ("this league does not aim to acquire any power of the state"; 8: 356), which will then expand gradually into a stronger worldwide federation of all states with at least some coercive authority at the federal level—presumably, the authority to enforce peace between nations as well as to prosecute fundamental human rights violations within states.[29] The stronger alternative of a universal "state of peoples [*Völkerstaat*]," while "correct *in thesi*" (8: 357), is neither a realistic nor a morally desirable option. Sovereign states "are not to be fused into a single state" (8: 354), for a world state is likely to result only in "a soulless despotism" (8: 367). However, while Kant prudently declines to speculate about the precise political contours of humanity's future cosmopolitan condition, it is clear that a political dimension forms a necessary part of his cosmopolitan conception of human nature. For instance, in the final sentence of *Anthropology from a Pragmatic Point of View*, he urges readers to work for the "progressive organization of the citizens of the earth [*Erdbürger*] into and toward the species as a system that is cosmopolitically united [*kosmopolitsch verbunden*]" (7: 333).

MORAL MOTIVES

Finally, let us examine the moral dimension of Kant's cosmopolitan conception of human nature, a dimension which, to the best of my knowledge, has been overlooked, indeed denied, by other scholars who have discussed it.[30] Here as elsewhere, we see clear signs of a moral agenda within Kant's anthropology.[31] By means of his cosmopolitan conception of nature, Kant intends to provide readers with a conceptual orientation and a delineation of where humanity as a species is headed, as well as to indicate what human beings need to do in order to reach their destination. The cosmopolitan conception of human nature is in effect a teleological moral map, a practical guide by means of which human beings are to orient themselves in both the present and the future.

A second moral motive behind the cosmopolitan conception is simply to stress what all members of the human species share in common with one another, rather than to dwell on what sets them apart from one another. In this role, it serves as an anthropological reminder that all human beings have rights simply in virtue of their shared humanity, and that these rights "must be held sacred, however great a sacrifice this may cost the ruling power" (*Frieden* 8: 380).

Third, the *Bestimmung* (vocation, destiny, determination—each of these meanings is present in Kant's use of the term) of humanity in a cosmopolitan condition is something that only the species as a whole can achieve. And in this respect, human beings differ markedly from other animals: "with the animal species each individual reaches its *Bestimmung*, but in the human race a single individual can never do this, rather only the whole species can reach its *Bestimmung*, despite the fact that the human being is equipped by nature like an animal" (*Menschenkunde* 25: 1196; see also *Mrongovius* 25: 1417; *Anth* 7: 324). Here, Kant indicates that the empirical and comparative study of different terrestrial beings supports the case for human exceptionalism. Human beings *are* different from other animals: we have collective cultural, political, and moral vocations that they lack.

It is true that Kant's anthropology, like other anthropologies past and present, is infected by multiple ethnic, racial, religious, and sexist prejudices that continually threaten to undermine its core progressive principles. But it is also important not to lose sight of the core progressive principles, and the cosmopolitan conception of human nature is ultimately what anchors them. In placing what the members of the human species share in common with one another at the center of his anthropology, and in trying to show that "there is a cosmopolitical predisposition [*cosmopolitische Anlage*] in the human species," one which, "even with all the wars . . . gradually wins the upper hand over the selfish predispositions of peoples in the course of political affairs" (*Anth* 7: 412),[32] Kant gives readers rational grounds both for adopting a stance whereby "a violation of right [*Rechtsverletzung*] on *one* place of the earth is felt in *all*" and for believing that "the idea of a cosmopolitan right is no fantastic and exaggerated way of representing right" (*Frieden* 8: 360). At the same time, anthropology from a Kantian point of view stresses that whether human beings ever will in fact become "cosmopolitically united" (*Anth* 7: 333) and enter into a condition where "a universal peace rules the world" (*Mrongovius* 25: 1429) depends ultimately on what they choose to do. Peace is by no means guaranteed. But this too is eminently appropriate for a project that sets out to investigate what human beings as free-acting beings make of themselves, or can and should make of themselves (see *Anth* 7: 119).

8

Making the Law Visible

THE ROLE OF EXAMPLES IN KANT'S ETHICS*

INTRODUCTION: EXAMPLES IN PURE MORAL PHILOSOPHY

NOWHERE IS THE stringency of Kant's *Groundwork of the Metaphysics of Morals* more evident than in his blunt statement that one could not "give worse advice to morality than by wanting to derive [*entlehnen*][1] it from examples" (*Gr* 4: 408). Was the sage of Königsberg oblivious to the power of examples? Was he indifferent to the adage that it is always "personalities, not principles, that move the age"?[2] The outspokenness of the message becomes even more apparent when Kant applies it to some of the most fundamental commitments of his largely Christian eighteenth-century readership. "Even the Holy One of the Gospel," he remarks pointedly, is unable to serve as a defensible norm in ethics (*Gr* 4: 408). A popular late twentieth-century bumper sticker to the contrary, the question is not "What would Jesus do?" Raising the religious ante still further, Kant next turns his sights on theists of all persuasions who look upon the deity as the ultimate criterion of moral norms: "But where do we get the concept of God as the highest good?" (4: 408–9). Even though Kant frequently claims to arrive at his own foundational moral principle simply by analyzing "the moral cognition of common human reason [*die gemeine Menschenvernunft*]" (4: 403, cf. 402),[3] the "divine command theory of ethics," according to which our moral duties are simply what God commands—subscribed to by a strong majority of people in all times and places, and hence still today the planet's dominant theory of normative ethics—is quickly rejected. Echoing Socrates' famous dispute with Euthyphro,[4] Kant too argues that human beings ought not to derive their moral norms from God. No one—not even Jesus or God—can give morality to us.

Why does Kant make these radical claims? In the *Groundwork*, his major objections to deriving moral principles from examples, while severely compressed, are both clear and compelling. First, whenever we judge an example (be it person or event)[5] to be of moral value, we judge it so—sometimes explicitly, but more often only implicitly—in virtue of a preexisting standard. To call x right or good (or pious, courageous, generous, etc.) presupposes that we first have a general conception of right or good (or pious, courageous, generous, etc.). This is what Kant means when he states that "every example [*jedes Beispiel*]" of morality "must first be judged by principles of morality" (4: 408). This point too is Socratic,[6] and while particularists of many persuasions continue to protest it,[7] their protests are unpersuasive. In order to judge x to be right or good, we must first be in possession of a general concept of rightness or goodness.

Kant's second objection to deriving morality from examples has roots in Enlightenment culture, particularly in his own definition of enlightenment. At the beginning of his essay *An Answer to the Question: What Is Enlightenment?* for instance, he offers the following as a motto for the Enlightenment: "Have courage to make use of your *own* understanding!" (8: 35; see also *KU* 5: 294; *Anth* 7: 228). When applied to the ethical sphere, the resultant advice is to make use of our own understanding in order to think about what is right and wrong, good and bad, rather than blindly following others. This is Kant's point when he states tersely in the *Groundwork* that "imitation [*Nachahmung*] has no place at all in ethics" (4: 409).

A third, related argument against examples stems from Kant's view concerning the importance of autonomy in ethics. On Kant's view, autonomy or self-legislation—the capacity of rational beings to act in accordance with principles that they themselves create—is "the supreme principle of morality" (*Gr* 4: 440) as well as "the ground of the dignity of human nature and of every rational nature" (4: 436). If we allow any external sources—be they persons (again, even the "Holy One of the Gospel" or God himself) or things (e.g., the beauty and sublimity of nature, to which Kant himself was by no means blind)[8]—to determine our moral principles, we run the risk of forfeiting our autonomy. Instead of correctly grasping the fact that the ground of morality lies in our own practical reason, we may begin to assume falsely that it lies in heteronomous sources.

A fourth Kantian objection to grounding morality in examples is briefly hinted at toward the end of the famous paragraph in *Groundwork* 4: 408–9, but elaborated on at greater length elsewhere. Because moral norms are categorical and involve concepts of necessity and universality, they cannot be grounded in experience. Rather, "necessity and strict universality," as he notes in the introduction to the *Critique of Pure Reason*, are "sure signs [*sichere Kennzeichen*] of an *a priori* cognition" (B 4; see also *Collins* 27: 333). This is essentially Kant's point in the *Groundwork* when he states that the "true original" of morality "lies in reason" rather than in experience (4: 409). Or, as he puts it at the beginning of the next paragraph, there exists "a genuine supreme principle of morality" that "must rest on pure reason independently of all experience" (ibid.).

Finally, a fifth objection to grounding morality in examples stems from Kant's methodological dispute with the popular philosophers (*Popularphilosophen*) of the time.[9]

As we have seen, Kant holds that moral norms, because they involve necessity and universality, cannot be derived from experience. This in turn convinces him "of the utmost necessity to work out for once a pure moral philosophy, completely cleansed of everything that may be only empirical" (*Gr* 4: 389). However, the popular philosophers of Kant's day (and this strategy continues to find support in many circles at present) tried to ground their ethical theories in experience, and were thus opposed to the very idea of a pure moral philosophy. In Kant's words, popular philosophy "goes no further than it can get through groping [*durch Tappen*] by means of examples," and is thus unable to arrive at a metaphysics of morals, "which no longer lets itself be held back by anything empirical" (4: 412). The title of section II of the *Groundwork* is "Transition [*Übergang*] from Popular Moral Philosophy to Metaphysics of Morals" (4: 406), and Kant's arguments against deriving morality from examples are themselves part of this larger project of defending the need for, and showing the way to, a metaphysics of morals.

One should not infer from what has been said thus far that Kant's position on the role of examples in ethics is entirely negative. But unfortunately, in the *Groundwork* his estimation of their positive role is even more compressed than is his criticism of their weaknesses. For example, after stating his *Aufklärung* conviction that imitation has no place in morality, he notes: "Examples serve only for encouragement [*Aufmunterung*], that is, they put beyond doubt the feasibility [*Tunlichkeit*] of what the law commands" (4: 409).[10] His point here is that when we are confronted by a truly virtuous person, this helps to convince us that what morality demands is humanly possible (see *KpV* 5: 158; *MdS* 6: 480). Still, the primary lesson to be learned from moral exemplars is one of encouragement, not imitation. As he states in *Collins*:

> An example is not for imitation, but it is certainly for emulation [*Nachfolge*]. The ground of the action must not be derived from the example, but rather from the rule. But if others have shown that such an act is possible, we must emulate their example, and also exert ourselves to perform such moral actions, and not let others surpass us in that respect.
>
> (27: 334)

A second (and even terser) argument in defense of examples in ethics presented in the *Groundwork* is located in the same sentence quoted in the previous paragraph. Examples also "make visible [*machen ... anschaulich*]"—the second word also means "clear," "vivid," "concrete," "perceptible," "intuitive"—"what the practical rule expresses more generally" (4: 409; see also *KpV* 5: 77). A sharp and vivid example brings the moral point home for human beings in a way that the abstractions of theories, principles, and rules often cannot. Again though, the example itself does not ground or justify the principle—quite the contrary. Rather, the right kind of example helps human beings to see what is at stake in the principle. Examples help to make the moral law visible to human beings.

However, this is certainly not the whole story about the role of examples in ethics. Kant's *Groundwork* has a tightly focused and limited aim. As he writes toward the end of the Preface: "the present groundwork is ... nothing more than the search for and establishment of the *supreme principle of morality*, which constitutes by itself a business that in its purpose is complete and to be kept apart from every other moral investigation" (4: 392). Once this specific goal of finding and justifying the supreme principle of morality has been reached, additional investigations—e.g., how do we apply the principle to the contingencies of human life?—can then be undertaken. And when Kant undertakes this latter task, he has much more to say about the role of examples in ethics.

EXAMPLES IN THE MORAL LIFE OF HUMAN BEINGS

Given Kant's specific and limited aim in the *Groundwork*, it is easy to see why he devotes so little discussion to the role of examples in ethics. Because he is trying to justify a moral principle that "must hold, not only for human beings, but for all *rational beings as such [alle vernünftigen Wesen überhaupt]*" (4: 408), and because he believes that this principle also must hold "not merely under contingent conditions and with exceptions but with *absolute necessity*" (ibid.), it is clear both that any references to specific persons and actions drawn from human life will be too weak to justify the principle and that such examples will fail to offer the right kind of moral guidance.

However, when Kant turns to what he variously calls "practical anthropology" (*Gr* 4: 388), "moral anthropology" (*MdS* 6: 217), and "the second part of morals" (*Moral Mrongovius II* 29: 599), his remarks about the place of examples in ethics are much more extensive. For here he he is concerned with "the subjective conditions in human nature that hinder people or help them in carrying out the laws of a metaphysics of morals" (*MdS* 6: 217).[11] In other words, the question now becomes: What are the specific features of human nature that make it difficult or easy for human beings to act morally?

Moral Education

One morally relevant fact about human nature concerns our biological and cognitive development. We are not born as autonomous moral agents; rather, we develop our moral reasoning capacities slowly over a number of years. Young children do not yet possess the ability to reason autonomously about moral matters, and, at least at the beginning, they do learn best by imitation. Hence, their ability to reason autonomously about ethics can only be fostered effectively through exposure to concrete examples. Parents and moral educators need to take these developmental factors into account. For instance, in a section called "Ethical Didactics" in the *Metaphysics of Morals*, Kant writes:

> The *experimental* (technical) means for cultivating virtue is [a] *good* example on the part of the teacher (his exemplary conduct) and [a] *cautionary* example in others, since, for a still undeveloped human being, imitation is the first determination of his will to accept maxims that he afterwards makes for himself.
>
> (6: 479)

Similarly, in the *Methodenlehre* section of the second *Critique*, which is concerned with "the way in which one can provide the laws of pure practical reason with *access* to the human mind and *influence* on its maxims" (5: 151)—in other words, with how to make moral principles efficacious in human life—Kant also refers several times to the need for concrete examples when discussing ethics with young people. Near the beginning of his discussion, for instance, he states, "it certainly cannot be denied, that in order to bring . . . a mind that is still uncultivated [*ungebildet*] . . . onto the track of the morally good in the first place, some preparatory guidance is needed" (5: 152).

However, in both the *Critique of Practical Reason* and in the *Metaphysics of Morals*, he warns that this strategy of teaching ethics by example, while humanly necessary, carries a danger: "not the conduct of other human beings, but rather the law must serve as our incentive [*Triebfeder*]" (*MdS* 6: 480; see also *KpV* 5: 152). Exposure to moral exemplars should help to set the child on the right moral track, but after a while the pupil must come to understand the norms by which these exemplars themselves are judged.

As we have seen, in the *Metaphysics of Morals* Kant stresses the role of teachers themselves as moral exemplars—not an easy assignment for any teacher. However, in the second *Critique* he advocates a different strategy, one that involves searching through "the biographies of ancient and modern times": "I do not know why educators of the young . . . have not, after first laying the foundation in a purely moral catechism, searched through the biographies of ancient and modern times in order to have at hand illustrations [*Belege*] of the duties presented" (5: 154). Here, the goal is to help the student "feel the progress of his power of judgment" (ibid.) by discussing different cases with him and helping him to gradually grasp the underlying principles by means of which the cases are properly appraised. By advocating the use of examples taken from real life rather than from fiction or the teacher's own imagination, Kant seems to reveal a preference for examples that are less "cooked," less theory-laden. And what real-life exemplars does he have in mind? Anne Boleyn, "an innocent but powerless person," is briefly singled out in the *Critique of Practical Reason* (5: 155), while in the *Metaphysics of Morals* Curtius and Seneca are referred to as heroes whose deaths perhaps constituted morally permissible exceptions to the prohibition against suicide—as was the carrying into battle of a fast-acting poison by "a great king who died recently" (6: 423; see also *Anth* 7: 258; Kant refers here to Frederick the Great), so that if and when he was captured by enemy troops, he could not be forced to agree to conditions that would prove harmful to his subjects.[12]

In his *Lectures on Pedagogy*, the major theme of which is *moral* education, Kant also refers several times to the importance of examples in discussing ethics with children. At one point, he advises parents not to place any value in fancy clothes, so that their children will do likewise: "for here as everywhere example is all-powerful and reinforces or destroys good teaching" (9: 486).[13] Later, he advises that "in order to ground a moral character in children, . . . one must teach them the duties that they have to fulfill as much as possible by examples [*so viel als möglich durch Beispiele*]" (9: 488).

However, none of these passages concerning the necessity of teaching ethics to children by example contradicts the controversial anti-example paragraph in the

Groundwork. For his point in the latter work is primarily *logical*, and concerns the impossibility of grounding an allegedly universal and necessary moral principle in empirical cases. His point in the former texts is *biological* and *psychological* (or what Kant would call anthropological), and concerns morally relevant facts of human nature. Because of the specific ways in which human cognitive development occurs, examples are necessary in their moral education.

Limitations of Human Reason

Even after human beings have reached adulthood and developmental maturity, there remain hindrances in human nature that make it difficult for them to act from moral principle. One of the most fundamental challenges is the fact that the developmentally mature human mind is still a finite intelligence rather than an infinite intelligence. The adult human mind is equipped only with "a discursive, image-dependent understanding" (*KU* 5: 408); in order to think abstractly, we need images. The finitude of the human condition thus poses a permanent challenge to the task of grasping ideas of pure reason, such as *a priori* moral norms or the concept of a morally perfect will.

Kant's basic response to this challenge of human finitude is to articulate various strategies for representing moral concepts analogically and symbolically through images. As he remarks in *Religion within the Boundaries of Mere Reason*, "for the human being the invisible needs to be represented through something visible (sensible)" (6: 192). In an important footnote in this same work, he elaborates:

> It is admittedly a limitation [*eine Beschränktheit*] of human reason, and one which is ever inseparable from it, that we can conceive of no considerable moral worth in the actions of a personal being without representing that person, or his manifestation, in human guise. This is not to assert that such worth is in itself (κατ' ἀλήθειαν) so conditioned, but merely that we must always resort to some analogy with natural beings in order to make supersensible qualities comprehensible [*faßlich*] to ourselves.
> (6: 64–65n)

This particular passage is complicated by the fact that the larger context of Kant's discussion concerns Jesus as the archetype (*Urbild*) of the perfectly good will. And as I noted at the beginning of the discussion, on his view even the "Holy One of the Gospel" must first be compared to a standard of moral perfection—one created by our own reason—before we are able to recognize him as a moral exemplar (see *Gr* 4: 408). However, the two passages are consistent with one another. His point at *Groundwork* 4: 408 is simply that any example—be it person or event—held to be morally good presupposes a standard by which it is judged to be morally good. At *Religion* 64–65n and in other supporting texts (which will be discussed below), his point is that the adult human mind needs concrete images in order to fully understand moral goodness. Due to our nature and because of the way our minds function, we need personal exemplars and tangible examples, not just principles. As he remarks later in *Religion*, there exists "a natural need of all human beings to demand for the highest concepts and grounds of reason something that *the senses can hold onto*, some confirmation from experience" (6: 109).

An additional complication in *Religion* 64–65n concerns Kant's difficult doctrine of schematism. In resorting to some analogy with natural being in order to make supersensible qualities comprehensible to ourselves, we are engaging in a "schematism of analogy"—adapting a concept to the spatial-temporal conditions of human experience by means of another object (in this case, Jesus), which in turn is a symbol for the original concept. However, in the *Critique of Practical Reason* Kant asserts that "no schema on behalf of its [viz., the moral law's] application *in concreto* is possible" (5: 69). No schema is possible for the categorical imperative, while a schema—or at least a "schematism of analogy," which differs from a "schematism of objective determination" in that it does not extend our knowledge but only helps us to make sense out of highly abstract concepts—*is* possible in the case of the perfectly good will. Has Kant contradicted himself here? Why is it possible to provide a schema for the concept of a morally perfect will, but impossible to provide a schema for the moral law? Both are concepts of pure reason, and if a schema is possible for one, then why not for the other?

I am not aware of a satisfactory Kantian solution to this conundrum,[14] but I am also not sure if one is necessary. For in the second *Critique*, after announcing that the moral law cannot be schematized, Kant offers a figurative substitution for the schematization of the moral law, which he calls "the typic of pure practical judgment" (5: 67, see also 69–70). And at bottom, the typification of the moral law achieves the same results as the schematization of the morally perfect will. In both cases, human beings, in order to better grasp abstract moral concepts, represent these concepts symbolically to themselves by making analogies to "something that the senses can hold onto."

Before moving on, it is important to underscore Kant's basic point that the finitude of the human condition implies a lifelong need for concrete moral examples and personal exemplars. With his second argument in defense of examples, we are no longer talking about a strategy of moral education that is to be applied only to children and that can be dispensed with once they reach adulthood. Adult human beings do have stronger powers of reflection and abstraction than do children. But even adults remain saddled with "a discursive image-dependent understanding," and thus they will always need examples in order to make the moral law visible to themselves.

Hope and Inspiration

Kant's third major argument in defense of examples in ethics is primarily psychological. The existence and availability of examples of moral goodness—be they persons or their deeds—give us hope and inspiration that what morality demands is achievable by human beings. Here as elsewhere, his argument in defense of the necessity of examples is based on certain facts about human nature. Examples provide us with palpable evidence that morality is humanly possible—that the actual carrying out of morality's demands is not a pipe dream but something achievable by real people like us.

Human beings need hope: without it, our lives become static; we lack goals and are unable to move under our own direction. In *Anthropology from a Pragmatic Point of View*, Kant notes that "overwhelming sadness (which is alleviated by no hope)" is an emotional state "that threatens life" (7: 254); and he repeatedly insists that the question "What may I hope?" is one of three or (in later formulations) four fundamental questions that philosophy is obligated to address.[15] Kant's best-known work in the philosophy of hope involves the attempt to show that the concepts of God and immortality are necessary presuppositions for a human moral life (albeit presuppositions that cannot be objectively proven). But his argument that examples in ethics serve to give human beings needed hope and inspiration constitutes an additional but underexplored contribution to the philosophy of hope—a more mundane and this-worldly contribution that is free of controversial religious assumptions.

Versions of this third argument appear in each of Kant's central writings on ethics. In the *Groundwork*, for instance, he states that examples "put beyond doubt [*außer Zweifel*] the feasibility [*Tunlichkeit*] of what the law demands" (4: 409); in the second *Critique* he discusses the specific example of someone who sacrifices his life for his country, noting that "we find our soul strengthened and elevated by such an example when we can convince ourselves, in it, that human nature is capable [*fähig*] of so great an elevation above every incentive that nature can oppose to it" (5: 158); and in the *Metaphysics of Morals* he states that the exemplary conduct of the teacher should serve as "proof of the feasibility of that which is in accordance with duty [*Beweis der Tunlichkeit des Pflichtmäßigen*]" (6: 480).

The strong language of "proof [*Beweis*]" in the last quotation deserves comment, for in certain respects it is very un-Kantian. As we have seen, one of Kant's central objections against trying to derive morality from examples is that empirical examples can never constitute proof of universal and necessary propositions. In the *Collins* moral philosophy lectures, for instance, he speaks directly to this issue, using the same German word *Beweis*, but there stating that an example can never serve as proof of an *a priori* proposition:

> What is apodeictically *a priori* needs no example, for there I perceive the necessity *a priori*. Mathematical propositions, for instance, need no examples, for the example serves not as proof, but as an illustration [*das Beispiel dient nicht zum Beweise, sondern zur Illustration*]. . . . All cognitions of morality and religion can be set forth apodeictically, *a priori*, through reason. We perceive *a priori* the necessity of behaving so and not otherwise; so no examples are needed [*nötig*] in matters of religion and morality.
>
> (27: 333)

From a *logical* point of view, examples are not necessary in ethics: moral principles, since they are *a priori* concepts involving necessity and universality, cannot be proven by means of empirical examples, and this is one of the main reasons that a pure moral philosophy needs to be "fully cleansed of everything that might in any way be empirical and belong to anthropology" (*Gr* 4: 389). But from an *anthropological* point of view, examples are necessary in ethics. Given our subjective nature, we do need examples. Human beings cannot function without hope, and examples help to convince us of the feasibility of moral demands. Thus in the *Metaphysics of Morals*, when Kant asserts that examples can serve as proof, "proof" is intended in a more informal, anthropological sense, while in *Collins* (and elsewhere), when he asserts that examples cannot serve as proof, "proof" is meant in a formal, logical sense. Alternatively stated, examples can serve as proof that it is possible for human beings to act in accord with duty, but they cannot be used to prove or justify an *a priori* moral principle.

There is also an important flip side to Kant's argument that examples in ethics give us hope and inspiration. If no plausible examples can be found, then we have an excuse that morality is impossible—what it demands is not feasible for human beings, for no examples can be found of people who have lived up to its demands. As he states in *Collins*: "Human beings like, in general, to have examples, and if none exists, they are happy to excuse themselves, on the ground that everybody lives that way" (27: 334). If no cogent examples can be found of persons who have lived up to morality's demands, then we are liable to avoid morality on the ground that it is simply beyond our capacities.

Kant's hope-and-inspiration argument in defense of examples may appear to overlap a bit with the limitations-of-human-reason argument (discussed above), for in both cases we do find support for the claim that concrete examples are necessary for human morality. But there is a key difference. The limitations-of-human-reason argument is primarily *epistemological*. Here, Kant's main point is that human beings, due to their discursive intellects, need to think analogically and metaphorically. The hope-and-inspiration argument is more *psychological*. Here, Kant's central point is that human beings are creatures who cannot function without hope, and that examples fulfill this function in the sphere of ethics. Examples serve to give human beings hope that what the moral law demands is feasible.

Emulation

Finally, Kant has a fourth major argument in defense of examples in ethics, which I will call the "emulation argument." When human beings are presented with a viable moral example, they have something specific to emulate. Examples of moral goodness give us a concrete goal to aim at, a tangible ideal for us to emulate. In *Collins*, for instance, Kant states: "Examples serve us for encouragement and emulation [*zur Aufmunterung und zur Nachfolge*], but must not be used as a model [*Muster*]. If I see a thing *in concreto*, I recognize it all the more clearly" (27: 333).

Here, we see a complication in Kant's emulation argument. We are urged to emulate examples, but we are also told not to use them as a model. We should strive to be like them, but we must not simply imitate or copy them. But how does one emulate something without imitating it? This complication is referred to again on the next page of the *Collins* lecture:

> An example [*ein Beispiel*]¹⁶ is not for imitating [*Nachahmung*], though it is certainly for emulation [*Nachfolge*]. The ground of the action must be derived, not from the example, but from the rule; yet if others have shown that such an act is possible, we must emulate their example [*ihrem Beispiel nachfolgen*] and not let others surpass us in that respect.
>
> (27: 334)

We are guilty of imitating or copying an example in Kant's sense if we simply mimic it without reflecting on *why* it is a good example in the first place. It is wrong to copy or imitate examples in this manner, because when we do so we are not thinking things through for ourselves. We have failed to grasp that the true standard of moral assessment lies within our own autonomous reason. In the *Anthropology* he notes: "The *imitator* [*Nachahmer*] (in moral matters) is without character; for character consists precisely in originality in the way of thinking. He who has character derives his conduct from a source that he has opened by himself" (7: 293). The same thought occurs in the *Groundwork*: "Imitation [*Nachahmung*] has no place at all in matters of morality," and even though examples serve many humanly necessary and important functions in ethics, "they can never justify setting aside their true original, which lies in reason" (4: 409).

Kant also seeks to differentiate emulation (or imitation in the good sense) from mere copying (or imitation in the bad sense) by reminding readers that ultimately it is not any actual person or event that we should try to emulate, but rather an ideal of reason created by rational agents, an ideal which the person or event merely represents or makes visible to us. As he writes in the *Metaphysics of Morals*: "it is not comparison with any other human being whatsoever (as he is), but with the *idea* (of humanity), as he ought to be [*wie er sein soll*], and so with the law, which must serve as the constant standard of the teacher's instruction" (6: 480). Comparing ourselves to other people is always to be avoided,¹⁷ because it can only lead to two bad outcomes: envy, in cases where we decide that they actually are better than us, or ridicule, in cases where we conclude that we are better than them. As Kant states in his *Lectures on Pedagogy*:

> When the human being values his worth according to others, he seeks either to raise himself above others or to diminish the value of the other one. The latter, however, is envy [*Neid*]. One then always tries to impute a wrong to the other one.... The inappropriate spirit of emulation [*Geist der Ämulation*] merely stirs up envy. The case in which emulation could be of some use would be to convince someone of the feasibility of a thing, for example, if I demand of a child that a certain lesson be learned and show the child that others can do it.
>
> (9: 491)

Ultimately, we should seek to compare ourselves only to the moral law itself, never to other people. Similarly, in the final analysis it is the moral law that we should seek to emulate, not other people or their actions. The latter merely help to make the former visible to the human eye.

The emulation argument may appear to overlap with the previously discussed hope-and-inspiration argument, in the sense that both of them involve the general claim that reflection on actual examples can help us to achieve what moral principles demand of us. (Indeed, at the end of the passage just cited from *Pedagogy* 9: 491, Kant—in saying that emulation is useful when it convinces us of the feasibility of a thing—blends the two arguments together. See also *Gr* 4: 409.) But there is a fundamental difference. The emulation argument functions as a strategy for moral improvement: we should strive to equal and surpass the achievements and qualities of moral exemplars, and when presented with actual examples of moral goodness, we can see which aspects of our character and conduct need improvement. The hope-and-inspiration argument, on the other hand, functions more as a grounding for possibility. When we are presented with real exemplars and plausible examples, we become convinced that what morality demands is humanly feasible.

Once we step back from the *Groundwork*'s tightly focused aim of locating and justifying a supreme principle of morality that holds for all rational beings and redirect our attention to the more terrestrial task of finding out how human beings can become morally better, we see that Kant offers four distinct arguments in defense of the necessity and importance of examples in the moral life of human beings. First, examples play a necessary role in the moral education of young people, for the immature human mind is not yet able to apply abstract moral principles effectively. Second, moral examples remain epistemologically necessary even for adult human beings. Human beings are saddled with a "discursive, image-dependent understanding," and because of this they need to represent abstract moral concepts symbolically and analogically. Third, examples provide us with hope and inspiration that what morality demands is humanly feasible. And fourth, examples give us something concrete on which we can focus our own efforts—a mark to emulate and perhaps even to surpass.

WHY EXAMPLES ARE NOT ENOUGH

We have seen that on Kant's view examples perform necessary and important functions throughout the moral life of all human beings; they are essential not only for children but for adults as well. And they perform these functions due to certain basic facts of human nature. It is because of our all-too-human biological, psychological, and epistemological makeup that we need examples in ethics. If we were nonhuman rational beings with a different biology, psychology, and epistemology (and Kant did think that such creatures existed),[18] then his arguments in defense of examples would not apply to us at all.

But it remains the case that examples alone are insufficient for human morality. When Kant asserts in the *Groundwork* that morality cannot be legitimately derived from examples, he is on the one hand referring to moral principles that in his view hold "not merely for human beings, but for all *rational beings as such*" (4: 408, see also 389). However, at the same time he is urging his human readers (and as far as we know, this is the only kind of reader he has yet had) not to fall into the trap of supposing that examples alone are enough in ethics. Any feasible human morality requires both general principles and concrete examples. Both components are necessary to develop our moral outlook; neither on its own is sufficient.

In order to gain a more balanced perspective on Kant's final assessment of the place of examples in human morality, let us return briefly to some of the points raised in the Introduction concerning Kant's objections to assigning examples a foundational role in pure moral philosophy. I will then conclude by adding to this list of objections an additional Kantian criticism of examples in ethics which is not raised in the *Groundwork*.

Examples Presuppose Standards

First, any moral example—e.g., of right conduct or good character—presupposes a general standard by means of which it is judged to be right or good. This is a fundamental point that Kant defends not only in the *Groundwork* (4: 408) and *Collins* (27: 333), but also in the *Critique of Pure Reason* (A 315/B 372).

Think for Yourself

Second, any critical approach to morality requires that we think for ourselves about the criteria of moral rightness and goodness. If we allow others to do our moral thinking for us by blindly following their example, we are cowards: we lack the courage to use our own understanding, and we have violated the motto of enlightenment. This is why Kant states repeatedly that "imitation has no place at all in matters of morality" (*Gr* 4: 409; see also *Collins* 27: 334; *MdS* 6: 480; *Anth* 7: 293). As he notes in the *Anthropology*:

> The most important revolution from within the human being is "his exit from his self-incurred immaturity." Before this revolution he let others think for him and merely imitated others or allowed them to guide him by leading-strings. Now he ventures to advance, though still shakily, with his own feet.
> (7: 229; see also *Aufklärung* 8: 35; *KU* 5: 294)

Autonomy

Third, if we rely too much on examples we run the risk of forfeiting our autonomy. The true source of morality lies within our own reason and not in any heteronomous sources, regardless of whether these sources be persons (even the "Holy One of the Gospel" or God himself) or actions. Even in the moral education of children, where examples are particularly important due to the inability of young people to think conceptually, Kant urges that moral education be an education *toward autonomy*. Students must come to see that the true norm of their conduct lies in their own reason—not in other people's behavior. For instance, in his discussion of moral culture in the *Lectures on Pedagogy*, Kant states: "everything is spoiled if one tries to ground this culture on examples [*Exempel*].... One must see to it that the pupil acts from his own maxims. . . . He must at all times comprehend the ground of the action and its derivation from the concepts of duty" (9: 475). Similarly, in the "Fragment of a Moral Catechism" (essentially, an imaginary conversation between a teacher and a student) that Kant presents toward the end of the *Metaphysics of Morals*, the teacher at one point reminds his pupil:

> As to how you should set about sharing in happiness and also becoming at least not unworthy of it, the rule and instruction in this lies in your *reason* alone. This amounts to saying that you need not learn this rule for your conduct from experience or from other people's instruction. Your own reason teaches you and directly commands you what you have to do.
>
> (6: 481)

Moral Norms Are A Priori

Fourth, genuine moral principles involve necessity and universality, and thus cannot be grounded in experience. Empirical examples alone are insufficient to justify *a priori* concepts and propositions. As Kant states in the second *Critique*: "It is an outright contradiction to want to extract necessity from an empirical proposition (*ex pumice aquam*) and to give a judgment, along with necessity, true universality" (5: 12).

Groping in the Dark

Finally, the methodology of popular philosophy, which seeks to ground ethics in examples, is defective and unable to arrive at a metaphysics of morals. But it is only within a metaphysics of morals that moral principles, as *a priori* propositions, can receive their necessary support. In order to reach the destination of a metaphysics of morals, a better philosophical method is needed, one that does not place more philosophical weight on examples than they are able to carry. "Groping by means of examples" (*Gr* 4: 412) cannot take us where we need to go.

Overreliance on Examples Weakens Judgment

Kant has an important additional argument against examples which he does not discuss in the *Groundwork*. Related to the autonomy argument is a more specific warning: overreliance on examples weakens our native power of judgment. "Examples [*Beispiele*]," Kant proclaims in a famous passage from the first *Critique*, "are the go-cart [*Gängelwagen*] of the power of judgment, which he who lacks the natural talent for judgment can never do without" (A 134/B 174). Concrete examples help us to learn how to exercise our judgment, just as a go-cart (a two-wheeled cart that was formerly used to teach children to walk, the way training wheels are used on bicycles) provides support for children when they are first beginning to walk. But overreliance on examples in turn weakens our ability to make independent judgments. As Kant remarks in the first *Critique*:

> [A]s far as the correctness and precision of the insight of the understanding is concerned, examples more usually do it some damage, since they only seldom adequately fulfill the condition of the rule (as *casus in terminis*) and beyond this they often weaken the effort of the understanding to gain sufficient insight into rules in the universal and independently of the particular circumstances of experience, and thus in the end accustom us to use those rules more like formulas than like principles.
>
> (A 134/B 173; see also *Aufklärung* 8: 36)

Similarly, an overreliance on go-carts may hinder a child's natural ability to walk. In the *Lectures on Pedagogy*, Kant notes: "It is customary to employ leading-strings and go-carts in order to teach children how to walk. But it is striking that one should want to teach children how to walk, as if any human being could not have walked for lack of instruction" (9: 461).

Kant's Rousseauian conviction[19] that teachers and parents should not interfere with the organic development of natural human capacities lies behind this particular argument against examples. Examples can become crutches; if we rely too much on them, our cognitive muscles may weaken and atrophy to the point where we are unable to think critically and independently about the principles by means of which the examples are judged. Overreliance on examples—as well as on go-carts—must be avoided:

> The first and foremost rule here is that all tools be dispensed with as far as possible. Thus leading-strings and go-carts should be done without right from the beginning, and the child should be allowed to crawl about on the ground until it learns to walk by itself, for then it will walk all the more steadily. For tools only ruin natural skill.
>
> (9: 466)

In conclusion, examples are necessary and important in the moral life of all human beings, but they are not sufficient. Examples help to make the moral law visible for human beings; without them, we are unable to see the law clearly. But examples do not make the moral law. We, as self-legislating rational beings, make this law. We are its co-authors, and we give it to ourselves by means of our own reflection and deliberation (see *Gr* 4: 431).

PART THREE

Extensions of Anthropology

If someone like that did all this, then there is really no chance. That's the biggest evil, that it was not someone from far away. It was one of us.

—AHMED KULENOVIC, a Muslim, commenting on his childhood friend Dusan Tadic, a Serbian. (Tadic, currently in prison, is the first person to be convicted of crimes against humanity by an international court since the Nuremberg trials after World War II.)

The human being is by nature evil.
—KANT, *Religion within the Boundaries of Mere Reason*

9

Evil Everywhere

THE ORDINARINESS OF KANTIAN RADICAL EVIL*

SINCE 9/11, AMERICAN POLITICIANS, preachers, journalists, and academics have all invoked the word "evil" with a frequency that has not been seen since the Holocaust. Philosophers too have contributed to this phenomenon in their customary way, issuing a small spate of monographs and anthologies on the topic.[1] Most of these books do not devote serious attention to Kant's account of radical evil,[2] in part because of the authors' shared belief, as one critic puts it, that "when faced with the question of evil," Kant, "the quintessential modern Enlightenment philosopher," is "confused, . . . eventually confesses defeat," and offers only "confused chatter about the rooting of radical evil in human nature."[3]

My view is that we still have much to learn from Kant's account of radical evil. While no author will ever have the last word on such a perplexing and pervasive feature of human existence, Kant's discussion of radical evil is still very much relevant today. For as others have noted,[4] his theory of radical evil is the first distinctly *modern* account of evil: he coined the evocative expression "radical evil," a term which has been repeatedly invoked (albeit sometimes in ways that differ strongly from his intended meaning) in contemporary efforts to make sense of the horrors of the twentieth and twenty-first centuries; he is "the modern philosopher who initiates the inquiry into evil without explicit recourse to philosophical theodicy"[5] (albeit in a manner that definitely does not foreclose religious responses to evil); and he is the first writer to place human responsibility for moral evil at the center of his account of evil.

Kantian radical evil is a huge topic, and my aim in what follows is by no means to cover all of this difficult and bewildering terrain. Rather, I will focus on four basic criticisms of his account of radical evil. In each case, I have two goals: first, to defuse the criticisms by explaining Kant's position in a way that is consistent both with his texts and with common sense; and second, to show—contrary to what critics claim—that Kant's position on these matters, correctly interpreted, is not a weakness but a strength.

EXPLANATORY IMPOTENCE AND HUMAN FREEDOM

One common criticism of Kant's doctrine of radical evil is that ultimately it does not explain anything. Once we have worked our way beneath its forceful rhetoric, we are left with something obvious and unenlightening. For all that remains beneath the surface is the simple claim that radical evil refers to our propensity to knowingly do what is morally wrong, to intentionally violate fundamental moral principles. As Kant puts it: "The statement 'The human being is *evil*,' cannot mean anything else than: he is conscious of the moral law and yet has incorporated into his maxim the (occasional) deviation from it" (*Rel* 6: 32).

We have already seen an oblique version of this criticism in William McBride's complaint (see n. 3 in this chapter) that, when faced with the question of evil, Kant "eventually confesses defeat." Gordon E. Michalson Jr. also hints at it when he notes that despite the "complex conceptual and terminological gridwork" attending Kant's account of radical evil, in the end we are left with "an unhelpful result"[6]—one that does not ultimately explain why we choose evil. But Richard Bernstein has developed the most detailed version of the explanatory impotence criticism. In *Radical Evil*, he writes:

> The more we focus on the details of Kant's analysis of radical evil, the more innocuous the concept seems to be.... We do not always follow the moral law *because*, as human beings, we have an innate propensity to evil. Our wills are corrupted at their root. But does this "because" really explain anything? Does it do any conceptual work? I do not think so. When stripped down to its bare essentials, it simply reiterates the fact that human beings who are conscious of the moral law sometimes (freely) deviate from it.... In short, radical evil—the alleged propensity to moral evil which is a universal characteristic of human beings—does not have *any* explanatory force (practical or theoretical) at all![7]

A few pages later, Bernstein raises the ante further by claiming that in his analysis of radical evil Kant has unconsciously caught himself in a dialectical illusion—the diagnosis of which is one of the main themes of the *Critique of Pure Reason*, indeed of Kant's work in general. In the first *Critique*, Kant warns readers that in addition to empirical or optical illusions (where our imagination leads us to think we see things that are not there) and logical illusions (where, because we have made a fallacious inference, we make a false judgment about something), there also exists a much more fundamental and dangerous kind of illusion—one that occurs when we try to employ concepts of the understanding beyond the limits of possible experience. This latter dialectical illusion is "*natural* and unavoidable"; it is "attached irremediably to human reason, so that even after we have exposed the mirage it will still not cease to lead our reason on with false hopes, continually propelling it into momentary aberrations that always need to be removed" (*KrV* A 298/B 355). Similarly, Bernstein claims, the concept of radical evil has caught Kant (and all those who accept his doctrine) in a dialectical illusion, because "it seduces us into thinking that we can *explain* something that we cannot possibly explain." It is an illusion to think that the doctrine of radical evil "enables us to explain or account for why we adopt evil maxims, why we sometimes succumb to this temptation. This alleged explanation turns out to be vacuous."[8]

However, the explanatory impotence criticism misses its target completely. For Kant is quite clear in stating that his doctrine of radical evil is in no way intended to explain *why* human beings choose to adopt evil maxims. The adoption of evil (or good) maxims is always a free choice, one for which each person is responsible. Without this assumption of freedom, it does not make sense to hold us morally responsible for any of our actions. As Kant states in the *Religion*: "The human being must make or have made *himself* into whatever he is or should become in a moral sense, good or evil. Both conditions must be an effect of his free choice [*freie Willkür*], for otherwise they could not be imputed to him and, consequently, he could be neither *morally* good nor evil" (6: 44; see also *KpV* 5: 98). In short, on Kant's view it is fundamental to our self-conception as moral agents that we are free-acting beings (see *Rel* 6: 37; *Anth* 7: 119). In any given choice situation, we can hypothesize about the roles that various environmental and genetic factors may have played in leading a person to make the choice that she made, but ultimately no causal explanation is fully satisfactory, for the simple reason that the choice was free. In many cases, we simply do not know why people choose to do what they do—this is something, as Kant famously remarks, that "remains inscrutable [*unerforschlich*] to us" (*Rel* 6: 43). For each human being, "the depths of his own heart (the subjective first ground of his maxims) are to him inscrutable [*ihm selbst unerforschlich*]" (6: 51; see also *MdS* 6: 392). Our assessment of others' motives and acts is also always fallible. Indeed, at one point in the *Groundwork of the Metaphysics of Morals* Kant insists that we do not know "with complete certainty" whether anyone in the entire history of the human race has ever succeeded in performing an act from the motive of duty (4: 407).[9]

Ironically, Bernstein fully endorses this particular aspect of Kant's position on radical evil. On the last page of his book, he states:

> *The ultimate ground for the choice between good and evil is inscrutable.* We initially encountered this thesis in Kant's reflections on radical evil, when he claimed that the ultimate subjective of the adoption of moral maxims is inscrutable. I consider this to be one of Kant's most profound and important insights about morality.[10]

However, in making this assertion, Bernstein completely undercuts his earlier explanatory impotence criticism. As he notes: "Human beings are responsible for the choices they make, but *ultimately*, we cannot explain why they make the moral choices they do. . . . Not only is this inscrutable; it *must* be inscrutable, because this is what it means to be a free and responsible person."[11] Ultimately, the explanatory impotence criticism will only persuade hard determinists who, because they assume that every event in the universe has antecedent causes, conclude that a complete and accurate causal account of every human action is in principle always available and that moral responsibility is therefore impossible.[12]

Kant's position regarding the ultimate inscrutability of human motives is a strength rather than a weakness in his doctrine of radical evil. Human action often does have an indecipherable character. Particularly in cases where people have committed horrendous acts of moral evil, we are often simply at a loss to explain definitively why they did what they did. Even the most ordinary people are capable of the most horrendous deeds,[13] and it is to Kant's credit that he recognizes this disturbing fact of human life.

Finally, Kant's stance with regard to the inscrutability of freedom is by no means novel or extreme. It has a long and distinguished pedigree that tracks back at least as far as Augustine. In *The City of God*, Augustine too warns readers against attempts to offer causal explanations for moral evil: "the truth is that one should not try to find an efficient cause for a wrong choice." Trying to find explanatory causes in cases where people have made a free choice, he adds, in a famous analogy, "is like trying to see darkness or to hear silence."[14] Free actions—whether for good or for evil—are fundamentally inexplicable.

SELF-LOVE AND THE MORAL LAW

In the previous section I argued in part that Kant's account of radical evil is not primarily a theory about *why* people commit acts of evil, and that he has good reasons for not offering a theory of this sort. Because of his dual commitments to human freedom and to the ultimate inscrutability of our motives, he does not have a lot to say about what specifically drives people to do evil. For some readers, this result is understandably unsatisfying. What they want from a theory of evil is an explanation of why people commit acts of evil. However, on Kant's view this is an illegitimate request that is foreclosed by our awareness that we are free beings whose actions are not causally determined. When it comes to human motivations to do evil, all that we can safely and accurately say is that whenever people commit evil, they have intentionally violated fundamental moral norms—they are "conscious of the moral law" but have willfully deviated from it (see *Rel* 6: 32).

However, this is not quite the complete Kantian story regarding human motives. Kant does secondarily address issues of motivation in his discussion of radical evil, but critics have not been happy with this part of his analysis either. For instance, in the *Religion* he asserts bluntly that "self-love [*Selbstliebe*]," "when adopted as the principle of all our maxims, is precisely the source of all evil [*gerade die Quelle alles Bösen*]" (6: 45, see also 30–31, 36). This assertion that self-love is the sole source of evil has led many commentators to criticize Kant for his allegedly simplistic and naïve account of human nature.

Perhaps the most famous example of the self-love criticism is in Hannah Arendt's book *The Origins of Totalitarianism* (1951). In referring to an allegedly new kind of non-Kantian radical evil—one that "breaks down all standards we know," cannot be explained "by comprehensible motives," and occurs within totalitarian regimes "in which all men have become equally superfluous"—she states that this new type of radical evil can "no longer be understood and explained by the evil motives of self-interest, greed, covetousness, resentment, lust for power, and cowardice."[15] Shortly after her book appeared, Arendt also wrote, in a letter to her former teacher Karl Jaspers (to whom she had sent one of the first copies of her book):

> [T]he Western tradition is suffering from the preconception that the most evil things human beings can do arise from the vice of selfishness. Yet we know that the greatest evils or radical evil has nothing to do anymore with such humanly understandable, sinful motives. What radical evil really is I don't know, but it seems to me it somehow has to do with the following phenomenon: making human beings as human beings superfluous.[16]

Bernstein uses this quotation to support his claim that one of Arendt's "most characteristic thought-trains" is the view that "the most evil deeds that human beings perform do not arise from the vice of selfishness,"[17] a thought-train that he endorses and then uses to make a further criticism of Kant's account of radical evil. Kant is wrong, Bernstein argues, in holding that evil always arises from selfishness. Rather, Bernstein notes, we should

> recognize that there are other incentives that are not easily assimilated to "self-love." It is difficult to see how the incentives that motivate fanatics and terrorists who are willing to sacrifice themselves for some cause or movement can be accounted for by self-love. The horrors of the twentieth century (and not just this century) have opened our eyes to the variety of types of incentives that motivate evil actions.[18]

The self-love criticism of Kant's account of radical evil would seem to have common sense on its side. As I remarked in an earlier discussion, "people are evil for many different reasons," and "the possibilities for evil are infinite."[19] Why reduce all of these reasons to self-love? But I think now that Kant's claim that self-love is "the source of all evil" is not so easy to dismiss, once it is placed within the proper context of his moral theory.

First of all, "self-love" in Kant's sense—Arendt and Bernstein to the contrary—is not synonymous with what is normally meant by "selfishness." Kantian self-love is a broader motivational tendency that encompasses a wide variety of desires and inclinations, many of which can be and are used to promote decidedly nonselfish purposes. As Andrews Reath notes:

> Self-love is a concern for well being which modifies an inclination only when it conflicts with one's overall happiness. It is opposed to the moral disposition, not due to the inclinations involved, but because it recognizes no moral restrictions. The inclinations may be good in that they can ground morally permissible ends,

when properly limited. But in recognizing no moral restrictions, self-love makes the moral law a subordinate principle.[20]

The main problem with self-love, according to Kant, is simply that it does not recognize the supremacy of the moral law. Whenever we act from a maxim of self-love, we have freely chosen to subordinate the incentives of morality to those of inclination. In some cases (e.g., with people who are "so sympathetically attuned that without any other motive of vanity [*Eitelkeit*] or self-interest [*Eigennutz*] they find an inner satisfaction in spreading joy around them"; *Gr* 4: 398), the purpose of the act may even be to *help* other people. Kant's naturally kind-hearted person is not selfish, and Bernstein's fanatics and terrorists who are "willing to sacrifice themselves for some cause or movement" are probably not either. ("Probably not" because, again, human motives are ultimately inscrutable. Some fanatics and terrorists do seem to be selfish, but we can certainly imagine others who are not.) However, neither Kant's naturally kind-hearted persons nor Bernstein's hypothetical fanatics and terrorists, despite their nonselfish motivations, are acting from moral maxims, that is, from maxims derivable from the categorical imperative. For instance, they all clearly violate the first formula of the categorical imperative: "*act only in accordance with that maxim through which you can at the same time will that it become a universal law*" (*Gr* 4: 421). Their maxims are not universalizable, and because they have subordinated the moral law to their own non-moral inclinations they are all acting from self-love in Kant's sense of the term.

One very common type of evil person in Kant's sense (and for him the term "evil" has extremely wide scope: there are *a lot* of evil people in the world, only some of whom count as evil according to non-Kantian theories of evil) is someone who "makes the incentives of self-love and their inclinations [*die Triebfeder der Selbstliebe und ihre Neigungen*] the condition of compliance with the moral law" (*Rel* 6: 36). Such a person says, in effect: "I will do what I desire and what is morally required, as long as the moral law doesn't conflict with my self-love." The morally good person, on the other hand, says: "I will do what is morally required and what I desire, so long as my desires don't conflict with the moral law."[21]

When the self-love criticism is placed within the larger context of Kant's moral theory, the claim that self-love "is precisely the source of all evil" loses much of its counterintuitive air. What it amounts to is simply the claim that morally good people put the moral law first, while the rest of us don't. This claim, I submit, is true, even if it does not count as one of the most profound statements of moral psychology to come from a philosopher's pen. Admittedly, Kant here "has not dared to descend into the depths,"[22] but that was not his intent. For again, his account of radical evil is primarily a theory about *what* evil is (and *how* we should respond to it)—not a theory about *why* people do evil. However, given the indecipherable character of much human action, perhaps it is best not to speak presumptuously about why people commit evil. Those who think they have succeeded in descending into the depths here are often mistaken. Unfortunately, it is very difficult to ever reach bottom in this particular line of work, for the depths of human evil are unfathomable.

DIABOLICAL EVIL AND MORAL RESPONSIBILITY

Another area within Kant's analysis of radical evil where the issue of motives comes up secondarily concerns his claim that the concept of "a *diabolical* being [*ein teuflischer*[23] *Wesen*]" is not "applicable to the human being" (6: 35). Here too, he has been criticized by many; here too, the central criticism is that his moral psychology is shallow and naïve, and does not adequately reflect the true depths of human depravity.

John Silber has developed the best-known version of the diabolical evil criticism. In "The Ethical Significance of Kant's *Religion*" (1960), he writes:

> [I]n dismissing the devilish rejection of the law as an illusion, Kant called attention to the limitations of his conception of freedom rather than to the limits of human freedom itself. . . . Kant's insistence to the contrary, man's free power to reject the law in defiance is an ineradicable fact of human experience.[24]

And in a subsequent essay, "Kant at Auschwitz" (1991), Silber reiterates the criticism:

> Kant's ethics is inadequate to the understanding of Auschwitz because Kant denies the possibility of the deliberate rejection of the moral law. Not even a wicked man, Kant holds, can will evil for the sake of evil. His evil, according to Kant, consists merely in his willingness to ignore or subordinate the moral law when it interferes with his nonmoral but natural inclinations. His evil is expressed in abandoning the conditions of free personal fulfillment in favor of fulfillment as a creature of natural desire.[25]

Similarly, Bernstein, after citing Silber's criticisms, concludes that Kant's "analysis of evil and radical evil is disappointing," that one of the primary reasons it is disappointing stems from a failure to consider that there do exist people who "incorporate into their maxims the primary incentive to *defy* the moral law," and that this failure ultimately "is rooted in Kant's limited moral psychology, in the narrow range of types of incentives that he acknowledges."[26] Finally, Claudia Card has argued that Kant was "wrong in his insistence that evil is never 'diabolical' in human beings (that we never do wrong for its own sake)," and that "diabolical evil in human beings is very real."[27]

In order to assess the diabolical evil criticism, we need first to get an accurate sense of both what Kant means by "diabolical evil" and why he rejects its possibility in human beings. I believe that once these preliminary tasks have been accomplished, some versions of the diabolical evil criticism can be dismissed, simply because they are off target.

As is well known, Kant divides the human propensity to evil into three different degrees or steps (*Stufen*) (*Rel* 6: 29). The lowest or most common degree is *frailty* (*Gebrechlichkeit, fragilitas*), which corresponds roughly to what is traditionally meant by weakness of will. Agents at this first level of evil intend to act from moral motives and often succeed in doing so, but sometimes at the last moment they weaken their resolve and act from nonmoral motives. The second degree of evil is *impurity* (*Unlauterkeit, impuritas, improbitas*), which is basically a case of acting from mixed motives. Here, agents want to do the morally right thing and to do so from morally right motives, but the presence of moral motives alone is often not sufficient to get them to do the right thing. As a result, they frequently need to turn to nonmoral motives in order to do the right thing (e.g., help others not from the motive of duty but out of sympathetic feeling). Because they need nonmoral motives in order to get themselves to do the right thing, their motives are "not purely moral [*nicht rein moralisch*]" (*Rel* 6: 30). The third and most severe degree of evil is *wickedness* or *depravity* (*Bösartigkeit, vitiositas, pravitas*). Agents at this level deliberately and consistently act on nonmoral maxims in virtually all of their behavior—they simply do not want to act from moral maxims at all. As a result, they represent "the *perversity* [*Verkehrtheit, perversitas*] of the human heart," and their mental attitude is "corrupted at its root" (ibid.).

We can see already—contra some versions of the diabolical evil criticism—that Kant by no means denies that some people do "reject the moral law in defiance"[28] and do "deliberately and consistently reject the moral law."[29] This is precisely what the third *Stufe* of evil is all about. People at this third level do openly, directly, regularly, and intentionally reject the moral law, and this is why they are wicked and corrupt. However, it remains the case that Kant does assert that the concept "diabolical being" is not "applicable [*anwendbar*] to the human being" (*Rel* 6: 35). If, as I argued above, he does not simply mean here that human beings are unable to openly and defiantly rebel against the moral law, then what exactly does he mean?

The answer is not terribly complicated, and is located in a simple contrast Kant draws between a diabolical being, "an absolutely evil will [*ein schlechthin böser Wille*]," or "a purely *animal* being [*ein blos tierischer Wesen*]" (*Rel* 6: 35), on the one hand, and a human being, on the other. Something important is missing in diabolical and animal beings—viz., they lack a moral personality that enables us to hold them accountable for what they do. In both cases, they do not make free choices and hence cannot be held legally or morally accountable for their behavior. Human beings, on the other hand—"even the worst [*selbst der ärgste*]" (*Rel* 6: 36)—do possess this capacity, and so can be held accountable for their actions.[30]

Here too (see my earlier discussion of the self-love criticism), it is important to keep in mind that Kant's primary goal is not to offer a detailed account of why people do evil. His discussion takes place on an entirely different level. As Henry Allison notes: "Kant's denial of a diabolical will is not a dubious piece of empirical moral psychology, but rather an *a priori* claim about the conditions of the possibility of moral accountability."[31]

Part of the point of Kant's (admittedly somewhat counterintuitive) diatribe against the possibility of diabolical evil in human beings, I submit, is that he does not want us to romanticize evil. We must not be seduced by *schwärmerische* historians, novelists, movie directors, etc., into thinking that some human beings, in virtue of their "strong" and "potent" personalities,[32] are somehow above the rest of us and are not to be judged by the same laws and principles that apply to ordinary human beings. Karl Jaspers, in a letter to his former student Hannah Arendt, put the point well when he criticized an early version of her notion of an allegedly new type of radical evil that "breaks down all standards we know" and "oversteps and shatters any and all legal systems":

> You say that what the Nazis did cannot be comprehended as "crime"—I'm not altogether comfortable with your view, because a guilt that goes beyond all criminal guilt inevitably takes on a streak of "greatness"—of satanic greatness—which is, for me, as inappropriate for the Nazis as all the talk about the "demonic" element in Hitler and so forth. It seems to me that we have to see these things in their total banality,[33] in their prosaic triviality, because that's what truly characterizes them. Bacteria can cause epidemics that wipe out nations, but they remain merely bacteria. I regard any hint of myth and legend with horror, and everything unspecific is just such a hint. . . . The way you do express it, you've almost taken the path of poetry. And a Shakespeare would never be able to give adequate form to this material—his instinctive aesthetic sense would lead to falsification of it—and that's why he couldn't attempt it.[34]

In short, we must resist the temptation to aestheticize evil. This is one reason why Kant rejects the strategy of attributing diabolical or demonic motives to human beings who commit evil. But his central point is simply to underscore the necessity of legal and moral responsibility when talking about human evil. He does not want to let perpetrators of evil—particularly the most extreme perpetrators of evil—off the hook. As long as they are aware of what they are doing and freely choose to do it, they should be held responsible for their conduct. Even the most wicked and depraved individuals are still rational beings who understand morality and the law, and because they possess this understanding they must be held accountable for their deviations from morality and the law. They have the capacity to recognize the criminality and immorality of their acts. To label someone a diabolical being in the sense described by Kant is to grant him the status of a being who is no longer legally and morally accountable. And no sane human being should be granted this status.

ANTHROPOLOGY AND THE UNIVERSALITY OF EVIL

The last criticism of Kant's account of radical evil that I will examine concerns his curious claim that this evil is both "innate [*angeboren*]" throughout the entire human species (*Rel* 6: 32, see also 25, 29, 38, 43, 50) and yet freely chosen by each individual ("brought upon us by ourselves [*uns von uns selbst zugezogen*]"; 6: 32), and his even more curious effort to convince readers of the truth of this paradoxical claim by appealing to experience. Its truth is allegedly evident "from what one knows of the human being through experience [*durch Erfahrung*]" (ibid.); it "can be established through experiential demonstrations [*durch Erfahrungsbeweise*]" (6: 35). How can something be innate and yet freely chosen, and how can the claim that a propensity present in every human being, past, present, and future—"even the best" (6: 32)—be established by appealing to experience? For as every student who has read at least the first paragraph of the introduction to the *Critique of Pure Reason* knows, experience "gives us no true universality [*keine wahre Allgemeinheit*], and reason, which is so desirous of this kind of cognitions, is more stimulated than satisfied by it" (*KrV* A 1). Empirical universality is not true or strict universality (*strenge Allgemeinheit*) but "only an arbitrary increase in validity from that which holds in most cases to that which holds in all" (B 4). Strict universality can never be justified by an appeal to experience; indeed, this is why Kant insists that it is one of the two "sure signs [*sichere Kennzeichen*] of an *a priori* cognition" (B 4).[35]

Critics and sympathetic commentators alike have had a field day with this issue. For instance, Allison remarks sensibly that "the *most*" that an appeal to experience "can show is that evil is widespread, not that there is a universal propensity to it," and concludes that Kant's argument is "quite disappointing."[36] Michalson, noting "the peculiarity of this appeal to experience, one which cannot possibly support the argumentative weight Kant seems to be placing on it," bemoans "the absence of genuine argumentation for this crucial point."[37] And Bernstein, after citing Allison and reminding readers that Kant himself says that "we can spare ourselves the formal proof [*uns . . . den förmlichen Beweis ersparen*]" (*Rel* 6: 33), simply asserts that Kant has thrown in the towel:

> When Kant reaches this crucial stage in his exposition, when we expect some sort of proof or justification of radical evil as a *universal* characteristic of human beings, *no* such proof is forthcoming. . . . Kant never gives—or even attempts to give—a *proof* of his controversial and bold claim that man is evil by nature.[38]

Indeed, criticism of the paradoxical nature of Kant's argumentation on this particular point is by no means a recent phenomenon, and goes back at least as far as 1794. For instance, Johann August Eberhard (1739–1809), one of Kant's early rationalist critics, in his essay "Ueber das Kantische radicale Böse in der menschlichen Natur" (On Kantian Radical Evil in Human Nature), asks:

> Now how does Herr Kant prove that such a radical evil exists, or that the human being is evil by nature? He does not carry out this proof, as would be expected, from principles of pure reason; rather, it rests merely on experience [*bloß auf die Erfahrung*]: he refers first to savage peoples, then to civilized nations, and tries to show through their well-known manner of acting that they are all afflicted with radical evil.[39]

Previous attempts to extricate Kant from these difficulties, while ingenious, have often seemed as paradoxical as the problem for which they are the alleged solution. Thus Allison sidesteps Kant's appeal to experience entirely, encouraging readers to treat Kant's claim as a synthetic *a priori* postulate,[40] while Robert Merrihew Adams suggests that we can solve the dilemma of a freely chosen but innate propensity by conceiving it noumenally as something that "originated in a free and voluntary act that was not in time."[41]

My counterstrategy begins by insisting that we take seriously Kant's frequent appeals to experience and anthropology in his discussion of radical evil. These appeals ought not to be jettisoned, regardless of the philosophical troubles they seem to land him in, for the simple reason that they pervade his entire analysis of evil in the *Religion*, and thus cannot be dismissed as an unnecessary aberration. For instance, as I noted in a previous discussion, we find either the term "human nature [*menschliche Natur*]" or "human being [*Mensch*]" not only in the title of part I of *Religion* but in all four section titles of part I as well.[42] In using this language, Kant makes it very clear to readers that in his discussion of radical evil he is concerned specifically and solely with human beings, and not—as is often the case in his canonical ethical theory writings—with the much larger set of rational beings in general, of which human beings constitute only a subset.

Furthermore, as noted earlier, when Kant discusses radical evil, he insists that he is concerned with a kind of moral evil that we actually encounter in our daily experience: "the existence of this propensity to evil in human nature can be established through experiential demonstrations of the actual resistance in time of human choice [*menschliche Willkür*] against the law" (*Rel* 6: 35). Indeed, as Michelle Kosch observes: "The claim that evil is given empirically (and only empirically) is reiterated throughout *Religion*."[43] At the very beginning of part I, he appeals to the collective experience of humanity to support the thesis that human beings are by nature evil (*Rel* 6: 19), and he criticizes certain overly optimistic Enlightenment philosophers for failing to offer empirical support for their counterposition that human beings are by nature good—their view, he notes pointedly, has "certainly not been drawn from experience [*sicherlich nicht aus der Erfahrung geschöpft*]" (6: 20). And when he does attempt to convince readers that there exists a corrupt propensity to evil "entwined with humanity itself and, as it were, rooted in it" (6: 32) (if indeed any convincing is needed), he says that "we can spare ourselves the formal proof" and invites us to look instead at "the multitude of woeful examples that the experience [*die Erfahrung*] of human *deeds* parades before us" (6: 32–33)—viz., the horrendous acts of evil that people continually commit against one another in "the so-called *state of nature*,"[44] in the "civilized state" (6: 33) (which turns out to be not so civilized), and last but not least in the international arena, where nations (then as well as now) remain in "a state of constant readiness for war [*ein Stand der beständigen Kriegsverfassung*]" (6: 34).

By 1793, the year *Religion* was published, Kant had been teaching an annual lecture course in anthropology for over twenty years. Described early on as an "empirical study" or observation-based doctrine (*Beobachtungslehre*) (Kant to Marcus Herz, toward the end of 1773, 10: 146) in which "the grounds of cognition are taken from observation and experience [*Beobachtung und Erfahrung*]" (*Collins* 25: 7), Kantian anthropology, as is well known, is designated by its creator as a *pragmatic* anthropology. Pragmatic anthropology in turn is distinguished from the *physiological* anthropology that the German physician Ernst Platner (1744–1818) and others were already advocating when Kant first began lecturing on anthropology in 1772. In the preface to *Anthropology from a Pragmatic Point of View* (1798)—essentially his last set of lecture notes for the course that he taught annually for twenty-four years until his retirement from university lecturing in 1796—Kant distinguishes pragmatic anthropology from physiological anthropology:

> A doctrine of knowledge of the human being, systematically formulated (anthropology), can exist either in a physiological or in a pragmatic point of view. —Physiological knowledge of the human being concerns the investigation of what *nature* makes of the human being; pragmatic, the investigation of what *he* as a free-acting being makes of himself, or can and should make of himself.
>
> (7: 119)

However, in order to adhere to its self-imposed constraint of being a *Beobachtungslehre*, pragmatic anthropology's investigation of the human being as a free-acting being must be conducted empirically, not transcendentally. Pragmatic anthropology studies the phenomenal effects of human freedom in the empirical world, not freedom's allegedly noumenal origins.

Also central to Kantian pragmatic anthropology is its emphasis on a particular understanding of human nature, which I call a *cosmopolitan* conception of human nature.[45] For instance, in the preface to *Anthropology from a Pragmatic Point of View*, Kant states that anthropology is only properly called pragmatic "when it contains knowledge of the human being as a *citizen of the world* [*Erkenntnis des Menschen als Weltbürgers*]" (7: 120). Similarly in the preamble to the *Friedländer* anthropology transcription (1775–1776), he states:

> Anthropology is not however a local but rather a general anthropology. In it one comes to know not the state of human beings but rather the nature of humanity, for the local properties of human beings always change, but the nature of humanity does not. Anthropology is thus a pragmatic knowledge of what results from our nature, but it is not a physical or geographical knowledge, for that is tied to time and place, and is not constant. . . . Anthropology is not a description of human beings, but of human nature.
>
> (25: 471)

Essentially, what Kant strives for in his anthropology is a wide conception of human nature that is not tied to time and place, one that focuses on what human beings share in common with one another. Again though, because Kantian anthropology is a *Beobachtungslehre*, this conception of human nature must be arrived at empirically, through collective reflection on the chief tendencies and characteristics of the species as a whole. It is not an *a priori* cognition but rather *a posteriori*: something "known from the experience of all ages and by all peoples [*aus der Erfahrung aller Zeiten und unter allen Völkern kundbar*]" (*Anth* 7: 331).

But while empirical, the cosmopolitan conception of human nature also has an important normative status within Kant's anthropology. In effect, it functions as a teleological moral map, a practical guide by means of which human beings are to orient themselves toward both the present and the future. For instance, in the final sentence of his *Anthropology*, Kant summarizes the human species' character as "a species of rational beings that strives among obstacles to rise out of evil," but he then adds that we can only be expected to reach that goal (*Zweck*) "by a progressive organization of citizens of the earth into and toward the species as a system that is cosmopolitically united" (7: 333).

Kant's discussion of radical evil in *Religion*, I submit, fits well with his extended anthropological investigations into human nature. In both his anthropology lectures and in part I of *Religion*, he is concerned with what our experience tells us about the human species as a whole—with what human beings past, present, and future share in common with each other. But there is also a fundamental difference between the anthropology and *Religion* discussions. In the various anthropology lectures (the following point also holds for Kant's writings on the philosophy of history), the discussion of human nature focuses primarily on the *future*—on humanity's cosmopolitical vocation and the gradual realization of a global society that administers justice universally. However, in part I of *Religion*, the primary focus is more on the *past*.[46] The propensity to evil "is detectable as early as the first manifestation of the exercise of freedom in the human being" (6: 38); our ancestors saw it "at the beginning of the world [*im Weltanfange*]" (6: 43).

In sum, Kant is serious when he encourages us to examine the woeful examples of radical evil "that the experience of human *deeds* parades before us." Empirical "anthropological inquiry [*anthropologische Nachforschung*]" (*Rel* 6: 25) of this sort is as close as we are going to get to a formal proof of the universality of a propensity to evil within the human species, and it is no doubt closer than many of us want to get. Throughout history and in every culture, human beings have continually revealed their propensity to evil in their conduct toward one another. Evil is truly everywhere.

Kant's account of radical evil, like many other aspects of his philosophy, is certainly not without its paradoxes and counterintuitive claims. But I hope I have succeeded in showing that four of the most frequently voiced criticisms of this account are often wide of the mark, and that when we take the time to determine what Kant is trying to say, his position still makes a lot of sense. To summarize my responses to the four criticisms: (1) Even the most ordinary people are capable of the most horrendous deeds, but in many cases we will never know for sure what drives people to evil. Human action, particularly evil human action, often has an indecipherable character, and because of this it is unrealistic to demand that a plausible theory of evil explain why people commit evil. In order to hold rational agents responsible for their conduct, we must assume that they have the capacity of free choice. But this very capacity of free choice implies that in many cases the ultimate motives of human conduct will be inscrutable. (2) Morally good people put moral principle first, and the rest of us don't. Beyond this, it is unwise to speculate about whether we have succeeded in plumbing the depths of human depravity. When confronted with cases of evil, all that we can safely say is that the perpetrator has knowingly violated fundamental moral norms. (3) We must resist the temptation to aestheticize evil by attributing motives of satanic evil to all-too-human criminals. To label perpetrators of evil demonic or diabolical is merely to offer them an escape route from responsibility for their deeds. (4) Finally, as human beings whose intentions are opaque, we have no choice but to try and extract invisible moral dispositions from the visible deeds before us (see *Rel* 6: 71, 77). And when we do look carefully at human deeds in different times and places, we find ample evidence of a universal human propensity to evil.

10

"The Play of Nature"

HUMAN BEINGS IN KANT'S GEOGRAPHY*

A NEW COURSE

IN THE SUMMER semester of 1756—Kant's second semester as a lowly *Privatdozent* at the University of Königsberg—he began lecturing regularly on physical geography, a practice that he continued until he retired from teaching in 1796, and one that grew directly out of his first publications in geography and natural science. Geography was a new academic discipline at this time, and Kant was one of the first university lecturers to offer independent courses in this field.[1]

Broadly speaking, Kant's geography lectures match Charles Withers's description of Enlightenment geography as a project that "in one way or another reflected the voyages of exploration and discovery that characterized the period and provided a wealth of information about the natural diversity of the world and its peoples," an enterprise that was "part of the process of enlightening the world through its inventory and description."[2] But once we look below the surface, we find features of the course that mark it as uniquely Kantian. What were these distinctive features of Kant's geography course, and what were his main aims in presenting these lectures?

First, the geography course was unusual in that it was based not on an official textbook, as was generally required at all Prussian universities at the time, but rather on Kant's own intentionally eclectic collection of materials, to which he added and subtracted over the years. As he notes in his first *Announcement* about the course, published in 1757: "useful information is scattered over numerous and voluminous works, and a textbook suitable for academic use is still lacking. Therefore I decided at the very beginning of my academic teaching to report on this science in special lectures [*in besonderen Vorlesungen*] after the guidance of a summary sketch" (2: 4). And in two later announcements about the course, published in 1758 and 1759, he also makes a point of saying, "I have read aloud from my own essays" (2: 25) and "lectured from my own manuscript" (2: 35). Indeed, in October 1778, Minister of Education Karl Abraham von Zedlitz specifically exempted Kant's physical geography course from the traditional required-textbook regulation:

> The worst compendium is certainly better than none, and professors may improve upon the author as much as they can, but lecturing from one's own notes [*das Lesen über Dictata*] must absolutely be stopped. However, from this, Professor Kant and his lectures on physical geography are exempted, because it is known that no entirely suitable textbook is yet available.[3]

At any rate, what several commentators have bemoaned as the "intellectual and political embarrassment," the "unbelievable hodge-podge of heterogeneous remarks, of knowledges without system, of disconnected curiosities"[4] in Kant's physical geography lectures seems to have been part of his intent all along. One of his key aims was simply to summarize current developments in the emerging field of geography. As he remarks in the 1757 *Announcement*, he wanted to explore topics with students "not with that completeness and philosophical exactitude in areas that is the business of physics and natural history, but with the reasonable curiosity of a traveler who seeks out everywhere what is noteworthy, peculiar, and beautiful, and then compares his collected notes and reflects on his plan" (2: 3).

This last quotation points to a second distinctive feature: Kant's geography course was designed to be popular and entertaining—not dry and rigidly academic. For instance, in the 1765–1766 *Announcement* for the course, he relates that he wants to make geography "into an entertaining and easy compendium [*Inbegriff*]" (2: 312), a "great diversity of entertaining, instructive, and easily understood knowledge" which will be well suited to a "sociable century" (2: 313). Similarly, at the end of the introduction to Rink's edition of the *Physical Geography* lectures (which, according to Adickes, stems from a 1775 course),[5] Kant remarks that his lectures "serve for our own enjoyment [*Vergnügen*] and provide rich material for social conversation" (9: 165).

At the same time, the goals of popular entertainment and enlightenment through science are by no means mutually exclusive. Kant also envisioned his geography course as a kind of popular science for laypeople, and this popular science goal constitutes a third distinctive feature. For instance, he opens the 1757 *Announcement* by saying that "the rational taste of our enlightened time" has brought us to a point where we are now "no longer in danger of losing ourselves in a world of fables [*Welt von Fabeln*] instead of attaining a correct science of natural curiosities [*richtige Wissenschaft der natürlichen Merkwürdigkeiten*]" (2: 3). And in the 1765 *Announcement* he stresses that the first part of the course, which explores "the natural relationship that holds between all the countries and seas of the world, and the ground for their connection, constitutes the real foundation [*das eigentliche Fundament*] of all history, without which history is scarcely distinguishable from fairy tales [*Märchenerzählungen*]" (2: 312).

Fourth, Kant's physical geography lectures were also intended to be useful and pragmatic. Indeed, though readers normally associate the term "pragmatic" with Kant's 1798 work, *Anthropology from a Pragmatic Point of View*, if his declining health had not prevented him from editing the geography lectures on his own,[6] he could just as well have entitled them *Physical Geography from a Pragmatic Point of View*. For instance, in the 1758 *Announcement*, he describes the course as a "useful [*nützlich*] and agreeable science" (2: 25), while in 1765 he states that the course should prepare students "and serve them for the exercise of practical reason," adding later that he has recently introduced changes in the lectures "which are of even greater utility [*noch gemeinnütziger*]" (2: 312). At the beginning of the 1775 *Announcement*, he calls the geography course "more of a useful entertainment [*nützliche Unterhaltung*] than a laborious business" (2: 429), and at the end, in one of his most famous descriptions, he calls geography a form of

> useful academic instruction [*nützliche akademische Unterricht*] . . . which I may call the preliminary exercise in the *knowledge of the world*. This knowledge of the world serves to procure the *pragmatic* element for all otherwise acquired sciences and skills, by means of which they become useful not merely for the *school* but rather for *life* and through which the accomplished apprentice is introduced to the stage of his destiny, namely, the *world*.
>
> (2: 443)

Similarly, in the introduction to Rink's edition of the lectures, Kant stresses that he intends to show students "how to make our knowledge *practical*[7] [*das Praktische zu geben*]. And this is *knowledge of the world*" (9: 158). He concludes the introduction by stressing that "the usefulness [*der Nutzen*] of this study is very extensive" (9: 165).

Related to this emphasis on usefulness and pragmatic applications is a fifth feature that I call the *orientation aim* of the lectures: Kant wanted to give students an empirically informed orientation toward the world at large, a sense of what to expect after they leave the narrow confines of home and school.[8] For instance, in the introduction to Rink's text he criticizes the cosmopolitan tourist who thinks he has acquired *Weltkenntnis* simply because he has been fortunate enough to travel widely: "there is more to knowledge of the world than just seeing the world. He who wants to draw utility [*Nutzen ziehen*] from his travels must have a plan [*ein Plan*] in advance of his travel" (9: 157; see also *Anth* 7: 120). Granted, as he acknowledges later, "through travel one can broaden one's knowledge of the external world, but this is of little use if one has not already received a certain preliminary exercise through instruction [*durch Unterricht eine gewisse Vorübung*]" (9: 158). Kant's geography course—along with the later anthropology course, which to a certain extent grew out of the geography lectures before splitting off as an independent course in 1772—was supposed to provide students with this preliminary exercise. Without this preparatory orientation, the results of the cosmopolitan's travels will form merely an unsystematic aggregate (ibid.), a hodgepodge that "can yield nothing more than fragmentary groping around and no science" (*Anth* 7: 120). This need to orient oneself by means of an accurate conception of the world and its inhabitants is stressed particularly in the 1765 *Announcement*, when Kant describes "the second part" of the geography course,

> which considers the *human being*, throughout the world, from the point of view of the variety of his natural properties and the differences in that feature of man which is moral in him [*was an ihm moralisch ist*], a very important and also highly stimulating consideration, without which universal judgments about the human being would scarcely be possible, and where the comparison of human beings with each other and with the moral state of earlier times furnishes us with a comprehensive map of the human species [*eine große Karte des menschlichen Geschlechts*].
> (2: 312–13)[9]

Finally, related to the orientation aim is what Kant calls the "cosmological" aim of his geography lectures. Both parts of *Weltkenntnis* (nature and the human being) are to be treated cosmologically, that is, from a broad, holistic perspective rather than a partial or local one. The cosmological goal is to acquire an overall sense of nature as a systematic and integrated whole, so that we may better find our way in the world and in our interactions with other people. In the 1775 *Announcement*, for instance, Kant stresses that both nature and the human being "must be considered *cosmologically*, namely, not with respect to the noteworthy details that their objects contain (physics and empirical psychology) but with respect to what we can note of the relation as a whole in which they stand and in which everyone takes his place" (2: 443, see also *Geo* 9: 157). The main stress of the adjective "cosmological" is on the need to understand the whole and how the parts relate to the whole. Without this broader perspective—which Kant believes must precede travel and social interaction rather than issue out of them—students are lost. Without a preparatory cosmological outline, any information about the world and its products and inhabitants gleaned from travel will constitute merely an unsystematic aggregate, a "fragmentary groping around" that can never yield science or true understanding. As Kant states in the introduction to Rink's text: "we must know the objects of our experience *as a whole* so that our knowledge does not form an *aggregate* but rather a *system*; for in a system the *whole* is there before the parts, on the other hand in an aggregate the *parts* are there earlier" (9: 158). However, this cosmological whole is arrived at empirically; it contains not the "strict universality [*strenge Allgemeinheit*]" that Kant identifies as one of the "sure signs [*sichere Kennzeichnen*] of an *a priori* cognition" in the first *Critique*, but only "empirical universality" (B 4).

HUMAN BEINGS IN KANT'S GEOGRAPHY AND ANTHROPOLOGY
A Distinction without a Difference?

In 1772, Kant began to separate anthropology from geography, offering an annual course in each subject after this point. But drawing a clear line between these two new Kantian disciplines is easier said than done. One might suppose that geography simply concerns "earth description" (*geo*, earth + *graphein*, to write = *Erdbeschreibung*; see *Geo* 9: 157) and that anthropology is the study of human beings (*anthropos*, human being + *logos*, word, reason = *Anthropologie*) and leave it at that. And Kant himself does occasionally distinguish the two disciplines in this manner. For instance, in the *Pillau* anthropology lectures (1777–1778), he states: "In physical geography we consider nature, but in anthropology the human being, or human nature in all of its situations. These two sciences constitute knowledge of the world" (25: 733; see also 2: 443, 9: 156).

However, because human beings are also part of nature and because they also live on the surface of the earth, this way of distinguishing the two disciplines won't work. "Geography," as defined by both Kant and contemporary geographers, also considers human beings.[10] For instance, in the 1757 *Announcement* he states that "physical geography examines only the natural condition of the earth, and what is located on it: seas, continents, mountains, rivers, the atmosphere, the human being [*der Mensch*], animals, plants, and minerals" (2: 3). And later in this same *Announcement* he notes that he intends to take up

> in the geographical way of teaching all the countries of the earth, in order to display the inclinations of human beings [*die Neigungen der Menschen*], as they flow from the region in which they live; the variety of their prejudices and way[s] of thinking [*Vorurteile und Denkungsart*], insofar as all of this can serve to make the human being more closely acquainted with himself; a brief idea of their arts, commerce, and science, a description of the products of the countries, . . . in a word, everything which belongs to physical geography.
>
> (2: 9; see also 2: 312–13)

In Rink's edition of the *Physical Geography*, human beings are also featured prominently. In the introduction, Kant states that his course will deal with five different types of geography: mathematical, moral, political, economic [*mercantilische*], and theological (9: 164–65). All but the first (which deals with "the shape, size, and motion of the earth, and its relationship to the solar system in which it is located"; 9: 164) of these five geographies clearly concern human beings. And at the beginning of the second part of these lectures, there occurs a ten-page section entitled "Concerning the Human Being" (9: 311–20). Human beings also make frequent appearances in other parts of Rink's text. For instance, they are described as one of the principal causes of changes in the shape (*Gestalt*) of the earth (9: 296–98); the importance of knowledge concerning coastlines, depths of oceans, causes of winds and storms, etc., to sailors is stressed (9: 306–8); various trees and plants are discussed in terms of their usefulness to human beings (9: 356–65); and his concluding discussion of the countries of the earth is largely a comparative survey of human cultures (9: 377–436).

In short, in all descriptions and records of Kant's physical geography lectures that are currently available to us, human beings play a prominent role. It is simply not the case that Kant's physical geography course deals exclusively with the earth itself, nor is it the case that his anthropology course deals exclusively with human beings. (For instance, in the *Anthropology* he occasionally discusses nonhuman animals; 7: 135, 266,

269n, 327.) Insofar as Kant's physical geography and anthropology lectures are both concerned with human beings, there is considerable overlap between the two disciplines.

Perhaps we can then distinguish them by emphasizing the particular manner in which they treat human beings? Emil Arnoldt, for instance, claims that Kant's

> physical geography chiefly takes into consideration uncivilized human beings; the anthropology, civilized human beings, and . . . the difference between the consideration of the human being in the physical geography and in the anthropology in general can thus be formulated as follows: physical geography considers human beings primarily from the outside, anthropology from the inside.[11]

But we have seen already that this is false. Kant planned to investigate various aspects of "civilized" human life (e.g., economics, politics, ethics, theology) in his geography lectures, and his anthropology lectures by no means consider only "civilized" human beings. For instance, in the *Anthropology* Kant discusses the patience and courage of the Indians of America, and asks later whether their forehead, "overgrown with hair on both sides, is a sign of an innate feeble-mindedness" (7: 257, 299). Contra Arnoldt, "the line of demarcation between the physical-geographical and anthropological consideration[s] of the human being" is by no means "easy to draw."[12]

Similarly, it is often asserted that Kant's anthropology considers human beings pragmatically, whereas his physical geography treats them nonpragmatically—as J. A. May puts it, "in a physical and 'external' sense" that is concerned only "with unreflective behaviour," "as a part and product of nature, viewed from the perspective of the natural environment."[13] Or, as Alix Cohen remarks, in Kant's geography course the human being is considered not "as a free being, but rather [as] an inhabitant of the earth like plants, animals, and minerals—it considers man as one type of 'thing' on earth."[14] But this attempt to demarcate the two disciplines, while closer to the truth than Arnoldt's, is also problematic for at least two reasons.

First, as noted earlier, Kant's physical geography lectures are also pragmatic. Geography (like anthropology) "serves to procure the *pragmatic* element for all otherwise acquired sciences and skills" and is "useful not merely for *school* but rather for *life*" (Racen 2: 443); geography (like anthropology) is a "useful and pleasant science" (2: 25); geography (like anthropology) is intended to "prepare and serve students for the exercise of a practical reason" (*Nachricht* 2: 312).

Second, when Kant defines "pragmatic anthropology" in *Anthropology from a Pragmatic Point of View* he is not distinguishing geography from anthropology, but rather the *physiological* anthropology of Ernst Platner (1744–1818) and other "philosophical physicians" from his own anthropology. Physiological anthropology, Kant asserts, "concerns the investigation of what *nature* makes of the human being; pragmatic, the investigation of what *he* as a free-acting being makes of himself, or can and should make of himself" (7: 119). However, all versions of Kant's anthropology lectures contain extensive discussions of human characteristics that stem from their biological composition rather than their free choices. For instance, much of the material on individual temperament and (physical) character, as well as the subsequent material on the character of the sexes, the peoples, and the species, is not about free human action but rather about what nature makes of human beings. What Kant chiefly objects to in the physiological approach to anthropology is its "eternally futile inquiries as to the manner in which bodily organs are connected with thought" (Kant to Herz, toward the end of 1773, 10: 145; see also *Anth* 7: 119, 176)—that is, its ungrounded speculations concerning the causal processes of human thought. What he proposes in its place is an empirical account of human nature that emphasizes pragmatic applications. But insofar as major portions of the anthropology lectures view human beings as products of nature, we also can't distinguish Kantian geography from anthropology by asserting that the former treats human beings as products of nature while the latter does not. Both sets of lectures at times treat human beings as products of nature. Similarly, when Kant in his geography lectures sets out to examine "the differences in that feature of the human being which is *moral* in him [*was an ihm moralisch ist*]" (*Nachricht* 2: 312; my emphasis), it would seem that he must at least occasionally consider free human choices.

Several commentators have also tried to distinguish Kant's geography from his anthropology by means of his doctrine of outer and inner sense. May, for instance, writes:

> This distinction [viz., between outer and inner sense] is of crucial importance for... [Kant's] separation of anthropology from geography, since the world as the object of outer sense is nature, and hence the concern of geography, whereas the world as the object of inner sense is man conceived as soul or self, and is the concern of anthropology.[15]

Similarly, Emmanuel Eze contends that "while anthropology studies humans or human reality as they are available to the *internal* sense, geography studies the same phenomena as they are presented or available to the *external* sense."[16] And there is at least one Kantian text that supports this reading. In Rink's edition of *Physical Geography*, Kant states: "The world as *object of outer sense* is **nature**; as *object of inner sense*, however, it is **soul** or *the human being*. . . . *Anthropology* teaches us *knowledge of the human being; knowledge of nature* we owe to *physical geography* or *description of the earth* [*Erdbeschreibung*]" (9: 156–57).

But this attempt to demarcate geography from anthropology also fails for at least two reasons. First, what I said earlier about Kant's treatment of temperament, the sexes, peoples, and the human species at large in the anthropology lectures is also relevant here. His discussion of these topics primarily involves data gathered from outer sense (viz., the way that external objects distinct from ourselves—in this case, other human beings—are made available to us in intuition). Much of the material in the anthropology lectures does not involve inner sense (viz., the way our own mental states are made available to us in intuition) at all.

Second, Kant's famous argument in the first *Critique* that inner sense and outer sense are necessarily bound up with each other spells additional trouble for any attempt to distinguish geography from anthropology by means of inner versus outer sense. "Inner experience itself," he notes,

> depends on something permanent, which is not in me, and consequently must be outside me, and I must consider myself in relation to it; thus for an experience in general to be possible, the reality of outer sense is necessarily bound up with that of inner sense: i.e., I am just as certainly conscious that there are things outside me to which my sensibility relates, as I am conscious that I myself exist determined in time.
> (B xl–xli n)

Contra May and Eze, it is simply not the case that Kant's anthropology is concerned exclusively with human beings' "self-consciousness"[17] or their "psychological, moral, internal aspect"[18] and that his geography is not.

Nor can we successfully distinguish Kant's geography from his anthropology by asserting that the former deals exclusively with "unconsciously held mores, with man's 'second nature' as it conditions his behaviour unconsciously, through the peculiar exigencies of place and custom."[19] For Kant also discusses unconsciously held mores in his anthropology lectures. The French nation, for instance, "is characterized among all others by its taste for conversation" (*Anth* 7: 313), while the Spaniard "displays in his public and private behavior a certain *solemnity*" (7: 316), and the German "submits most easily and permanently to the government under which he lives" (7: 317). Indeed, Kant's chapter on "The Character of the Peoples" is at bottom nothing but a mélange of human customs and mores. Granted, his aim here is to put this allegedly empirical data to pragmatic use: to show his listeners "what each can expect from the other and how each could use the other to his own advantage" (7: 312). But, again, his geography is also pragmatic. It too aims to show us how to apply our knowledge of the world and its inhabitants to practical purposes.

In sum, there is no bright, clear line to be drawn between Kant's physical geography and anthropology lectures, particularly when we use human beings as the intended line of demarcation. Obviously, the anthropology lectures are much more concerned with human beings than are the geography lectures, but the study of human beings is not the exclusive domain of either discipline. The most we can say is something like the following: in the geography lectures, human beings are treated primarily (though by no means exclusively) as "*things* in the world" that are "products belonging to the play of nature" (*Anth* 7: 120), whereas in the anthropology lectures, the human being is considered primarily (though by no means exclusively) as "a *citizen of the world*" (7: 120) who is "a free-acting being" (7: 119)—a creature who is not completely determined by his natural environment and regional habitat and who thus, "as a rational being endowed with freedom" (7: 285), can, at least to some extent, make his own character and determine his own way of life.

OTHER GEOGRAPHIES: HUMAN CULTURE AND NATURAL ENVIRONMENT

In the introduction to Rink's edition of the geography lectures, Kant states that physical geography is "the ground [*Grund*] of all other possible geographies" (9: 164, see also *Nachricht* 2: 312). Specific geographies mentioned under the category of "other" include mathematical geography, "in which the shape, size, and motion of the earth as well as its relation to the solar system are treated" (9: 164); moral, "in which the different customs and characters of human beings according to different regions [*Sitten und Charakteren der Menschen nach der verschiedenen Gegenden*] are discussed" (ibid.); political, in which "laws that are connected with [*beziehen . . . auf*] the nature of the soil and of the inhabitants" are treated (ibid.); economic [*mercantilische*], or geography of trade [*Handlungsgeographie*], in which is indicated "why and from what source one land has in excess that which another lacks" (9: 165); and theological, where theological principles that undergo changes "according to differences of soil [*nach der Verschiedenheit des Bodens*]" (ibid.) are considered.

Although mathematical geography does not necessarily require the presence of human beings (the earth has a certain shape, size, and motion regardless of whether human beings are present), the remaining four geographies all focus exclusively on certain aspects of human culture in relation to the natural environment. And in each case Kant makes the surprising claim that the cultural practice itself—or at least the specific part of it that concerns him in these lectures—is causally determined by the natural environment. (Political laws "connect with the nature of the soil," theological principles change "according to differences of soil," moral customs and characters "vary according to region," etc.) What does Kant say about these other four geographies after the introduction? How, if at all, does he support his ambitious determinist claims with respect to them?

Unfortunately, in the third part of the lectures, where Kant discusses "the principal natural curiosities of all lands according to geographical order" (9: 377), he offers no detailed presentation of any of these four geographies. For the most part, his brief discussions of moral, political, economic, and theological geography are simply blended into the general country entries. Thus, in the entry on Ceylon we are told that "the women throw their children away or give them away, if they fancy they were born at an unlucky hour" (9: 394–95); and in the entry on Madagascar we are informed that the inhabitants "have no divinity [*Gottheit*] other than a cricket they feed in a basket, into which they put evil things. . . . This they call their '*Oly*'" (9: 411). Similarly, in the entry on Italy Kant notes that the inhabitants "are jealous, vengeful, and secretive, but otherwise inventive, clever, and political" (9: 423); while in the section on South America he states that the Tapeje people in Brazil "have no concept of God, no word that designates him, go naked, devour captured enemies, although not with such cruel torture as the Canadians, drill a hole through their lips and put a kind of green jasper into the opening" (9: 430).

The exceptions to this minimalist treatment occur in the somewhat longer discussions of China, Arabia, the Russian Territory, and Africa. For instance, the entry on China includes separate sections on "Customs and Character of the Nation," "Eating and Drinking," "Compliments," "Agriculture, Fruits, and Manufacturing," "Concerning the Sciences, Language, and Laws," "Religion," and "Marriages." In the first section, we are told that the Chinese "is of an uncommonly serene demeanor" (9: 378), but that he is also "cowardly, very industrious, very obsequious, and devoted to compliments to an excessive degree" (ibid.).[20] In "Religion," we are told that religion "is treated in a fairly cold manner [*ziemlich kaltsinnig*]. Many believe in no God; others, who accept a religion, do not concern themselves much with it" (9: 381).

Similarly, under the entry on Arabia there is a separate section on "Religion." Here, Kant focuses primarily on Mohammed's life, stating that while Mohammed "admitted that he could not perform any miracles [*keine Wunder tun könne*], . . . he is reputed to have split the moon into two parts" (9: 399). And the entry on the Russian Territory includes separate sections on "The Character of the Nation in Siberia" and on "Religion." In the former, Kant proclaims that "the laziness [*die Faulheit*] in these lands is astonishing" (9: 402), and in the latter he states that "if one excludes the Russians of these regions and the Mohammedans, the other peoples have nothing to do with any divinity other than the devil; for, although they maintain that there is a supreme God, he lives in heaven and is far too far away. However, devils rule the earth" (ibid.). Finally, in his opening discussion of Africa, Kant includes a short section entitled "Products of the Land," where he states that "cinnabar and some gold is found there" (9: 409), and that "the wine is splendid" (9: 410).

What should we make of Kant's abrupt but frequent forays into moral, political, economic, and theological geography? Answer: not much. His discussions of these other geographies are extremely undeveloped and unsystematic. In his 1765 *Announcement* for the geography course, Kant states that he intends to condense "that part of the subject which is concerned with the physical features of the earth [*physische Merkwürdigkeiten der Erde*], to gain the time necessary for extending my course of lectures to include the other parts of the subject which are of even greater utility. This discipline will therefore be a *physical*, *moral*, and *political* geography" (2: 312). However, in none of the various geography lecture transcriptions edited by Werner Stark for inclusion in the German Academy edition does Kant offer us an extended moral and political geography. Physical geography always looms larger than moral and political geography.[21] Likely causes for this failure to enlarge the cultural geography dimension of the lectures include both Kant's increased preoccupation, after the "critical turn" in 1770, with "pure" philosophy (which resulted in a diminished interest in empirical studies), and, after 1772, his new anthropology course, which effectively displaced cultural geography.

Furthermore, nowhere in these discussions—or anywhere else—does Kant make the slightest effort to support the strong environmental determinism to which he commits himself in the introduction to Rink's edition of the *Geography*. Regardless of whether the Chinese are or are not cowardly, industrious, and obsequious; regardless of whether the inhabitants of the Russian Territory are or are not lazy and do or do not have anything to do with any divinity other than the devil; regardless of whether the inhabitants of Madagascar do or do not have any divinity other than a cricket; and regardless of whether the Tapeje of Brazil do or do not have a concept of God, Kant provides no arguments that such beliefs and dispositions are caused by the natural environment.

At the same time, it is instructive to compare these comments about cultural practices with similar ones found in the *Anthropology*. In some cases, the remarks are virtually interchangeable. For instance, in the *Geography*, as we saw earlier, Italians are described as "jealous, vengeful, and secretive" (9: 423), while in the *Anthropology* Kant bemoans their "*bad* side": "knifings, bandits, assassins taking refuge in hallowed sanctuaries, neglect of duty by the police, and so forth" (7: 317). In the *Geography* Kant informs us that the inhabitants of Greece "have greatly declined from their previous good character" (9: 422), while in the *Anthropology* he laments "the fickle and groveling character of the modern Greek" (7: 320). This interchangeability constitutes additional support for my earlier claim that when it comes to human beings, there is no bright, clear line of demarcation between Kantian geography and anthropology. Kant sometimes makes virtually identical comments about the same human beings in both sets of lectures.

Nevertheless, there are some significant differences. The discussion of peoples in the *Anthropology* is very Western Eurocentric. The only featured people are the French, English, Spanish, Italians, and Germans. After the separate sections on each of the "big five," Kant concludes his chapter on "The Character of the Peoples" with a few brief, dismissive remarks regarding Russians, Poles, Turks, Greeks, and Armenians.[22] In Rink's edition of the *Geography*, on the other hand, Kant claims to provide entries on "*all* lands according to geographical order" (9: 377; my emphasis), and his entries on some non-European lands (e.g., China) are much more detailed than the entries on European countries. Indeed, in the *Geography*—despite the announced focus on "all lands"—Kant neglects to even include entries on England and Germany.

Also, in *Anthropology from a Pragmatic Point of View* Kant abandons the environmental determinism that he asserts in the introduction to Rink's edition of the *Geography*. At the beginning of the chapter on "The Character of the Peoples," he warns readers that "climate and soil [*Klima und Boden*] . . . cannot furnish the key here" (7: 313). But in its place he inserts an even darker biological determinism. In the *Anthropology* Kant professes to be describing the "innate, natural character [*angeborener, natürliche Charakter*]" (7: 319) of peoples—yet another sign that his *Anthropology*, contrary to received opinion, does not simply consider human beings as "free-acting beings" (see 7: 119).

RACE: DISTORTIONS IN THE *GROßE KARTE*

The part of Kant's geography lectures where human beings are featured most prominently is a section called "Vom Menschen"—"Concerning the Human Being." All extant versions of the geography lectures, including Rink's edition and the various student and auditor transcriptions edited by Werner Stark, contain a variant of this important section.

Race is the main topic in "Vom Menschen," and it has understandably cast a pall over all of Kant's work in geography. Two of the most notorious and frequently criticized passages from Kant's *Geography* appear in this short section. First, we are informed that "humanity is in its highest degree of perfection in the white race. The yellow Indians already have a somewhat lesser talent. The Negroes are much lower, and lowest of all is a part of the American races" (9: 316). Second, we are told:

> The inhabitant of the temperate zone . . . is more beautiful in body, harder working, more witty [*scherzhafter*], more moderate in his passions, more intelligent [*verständiger*] than any other kind [*Gattung*] of people in the world. Consequently, these people have at all times taught the others and vanquished them by the use of weapons. (9: 317)

This particular part of the lectures, according to Adickes, dates from 1758–1759, and at this early stage of his career Kant appears to have held that climate was the major causal factor behind race. For instance, in subsection 3, "Opinions as to the Cause of This Color" (viz., black), he states: "it is obvious that the *hot* climate is the cause. But it is certain that a large number of generations had to pass for it to become handed down and hereditary" (9: 314). Speculation about the role of climate in determining not only human skin color but also mental and moral capacities was rampant during the Enlightenment, and geography's unfortunate association with race also stems from this concern with climate. The most influential author here was "the celebrated Montesquieu, a great champion for the climate,"[23] who, in book XIV of *The Spirit of the Laws*, set out to show that "the temper of the mind and the passions of the heart" vary significantly according to climate, and that "the laws ought to be in relation both to the variety of those passions and to the variety of those tempers."[24] But Montesquieu was not the only Enlightenment advocate of climatology. Buffon also held that "climate is the principal cause of the varieties of mankind" and "the chief cause of the different colors of men."[25] In his *Anthropology*, Kant pays tribute to Buffon as "the great author of the system of nature" (7: 221), and in his first major statement on race, he points to "Buffon's rule, that animals which produce fertile young with one another (whatever difference in shape there may be) still belong to one and the same physical species [*physische Gattung*]," as the correct "definition of a natural species [*Naturgattung*]" (Racen 2: 429).

Kant's most developed accounts about race occur in three separate essays: *Of the Different Races of Human Beings* (1775), *Determination of the Concept of a Human Race* (1785), and *On the Use of Teleological Principles in Philosophy* (1788).[26] The full title of the first essay was *Of the Different Races of Human Beings, in Announcement of the Physical Geography Lectures in Summer Semester 1775*, and it functioned as a kind of advertisement for his geography lectures of that year. The second and third papers were first published as freestanding essays in journals, and were not officially connected to the geography course. Overall, the contour of Kant's thinking about race is a gradual move away from climatological causes and toward biological ones. However, climate continues to play a secondary role even in his later statements about race, functioning as a circumstantial cause that triggers a more fundamental biologically predetermined development. At any rate, the geography lectures, while they contain some of Kant's earliest and most notorious remarks about race, do not constitute his most systematically developed statements on the topic.

Nevertheless, the geography lectures are never entirely detachable from Kant's work on race; discussions of race continue to appear in these lectures, year after year. The "Vom Menschen" section, for instance, appears both in the earliest surviving version of the geography lectures, the *Holstein* manuscript of 1758–1759 (although it differs in certain fundamental respects from the version in Rink's text),[27] and in the last version, the *Dohna* manuscript of 1792.

When he is careful, Kant restricts the concept of "race" to the single, physical, heritable trait of skin color. For instance, in the 1785 essay, he divides the human species into four races "with respect to their skin color" (*Menschenrace* 8: 93), and argues that "no other characteristic property is *necessarily hereditary*" (8: 94) in these four races except the skin colors of white, yellow, black, and copper-red. Unfortunately, he is not always careful, and does not consistently adhere to this modest skin-color-only conception of race. In the 1788 essay, for instance, he claims that the Native American is "too weak for hard labor, too indifferent for industry and incapable of any culture [*unfähig zu aller Kultur*] . . . and ranks still far below even the Negro, who stands on the lowest of the other steps that we have named as differences of the races" (*Gebrauch* 8: 176).

Kant was well aware that there were two very different faces to his race theory—a narrower physical one and a broader moral and intellectual one. In a revealing letter to Johann Jakob Engel, publisher of *Der Philosoph für die Welt* (The Worldly Philosopher), in which a revised and expanded version of the first race essay was published in 1777, Kant suggests that his broader moral characterization of race will be of more interest to the average reader: "the attached principles of a moral characterization [*moralische Charakteristik*] of the different races of the human species will serve to satisfy the taste of those who do not pay particular attention to the physical [*physische*] characterization" (Kant to Engel, July 4, 1779, 10: 239).[28]

But the moral characterization of race seems also to have satisfied the taste of the sage of Königsberg, for it is not clear that he ever abandoned it. And it has proved to be a major interpretive problem ever since, for both Kantians and non-Kantians alike. How are we to reconcile the Kant who claims that Native "Americans and negroes cannot govern themselves. Thus they serve only as slaves" (*Refl* 1520, 15: 878) with the Kant who proclaims that "the human being and in general every rational being *exists as an end in itself, not merely as a means* to be used by this or that will at its discretion" (*Gr* 4: 428)?

At present, three competing interpretive strategies are offered. One group accuses Kant of "inconsistent universalism"[29]—in some places he says that *all* human beings must be treated as ends in themselves, while in others he asserts that nonwhite races should serve as slaves for whites. But the universalist strand, according to this first group, is more central to Kant's core commitments than the racist strand. A second group accuses Kant of "consistent inegalitarianism," and holds that the racist strand is in fact dominant. Kant, on Charles Mills's reading, "makes whiteness a prerequisite for full personhood and . . . limits nonwhites to 'subperson' status."[30] So when Kant says that all persons are ends in themselves, he in fact means only whites. A third group acknowledges that Kant's position on personhood is inconsistent in his earlier writings, but holds that in his late works he abandons racial hierarchy and finally espouses both a consistent universalism and a consistent egalitarianism. Sankar Muthu, for instance, writes: "In Kant's later years . . . the hierarchical and biological concept of race disappears in his published writings. . . . In his last published discussion of race, . . . Kant makes no arguments about the preeminence of whites or Europeans over other human races."[31] More recently, Pauline Kleingeld, while taking issue with certain aspects of Muthu's ameliorative account, has also argued that "during the 1790s Kant restricts the role of the concept of race, and drops his hierarchical account of the races in favor of a more genuinely egalitarian and cosmopolitan view."[32]

The geography lectures, which span Kant's entire writing career, provide us with a way to test the claims of this third group. Did Kant change his mind about race over the years, and does he in fact make no mention of racial hierarchy in his works from the 1790s?

In the version of "Vom Menschen" that occurs in the last of the geography lectures currently available, the *Dohna* lectures of 1792, Kant repeats a version of Hume's infamous footnote about Negroes,[33] which he had also cited with approval in his 1764 work, *Observations on the Feeling of the Beautiful and Sublime* (2: 253). The *Dohna* version reads:

> Hume says, that of the many thousands of Negroes who have gradually been freed, there is no example of one who has distinguished himself with a special skill. Something essential in the character of the Negro is a kind of vanity, arrogance—this is why no freed Negro cultivates the land, he prefers to live in a monkey-house or to become a servant.
>
> (105)

Clearly, in the *Dohna* lectures of 1792 Kant still "employs a hierarchical account of the races." Isn't the assertion that "Kant changed and improved his position [on race] during the 1790s"[34] therefore false?

Kleingeld acknowledges that in *Dohna* Kant "still endorses Hume's claim that blacks are naturally inferior," and as a result she qualifies her position concerning Kant's second thoughts about race by saying that he changed his mind "most likely *after* 1792" and that he "makes no mention of racial hierarchy anywhere in his *published* writings of the 1790s."[35] But I think the *Dohna* passage should lead us to be more circumspect in making any pronouncements about Kant's second thoughts on race. While it is certainly true, as Kleingeld and others have pointed out, that Kant explicitly condemns colonialism in publications of the 1790s such as *Toward Perpetual Peace* (1795; see 8: 358) and the *Metaphysics of Morals* (1797; see 6: 266, 353), nowhere in either his published or unpublished works of the 1790s does he issue any sort of explicit mea culpa nor acknowledge to readers that he has changed his mind about race. Accordingly, I think it is more probable that Kant, like Thomas Jefferson and other leading Enlightenment intellectuals, while firmly opposed to colonialism, also continued to hold that "the blacks . . . are inferior to the whites in the endowments both of body and mind."[36]

There is much to admire in Kant's geography lectures—particularly his emphasis on "how to make our knowledge *practical*" (9: 158) and his goal of introducing students to the stage of their "destiny, namely the *world*" (2: 443). But his heavy reliance on racial stereotypes when attempting to provide students with "a comprehensive map [*große Karte*] of the human species" (2: 313) results only in a severely distorted map of humanity. Far better is the moral map of Kant's anthropology and history essays, which describes the vocation of the human species as the "progressive organization of the citizens of the earth into and toward the species as a system that is cosmopolitically united" (7: 333). If and when our species *is* cosmopolitically united, local contingencies of climate and soil will play a smaller role in people's lives.[37]

11

Becoming Human

KANT AND THE PHILOSOPHY OF EDUCATION*

BACKGROUND OF KANT'S *LECTURES ON PEDAGOGY*[1]

Kant's *Lectures on Pedagogy* stems from a course on practical pedagogy that the philosophy faculty at the University of Königsberg was required to offer, which rotated among its faculty. Kant taught the course four times: winter semester 1776–1777, summer semester 1780, winter semester 1783–1784, and winter semester 1786–1787. His text the first time he offered the course was Johann Bernhard Basedow's *Methodenbuch für Väter und Mütter der Familien und Völker* (1770). In 1774, under the patronage of Prince Friedrich Franz Leopold III of Anhalt-Dessau, Basedow (1723–1790) founded the Philanthropinum in Dessau, a Rousseau-inspired educational experiment that Kant greatly admired. From 1780 on, Kant was required to use his senior colleague Friedrich Samuel Bock's (1716–1785) book *Lehrbuch der Erziehungskunst zum Gebrauch für christliche Eltern und künftige Jugendlehrer* (1780). However, in keeping with his general practice regarding the required-text rules that all German professors were expected to follow at this time, Kant's lecture notes follow neither Basedow nor Bock at all closely.

Friedrich Wilhelm Schubert, co-editor of the first collected edition of Kant's works, reports that toward the end of his life Kant offered his lecture notes on pedagogy—"which according to the habit of the philosopher consisted in individual scraps of paper [*einzelne Papierschnitzel*]"—to his younger colleague Friedrich Theodor Rink, "in order to select out from them the most useful ones for the public."[2] Rink (1770–1811) studied theology at Königsberg from 1786 to 1789 (during which time he attended some of Kant's lectures), returning in 1792 to lecture as a *Privatdozent*. During

1792–1793 and 1795–1801 he was a frequent dinner guest at his former professor's home. In 1794 Rink was appointed associate professor of oriental languages at the university, he was promoted to full professor in 1797, and in 1800 he became a full professor of theology. From 1801 until the end of his life, he served as a pastor in Danzig. Kant also entrusted Rink with the editing of his *Lectures on Physical Geography*.[3] Other publications of Rink concerning Kant include a biography, an edited anthology of some of Kant's essays, and a defense of Kant's philosophy against criticisms raised by Johann Georg Hamann (1730–1788) and Johann Gottfried Herder (1744–1803).[4]

Unfortunately, the original *Papierschnitzel* that Kant handed over to Rink have not survived. As a result, it is not possible to know for certain whether Rink published all or only some of Kant's notes, whether he rearranged the order of those that he did publish, whether words or phrases were added or deleted, etc. What *is* certain is that the resulting book published by Rink in the year before Kant's death in 1804[5] is not well organized and is at times repetitive. Similar criticisms have also been made of Rink's editing of other works of Kant, particularly the *Lectures on Physical Geography*. Over the years, various attempts have been made to improve upon Rink's efforts, chiefly by rearranging portions of his text. However, without Kant's original notes, all such interpretive speculations seem imprudent at best. As Paul Natorp, editor of the Academy edition of *Über Pädagogik*, writes: "as regards the arrangement of the material, in the absence of a secure basis of possible correction it seems necessary to reprint Rink's text without alterations" (9: 570).

The *Lectures* have been translated into English twice before my version—first by Annette Churton (1899) and then by Edward Franklin Buchner (1904).[6] However, both Churton and Buchner base their translations on Theodor Vogt's edition, *Über Pädagogik: Mit Kant's Biographie* (1878). Because Vogt's edition is the most influential of the editorial rearrangement efforts referred to earlier, the order in which they present Kant's lecture notes differs somewhat from my own.

In sum, *Lectures on Pedagogy* is not a book that Kant himself published, but rather a poorly edited compendium of his views on education culled from lecture notes that he prepared and used for a course on practical pedagogy at the University of Königsberg. Nevertheless, despite its flaws, *Lectures on Pedagogy* remains Kant's central work on education. Although he gave considerable and repeated attention to educational questions in many of his published writings, particularly the essays on the philosophy of history, the popular anthropology lectures, and the famous works on ethics, aesthetics, and philosophy of religion, his discussions of pedagogical issues in these works are often sporadic and subsidiary to his central concerns. On the other hand, in *Lectures on Pedagogy* educational concerns are always front and center, even when the authorial integrity of some of its specific claims have been challenged. Thus, in order to arrive at a fully developed and authentically Kantian philosophy of education, one really needs to study Rink's short text in conjunction with Kant's voluminous and difficult published writings—a daunting task for even the most dedicated student. In what follows, I will offer some signposts through this difficult territory.

STAGES OF EDUCATION, STAGES OF HISTORY

In comparison with Kant's most famous work, the *Critique of Pure Reason* (which he, in the *Prolegomena to Any Future Metaphysics*, refers to as "dry, . . . obscure, opposed to all familiar concepts, and long-winded as well"; 4: 261), the *Lectures on Pedagogy* is not a difficult book to read. But as noted earlier, it is poorly edited and at times repetitive. In his *Lectures*, Kant makes numerous distinctions between different types of educational activities, processes, and divisions, not all of which are clearly developed and some of which are inconsistent with each other. In this section I draw attention to the central and most compelling pattern of organization in the *Lectures*, a pattern that is not always clearly presented in Rink's text and one that, as a result, has been analyzed in different ways by different commentators.[7]

In the opening paragraph of the *Lectures*, Kant announces that what he means by "education" is a three-stage process of care, discipline, and formation (9: 441). Later, he asks whether the education of individuals should "imitate the course followed by the development of humanity in general through its generations" (9: 446), and at this point it becomes clear that his position on the stages of education essentially mirrors his conception of the stages of world history. In other words, Kant's educational theory is strongly influenced by his philosophy of history.

The root idea behind Kant's schema of the stages of both education and history is the gradual development of humanity out of natural predispositions. As he states in the *Lectures*: "Many germs [*Keime*] lie within humanity, and now it is our business to develop the natural predispositions proportionally and to unfold humanity from its germs and to make it happen that the human being reaches his vocation [*Bestimmung*; this important term can also be rendered as 'destiny']" (9: 445). An explicit teleology is thus always present in Kant's discussions of education and history—both aim at the perfection of humanity. But "humanity" is meant here primarily in a cultural and moral sense: how do individual members of the biological species *Homo sapiens* become fully human? At bottom, it is an extremely ambitious story of the growth of freedom out of nature through rational control of instinct and desire, culminating eventually in a single world community where all human beings are accorded a dignity that is beyond price. And on Kant's view education has a major role to play in achieving this goal: "the human being can only become human through education. He is nothing except what education makes of him" (9: 443).[8]

The first stage of education is *care*. Kant defines it at the beginning of the *Lectures* simply as "the precaution of the parents that children not make any harmful use of their powers" (9: 441), and the primary stress here is simply on protecting the young so that they do not injure themselves in the course of their natural development. But later, in discussing the distinction between physical and practical education, he also includes under "care" (which is part of physical education) numerous bits of advice about what foods, drinks, and activities are appropriate for young children. Much of his advice concerning care appears to be borrowed from Rousseau's *Émile*,[9] and is today perhaps of only antiquarian interest, in part because it is sometimes based on false empirical data.[10] At the same time, it is possible that some of his remarks concerning the care of young children may stem from his personal experiences as a tutor or private teacher (*Hofmeister*) in the homes of two or three families near Königsberg from 1748 to 1754, after his student years. In later life, Kant is said to have remarked that "in the whole world there was never a worse tutor" than he,[11] but the testimony of the families who employed him suggests that he was in fact a much better tutor than he thought.

In terms of the history of humanity, this first stage of education corresponds to the very earliest period of human existence, when (Kant conjectures) our ancestors were still purely instinctual creatures who blindly and unreflectively obeyed the promptings of their natural inclinations and desires—a time before humans were conscious of "reason as a faculty that can extend itself beyond the limits within which all animals are held" (*Anfang* 8: 112). Once they became aware of their capacity to choose between alternative courses of action and ways of life, early humans were freed from the limitations of instinct that nature imposes on other animals. They crossed an abyss from which there was no turning back.

The second stage of education is *discipline*, which "changes animal nature into human nature" (9: 441). Changing animal into human nature by no means entails eradicating or demolishing instincts, desires, and inclinations—a radical change of this sort would result in beings who were no longer human. Rather, it refers to the ability (an ability which itself is one of humanity's germs or natural predispositions) to control them through the exercise of reason. As Kant remarks in a later work, *Religion within the Boundaries of Mere Reason* (1793):

> *Considered in themselves* natural inclinations are *good*, i.e., not reprehensible, and to want to extirpate them would not only be futile but harmful and blameworthy as well; we must rather only curb them, so that they will not wear each other out but will instead be harmonized into a whole called happiness.
>
> (6: 58)

Or, as he puts it in the *Lectures*: "to discipline means to seek to prevent animality from doing damage to humanity, both in the individual and in society. Discipline is therefore merely the taming of savagery" (9: 449).

But even Kant's counsel to curb rather than extirpate our animal inclinations fails to capture fully the enormous task of discipline. As Aristotle emphasized, human beings need to train their inclinations and emotions so that the right feelings are expressed in the right way at the right time, about the right things, and toward the right people (see *Nicomachean Ethics* II.6 1106b21–24). Kant is often accused of ignoring the positive role of feeling in human development in both his ethical and educational theories,[12] but this is a misreading. For instance, in the *Metaphysics of Morals* (1797) he stresses, "what is done not with pleasure but merely as compulsory service has no inner worth for him who so responds to his duty" (6: 484). Virtuous people take pleasure in doing what is morally required.

Discipline, like care, forms part of what Kant calls "negative" education. The main goal is not to interfere with nature except when absolutely necessary: "In general it should be observed that the first stage of education must be merely negative, i.e., one should not add some new provision to that of nature, but merely leave nature undisturbed" (9: 459). "From earliest childhood the child must be allowed to be free in all matters (except those where it might injure itself . . .)" (9: 454). Here as well, Kant echoes Rousseau. In *Émile* we read:

> [T]he education of the earliest years should be merely negative. It consists, not in teaching virtue or truth, but in preserving the heart from vice and from the spirit of error. . . . Exercise his body, his limbs, his strength, but keep his mind idle as long as you can. . . . Leave childhood to ripen in your children.[13]

However, despite Kant's Rousseauian emphasis on the negative character of discipline, there are also positive dispositions to be fostered during this second stage, e.g., obedience, truthfulness, sociability (9: 481–84), and, above all, self-control.

The corresponding second stage in the history of humanity is *civilization*. Human beings at this level of development have begun "the transition from the crudity of a merely animal nature into humanity, from the go-cart of instinct to the guidance of reason" (*Anfang* 8: 115). They have begun to replace the rule of instinct with the rule of law, and they have developed an immense variety of cultural practices and institutions in their dispersion to all corners of the globe. But as for the grounding of moral character, the ultimate goal in Kant's philosophy of history, they still have a long way to go: "We are *cultivated* in a high degree by art and science. We are *civilized*, perhaps to the point of being overburdened, by all sorts of social decorum and propriety. But very much is lacking before we can be held to be already *moralized* [*moralisiert*]" (*Idee* 8: 26).

The third stage of education is *formation* (*Bildung*, also rendered as "culture"). The important term *Bildung*, which is often said to embody "the German theory of education,"[14] is used very broadly by Kant and later writers to refer not only to education and culture generally, but also to the entire process of self-realization, the ultimate goal of human existence. For instance, Wilhelm von Humboldt (1767–1835), one of the most influential writers in this German tradition, declares in *The Limits of State Action* that "the true end of the human being . . . is the highest and most proportional *Bildung* of his powers into a whole."[15] Kant also occasionally uses the more familiar term *Kultur* as a synonym for *Bildung*.

Discipline, as we saw earlier, involves the negative task of curbing the natural inclinations to make way for humanity; formation or culture is the positive stage of education, and involves fostering human beings' natural talents and abilities. At one point in the *Lectures on Pedagogy*, Kant defines culture tersely by stating that "it is the procurement of skillfulness" (9: 449, see also 466). Human beings are skillful when they can attain their chosen ends, whatever these ends may be. Culture imparts skill, and skill enables us to achieve our goals. As he states in the third *Critique*, "the production of the aptitude of a rational being for any ends in general (thus those of his freedom) is *culture* [*Kultur*]" (5: 431). Kant draws a similar negative-positive distinction between discipline and culture in the following passage from the first *Critique*:

> The *compulsion* through which the constant propensity to stray from certain rules is limited and finally eradicated is called *discipline*. It is different from *culture* [*Kultur*], which would merely produce a *skill* without first canceling out another one that is already present. In the formation of a talent [*Bildung eines Talents*], therefore, which already has by itself a tendency to expression, discipline will make a negative contribution, but culture and doctrine a positive one.
>
> (A 709–10/B 737–38)

Under the broad terms *Bildung* and *Kultur*, Kant also includes more specific educational activities such as instruction (*Unterweisung*; 9: 441, 449, 452), teaching (*Belehrung*; 9: 449), and guidance (*Anführung*; 9: 452).

In his philosophy of history writings, Kant usually refers to the third stage of human history as "moralization [*Moralisierung*]," a future level of development where all members of the species will consistently act from moral motives. However, while he does include a fairly detailed discussion of moral education at the end of the *Lectures* (9: 486–99), and while he certainly holds that moral character is the ultimate goal of human development, *Bildung*, the third stage of education, does not actually correspond to moralization, the third stage of history. For moral character as Kant understands it is ultimately a free choice for which each moral agent is responsible—a choice that is not causally determined by nature or nurture. The development of moral character can be and is fostered by a variety of cultural factors, including not only good educational institutions but also the establishment of an effective international justice system that successfully restrains nation-states' "vain and violent aims of expansion," aims which "ceaselessly constrain the slow endeavor of the inner *Bildung* of their citizens' way of thinking" (*Idee* 8: 26). But these needed external institutions alone cannot guarantee moral character. Rather, what is called for is "the transformation of one's way of thinking [*Umwandlung der Denkungsart*] and the founding of a character" through an act of freedom, "a *revolution* [*Revolution*] in the disposition of the human being" (*Rel* 6: 48, 47). Moral education and institutional reform can help to prepare the way for the radical transformation that Kant calls moralization by securing "the completion of empirical practical reason,"[16] but they alone cannot bring it about. Ultimately, moralization is a free choice on the part of each individual.

On Kant's view, civilization and culture are essentially coterminous stages of human historical development. Both have occurred together ever since our ancestors first broke free from the dominion of instinct. And culture, the third stage of education, is still part of this second stage of history: "We live in a time of disciplinary training, culture [*Kultur*], and civilization, but not by any means in a time of moralization [*Moralisierung*]" (*Päd* 9: 451).

In sum, Kant understands both education and history as a developmental process involving the gradual realization of inherent human powers and capacities, the growth of freedom through rational control of instinct and desire. The final goal is human perfection, where "perfection" is understood not just as technical and cultural achievement but, ultimately, moral transformation.

REVOLUTION, EXPERIMENTALISM, NATURALISM[17]

Readers who know Kant only through his major philosophical works and the endless commentaries on them are in for some surprises when they turn to his writings on education. For in these texts he espouses several unexpected doctrines, each of which can be traced to his strong endorsement of Basedow's Philanthropinum project. In 1776–1777 Kant published two short pieces, known today as the *Essays Regarding the Philanthropinum* (2: 445–52),[18] both of which are in large part fundraising appeals for the project, and in the *Friedländer* anthropology transcription (1775–1776) he refers to Basedow's school as "the greatest phenomenon which has appeared in this century for the improvement of the perfection of humanity" (25: 722–23).

Revolution

One of Kant's least popular doctrines in his political philosophy is his firm rejection of the right to revolution. For instance, in the *Metaphysics of Morals* he states plainly that "a people cannot offer any resistance to the legislative head of a state which would be consistent with right [*Recht*]" (6: 320, see also 322). However, in his educational theory he advocates not gradual reform but revolution. In the second *Essay Regarding the Philanthropinum*, he writes:

> It is futile to expect this salvation of the human species from a gradual improvement of the schools. They must be transformed [*umgeschaffen*] if something good is to come out of them because they are defective in their original organization, and even the teachers must acquire a new *Bildung*. Not a slow *reform*, but a swift *revolution* [*eine schnelle Revolution*] can bring this about.
>
> (2: 449)

Baesdow's school, Kant notes, was organized "in a radically new way according to the genuine method" (2: 449). And this is precisely what was needed, for it is widely acknowledged that the existing schools were grossly deficient. According to one frequently cited account:

> Youth was in those days, for most children, a sadly harassed period. Instruction was hard and heartlessly severe. Grammar was beaten into the memory, so were portions of Scripture and poetry. A common school punishment was to learn by heart Psalm 119. Schoolrooms were dismally dark. No one conceived it possible that youth could find pleasure in any kind of work, or that they had eyes for anything but reading and writing. The profligate age of Louis XIV inflicted on the poor children of the upper classes hair curled by the barber and smeared with powder and pomade, laced coats, knee-breeches, silk stockings, and a dagger at the side—for active, lively children the severest torture.[19]

Basedow and his followers were opposed to all of this. In their schools (the original Philanthropinum in Dessau was soon imitated by a number of other schools in Germany and Switzerland), memorization was kept to a minimum, pupils were not forced to study, and teachers did not use corporal punishment. Learning through games was stressed, and physical education became an important part of the curriculum. Instruction was given in the pupils' native tongue, and Latin and French were taught by the conversational method. Last but definitely not least, the Philanthropinum schools were cosmopolitan rather than nationalist in orientation, free from religious indoctrination (even Jewish students were admitted), and open to students from all social classes.

Unfortunately, Basedow's school never attracted sufficient students or funding, despite Kant's strong efforts on both fronts. And part of the blame must be placed on Basedow's lack of administrative and people skills. Goethe, who spent some time with Basedow in 1774, shortly before the founding of the Philanthropinum, later wrote that Basedow "was not the man, either to edify souls or to lead them," and while acknowledging that Basedow could speak eloquently about education, concluded that his fundraising efforts were frequently hampered by "the most incomprehensible way he injured the feelings of the men whose contributions he wished to gain; indeed, he offended them unnecessarily, because he could not hold back his opinions and fancies [*Grillen*] on religious topics."[20] Kant, in an anthropology transcription from 1791–1792, put matters more bluntly when he stated: "Basedow's shortcoming was that he drank too much Malaga" (25: 1538, see also 1561).[21]

Kant worked fervently as a supporter and fundraiser for the Philanthropinum from 1776 to 1778, during which time the school had three different directors: Basedow, Joachim Heinrich Campe, and Christian Heinrich Wolke. But in the summer of 1778 he cut his ties with the school, after persuading an influential local minister (Wilhelm Crichton, court chaplain in Königsberg) to take over the money-raising effort (see Kant's letter to Crichton of July 29, 1778; 10: 217–18).

Although Kant remained firmly committed to the need for fundamental educational change throughout his career, his early revolutionary zeal softened somewhat in his later years. In addressing the question of how human progress is best achieved in the *Conflict of the Faculties* (1798), he notes that to believe it "will eventually happen by means of the *Bildung* of youth in domestic instruction, then in schools on both the lowest and highest level, in intellectual and moral culture fortified by religious doctrine, . . . is a plan which is scarcely likely to achieve the desired success" (7: 92). Rather, he continues, "progress is to be expected only on the condition of a wisdom from above [*nur in einer Weisheit von oben herab*] (which bears the name of providence if it is invisible to us)" (7: 93). This starkly religious appeal would have surprised the radical Basedow, but Kant adds a final cosmopolitan note on which the two would agree: human beings must also learn to "renounce wars of aggression altogether" (ibid.), so that governments will be able to invest more in education.

Experimentalism

Like other philosophers in the German idealist tradition, Kant normally advocates an extremely top-heavy relationship between theory and practice, according to which reason and theory must always guide practice—never vice versa. For instance, in the *Critique of Pure Reason* he praises Galileo and other scientists for discerning that "reason has insight only into what it itself produces according to its own design; that it must take the lead with principles," and for compelling "nature to answer its questions, rather than letting nature guide its movements" (B xiii). And in his practical philosophy he also insists that "the worth of practice rests entirely on its conformity with the theory underlying it" (*Gemeinspruch* 8: 277). Human beings must realize that they do not have "moles' eyes fixed on experience"; rather, their eyes "belong to a being made to stand erect and look at the heavens" (ibid.).

But another surprise in the *Lectures on Pedagogy* is Kant's demand for experimentalism. Experiments are needed in education, and the kind of experiments called for should not simply be viewed as handmaidens of preordained theory. In defending Basedow's Philanthropinum against its conservative critics, Kant states:

> It is even commonly imagined that experiments in education are not necessary, and that one can already judge by reason alone whether something will be good or bad. But this is very mistaken, and experience teaches us that our experiments often show quite different effects from the ones expected. One sees therefore that since experiments matter, no one generation can present a complete plan of education. The only experimental school which to an extent made a beginning in establishing a course was the Dessau Institute. We must let it keep this glory regardless of the many mistakes of which one could accuse it (mistakes found in all conclusions that come from experiments)—viz., that new experiments are always required.
>
> (9: 451)

What is most surprising about this passage is its strong empirical tone—its denial that reason must always lead the way over experience, and its assertion that experiments are valuable precisely because they sometimes lead to results that reason did not foresee. In his more canonical writings, Kant defends an anti-empiricist model of scientific inquiry, one that "sees science as from the beginning a product of reason, guided by *a priori* principles both in setting its aims and in setting the guiding principles for making its observations and its systematic presentation of their results."[22] Although Kant, like many optimistic educational theorists before and since, does express the hope that the art of education will eventually be "transformed into science [*Wissenschaft*]" (9: 447), the picture of science defended in the *Lectures on Pedagogy* is a refreshingly open-ended and empirical one.[23]

Naturalism

Insofar as he maintains that moral principles cannot be derived from facts of nature, Kant is a stern anti-naturalist in his ethical theory. For instance, the concept of a "moral ought," he asserts in the *Critique of Pure Reason*, expresses a species of necessity and a connection with grounds which does not occur anywhere else in the whole of nature. In nature the understanding can only cognize *what exists*, or has been, or will be. It is impossible that something in it *ought to be* other than what, in all these time relations, it in fact is; indeed, the *ought*, if one has merely the course of nature before one's eyes, has no significance whatsoever.

(A 546/B 575)

And because he holds that moral principles cannot be derived from empirical facts, Kant is also adamantly opposed to any and all moral theories that are based merely on biological or cultural-historical facts about human beings. He insists on a "pure moral philosophy," one that is "completely cleansed of everything that may be only empirical and belongs to anthropology" (*Gr* 4: 389).

But a third surprise in Kant's writings on education is his refreshing appeal to a kind of naturalism. ("A kind" because, as Hume famously remarked, "nature" is a word "than which there is none more ambiguous and equivocal."[24] There are many kinds of naturalism.) In his second *Essay Regarding the Philanthropinum*, he asserts that all schools save one "were spoiled at the outset, . . . because everything in them works against nature" (2: 449). Basedow's Philanthropinum alone employs the correct educational method, which "is wisely derived from nature itself and not slavishly copied from old habit and unexperienced ages" (ibid.).

The kind of naturalism invoked here is one that we encountered earlier, in the discussion of the "negative" education advocated by Rousseau. At bottom, it hints of a proto-Romantic glorification of nature, a conviction that natural processes are good and departures from them bad. However, at least on Kant's understanding, this naturalism is not an outlook that seeks to derive the ethical from the natural. Even in his pre-critical *Lectures on Pedagogy*, Kant insists that one must sharply differentiate the realms of nature and moral freedom: "One must . . . distinguish between nature and freedom. Giving laws to freedom is something entirely different from forming nature" (9: 469–70). The concept "good" is not derived from nature; rather, nature is simply viewed as good. Ultimately, the naturalism of his educational writings is a species of *weak* naturalism: much that we find in nature is good, though natural facts in themselves do not establish or justify moral principles. And any moral theory that is to be applied successfully to human beings needs to be consistent with the facts of human nature. Accordingly, education, one of the primary external influences on human moral development, needs a method that is "wisely derived from nature itself."

MORALITY AND EDUCATION

Morality occupies the biggest space in Kant's theory of education, in large part because of the explicit teleology behind his concepts of education and history. As we have seen, education and history both aim at the realization of morality throughout the human species. As he declares at the end of the *Collins* lecture on ethics: "The final end of the human race is moral perfection. . . . How then are we to seek this perfection, and from where is it to be hoped for? From nowhere else but education" (27: 470–71). At the same time, as also noted earlier, education ultimately plays only a preparatory role in the grounding of moral character, because even the best educational institution cannot guarantee that its graduates will become morally good people. Moral character on Kant's view is not causally determined by nature or nurture, but is rather a free choice for which each individual bears responsibility. In the language of his mature philosophy, educational institutions affect human beings' empirical or phenomenal character, but not their nonempirical or noumenal character. Keeping these two background points in mind, let us now turn to Kant's perspective on the methods and goals of moral education.

Methods of Moral Education

Kant's position on the methods of moral education is fairly straightforward, although—as is often the case in his educational theory—the full story does not emerge from the *Lectures on Pedagogy* alone. To a certain extent, his views on how to teach ethics are the same as his views on how to teach other subjects. The student's level of emotional and cognitive development should be the primary criterion in choosing a teaching method, not the subject matter or the instructor's personal preference. For instance, in his discussion of the "Doctrine of the Method of Ethics" at the end of the *Metaphysics of Morals* (one of his best texts on moral education), he advocates what he calls an "erotematic" teaching method (from the Greek *eromai*, "to ask or inquire")—essentially, question-and-answer rather than lecture. For the primary goal of moral education is to show the student "that he himself can think" (6: 478) about morality rather than just listen to other people's (including his teachers') opinions about it. Kant then subdivides the erotematic method into the dialogical approach, "where the teacher questions the pupil's *reason*," and the catechistic, "where he merely questions his *memory*" (ibid.). He also discusses these two varieties of the erotematic teaching style (along with its counterpart, the lecture or "acroamatic" approach—from the Greek *akroamai*, "to listen to") in many of his logic lectures (see, e.g., *Jäsche* 9: 149–50; *Pölitz* 24: 599; *Busolt* 24: 684; *Dohna-Wundlacken* 24: 780). His main point concerning the two varieties of erotematic teaching is that the catechistic method is most appropriate for younger pupils, who need first to learn the basic concepts and ideas of a subject, while the dialogical method should come later.

Accordingly, "the first and most essential" instrument for teaching ethics to young students is "a *moral* catechism" (*MdS* 6: 478; see also *KpV* 5: 154) or "catechism of right" (*Päd* 9: 490). Catechisms—summaries of the main principles of a doctrine presented in the form of question-and-answer—had already been used for centuries by Christian educators to teach young people about the main tenets of that faith, and Kant is borrowing from this earlier tradition of moral education. But his moral catechism differs from Christian catechisms in two basic ways. First, it is "purely moral" (*KpV* 5: 154)— i.e., unmixed with religious or theological doctrines. On Kant's view, the validity of moral principles is not contingent on religion but is rather a matter of rational argument and agreement: "on its own behalf morality in no way needs religion . . . but is rather self-sufficient by virtue of pure practical reason" (*Rel* 6: 3). Second, and related, the moral catechism must precede any religious education in the student's life. Again, moral principles are to be rationally justified independently of religious faith. And religion itself needs to be grounded in morality, for "if religion is not combined with morality, then it becomes nothing more than currying favor.... Morality must therefore come first" (*Päd* 9: 494–95).

In the *Lectures* Kant offers only a brief summary of what a moral catechism should look like: "it would have to contain cases which would be popular, which occur in ordinary life, and which would always naturally raise the question [of] whether something is right or not" (9: 490). In the *Metaphysics of Morals*, he presents a fragment of an actual catechism, one that stresses basic moral concepts such as the nature of happiness, inclination, autonomy, and duty (6: 480–82). A complete catechism, which he does not provide, would be extensive, "for it must be carried out through all the articles of virtue and vice" (6: 482).

Kant's employment of case studies in his moral catechism is based on the cognitive development and natural curiosity of children. Children are not yet able to reason autonomously about moral principles, and at the beginning their ability to think about moral issues is best fostered through contact with concrete examples. But even though the pupil is "not yet ready for speculation" about the rational foundations of ethics, he naturally takes an interest in specific moral questions, and in analyzing them with a teacher he will "feel the progress of his power of judgment" (*KpV* 5: 154). However, while discussing case studies does help to foster students' native interest in morality, Kant stresses that what is most important are the underlying principles by which the cases are properly appraised. Ultimately, it is not specific examples of virtuous human beings or morally right actions but rather the moral law itself "that must serve as the constant standard of a teacher's instruction" (*MdS* 6: 480).[25]

With the introduction of dialogue, the second stage of the erotematic teaching method, students adopt a more active role in their moral education, asking questions of teachers in addition to providing answers to the teachers' questions. In the *Critique of Practical Reason*, Kant offers a brief hint of what he has in mind. Describing a discussion with a ten-year-old boy concerning "the mark by which pure virtue is tested," Kant advocates using real examples drawn from "the biographies of ancient and modern times" in a manner that encourages the student to reach his own conclusion "without being directed to it by a teacher" (5: 154–55).

Taken together, the moral catechism and the dialogical method form half of what Kant calls "ethical didactics"—essentially, moral education strategies for teachers to use with students. The "practical counterpoint" to these two techniques is what Kant calls "ascetics," "in which is taught not only the concept of virtue but also how to put into practice and cultivate the *capacity for* as well as the will to virtue" (*MdS* 6: 411–12). Moral ascetics (from the Greek *askētēs*, "one who practices an art") in Kant's etymological sense refers not to rigorous self-denial, renunciation of the flesh, etc., but merely to the practice rather than the theory of virtue. But it is largely a self-discipline that students must practice on themselves. The teacher's role here is limited to helping students to grasp the correct principles for cultivating and practicing virtue. The main principle

Kant stresses is the importance of taking pleasure and joy in doing one's duty (6: 484)—ironically, the exact opposite of what some critics claim to find in Kant's ethics.

Didactics and ascetics form the two divisions of Kant's "doctrine of method" for ethics, and they can both "be presented as a *science [Wissenschaft]*" (6: 478); in this context, "science" is a body of knowledge that can be set forth systematically and taught by means of rules. Casuistry, the art of resolving particular cases by applying general principles (from the Latin *cāsus*, "case"), forms the final component in Kant's methods of moral education. It "is neither a science nor a part thereof . . . and is not so much a method concerning how something is to be *found* as an exercise concerning how truth is to be *sought*. Therefore it is *woven into ethics fragmentarily*, not systematically . . . , as scholia are added to the system" (6: 411). Casuistry is needed in moral education because rules are never self-deploying.[26] There are no rules that can show us how to apply principles to specific cases; thus good judgment—which is always needed in ethics but rarely found—remains an art to be cultivated through practice rather than a science to be learned through study.

Goals of Moral Education

Kantian moral education of course aims to teach children "the duties that they have to fulfill" (*Päd* 9: 488), but, more important, it also strives to foster a number of interconnected attitudes and dispositions that are preliminary to but essential for morality as Kant understands it. Perhaps the clearest example of the latter is the goal of instilling cosmopolitan dispositions in students. Students must learn to become citizens of the world, and to respect the inherent dignity and moral equality of all human beings: "they must rejoice at the best for the world [*das Weltbeste*] even if it is not to the advantage of their fatherland or to their own gain" (9: 499). Education everywhere must aim not at national or parental goals (both of which are usually vocational in nature), but at human perfection. As Kant stresses in the *Lectures*:

> Parents usually care only that their children get on well in the world, and . . . princes regard their subjects merely as instruments for their own designs. Parents care for the home, princes for the state. Neither have as their final end the best for the world and the perfection to which humanity is destined, and for which it also has the predisposition. However, the design for a plan of education must be made in a cosmopolitan manner.
>
> (9: 448)

This strong cosmopolitan orientation is also present in several other Enlightenment educational reform efforts, e.g., Basedow's Philanthropinum. But in Kant's case it connects directly to a core theme in his ethical theory. Educational plans that serve merely parental or national purposes are morally objectionable because they violate the categorical imperative to treat all human beings as ends in themselves: they treat students as tools (see *Gr* 4: 429).

The most important task of moral education is what Kant calls "the grounding of character," and this too is essentially shorthand for instilling a number of interrelated dispositions. At one point in the *Lectures* he states: "the first effort in moral character is the grounding of character. Character consists in the aptitude of acting from maxims" (9: 481). In the generic sense, a "maxim" is simply the underlying principle that guides one's action—thus, every action has a maxim. But Kant adds that the person who has character acts from a special type of maxim, one that originates "from the human being's own understanding" (ibid.). People who have character act autonomously from principles that originate in their own reason rather than from rules that are externally imposed by others. As he remarks in *Anthropology from a Pragmatic Point of View*: "He who has character derives his conduct from a source that he has opened by himself [*als einer von ihm selbst geöffneten Quelle*]" (7: 293). Later in the *Lectures* he states that the grounding of character "consists in the firm resolution of willing to do something, and then also in the actual performance of it" (9: 487). Now, the stress is on strength of will and control of one's desires and passions, perseverance in the face of adversity.

Evil as well as good people, however, may possess independent judgment and strength of will. On Kant's view, the crucial distinguishing mark of morally good people is that they consistently act from maxims that can be "universalized"—that is, they act from principles that could be accepted and acted on by everyone. Those who are not morally good do not act from universalizable maxims. Human beings are moralized when they have acquired deep-seated dispositions to act on universalizable maxims, to treat all human beings as ends in themselves, and to regard all people as lawgiving members in a universal kingdom of ends—in other words, when they have internalized the norms expressed in the different formulas of the categorical imperative (see Gr 4: 421–37). The moral educator's task is to instill these dispositions in individual students. Kant's philosophy of history points to a future condition when all members of the human race have acquired them.

Many Enlightenment intellectuals believed that human beings would be morally transformed through the growth of education, participation in democratic polities dedicated to the rule of law, free trade between nations, and the establishment of an effective international justice system that would stand up for human rights everywhere and eventually put an end to war.[27] Gradually, the right sort of external institutional development would lead to inner moral transformation. But while he is certainly sympathetic to this global reform movement, Kant's metaphysical commitment to free will prevents him from being a full-fledged member. External change does not guarantee internal change; good moral character is ultimately a free choice and not a causal outcome of social reform efforts.

John Dewey, in a famous passage in *Democracy and Education*, defines all of philosophy as philosophy of education.[28] Kant does not go quite that far, but in the preceding account I have tried to indicate some of the strong connections that exist between his philosophy of education, his philosophy of history, his ethical theory, and his anthropology. At bottom, education for Kant is about the effort to realize our humanity: "the human being can only become human through education" (9: 443).

The first rule to be followed is the principle of national character [*caractère national*]; for each people [*peuple*] has, or ought to have, a national character; if it did not, we should have to start by giving it one.
—ROUSSEAU, *Project of a Constitution for Corsica* (1765)

With us, God be praised! all *national characters* [*Nationalcharaktere*] have been extinguished! We *all* love each other, or rather, none of us *needs* to love the other. *We socialize with each other*, are completely each other's *like—well-mannered, polite, blissful!*; indeed have no fatherland, no *our-people* for whom we live, but we are *friends of humanity* and *citizens of the world*. All of the rulers of Europe are speaking French already, and soon we will *all* be doing so! And then—bliss!—the Golden Age begins again "when *all the world* will have *one tongue* and *language* and there shall be *one flock* and *one shepherd*." National characters, where have you gone?
—HERDER, *Another Philosophy of History for the Education of Mankind* (1774)

12

National Character via the Beautiful and Sublime?*

⁂

THE *OBSERVATIONS* AS ANTHROPOLOGY

IN A LETTER TO Goethe of February 19, 1795, concerning Kant's *Observations on the Feeling of the Beautiful and Sublime*, Schiller complained that "the exposition is merely anthropological, and as concerns the ultimate grounds of the beautiful one learns nothing in there,"[1] so perhaps by now it is time to concede that Kant's 1764 work—in spite of its title—is not fundamentally a project in aesthetics at all but "really a work in what Kant would later call 'anthropology from a pragmatic point of view.'"[2] The specific features of the *Observations* that bring it into closest proximity with Kantian pragmatic anthropology are the following:

First and foremost is its extensive discussion of human varieties and differences. The lead concepts of the beautiful and sublime stressed in the book's title (which of course *do* suggest an aesthetics project) are in fact analyzed only briefly in the short first section (*Beob* 2: 207–10), while the rest of the book (2: 211–56) applies these concepts to different characters and attitudes among individual humans (second section), to the two sexes of human beings (third section), and to national characters (fourth section).

Second is its unabashedly popular rather than academic orientation. The book's aim, as Kant notes in his opening paragraph, is to report on "discoveries that are as charming as they are instructive," and to do so "more with the eye of an observer than of the philosopher" (2: 207).³ The later anthropology lectures share this popular aim: their goal is not "science for the academy" but rather "enlightenment for common life" (*Menschenkunde* 25: 853).

Third is its goal of conveying knowledge of human nature and human differences to readers so that they will learn what to expect from each other and how to deal with each other. For instance, in *Anthropology from a Pragmatic Point of View*, Kant opens the section on "The Character of the Peoples" (7: 311–20) by emphasizing that his concern is not the social science goal of locating the causal factors that determine collective character formation. Rather, "in an anthropology from a pragmatic point of view, . . . the only thing that matters to us is to present the character [of different peoples] as they are now, . . . which makes it possible to judge what each can expect from the other and how each could use the other to its own advantage" (7: 312).⁴ This same pragmatic intent informs the various discussions of human difference in the *Observations*. For instance, in a footnote at the beginning of the discussion of national characters, Kant stresses that he "will not investigate here whether these national differences [*Nationalunterschiede*] are contingent [*zufällig*] and depend upon the times and types of government, or whether they are connected with a certain necessity [*mit einer gewissen Nothwendigkeit*] with the climate" (2: 243n).

Kant first began lecturing on anthropology in the winter semester of 1772–1773, and definite traces of the *Observations* sections on gender and national characters are detectable in all of the surviving transcriptions of these lectures and in his 1798 published version, *Anthropology from a Pragmatic Point of View*. As Paul Guyer remarks in two of his notes to his English translation of the *Observations*, "differences between the sexes would remain a constant theme in Kant's anthropology," and "discussion of national characters was a standard part of Kant's lectures on anthropology."⁵ For instance, *Collins*, one of the earliest surviving anthropology transcriptions (1772–1773), includes sections entitled "On the Character of the Sexes" (25: 234–38) and "On National Character" (25: 232–34), and Kant's *Anthropology from a Pragmatic Point of View* has sections entitled "The Character of the Sexes" (7: 303–11) and "The Character of the Peoples" (7: 311–20).

At the same time, a closer look at the relevant sections of the *Observations* and the various anthropology lectures reveals that, while clear traces of the former do exist in the latter, surprisingly little exact duplication can be found. For instance, in the various discussions of national characters (on which I will focus for the remainder of this essay), Kant bemoans the German's "tendency to imitation and his low opinion of his own ability to be original" in the *Anthropology* (7: 318–19; see also *Friedländer* 25: 658), while in the *Observations* he notes that the German "does not dare to be original" and is "too concerned with the opinion of others" (2: 248). In both texts he criticizes the cruelty of the Spaniards, pointing to their endorsement of *auto-da-fé* (public burning of heretics) as evidence (7: 316, 2: 245). In his comments on the English people in *Friedländer* (1775–1776), he remarks that "no imitators [*keine Nachahmer*] are found among them" (25: 660), while in the *Observations* he notes that the Englishman "is a poor imitator [*ein schlechter Nachahmer*]" (2: 247). In the *Menschenkunde* (1781–1782), which is unique among the anthropology transcriptions in that it was first published in 1831 and not in the 1997 Academy edition, Kant states that the Italian "appears to keep to the middle street between the French and the Spaniard" (25: 1185), while in the *Observations* he says that "the Italian seems to have a feeling which mixes that of a Spaniard and that of a Frenchman" (2: 245).

The closest we come to an example of direct word-for-word duplication between the national characters discussion in the *Observations* and the later ones in the anthropology lectures is the following: in *Collins*, Kant notes that "the Persians are the French of Asia [*Die Perser sind die Franzosen von Asien*]" (25: 203); in *Parow* he says that "the Persians are the French in Asia [*Die Perser sind die Franzosen in Asien*]" (25: 400); and in the *Observations* we read: "the *Persians are the French of Asia* [*so sind die Perser die Franzosen von Asien*]" (2: 252). *Collins* and *Parow* are both assigned dates of 1772–1773—the first year that Kant lectured on anthropology—and they are also the closest temporally to his 1764 *Observations*. So it is not surprising that a virtually identical sentence occurs in each text. Still, given Kant's heavy teaching load and enormously ambitious research program, it is remarkable that so little direct duplication exists between these different discussions of national characters.

THE *OBSERVATIONS* AS GEOGRAPHY?

But while these connections between Kant's *Observations* and his anthropology lectures are readily acknowledged at present, another important connection—viz., that between the *Observations* and the geography lectures—remains severely underexplored. Kant began lecturing regularly on geography in 1756—sixteen years before the anthropology course commenced in 1772 and eight years before the *Observations* were published. In addition to asking how the *Observations* may have influenced the later anthropology lectures, it is also important to ask how the pre-1764 geography lectures may have influenced the *Observations*.

However, the geography-*Observations* relationship question is complicated by the fact that Kantian geography and anthropology are not separate and distinct disciplines but interconnected parts of a larger whole that Kant calls *Weltkenntnis* or "knowledge of the world" (*Racen* 2: 443). They are both intended to be popular and entertaining sciences rather than purely scholarly or academic undertakings. For instance, in his 1765 *Announcement* for the geography course, Kant notes that he conceives of it as "an entertaining and easy compendium of the things which might prepare . . . [students] and serve them for the exercise of practical reason" (2: 312). This "popular science for young people" perspective of the geography lectures is also stressed at the beginning of the first *Announcement* for the course, published in 1757, when Kant predicts that "the rational taste of our enlightened time" is no longer in danger of losing itself in "a world of fables" but may instead attain "a correct science of natural curiosities" (2: 3).

But he quickly adds that the kind of correct science he aspires to is not that which strives after "completeness and philosophical exactitude," but rather that which comes from "the reasonable curiosity of a traveler, who seeks everywhere the noteworthy, special, and beautiful, compares the collected observations [gesammelte Beobachtungen], and considers its plan" (ibid.).

Like his anthropology, Kant's geography is also intended to be a useful and pragmatic science, one that will provide students with helpful information about the world and its inhabitants and show them what to expect when they leave school and venture out beyond their local communities. For instance, in his 1758 *Announcement* for the course, he calls geography "a useful and agreeable science" (2: 25). And in the 1765 *Announcement*, he stresses that his goal is to furnish readers with "a comprehensive map of the human species" (2: 312–13). Geography and anthropology are both designed to provide students with an empirically informed orientation toward the world at large. In sum, Kantian geography and anthropology both aim to provide students with a pragmatically oriented knowledge of the world and all that it contains, communicated in an unabashedly entertaining and popular manner.[6] And the later sections of the *Observations* dealing with human beings share these features with both sets of lectures.

An even more surprising overlap between Kantian geography and anthropology concerns their respective treatments of human beings. Contrary to what Emil Arnoldt and other Kant scholars have often asserted, "the line of demarcation between ... [Kant's] physical-geographical and anthropological consideration of the human being" is by no means "easy to draw."[7] For instance, it is by no means the case that Kantian geography considers only "uncivilized" human beings and Kantian anthropology "civilized" ones. Both sets of lectures include discussions of Europeans and non-Europeans and of their arts and sciences. Nor are humans viewed merely as "products of nature" in the geography lectures and solely as "free beings" in the anthropology lectures. Kant's discussions of national characters in the various anthropology lectures are explicitly not about free human action but rather about what nature makes of humans. As he notes in the *Friedländer* anthropology transcription:

> The determination of the character [of a nation] must not be taken from contingent matters [*nicht von zufälligen Sachen*], for example, from religion, else it is based on chance [*Zufall*]; rather the hereditary peculiarity [*das erbliche eigenthümliche*], the uniform in the determination, which has yet remained an essential component among all the variations of the nation, must be picked out. That which is characteristic [*Das Characteristische*] refers here to what is distinctive in regard to the mind of the entire nation [*des gantzen Volcks*].
>
> (25: 654–55; see also Anth 7: 312)

And because the geography lectures also consider "the differences in that feature of man which is moral in character [*was an ihm moralisch ist*]" (2: 312), they too must at least occasionally consider free human actions.[8]

The best-known version of Kant's geography lectures is the one that his former student Friedrich Theodor Rink edited and first published in 1802, six years after Kant had retired from teaching at Königsberg University. Rink's text is reprinted in volume 9 of the German Academy edition (9: 151–436), and a long-overdue English translation is in the *Natural Science* volume of *The Cambridge Edition of the Works of Immanuel Kant*.[9] As is also the case with other Kantian texts edited by Rink (chiefly the *Lectures on Pedagogy*,[10] first published in 1803 and also reprinted in volume 9 of the Academy edition), the quality of Rink's editing work in the published version of *Physische Geographie* has been strongly criticized by Kant scholars. For instance, Erich Adickes argues that Rink in fact collated two entirely different sets of lectures, one from 1775, which is reprinted in 9: 156–273, and a second from 1758–1759, which is in 9: 273–436.[11]

However, volume 26 of the Academy edition includes two geography transcriptions that predate the 1764 publication of the *Observations*: *Holstein* (1758–1759, which is very close to 9: 273–436 of Rink's text) and *Herder* (1763–1764). Does the discussion of national character in the *Observations* reveal any traces of these earlier discussions of the same topic? Surprisingly, there is no direct duplication. The only clear similarities are the following:

In the section on Arabia in *Holstein*, Kant states that the Arabs are "honest, earnest, amiable, and charitable" (26: 246, see also 9: 398). In the *Observations*, he writes that the Arab is "hospitable, generous, and truthful" (2: 252). The two judgments about Arabian character are very similar, but the words used to express the judgment are not the same. Similarly, in the section on the native peoples of North America in Rink's text, Kant remarks that "the women here have great influence on the affairs of the state, but only the shadow of sovereignty" (9: 432). In *Holstein*, the text is very similar but contains a few additional words: "the women here and on other affairs of the state have great influence but only the shadow of sovereignty" (26: 311). In the *Observations* Kant writes:

> Among all the savages there are none among whom the female sex stands in greater regard than those of *Canada*. In this perhaps they even surpass our civilized part of the world. Not as if they pay the women their humble respects; that would be mere compliments. No, they actually get to command.
>
> (2: 255)

Here too, while the judgments about Native Americans' national character are quite similar, the words used to express the judgment are not exactly the same. However, in both cases it seems likely that Kant was indeed borrowing from earlier geography lecture material when he wrote the cited passages in the *Observations*.

The *Herder* geography lecture is the closest temporally to the 1764 *Observations*, and here is where one would expect to find the most overlap. But while *Herder* does include a short section on "The Characters of Nations" (ms. pp. 62–66),[12] the discussion there is very different from the fourth section of the *Observations*. I see no clear traces at all of the *Herder* material on national characters in the fourth section of the *Observations*.

In sum, the discussion of national characters in the *Observations* is very different from the discussion of the same topic in the pre-1764 geography lectures. While there are two passages in the *Observations* that are similar in content to what we find in the 1758–1759 lectures, there is no word-for-word duplication. And in the case of the 1763–1764 Herder manuscript, where one would expect to find the most duplication simply because the *Observations* was published less than a year after this lecture course ended, there are no noticeable similarities at all. The discussion of national characters in the *Observations* thus stands on its own. It is not derivative material borrowed from earlier geography lectures, but rather appears to be new material that Kant developed specifically for his own purposes in the *Observations*.

New and also different: Kant's approach to national character in the *Observations* marks an important transition. He attempts to survey all peoples and nationalities in the lectures on geography, but beginning with the *Observations* in 1764 he focuses primarily on "the peoples of our part of the world" (2: 243)—i.e., Western Europeans—a shift of perspective that he continues in the various anthropology lectures beginning in 1772. The scope of the other thus shrinks considerably in the *Observations* and later anthropology lectures, but here too a pragmatic motive may be at work. Kant knows more about Europeans, and he may also have believed that it is far more likely that his German readers would encounter, say, an Italian than a citizen of Siam (see *Geo* 9: 383–86).

NATIONAL CHARACTER FROM A KANTIAN POINT OF VIEW

Its originality notwithstanding, the concluding section on national characters in the *Observations* remains by far the least-discussed part of the book. Most commentators pass over it entirely in noticeable silence; those few who do discuss it more or less advise readers to skip it. Guyer, for instance, remarks that "there seems to be little that is redeemable in the fourth section of the work," and Manfred Kuehn cites several passages from the fourth section to illustrate his claim that

> much of the *Observations* must strike us as dated, as the expression of sentiments long since become passé. . . . Some of his observations seem silly to us today, others are annoying, and still others touching. . . . What we get is not so much heartfelt sentiments as the prejudices of an era.[13]

The single most decisive reason behind commentators' dismissal of the fourth section is undoubtedly Kant's endorsement of Hume's infamous footnote about Negroes. In "Of National Characters," Hume asserts that "the Negroes" are "naturally inferior to the Whites,"[14] and in the fourth section of the *Observations* Kant endorses the argumentation and alleged evidence behind Hume's claim before concluding with the following rhetorical flourish: "so essential is the difference between these two human kinds [*diese zwei Menschengeschlechtern*], and it seems to be just as great with regard to capacities of mind as with color" (2: 253).

Much ink has understandably been spilt over this offensive passage,[15] but in our eagerness to expose Kant's racism we seem also to have lost sight of his main concern in the fourth section—viz., national characters. Race is not the same as national character. And the topic of national character was of fundamental importance to Kant throughout his writing career, as it was to many other writers, both ancient and modern. For instance, in the *Pillau* anthropology transcription, he states:

> We find many books that present the characters of people, for we have a drive within us to know that which is characteristic [*das Characteristische*] of everything, which extends also to nations and peoples [*Nationen und Völcker*]. That which is characteristic of peoples is always a necessary condition of world knowledge [*Welt-Erkenntniß*], and this is also the final end in all histories that we read, and in all travels, where we become acquainted with nations.
>
> (25: 831)

Three distinct arguments in defense of knowledge of national characters are presented here. The first is a quasi-Aristotelian argument about human beings' innate desire to know the basic causes and principles of things. "All human beings by nature desire to know," Aristotle announces in the opening sentence of his *Metaphysics* (980a21), and unlike other animals humans live not just by appearances and memories but also by "art and reasonings [*technē kai logismois*]" (980b28). By means of the latter humans are able to form "one universal judgment about similar objects" (981a6–7), and this is essentially what Kant means by character or "that which is characteristic." The concept of national character is of course merely an empirical one rather than a Kantian "pure concept of the understanding" (see *KrV* B 89–169), but as an empirical rather than an *a priori* concept it still plays a vital role in the human desire for knowledge of the world.

The second argument is a pragmatic one, and thus more distinctly Kantian. An understanding of national characters is a necessary component of knowledge of the world, a type of knowledge that "serves to procure the *pragmatic* element for all otherwise acquired sciences and skills, by means of which they become useful not merely for the *school* but rather for *life* and through which the accomplished apprentice is introduced to the stage of his destiny, namely the *world*" (*Racen* 2: 443). Understanding national characters helps to prepare us to deal successfully with other peoples; it shows us what to expect from others.

Finally, a third argument in defense of national characters is hinted at in Kant's commonsense retort to the skeptic who holds that national character is merely a myth.[16] In the *Parow* transcription we read: "a national character is not a mere chimera.... Who does not clearly recognize a French person?" (25: 452). Kant's position is that national character is an undeniable fact of the human sociocultural world. Much as we might wish to think that we are each entirely free individuals who construct our own characters through a creative act of will (as Sartre would have it, "Man is nothing else but that which he makes of himself"),[17] in the end we are forced to recognize that each human being's character is strongly influenced by the cultural and political environments in which she lives. National character is not a myth.

NATIONAL CHARACTER VIA THE BEAUTIFUL AND SUBLIME?

The concept of national character became increasingly popular as the eighteenth century drew to a close. Montesquieu and Hume were two leaders in bringing the concept into vogue, and Kant explicitly acknowledges his debt to each author in the fourth section of the *Observations* (2: 247, 253). But many other writers, particularly among the French *philosophes*, also contributed to the discussion.[18]

Nearly everyone accepted the core assumption that each nation has its peculiar characteristics, but debate raged over the causes of these characteristics. Were they due to physical causes (e.g., climate), to what Hume called "moral causes" (e.g., government), or to some combination of the two?[19] Kant, as we have seen, for the most part[20] adopts a pragmatic stance on the causality issue. His goal is to present the characters of nations as they are at present, in order to inform readers regarding "what each can expect from the other and how each could use the other to its own advantage" (*Anth* 7: 312), and thus he sidesteps the debate about causes.

However, from the beginning, doubts were raised about the accuracy of attributions of national character. Are such attributions merely "unfounded stereotypes" and "myths"?[21] Kant was clearly aware of this objection, and warned readers at the beginning of his discussion in the *Observations* that he was by no means attributing the same character traits and behavior patterns to all individual citizens within the borders of a single country. "My intention," he notes,

> is not at all to portray the characters of the peoples in detail; rather I will only outline some features that express the feeling of the sublime and the beautiful in them. One can readily guess that only a mediocre accuracy [*nur eine leidliche Richtigkeit*] can be demanded in such a description, that its prototypes stand out only [*nur*] in the large crowds of those who lay claim to a finer feeling, and that no nation is lacking in casts of mind which unite the foremost predominant qualities of this kind.
>
> (2: 243n)

Stronger doubts were voiced a bit later by Kant's former student Herder, with whom the concept of national character is much more closely associated:

> No one in the world feels *the weakness of general characterizing* [*die Schwache des allgemeinen Charakterisierens*] more than I. One paints *a whole* people, age, region of the earth—*whom* has one painted? One draws together peoples and periods of time *that follow one another* in an *eternal succession* like waves of the sea—*whom* has one painted?, *whom* has the depicting word captured? Finally, one after all

draws them together into nothing but a *general* word in relation to which each person perhaps thinks and feels what he wants—imperfect *means of depiction!*, how one can be *misunderstood!*[22]

There are several specific problems stemming from Kant's decision to analyze national character from the perspective of the beautiful and sublime, concerning which he seems to be unaware. Let us now turn to these.

First and most obviously, how can Kant do justice to the diversity of national characters that we find among the peoples of the world by means of the dichotomy of the beautiful and sublime? In forcing all nations onto the procrustean bed of the beautiful and sublime, won't he inevitably need to grossly oversimplify and distort matters, thus contributing to the main objection that has been repeatedly raised against national character studies? And if so, won't he also have to sacrifice his pragmatic aim of accurately informing readers about what to expect from others?

But when Kant does finally settle down to describe the various national characters, the simple dichotomy of the beautiful and sublime is not strictly adhered to. Rather, each concept is subdivided—in the case of the beautiful, into two groupings; in the case of the sublime, into three. The resulting quintet of categories (surprise, surprise) just happens to form a one-to-one correspondence with the five major Western European nations that form the bulk of his opening discussion. Thus the Italians are said to distinguish themselves in the feeling of the beautiful "that is enchanting and moving [*bezaubernd und rührend*]," the French in the feeling of the beautiful that is "laughing and charming [*lachend und reizend*]," the Spanish in the feeling of the sublime "of the terrifying kind [*von der schreckhaftern Art*], which inclines a bit to the adventurous," the English in the feeling of the sublime that is "a feeling for the noble [*das Edle*]," and the Germans in the feeling of the sublime that is "a feeling for the magnificent [*das Prächtige*]" (2: 243, see also 209). However, these five categories implicitly allow for a sixth option—viz., "none of the above." And this is where Kant places Holland, a country that warrants only a few short sentences in his discussion of national character. Because the Dutchman "looks merely to what is useful [*lediglich auf das Nützliche*]," he has no perceptible taste for either the beautiful or the sublime (2: 248, see also 243).

But the resulting sextet seems forced and artificial. Why is the beautiful subdivided into two categories while the sublime manages to warrant three? And if utilitarian Holland can be said to have no feeling for either the beautiful or the sublime, why could not a seventh country be said to have a cast of mind in which "both feelings are united" (2: 211, see also 243n)? To make matters worse, one of the categories is in danger of disappearing into another. For the Italian brand of the beautiful that is "enchanting and moving [*rührend*]," we are informed, "has something of the sublime in it" (2: 243, see also 209). The conceptual boundaries of the labels are now called into question.

When Kant turns all too briefly to national characters outside of Western Europe, he employs the same six categories, and so the same set of problems comes up again.

Thus the Arabs are "as it were the Spaniards of the Orient" (i.e., they are marked by a feeling for the sublime of the terrifying kind), and the Persians, as noted earlier, are "the Frenchmen of Asia" (that is, they are distinguished by a feeling for the beautiful that is laughing and charming). The Japanese in turn are labeled as "the Englishmen of this part of the world" (their taste is for the kind of sublime that is a feeling for the noble). The Chinese and the Indians, on the other hand—along with "the Negroes of Africa" (though again, here Kant inexplicably shifts from national character to race)—are all relegated to the unenviable conceptual space occupied by Holland. In these latter nations or races we find no taste for either the beautiful or the sublime (2: 252–53).

The indigenous peoples of North America (another slide from national character to race?) are said to demonstrate a greater "sublime character of mind" than all other "savages [*Wilden*]" (2: 253). Kant does not explicitly invoke any of his three subdivisions of the sublime here, but since the Spanish and the English have already been taken, perhaps we can infer by a process of elimination that the Native Americans are the Germans of the New World (viz., their feeling for the sublime is a feeling for the magnificent). But what reasons does Kant give readers to accept his claim that non-European national characters mirror European ones so precisely? By this point, the procrustean bed of the beautiful and sublime seems to have reached its breaking point.

A second, more fundamental problem concerning Kant's decision to analyze national characters from the standpoint of the beautiful and sublime is the following: Why is the feeling of the beautiful and sublime the best gauge of national character? In virtue of what does this particular feeling constitute the best (or if not the best, at least a plausible) perspective from which to analyze national character?[23] One might think that an answer to this question would form part of the "rich lode . . . [of] discoveries that are as charming as they are instructive" (2: 207) to which Kant draws attention in the opening paragraph of the *Observations*, but in fact he does not address it at all. Granted, at a more general level this question concerning the privileging of the beautiful and sublime could be raised not only with regard to the fourth section of the *Observations* but also with regard to the entire book. However, at this broader level, a reply along the lines of "but the topic of the beautiful and sublime was in vogue among European authors during this time, particularly due to the influence of Burke"[24] seems to be apropos. In the fourth section the question jumps out more, for now Kant has clearly chosen to apply the concepts of the beautiful and the sublime to an area of human life where his contemporaries declined to do so, and it is odd that he does not pause to justify his decision.

A third oddity of the fourth section is that Kant does not actually stick very closely to his announced topic, viz., "national characters, insofar as they rest upon the different feeling of the sublime and the beautiful" (2: 243). I will discuss three examples of this straying tendency.

First, much of the discussion concerns not the different characters themselves, but rather different expressions or manifestations of these characters. "National character," for Kant as well as most other theorists, refers to alleged psychological characteristics of nationalities—to what Kant calls "the characters of mind of the nationalities [Gemüthscharaktere der Völkerschaften]" (2: 245) or "the mind of the entire people [Gemuth des gantzen Volcks]" (Friedländer 25: 655), or what Hegel would later famously call the "Volksgeist" or spirit of the nation.[25] But in addition to his attempts to describe the different collective characters of mind via the different subdivisions of the beautiful and the sublime, Kant also devotes considerable space to descriptions of some of the major expressions of these characters. For instance, he touches (albeit "only fleetingly [nur flüchtig]") on the arts and sciences, for they "can confirm [bestätigen] the taste of the nations that we have imputed to them" (2: 244). Similarly, at 2: 245 he announces that "the characters of mind of the nationalities are most recognizable [am kenntlichsten] in that in them which is moral [was an ihnen moralisch ist]." But it is visible, customary moral behavior (mores, Sitten) that he is referring to here, not internal moral character, which he describes later in the Anthropology as the developed capacity "to act according to firm principles" (7: 292). The same is true of the later brief discussion of religion, which Kant says can also "yield signs of the different national qualities [Zeichen von den verschiedenen Nationaleigenschaften abgeben]" (2: 250). That is, it is outward, religious behavior that concerns him, not internal spiritual attitudes.

Later German authors concerned with national character, such as Herder and Hegel, focus even more intently on national character's alleged visible expressions, and Kant seems to be setting a trend here. Which tangible manifestations of character receive the most attention in such discussions (e.g., in Herder's case, folklore, popular poetry, language; in Hegel's, law and constitutions) seems ultimately to have more to do with the individual author's personal interests than with any objective argument or evidence. But given both the earlier Enlightenment debate centering around Montesquieu and Hume concerning the causes of national character (physical or moral?) and Kant's pragmatic decision to sidestep this debate, it is odd that he devotes so much space to expressions of national character. For in asserting that the arts and sciences, morals, and religion are all expressions of national character, he seems to be implying that they are effects rather than causes of national character. And this would seem to put him on the side of Montesquieu and others who argue that national character is primarily caused by physical factors. In other words, he is forfeiting his professed pragmatic neutrality.

A second example of Kant's straying tendency in the fourth section occurs at 2: 255, when he casts "a few glances at history." The emphasis now is temporal rather than spatial—more Zeitgeist than Volksgeist—and the earlier discussion of different national characters has been replaced by a broader focus on European character. The first point that Kant makes in his digression on history is that "we see the taste of human beings, like Proteus,[26] constantly take on changeable shapes [wandelbare Gestalten]" (2: 255), and this remark introduces another tension with his discussions of national character. For national character—at least in the various anthropology texts—is held to be "unchangeable [unveränderlich]" (Anth 7: 312; see also Friedländer 25: 654; Menschenkunde 25: 1181), but here Kant claims that a people's character, as revealed in the feeling of the beautiful and sublime, changes frequently.

Essentially, what we find in Kant's glances at history is a proto-philosophy of history. To be sure, it is somewhat crude and lacks the sophistication of his later work in this area, but even here we can see that he is trying to "discover an *aim of nature* in this nonsensical course of things human," a "guiding thread for exhibiting an otherwise planless *aggregate* of human actions, at least in the large, as a *system*" (*Idee* 8: 18, 29). At this early stage of his career, Kant's reflections on history mirror a familiar Enlightenment narrative of high praise for the ancient Greeks and Romans ("who displayed clear marks of a genuine feeling for the beautiful as well as the sublime[27] in poetry, sculpture, architecture, legislation, and even in morals"; 2: 255); "extremely disparaging judgment of the Middle Ages,"[28] which are blamed for introducing "a certain perverted taste" and "degenerated feeling" (ibid.) into Europe that led to "an almost complete destruction" (2: 256); and finally a "palingenesis" or rebirth, where "we see in our own times the proper taste for the beautiful and noble[29] blossom in the arts and sciences as well as with regard to the moral" (ibid.). Like Kant's later philosophy of history, these pre-critical cursory glances at history are shaped by an underlying story of human progress and gradual enlightenment. However, he has not yet developed his famous dialectical account of the "unsociable sociability" of human beings, nature's primary means of developing all of the predispositions in the human species.

Kant's unexpected closing remarks about cosmopolitan education are my third example of his wandering tendency in the fourth section.[30] If the rebirth of a proper taste for the beautiful and sublime in the modern world is to become truly efficacious, he emphasizes, it is first necessary "that the as yet undiscovered secret of education should be torn away from ancient delusion in order early to raise the moral feeling in the breast of every young citizen of the world [*eines jeden jungen Weltbürgers*] into an active sentiment" (2: 256). When he refers to young *Weltbürgers*, Kant has clearly moved well beyond the nationalistic boundaries expressed in the title of the fourth section, and even beyond the pan-European focus assumed in his cursory glances at history. For a *Weltbürger*'s primary allegiance is to the world as a whole, not to any nation or region within it. This closing passage most obviously presages the cosmopolitan spirit of Kant's later political thought, a body of writing that points toward a future condition where the citizens of the earth will become "cosmopolitically united" (*Anth* 7: 333) and where "a violation of right [*die Rechtsverletzung*] in *one* place of the earth is felt in *all*" (*Frieden* 8: 360). But will national characters still exist if and when the citizens of the earth become cosmopolitically united, or will the "golden age" that Herder detests (see the epigraph to this chapter) begin again?

The *Weltbürger* passage also foreshadows Kant's strong interests in educational reform, which are traditionally associated with his teaching and writing activities in 1776–1777. In the winter semester of 1776–1777, he taught for the first time a course on practical pedagogy. On the final page of his lecture notes for this course, as edited by Rink, Kant emphasizes that teachers must stress both "philanthropy toward others" and "cosmopolitan dispositions [*weltbürgerliche Gesinnungen*]" to their students (9: 499). In 1776–1777 Kant also published two short fundraising appeals for the Philanthropinum, an experimental school that Johann Bernhard Basedow founded in

Dessau in 1774. Basedow introduced several innovations into his curriculum that eventually became part of mainstream educational practice—e.g., a conversation-based approach to the study of foreign languages, courses in physical education, and the banning of corporal punishment. But above all, it was the nonsectarian and cosmopolitan emphases of his new school that appealed most to Kant. As Basedow wrote in 1776 (and as the name Philanthropinum was meant to intimate), the main goal of the institute was to educate young people to be "citizens of our world."[31]

In his second *Essay Regarding the Philanthropinum*, Kant expresses a dissatisfaction with traditional educational methods that is very similar to what we find in the education passage from the *Observations*, combined now with a call for a revolution in education: schools "must be transformed if something good is to come out of them because they are defective in their original organization, and even teachers must acquire a new formation [*eine neue Bildung*]. Not a slow *reform*, but a swift *revolution* can bring this about" (2: 249).

Kant's closing emphasis on education in the *Observations* is, at least in part, yet another example of the strong influence that Rousseau exercised on his thought during this period. *Émile* and *The Social Contract* were both published in 1762, and references to Rousseau abound in the notes that Kant made in 1764–1765 in his own copy of the *Observations*. For instance, in one note he writes: "The chief intention of Rousseau is that education be free and also make a free human being" (20: 167).[32] However, the concluding emphasis on education can only be partly due to Rousseau's influence, for Rousseau's intensely nationalistic educational program is the polar opposite of Kant's cosmopolitan vision. For example, in his chapter on education in *Considerations on the Government of Poland* (1772), Rousseau writes: "It is education that must give souls a national formation, and direct their opinions and tastes in such a way that they will be patriotic by inclination, by passion, by necessity. When first he opens his eyes, an infant ought to see the fatherland, and up to the day of his death he ought never to see anything else."[33] To instill sufficient *amour de la patrie* in citizens, Rousseau advises that all subjects taught in Polish public schools (to be taught, of course, only by Polish teachers) must be imbued with a strongly nationalistic slant: students are to focus exclusively on Polish literature, Polish history, Polish law, and even Polish science. Rousseau has no sympathy whatsoever for "those supposed cosmopolites who . . . boast of loving everyone in order to have the right to love no one."[34]

I have drawn attention to some inconsistencies and problematic features in Kant's treatment of national character in the *Observations*, but I hope that I have also convinced readers that, contrary to present scholarly opinion, there is much that is redeemable in it. Knowledge of national character constitutes an integral dimension of Kant's pragmatic orientation to the world and its inhabitants, and if we forswear this dimension, much will be lost. Kant wants to inform readers "what each can expect from the other and how each could use the other to its own advantage" (*Anth* 7: 312), and this aim cannot be fulfilled if one forgoes discussions of national character.

At the same time, Kant is not as paranoid as Rousseau and Herder are when it comes to national character; he does not fear that the forces of globalization will obliterate the varieties of national character. To be sure, he is by no means blind to "the *spirit of commerce . . . which sooner or later takes hold of every nation*" (*Frieden* 8: 368) and strengthens social connectivity between peoples; indeed, he endorses this process in the hope that it will lead to "greater agreement in principles" in international law (8: 367) and, eventually, to the abolition of war. And he endorses it with a full awareness that there is an enormous price to be paid. Traditional cultures and languages *are* disappearing in the face of globalization, and (as he remarks in 1800 in his short *Postscript* to a Lithuanian-German dictionary, the last work he published himself), the attempt to preserve the peculiarity of a people and its language "is in itself already of great worth" (8: 445). But Kant's teleological assumption in his philosophy of history also includes the core convictions that nature wills progress through diversity and plurality, and that it employs cultural pluralism as a central means toward this goal. Nature itself seeks to preserve national character, whether human beings aim to or not. The variety of national characters will not be obliterated by the forces of globalization, for "*nature wills* it otherwise" (8: 367; see also *Anth* 7: 320). The best cosmopolitanism is one that recognizes that different states "are not to be fused into a single state" (8: 354), for this "soulless despotism" leads only to "the graveyard of freedom" (8: 367).[35]

NOTES

INTRODUCTION

1. Here as elsewhere (see *Pro* 4: 260–61), Kant may owe a debt to Hume, and certainly one to Enlightenment thought generally. In his introduction to *A Treatise of Human Nature* (1739–1740), Hume writes: "'Tis evident, that all of the sciences have a relation, greater or less, to human nature; and that however wide any of them seem to run from it, they still return back by one passage or another. Even *Mathematics, Natural Philosophy, and Natural Religion*, are in some measure dependent on the science of MAN; since they lie under the cognizance of men, and are judged of by their powers and faculties" (xv). Did Kant know about this Humean text when he proclaimed that all philosophical questions ultimately relate back to anthropology? Hume's *Treatise* was first translated into German in 1790–1792 by Ludwig Heinrich Jakob, a follower of Kant. The dates for Kant's three "What is the human being?" texts are 1800 (*Logik*), 1793 (letter to Stäudlin), and 1790–1791 (*Pölitz*). (However, the *Logik* notes that Jäsche edited extend over a forty-year period, and it is not always possible to accurately date some of their individual statements.) Furthermore, Hume also stresses the importance of "the science of human nature" in the opening sentence of his *Enquiry Concerning Human Understanding*, which first appeared in German in 1755. (For discussion of German translations of Hume, see Kuehn, *Kant: A Biography*, 353, 497n90, 108.) Another possible influence is Francis Hutcheson. In the opening sentence of the preface to his *Inquiry into the Original of Our Ideas of Beauty and Virtue* (1725), Hutcheson declares: "There is no part of philosophy of more importance than a just knowledge of human nature and its various powers and dispositions" (in *Philosophical Writings*, 3). This work was translated into German in 1762 as *Untersuchung unserer Begriffe von Schönheit und Tugend in zwei Abhandlungen*, and Kant's library contained a copy of the translation. However, even if one remains skeptical of a specific debt to Hume or Hutcheson on this point, it is common knowledge that many Enlightenment authors believed that the study of human

nature should occupy center stage. For instance, Alexander Pope, one of Kant's favorite authors, declares in his *Essay on Man* (1733) that "the proper study of mankind is Man," and Kant was certainly aware of Pope's text when he asked "What is the human being?"

2. Kant, *Vorlesungen über Anthropologie*; Kant, *Lectures on Anthropology*. For an extensive study of the development and nature of Kant's anthropology, see Sturm, *Kant und die Wissenschaften vom Menschen*.

3. For further discussion of the contribution that Kant's geographical writings make to his theory of human nature, see "'The Play of Nature': Human Beings in Kant's Geography," chapter 10 in this volume. Several different versions of Kant's classroom lectures on physical geography are included in volume 26 of *Kants gesammelte Schriften*. Volume 26.1, which contains the *Holstein* manuscript, was first published in 2009 as *Vorlesungen über Physische Geographie*, ed. Werner Stark (Berlin: de Gruyter).

4. For further discussion of the contribution that Kant's educational writings make to his theory of human nature, see "Becoming Human: Kant and the Philosophy of Education," chapter 11 in this volume.

5. Sartre, "Existentialism Is a Humanism," 290–91. "Even in Kant," Sartre notes correctly, we find the idea that "man possesses a human nature" (290).

6. Foucault, *The Order of Things*, 387. Foucault's critique of the human sciences and his own history of "man" are in no small part an outgrowth of his early encounters with Kant's anthropology. His secondary doctoral thesis, defended in 1961, was a "translation, with introduction and notes" of Kant's *Anthropologie in pragmatischer Hinsicht*. The translation was soon published as *Anthropologie du point de vue pragmatique*, but Foucault, on the advice of his dissertation committee, recast most of the commentary into what eventually became *The Order of Things* (*Les Mots et les choses: Une archéologie des sciences humaines*). However, in 2008 his original *Introduction* was published as *Anthropologie d'un point de vue pragmatique: Introduction à l'Anthropologie*, and an English translation quickly followed, *Introduction to Kant's Anthropology*.

7. Geertz, "Anti Anti-Relativism," in *Available Light: Anthropological Reflections on Philosophical Topics*, 50 and 44.

8. For further discussion of this particular aspect of Kant's theory of human nature, see "Anthropology from a Kantian Point of View: Toward a Cosmopolitan Conception of Human Nature" (chapter 7 in this volume).

9. Beck, "Extraterrestrial Intelligent Life," 3. (This essay was Beck's presidential address to the American Philosophical Association Eastern Division meeting in New York City, December 1971.) For further discussion of Kant's views on extraterrestrials, see Louden, *Kant's Impure Ethics*, 188n30, 212n89, 224nn10 and 13, 229n9.

10. Haraway, *When Species Meet*, 11, see also 32.

11. Brooks, *Flesh and Machines*, 179. However, unlike both Brooks and Haraway, Kant does believe that the boundary between humans and machines is a firm one: "an organized being is . . . not a mere machine" (*KU* 5: 374). Unless and until we find a way to replicate biological creatures who share our capacities for (among other things) self-consciousness, abstract thought, and free choice, artificial intelligence will remain a fantasy.

12. Wilson, *On Human Nature*, 13. In the following section I am indebted to Patrick Kain's informative discussion of Kant's views about the nature of animals in his essay "Duties Regarding Animals."

13. At one point Wilson does allow that "you and I are . . . free and responsible persons" in the restricted sense that it is very difficult for any finite intelligence to accurately predict the precise actions of an individual human being (*On Human Nature*, 77). However (as Wilson himself

recognizes), unpredictability is not the same as freedom. X's actions may be humanly unpredictable but nevertheless completely determined. Nor does predictability imply determinism. X's conduct may be predictable but nevertheless freely chosen.

14. E.g., de Waal writes: "I would never speak of 'discontinuities.' Evolution does not occur in leaps: new traits are modifications of old ones so that closely related species differ only gradually" (*Primates and Philosophers*, 161).

15. Wood, "Kant and the Problem of Human Nature," 51. See also Wilson, *Kant's Pragmatic Anthropology*, 39, 45.

16. Pico della Mirandola, *Oration on the Dignity of Man*, 9, 7. See also Cassirer's discussion of the "specifically modern pathos of thought" in Pico's oration in *The Individual and the Cosmos in Renaissance Philosophy*, 84ff.

17. Whiten et al., "Cultures in Chimpanzees," 682. See also de Waal, *The Ape and the Sushi Master*; and McGrew, *The Cultured Chimpanzee*.

18. Gould, "The Human Difference," A17.

19. Whiten et al., "Cultures in Chimpanzees," 682.

20. For discussion, see Catchpole and Slater, *Bird Song*. These authors appear to assume that bird songs should count as cultural (see esp. "Cultural Change," 265–70), but because they offer no definition of the highly debated concept of "culture," it is impossible to critically evaluate their position. As Geertz remarks: "no one is quite sure what culture is. Not only is it an essentially contested concept, like democracy, religion, simplicity, or social justice; it is a multiply defined one, multiply employed, ineradicably imprecise. It is fugitive, unsteady, encyclopedic, and normatively charged, and there are those, especially those for whom only the really real is really real, who think it vacuous altogether, or even dangerous, and would ban it from the serious discourse of serious persons. An unlikely idea, it would seem, around which to try to build a science. Almost as bad as matter" (*Available Light*, 11).

21. Tomasello, *The Cultural Origins of Human Cognition*, 5. Tomasello first presented the ratchet effect thesis in a 1993 article that was co-authored by Kruger and Ratner: "Cultural Learning."

22. Bekoff and Pierce, *Wild Justice*, 7.

23. de Waal, *Primates and Philosophers*, 162. For a response to this other-regarding conception of morality, see my "Morality and Oneself," in Louden, *Morality and Moral Theory*, 13–26.

24. De Waal, *Primates and Philosophers*, 6. De Waal appears to be echoing Darwin's famous claim that "any animal whatever, endowed with well-marked social instincts, . . . would inevitably acquire a moral sense or conscience, as soon as its intellectual powers had become as well, or nearly as well developed, as in man" (*The Descent of Man, and Selection in Relation to Sex*, I: 71–72). But although Darwin holds that the roots of a moral sense track back to social instincts, he also maintains that we do not arrive at a mature moral sense until certain developed intellectual powers are added to these instincts. Consequently, Darwin does not subscribe to the currently popular view that "animals have morality" (Bekoff and Pierce, *Wild Justice*, 1). As he writes: "I fully subscribe to the judgment of those writers who maintain that of all the differences between man and the lower animals, the moral sense or conscience is by far the most important" (*The Descent of Man*, I: 70).

25. Korsgaard, "Morality and the Distinctiveness of Human Action," 112.

26. Wood, "Kant and the Problem of Human Nature," 52.

27. For further discussion of what exactly Kant means by "pragmatic anthropology," see "Applying Kant's Ethics: The Role of Anthropology" and "Anthropology from a Kantian Point of View: Toward a Cosmopolitan Conception of Human Nature" (chapters 6 and 7 in the present volume).

28. Wilson defends the first view (*Kant's Pragmatic Anthropology*, 62), Wood the second ("Kant and the Problem of Human Nature," 52).

29. E.g., in part I of *Religion* Kant defends at length the claim that there exists a propensity (*Hang, propensio*) to evil in human nature, one that is absent in other terrestrial beings. But insofar as this propensity "is only possible as the determination of a free power of choice" (6: 29), it is best viewed as a corollary of the more fundamental capacities of free choice and morality discussed above. For related discussion, see "Evil Everywhere: The Ordinariness of Kantian Radical Evil" (chapter 9 in this volume). Similarly, in *Proclamation of the Imminent Conclusion of a Treaty of Perpetual Peace in Philosophy* (1796) and elsewhere, Kant refers to "the property of *self-consciousness*, by which the human being is to be distinguished above all other animals, and in virtue of which he is a *rational* animal" (8: 414; cf. *Anth* 7: 127). But this capacity seems best treated as a component of Kant's conception of rationality.

30. One valuable historical study which I believe adds strong support to my position is Linden, *Untersuchungen zum Anthropologiebegriff des 18. Jahrhunderts*. In an impressive twelve-page section entitled "Anthropologie als Teilgebiet der praktischen Philosophie" (Anthropology as a Branch of Practical Philosophy), she quotes extensively from the writings of eighteen different German authors from the second half of the eighteenth century, all of whom viewed anthropology as a branch of practical philosophy, and she says, "Kant appears to be the one who first made use of the concept of a moral or practical anthropology in the context of the division of his practical philosophy" (93).

CHAPTER 1

* The origins of this essay lie in conversations that I had with Warner Wick when I was a graduate student at the University of Chicago in the late 1970s. The virtue ethics movement was beginning to pick up speed then, and Kant's ethics was uniformly criticized in the growing virtue ethics literature. At the same time, English-speaking fans of Kant were finally beginning to pay more attention to his important late work the *Doctrine of Virtue* (*Tugendlehre*, 1797), due to the simultaneous appearance of its first two complete translations into English—*The Doctrine of Virtue*, trans. Mary J. Gregor (Philadelphia: University of Pennsylvania Press, 1964) and *The Metaphysical Principles of Virtue*, trans. James Ellington (Indianapolis, IN: Bobbs-Merrill, 1964). Ellington, who had studied earlier at Chicago, notes in his "Translator's Preface" that "it was Warner Wick who first encouraged me to undertake this translation so that the English reader not proficient in German might be able to appreciate the full range of Kant's ethical thought" (vi).

Shortly after completing my doctorate at Chicago (1981), I spent an enjoyable two months as a participant in a Council for Philosophical Studies summer institute organized by Jerry Schneewind and David Hoy at Johns Hopkins University entitled Kantian Ethics: Historical and Contemporary Perspectives (1983). Among the participants was Mary Gregor, and among the guest speakers were Onora O'Neill and Otfried Höffe. At this time Alasdair MacIntyre's *After Virtue* (1981) was attracting a lot of attention among moral philosophers, including Kantians, and many of us at the summer institute were trying to find ways to craft a Kantian response to MacIntyre's claim that Kant's ethics represented the worst-case scenario of a rule ethic. "Kant's Virtue Ethics," an early version of which was presented at the summer institute, was my first effort, and in it I attempted to integrate a number of Kant-and-virtue themes that I had discussed with others, particularly Wick, Gregor, O'Neill, and Höffe. Although I thought O'Neill's claim that "Kant offers primarily an ethic of virtue" was a bit too blunt, and while I was also not persuaded that her strategy of interpreting Kant's concept of maxims as "underlying intentions" (a variation of which Höffe and Rüdiger Bittner had defended earlier) was always true to Kant's texts, I was firmly convinced that the phrase "Kant's virtue ethics," suitably qualified, made sense. Determining what qualifications were needed in order to render the phrase plausible was a project that would continue to occupy me for many years. But in hindsight, the germ of my present position is latent in this early piece: Kant's theory of human nature is darker than that of classical virtue ethicists, and this results in a different kind of virtue ethics, one that places primacy on self-constraint.

1. MacIntyre, *After Virtue*, 219, see also 42, 112.
2. Foot, *Virtues and Vices*, 1.
3. Williams, *Moral Luck*, esp. 14, 19.
4. O'Neill, "Kant after Virtue," 397, see also 396. For an earlier interpretation which also stresses the prominence of virtue (but in a less either-or manner), see Wick, "Introduction: Kant's Moral Philosophy," xi–lxii (originally published as the introduction to Kant, *The Metaphysical Principles of Virtue*, trans. Ellington).
5. For a more detailed look at this issue, see my essay "On Some Vices of Virtue Ethics."
6. Wolff, *The Autonomy of Reason*, 56–57.
7. On strength and virtue, see *MdS* 6: 390, 392, 397, 405, 407–9; *Anth* 7: 147; *Collins* 27: 300. On the accomplishment of goals, see *Gr* 4: 394.
8. Harbison, "The Good Will," 59.
9. O'Neill, "Kant after Virtue," and "Consistency in Action," 159–86; and Höffe, "Kants kategorischer Imperativ," esp. 90–92.
10. O'Neill, "Kant after Virtue," 394.
11. Ibid., 393–94.
12. Ibid., 395; Höffe, "Kants kategorischer Imperativ," 91.
13. O'Neill, "Kant after Virtue," 394, 395.
14. Kant to the contrary, Aristotelian virtue is not a mechanical habit but rather a state of character determined by a rational principle (*Nicomachean Ethics* II.6 1107a1).
15. See also *MdS* 6: 219: "all duties, just because they are duties, belong to ethics."
16. Foot, *Virtues and Vices*, 10, 14.
17. Two examples of this view are Blum, *Friendship, Altruism and Morality*; and Hinman, "On the Purity of Our Motives."
18. *Nicomachean Ethics* VI.2 1139b4–5.
19. Ameriks, "The Hegelian Critique of Kantian Morality," 11.
20. *KpV* 5: 72. Here, I am following Ameriks, 12.
21. Earlier versions of this essay were presented at the Johns Hopkins University in August 1983 (in conjunction with the Council for Philosophical Studies summer institute, "Kantian Ethics: Historical and Contemporary Perspectives"), and at the 1984 Northern New England Philosophy Association meeting at Plymouth State College in New Hampshire. I would like to thank Marcia Baron, Ludwig Siep, Warner Wick, and the editor of *Philosophy* for valuable criticisms of earlier drafts.

CHAPTER 2

* This essay was originally presented at a conference called Moralische Motivation: Kants Ethik in der Diskussion, held at Philipps-Universität Marburg in Germany on March 24–27, 2004, in honor of the bicentenary of Kant's death. Two of the conference organizers—Heiner

F. Klemme and Manfred Kuehn—had included my essay "Kant's Virtue Ethics" in an earlier anthology that they co-edited, *Immanuel Kant II: Practical Philosophy*, and they suggested that I revisit the topic of Kant and virtue ethics in my conference paper. The virtue ethics literature had grown enormously since my earlier work in this area in the 1980s, and their invitation provided me with the opportunity to reassess my position by contrasting it with more recent work on the virtues. Back in 1991 I enjoyed a wonderful summer studying German in Marburg at a small language school (SPEAK + Write Gesellschaft für Sprachunterricht) as part of my sponsored research with the Alexander von Humboldt Fellowship program. On my return visit to Marburg, in part as a token of appreciation to my language instructors, I opted to present my paper in German. At first, my effort was enthusiastically embraced by the predominantly German audience. But during the discussion following my presentation, it quickly became apparent that I still had a long way to go in my quest to understand philosophical German. The year 2004 was a busy one for Kant scholars, and another bicentennial symposium in which I was invited to participate shortly after the Marburg conference was the Beijing International Symposium on Kant's Moral Philosophy, held at Peking University on May 17–19, 2004, and organized by Xu Xiangdong and Thomas Pogge. For this occasion, I prudently decided to present an English version of my Marburg paper. In "Moral Strength" I return to an important Kantian theme that I first learned about in conversations with Warner Wick at Chicago: the foundational role of duties to oneself. Kant's conception of ethics, or at least of ethics as it confronts human beings, is one of self-constraint, and his definition of virtue as moral strength (viz., the strength to constrain and govern oneself in order to act rightly) does establish a clear path for a virtue ethics reading of his ethics. But while this project of self-constraint and self-governance, when pursued properly, certainly entails a positive role for emotions such as pleasure, joy, and awe in human ethical life, it is also motivated by a darker view of human nature than one finds in both traditional and mainstream virtue ethics programs. Excavating further details of Kant's view of human nature, particularly as it relates to his ethical theory, would become the focus of my own work.

1. For Kant as deontologist, see, e.g., Rawls, *A Theory of Justice*, esp. 31n16; and Darwall, *Deontology*, "Part I: Classical Sources," 11–33. The anti-deontology remarks cited above are from Herman, "Leaving Deontology Behind," in her *The Practice of Moral Judgment*, 210; Hare, "Could Kant Have Been a Utilitarian?" 92; Guyer, "Kant's Morality of Law and Morality of Freedom," 133 (Guyer's essay was first published in *Kant and Critique*); and Wood, *Kant's Ethical Thought*, 414n14, see also 114, 327. For further discussion, see Cummiskey, *Kantian Consequentialism*; and Kagan, "Kantianism for Consequentialists."

2. Kuehn, *Kant: A Biography*, 402. Similarly, Christine Swanton writes: "the differences between virtue ethics and Kantianism have I think been overdrawn" (*Virtue Ethics*, 5).

3. See my "Kant's Virtue Ethics" (chapter 1 of this volume), and "Kantian Virtue," in Louden, *Morality and Moral Theory*, 41–44.

4. McAleer, "Kant and Virtue Ethics," 261. Here, McAleer is essentially applying Gary Watson's account of virtue ethics to Kant. Watson, in "On the Primacy of Character," states that an ethics of virtue is committed to "the claim that action appraisal is derivative from the appraisal of character. To put the matter another way, the claim is that the basic moral facts are facts about the quality of character" (452). For similar definitions of virtue ethics, see my "On Some Vices of Virtue Ethics," esp. 203 (a German version of this essay is available in *Tugendethik*, ed. Rippe and Schaber); Slote, "Agent-Based Virtue Ethics," 239; Oakley, "Varieties of Virtue Ethics," 129; and Hursthouse, *On Virtue Ethics*, 28.

5. Schopenhauer, *On the Basis of Morality* (1841), 58–60; Sidgwick, *The Methods of Ethics*, 7; Mill, *On Liberty* (1859), 77; Singer, *Generalization in Ethics*, 312 (this book reprints his earlier essay "On Duties to Oneself"); Williams, *Ethics and the Limits of Philosophy*, 50, 182; Williams, *Morality: An Introduction to Ethics*, 75. For discussion, see Denis, *Moral Self-Regard*.

6. Baier, in *The Moral Point of View*, asserts that "a world of Robinson Crusoes has no need for a morality and no use for one" (215).

7. Reath, "Self-Legislation and Duties to Oneself"; and Potter, "Duties to Oneself." See also Paton, "A Reconsideration"; and Arntzen, "Kant on Duty to Oneself."

8. Georg Ludwig Collins was enrolled as a student at the Albertina University in Königsberg in 1784, and the title page of these lectures in the Academy edition reads (in part): "Königsberg im Wintersemester 1784 und 1785" (27: 241). However, Werner Stark believes that they were actually delivered by Kant a decade earlier. In a brief discussion of *Collins*, he writes: "Datum der Vorlesung: 1774/75 [?]" ("Kants Moralkolleg der 1770er Jahre," 98). If the *Collins* lectures were indeed delivered in 1774–1775, then I think it is also the case that Kant's views about the importance of duties to oneself (and, by extension, his views about virtue) did not change substantially after 1774. Other ethics lectures in which duties to oneself are discussed include *Mrongovius* (29: 618–19) and, more extensively, *Vigilantius* (27: 510, 579, 583–87, 592–93, 600–668).

9. Cf. Paton, "A Reconsideration," 227; Potter, "Duties to Oneself," 388; and Reath, "Self-Legislation and Duties to Oneself," 349, who all agree on this point.

10. E.g., Paton, "A Reconsideration," 228; Reath, "Self-Legislation and Duties to Oneself," 352.

11. As Denis notes: "we should avoid taking Kant's comments about the importance of duties to oneself as having direct implications for a procedure for deciding between the performance of self—and other-regarding duties" (*Moral Self-Regard*, 160).

12. For a slightly more upbeat discussion, see my "Perfecting Others," in Louden, *Kant's Impure Ethics*, 56, 58–59. See also Frierson, *Freedom and Anthropology*, esp. chapter 4.

13. Schneewind, "The Misfortunes of Virtue," reprinted in *Virtue Ethics*, ed. Crisp and Slote, 199.

14. Watson, "On the Primacy of Character," 452. See also Swanton, *Virtue Ethics*, 5, and n. 4, above.

15. E.g., Hursthouse, in "Virtue Ethics and the Emotions," writes: "The virtues (and vices) are all dispositions not only to act, but to feel emotions" (108).

16. Nussbaum, *Upheavals of Thought*, 172, cf. 232. See also her "Virtue Ethics: A Misleading Category?" esp. 172–73.

17. It should be noted that Kant himself does not generally use the term "emotion," but rather other terms such as "inclinations," "affects," "passions," and "moral feelings." On his view, what we pre-analytically call "emotions" are a wide variety of states, each of which requires a different model of analysis. For discussion, see Borges, "What Can Kant Teach Us about Emotions?"

18. Rawls, *Lectures on the History of Moral Philosophy*, 232. See also Baron's discussion of these passages in her *Kantian Ethics Almost without Apology*, 199ff. According to Rawls, Kant's Manichean (or what I have called anti-emotion) moral psychology crops up only occasionally in *Gr* and *KpV*, and is later abandoned in the *Religion* (Rawls, *Lectures on the History of Moral Philosophy*, 291, 303; see also Silber, "The Ethical Significance of Kant's *Religion*," esp. cxii–cxiv). However, it is not at all clear that Kant's moral psychology undergoes a radical shift (from anti-emotion to pro-emotion or, as Rawls would have it, from Manichean to Augustinian) between the 1780s and the 1790s. E.g., in *Anthropology from a Pragmatic Point of View* (published five years after *Religion*), he still refers to "the deceiver in ourselves, the inclinations" (7: 151).

19. Cf. Stohr, "Virtue Ethics and Kant's Cold-Hearted Benefactor," 199–200; and Sherman, *Making a Necessity of Virtue*, 149. At the beginning of her essay, Stohr criticizes Sherman's account of Kant on virtue and emotion as being "mistaken in important ways" (187). But on this key point, Stohr is in agreement with Sherman.

20. Cf. Engstrom, "The Inner Freedom of Virtue," 313. See also Sherman's discussion of respect as a distinct moral emotion in *Making a Necessity of Virtue*, esp. 176; and in her "Concrete Kantian Respect."

21. Cf. Baron's discussion in "Kantian Ethics and Virtue Ethics," 45; and Sherman, "Kantian Virtue," esp. 276.

22. Contra Korsgaard, who claims that Kant "doesn't make the distinction between continence and virtue" ("From Duty and for the Sake of the Noble," 223).

23. Cf. Engstrom, "The Inner Freedom of Virtue," 307–8; and Munzel, *Kant's Conception of Character*, 167. See also Johnson, "Kant's Conception of Virtue," 375–77, for further differences between Kantian virtue and Aristotelian continence.

24. See also Engstrom's comment on this passage in "The Inner Freedom of Virtue," 289n2.

25. Cf. O'Neill, who writes in her "Kant's Virtues" that virtue is "enactable only through a certain sort of effort which nobody else can supply for us" (96). However, on Kant's view the self-acquisition of virtue is also compatible with its teachability. In *MdS* he writes: "That virtue can and must be *taught* already follows from its not being innate" (6: 477). But to make these views consistent, "teaching virtue" needs to be interpreted as consisting of attempts to get students to exercise their autonomous choice.

26. See, e.g., Nietzsche, *On the Genealogy of Morality*, "Third Treatise: What Do Ascetic Ideals Mean?" sec. 27.

27. See Johnson, "Kant's Conception of Virtue," 376–77.

28. Bernard Williams, "Evolution, Ethics, and the Representation Problem," in his *Making Sense of Humanity*, 104. For rejoinders, see Louden, *Kant's Impure Ethics*; and Louden, "The Critique of the Morality System."

29. Oakley, "Varieties of Virtue Ethics," 128.

30. Nussbaum, "Virtue Ethics: A Misleading Category?" 201, 168.

31. See, e.g., Louden, "Virtue Ethics and Anti-Theory"; and Louden, "Virtue Ethics."

32. Anscombe, "Modern Moral Philosophy," reprinted in *Virtue Ethics*, ed. Crisp and Slote, 26–44, at 26. (Anscombe's essay is often regarded as marking the beginning of the contemporary virtue ethics movement.) Hume, "My Own Life" (1776), xxxiv.

33. See O'Neill, "Kant's Virtues," 84n14.

34. See Wood, "Self-Love, Self-Benevolence, and Self-Conceit," 158.

CHAPTER 3

* This essay started out as a contribution to an Author Meets Critics session at the 2006 American Philosophical Association Pacific Division meeting in Portland, Oregon. Patrick Frierson and I were the critics, and we were invited to discuss author Jeanine Grenberg's book *Kant and the Ethics of Humility*. Grenberg's interpretation of Kant's ethics is similar to mine in many basic respects. For instance, we both read Kant's ethics as a kind of virtue ethics, we both believe that his empirical account of human nature is fundamentally important for his ethical theory, and we both hold that Kant's account of radical evil is an important chapter in his theory of human nature. But because my assigned role in the APA symposium was one of critic rather than supporter, this chapter focuses primarily on the differences between rather than the similarities of our respective readings of Kant's ethics. I discuss five points of disagreement in some detail, but I think the key difference in our perspectives can be summed up by saying that we disagree about the precise contours of Kant's virtue ethics. On Grenberg's view humility is Kant's central virtue; whereas on my view it is courage or what Kant often calls "moral strength." In arguing that courage rather than humility is Kant's central virtue, I am also claiming that his ethics owes important debts to Christian ethics and to ancient Greek and Roman ethics; Kant is somewhere in between Aristotle and Paul. After the APA session, Grenberg, Frierson, and I were invited to contribute shortened versions of our presentations for a book symposium discussion in *Philosophy and Phenomenological Research*. The present version of the essay restores most of the deletions that were made in the abridged version published in *Philosophy and Phenomenological Research*. It is not exactly the same as the original APA presentation, but it comes very close.

1. As Allen Wood notes, "in this passage there is every reason to believe that the Deity is explicitly to be included in the referent of the phrase 'whoever it may be.' One of Kant's most persistent criticisms of traditional religious services and petitionary prayer is the way extravagant praise of God and self-belittlement are combined with wheedling solicitations of (self-confessedly undeserved) divine aid" (*Kant's Ethical Thought*, 368n23).

2. See also the *Kaehler Nachschrift* in Kant, *Vorlesung zur Moralphilosophie*, where a virtually identical passage occurs on 184. (Future references to *Kaehler* are cited in the body of the text by title and page number.)

3. Hume, *An Enquiry Concerning the Principles of Morals*, in his *Enquiries Concerning Human Understanding and Concerning the Principles of Morals*, 270. See also Grenberg, *Kant and the Ethics of Humility*, 1–2 (hereafter cited in the body of the text by page number).

4. See also Kant's criticisms of "monkish ascetics [*Mönchsasketik*]" at MdS 6: 485 and of "distorted forms of virtue" at Anth 7: 282.

5. Langton, *Kantian Humility*, 14. See also Grenberg, *Kant and the Ethics of Humility*, 23.

6. Grenberg herself mentions yet another reason for being wary about Kantian moral humility when she writes: "Some may find it curious to appeal to Kantian themes to make sense out of humility. Kant's ideas are often linked to an excessive emphasis on autonomy of person, which leads to an unattractive image of the self-sufficient, hermetically sealed autonomous agent who needs no one but himself; and the thought that this same thinker could provide the tools for understanding the virtue of humility may strike some as curious and unlikely" (*Kant and the Ethics of Humility*, 144).

7. Mill, *On Liberty*, 59.

8. I defend this position in "Kant's Virtue Ethics," chapter 1 in this volume. See also Grenberg, *Kant and the Ethics of Humility*, 57, 58, 62.

9. O'Neill, "Kant's Virtues," 84, see also 94.

10. For related discussion, see "Moral Strength: Virtue as a Duty to Oneself," chapter 2 in this volume.

11. For a related discussion and references, see my "Morality and the Sublime," in Louden, *Kant's Impure Ethics*, 118–25.

12. A qualifying adjective of this sort is needed in talking about Kantian moral humility, since on Kant's view some sorts of humility are proper and others are not. For related discussion, see Hill, *Autonomy and Self-Respect*, 112–15. Hill writes: "By 'proper humility' I mean that sort and degree of humility that is a morally admirable character trait. How precisely to define this is, of course, a controversial matter; but the point for present purposes is just to set

aside obsequiousness, false modesty, underestimation of one's abilities, and the like" (112n13). See also Grenberg, *Kant and the Ethics of Humility*, 184, 199.

13. Hegel, *Elements of the Philosophy of Right* (1821), § 135.

14. Williams, *Making Sense of Humanity*, 104. For further discussion, see "The Second Part of Morals" and "Applying Kant's Ethics: The Role of Anthropology," chapters 5 and 6 in this volume.

15. Wood, *Kant's Ethical Thought*, 402n7.

16. Yet she also states later that "Wood is right, though, that it is not the simple fact of being desiring beings that accounts for radical evil. But this was never claimed by . . . Kant" (42). This latter claim strikes me as basically correct, but it unfortunately contradicts the passages on 31 and 32.

17. For further discussion, see my "On the Radical Evil in Human Nature," in Louden, *Kant's Impure Ethics*, 132–39. See also "Evil Everywhere: The Ordinariness of Kantian Radical Evil," chapter 9 in this volume.

18. Wood, *Kant's Ethical Thought*, 286. Here, Grenberg is closer to Henry Allison, who holds that it is impossible to attribute a propensity to good "to finite, sensuously affected agents such as ourselves" (*Kant's Theory of Freedom*, 155). Wood labels Allison's argument "especially unpromising" (402n7).

19. See Wood, *Kant's Ethical Thought*, 135–37.

20. Here, she parts ways with Wood, who holds that in Kant's ethics "every comparison between people drops out" (*Kant's Ethical Thought*, 137). See Grenberg, *Kant and the Ethics of Humility*, 212.

21. See my "Go-Carts of Judgment." See also "Making the Law Visible: The Role of Examples in Kant's Ethics," chapter 8 in this volume.

22. For discussion, see my "Morality and Oneself," in Louden, *Morality and Moral Theory*, 13–26. See also chapters 1 and 2 in this volume.

23. O'Neill, "Kant's Virtues," 95.

CHAPTER 4

* This essay began as an invited comment on Jeanine Grenberg's "The Social Dimensions of Courageous Humility in Jane Austen's *Mansfield Park*," presented at the Conference on Virtue and Social Diversity, Florida State University, March 2007. After the conference, the organizers, Joshua Gert and Victoria Costa, encouraged me to expand on my remarks and submit the results for a special issue of *Social Theory and Practice* for which they were guest editors. The essay is in part a further exploration of some of the virtue ethics themes first examined in "Kantian Moral Humility: Between Aristotle and Paul" (chapter 3 in this volume), approached this time not through Grenberg's book *Kant and the Ethics of Humility*, but through her interpretation of Austen's novel *Mansfield Park*. Essentially, Grenberg argues that the main character in the novel, Fanny Price, is Kantian in her moral orientation, while I offer several reasons for skepticism about this interpretation. Additionally, the broader theme of literature and ethics—to which Kantians are often thought to be hostile—also looms large in this piece. Does literature have unique moral insights to teach us, insights which the abstract arguments and principles of moral philosophy are unable to articulate? Is exposure to and reflection on moral dilemmas as presented in works of fiction sufficient for moral education, or is there a further need for exposure to and reflection on philosophical principles and theories of ethics? What were Kant's views about the role of novels in moral education? I argue that although Kant's published statements on these matters are somewhat inconsistent (and sometimes

hilarious), in his anthropology lectures he does speak strongly in defense of the new genre of novels as being one of the most important sources of insight into human nature. There is thus good reason to believe that, had he lived to see the publication of *Mansfield Park*, he would have welcomed rather than shunned it.

1. This term is related to *Schwärmerei*, traditionally rendered as "enthusiasm." Throughout the Enlightenment, "enthusiasm" had strongly negative connotations and was used in a sense closer to our "religious fanaticism." As Locke wrote: "This I take to be properly enthusiasm, which, though founded neither on reason nor divine revelation, but rising from the conceits of a warmed or over-weening brain, works yet, where it once gets footing, more powerfully on the persuasions and actions of men, than either of those two, or both together"; *An Essay Concerning Human Understanding* (1689), IV.xix.7.

2. Friedrich Theodor Rink, a former student and early biographer of Kant, also notes that Kant's observations about human nature in his anthropology lectures were sometimes "borrowed from the best English novel writers [*Romanschreiber*]" (*Ansichten aus Immanuel Kants Leben*, 46).

3. For related discussion, see my "Anthropology from a Kantian Point of View: Toward a Cosmopolitan Conception of Human Nature," chapter 7 in this volume. At the same time, Kant warns that care must be exercised in reading novels, "for novels heat up the passions and present humanity in exaggerated features" (*Mrongovius* 25: 1213; see also *Anth* 7: 121). When we turn to novels to learn about human nature, we need to factor in this "exaggeration factor." Kant's criticisms of novels were far from unique. Throughout the Enlightenment, as Robert Bledsoe notes, "the novel was often accused of over-stimulating the imagination, and excessive reading of novels was frequently associated with a loss of self-control" ("Harnessing Autonomous Art," 481).

4. However, "Elinor and Marianne," a first version of *Sense and Sensibility*, was written in 1795.

5. Fielding is referred to three times (7: 163, 164, 232), Richardson twice (7: 121, 163).

6. Grenberg, *Kant and the Ethics of Humility*, 7.

7. See "Kantian Moral Humility: Between Aristotle and Paul" (chapter 3 in this volume). For more on Kantian virtue as courage, see "Moral Strength: Virtue as a Duty to Oneself" (chapter 2 in this volume).

8. Grenberg, "Courageous Humility in Jane Austen's *Mansfield Park*," 650n12.

9. It is not entirely new. At two points in her earlier analysis of virtue in *Kant and the Ethics of Humility*, Grenberg refers to "courageous humility" (74, 91–93). However, as her book title indicates, in the earlier discussion she clearly gives pride of place to humility.

10. One important aspect of Grenberg's paper not addressed in my response concerns her discussion of Kant's thesis of radical evil. Briefly, while I agree with her that Kantian radical evil does have "nonsocial, individualistic dimensions" ("Courageous Humility in Jane Austen's *Mansfield Park*," 648), I do not endorse her view that evil can be reduced to "the general tendency to place concerns for self above concerns for morality" (ibid., 647). Evil is not mere selfishness. As Richard J. Bernstein notes, "It is difficult to see how the incentives that motivate fanatics and terrorists who are willing to sacrifice themselves for some cause or movement can be accounted for by self-love" (*Radical Evil*, 42). While Kant is not entirely consistent on this point, I do not believe that he simply equates evil with self-love. Rather, as he states, evil occurs whenever human beings act on "incentives other than the law (for example, ambition, self-love in general, yes, even a good-hearted instinct such as compassion" (*Rel* 6: 30–31). For discussion, see my "On the Radical Evil in Human Nature," in Louden, *Kant's Impure Ethics*, 132–39, and "Evil Everywhere: The Ordinariness of Kantian Radical Evil" (chapter 9 in this volume).

11. Grenberg, "Courageous Humility in Jane Austen's *Mansfield Park,*" 666.

12. The Latin *virtus* (virtue) comes from *vir* (man), and the Greek *andreios* (courageous) comes from *anēr* (man).

13. Kant seems to be on shaky ground here. On the one hand, he worries that people will "go into raptures" while reading novels (*Päd* 9: 473; see n. 1, above); yet, on the other hand, he approves of people being enraptured by a feeling of the sublimity of their own vocation. What gives? Note first that the relevant German term in each passage is different (*herumschwärmen*, *hinreißt*). Briefly, I believe his considered view is that if one is led to raptures through a *rejection* of reason (which is what *herumschwärmen* implies), then it is a bad thing. However, if one is led to raptures *by means of* reason (which is what happens in the *Religion* passage—here, agents are reflecting on their capacities of moral agency), then it is a good thing. I thank Joshua Gert for conversation on this topic.

14. Grenberg, *Kant and the Ethics of Humility*, 150; see also 116, 143.

15. This is the date that is listed in the Academy edition at 27: 240. However, Werner Stark has argued that this lecture dates from 1774–1775. See Kant, *Vorlesung zur Moralphilosophie*, ed. Stark, 403–4.

16. Stark, in his edition of this text, suggests that Kant is borrowing here from Erasmus, *Of Free Will* (1524). Erasmus cautions readers to avoid both the Scylla of pride and the Charybdis of despair or indifference (*Vorlesung zur Moralphilosophie*, 186n121).

17. Stark's hypothesis concerning the date of the lecture (see n. 15, above) is perhaps relevant here. Kant's conception of virtue as courage is definitely part of his mature (post-*Groundwork*) moral philosophy.

18. References to *Mansfield Park* (MP) are cited in the body of the text by page number in the following edition: Austen, *Mansfield Park*, ed. Sutherland.

19. Grenberg, "Courageous Humility in Jane Austen's *Mansfield Park,*" 656, quoting MacIntyre, *After Virtue*, 240. See also Emsley, *Jane Austen's Philosophy of the Virtues*, who argues that the answers that Jane Austen's heroines offer to questions about how to live are "consistent with the approaches to ethics proposed by Aristotle and St. Thomas Aquinas, rather than with a utilitarian or Kantian approach to ethics" (3–4). Samuel Louis Goldberg, on the other hand, is not persuaded: "Wanting to see Jane Austen as an 'Aristotelian' moralist like himself, MacIntyre gives little or no weight to all the pointed references to 'principle'" in *Mansfield Park* (*Agents and Lives*, 282).

20. Ryle, "Jane Austen and the Moralists," 118. For general discussion, see Knox-Shaw, "Philosophy."

21. Eva Dadlez, unpublished manuscript. I am grateful to Dadlez for allowing me to take a look at her manuscript on Austen and Hume. Ruderman, in *The Pleasures of Virtue*, also argues against an Austen-Kant connection. "Austen, unlike Kant," she claims, "goes out of her way to show how virtue benefits the doer" (6). "She [Austen] would not say, with Kant, that an action lacked moral worth if it was done out of inclination, and not purely from duty" (115).

22. Sutherland, "Introduction," in Austen, *Mansfield Park*, xvii.

23. Butler, *Jane Austen and the War of Ideas*, 298.

24. Tony Tanner, "The Quiet Thing: *Mansfield Park*," in Tanner, *Jane Austen*, 143. (Tanner's essay is also reprinted as an appendix to the Penguin edition of *Mansfield Park*.)

25. Description in Emsley, *Jane Austen's Philosophy of the Virtues*, 107. (Emsley goes on to argue that this view of Fanny is mistaken.)

26. Trilling, "Mansfield Park," in his *The Opposing Self*, 212. See also Emsley, *Jane Austen's Philosophy of the Virtues*, 180n1.

27. Another possibility, at least in the case of Kant: Kant asserts repeatedly that the moral principles he puts forward and defends are reached through a descriptive analysis of what "common human reason [*die gemeine Menschenvernunft*]" already holds to be true. For instance, when a proto-version of the categorical imperative is first introduced in the *Groundwork of the Metaphysics of Morals*, he asserts that "common human reason" always has this principle "before its eyes" and already uses it "as the norm for its appraisals" (4: 403–4). If Austen (or one of the characters in her novels) were to make a similar claim on behalf of the source of her own moral outlook, one could establish a "Kantian" connection in this manner. But even here, the connection would be merely coincidental, unless Austen or the character in question were to explicitly say: "And I follow Kant here." For discussion, see my "*Gemeine Menschenvernunft* and *Ta Endoxa*," in Louden, *Morality and Moral Theory*, 116–20. I thank Anthony Rudd for discussion on this topic.

28. Wilde, preface to *The Picture of Dorian Gray*, in *The Portable Oscar Wilde*, 138.

29. MacIntyre, *After Virtue*, 240. See Grenberg, "Courageous Humility in Jane Austen's *Mansfield Park*," 656. Goldberg, on the other hand, argues that MacIntyre's reading of Fanny's rejection of Henry Crawford is a "patent inaccuracy." See *Agents and Lives*, 282. For additional responses to MacIntyre, see Emsley, *Jane Austen's Philosophy of the Virtues*, 180n12.

30. MacIntyre, *After Virtue*, 236. For a rejoinder, see my "Kant's Virtue Ethics" (chapter 1 in this volume).

31. Grenberg, *Kant and the Ethics of Humility*, 7.

32. Grenberg, "Courageous Humility in Jane Austen's *Mansfield Park*," 656.

33. Ibid., 665.

34. Grenberg, I think, over-moralizes Fanny's decision not to marry Crawford when she states: "Fanny has good *moral* reasons *never* to feel love for Henry. Her choice to reject him is thus in at least short-term tension with her happiness, since rejecting him involves being at odds with everyone around her" (ibid., 664). Agreed, but sometimes one needs to accept a short-term tension with one's happiness in order to better promote, in the long term, one's greatest well-being. At bottom, Fanny simply does not love Crawford. "She told him [Crawford], that she did not love him, could not love him, was sure she never should love him: that such a change was quite impossible" (*MP*, 302). Also, by the end of the novel, it is clear that Fanny has made the right choice. For now, she is happy: "there was happiness . . . which no description can reach. Let no one presume to give the feelings of a young woman on receiving the assurance of that affection of which she has scarcely allowed herself to entertain a hope" (*MP*, 437).

35. See, e.g., *Apology* 38a. As Hilary Putnam notes, "the earlier Platonic enlightenment" shares with the "seventeenth- and eighteenth-century enlightenment, the Enlightenment with a capital 'E,' . . . the same aspiration to reflective transcendence, the same willingness to criticize conventional beliefs and institutions, and to propose radical reforms" (*Ethics without Ontology*, 94).

36. Eva Dadlez also analyzes this passage to good effect in her manuscript. She too concludes, though for different reasons from those that I offer, that it does not warrant us to assert a connection between the moral outlooks of Austen and of Kant.

37. See nn. 24–26, above. (I thank Simon Keller for raising this issue.)

38. Schiller, *Sämtliche Werke*, 1: 299–300. See also Paton, "Misunderstandings," in Paton, *The Categorical Imperative*, 48–50. For a more recent discussion, see Beiser, "Dispute with Kant," in his *Schiller as Philosopher*, 169–90. Beiser argues that many readers "have completely misunderstood Schiller's dispute with Kant" (170), and that "there was indeed a great deal of agreement between Kant and Schiller" (171).

39. See n. 25, above. On the last page of the novel, for instance, after Fanny and Edmund are married, their happiness is described as being "as secure as earthly happiness can be. – Equally formed for domestic life, and attached to country pleasures, their home was the home of affection and comfort" (*MP*, 439). Fanny's tranquility simply does not square with the derogatory picture of her that Trilling and others have painted.

40. I thank Claudia Schmidt and Nancy Gish for suggestions and advice on approaching *Mansfield Park*.

CHAPTER 5

* This essay was one of the first Kant pieces that I wrote after *Kant's Impure Ethics* (2000), and it went through several stages of development. It began as an invited paper presented to the North American Kant Society session at the American Philosophical Association Central Division meeting in Minneapolis, May 2001. In June 2002, I presented a revised version (under the title "'The Second Part of Morals': Kant's Moral Anthropology and Its Relationship to His Metaphysics of Morals") in Brazil—first as the keynote address to the IV Colóquio Kant at the Universidade Estadual de Campinas, and then as an invited lecture to the Philosophy Department at Universidade Federal de Santa Catarina. Zeljko Loparic and Maria Borges were my hosts for this visit. I had never traveled to Brazil before and was quite impressed with the high quality of Kant scholarship and discussion that I experienced during my trip. The English version of my Brazil lecture was later published in *Kant e-Prints* 1.2 (2002): 1–13; a Portuguese translation also appeared in *ethic@: Revista International de Filosofia da Moral* 1.1 (2002): 27–46 (www.cfh.ufsc.br/ethic/@). The final version of the essay was initially published in a volume devoted to Kant's lectures on anthropology: *Essays on Kant's Anthropology*, ed. Brian Jacobs and Patrick Kain.

In this piece, I pursue a key theme initiated in *Kant's Impure Ethics*: What is the import of Kant's lectures on anthropology for his ethical theory? What are the central connections between his work in anthropology and his moral philosophy? I am particularly concerned to elucidate Kant's claim that within his anthropological writings we find "the second part of morals," and to defend the coherence of his claim against a variety of criticisms of it by Kant scholars. In a broader sense—and this point holds for all of the essays in part II of this volume—my concern now is with the impact of Kant's views about human nature for his ethical theory. In what specific ways does his account of human nature influence his ethical theory? Any convincing positive answer to this question must also be made consistent with Kant's repeated remarks concerning the need for "a pure moral philosophy, completely cleansed of everything that may be only empirical and that belongs to anthropology" (*Gr* 4: 389).

1. For instance, in the opening section of the *Menschenkunde*, to which Brandt and Stark assign a tentative date of 1781–1782, Kant states: "Knowledge of the human being we designate with a general name 'anthropology,' which is not taught at any other academy" (25: 856; see also *Friedländer* 25: 472; *Mrongovius* 25: 1210–11). And in a frequently cited letter to Marcus Herz written toward the end of 1773, Kant announces: "this winter for the second time I am giving a lecture course on anthropology, which I now intend to make into a proper academic discipline" (10: 138).

2. In the letter to Herz cited in n. 1, Kant also asserts that his intention is "to disclose through anthropology the sources of all the sciences [*die Quellen aller Wissenschaften*], of ethics, of skill, of human relations, of the method of education and governing human beings, and therefore of everything that pertains to the practical" (10: 138). So even in 1773, he pins very high hopes on anthropology. But it is also the case that much of the material in the

lectures is best described as informal, empirical, layperson-friendly science rather than as *transcendental* anthropology.

3. Erdmann, *Reflexionen Kants zur Anthropologie*, 37. On this point, I think a comparative analysis of the different versions of the anthropology lectures falsifies Erdmann's claim.

4. Brandt, "Einleitung," xlvi. See also his "Ausgewählte Probleme der Kantischen Anthropologie," 29. Although I do concur with Brandt's basic contention that "pragmatic anthropology is not systematically integrated with Kant's philosophy" ("Einleitung," xlvii), I think it is a mistake to place so much weight on the issue of whether certain words do or do not appear in a text. A given topic can be addressed using many different words, and it would be unwise to conclude, for example, that an English author has nothing at all to say about the idea of God just because the word "God" doesn't appear in his texts.

5. Arnoldt, *Kritische Excurse im Gebiete der Kant-Forschung*, 351. See also Hinske's criticisms of Arnoldt's long-winded attempt to resolve this dilemma in "Kants Idee der Anthropologie," 426n30.

6. Here, I am basically in agreement with Wolfgang Becker, who notes that "a 'practical anthropology' must, in its conception, in its systematic method, and in its carrying-out, be tied much more tightly to moral philosophy than is the case with [Kant's] *Anthropology [from a Pragmatic Point of View]*." "Einleitung: Kants pragmatische Anthropologie," 14. I would also extend this remark to cover all of Kant's anthropology *Nachshriften* as well.

7. A familiar word of caution bears repeating here. Obviously, one needs to be careful in citing from Kantian lectures that Kant himself did not publish. Kant, in another letter to Herz (October 20, 1778), sounds an appropriate warning: "Those of my students who are most capable of grasping everything are just the ones who bother least to take explicit and verbatim notes; rather, they write down only the main points, which they can think over afterward. Those who are most thorough in note-taking are seldom capable of distinguishing the important from the unimportant. They pile a mass of misunderstood stuff under that which they may possibly have grasped correctly" (10: 242; cf. Kant's letter to Herz of August 28, 1778, at 10: 240–42).

8. Mellin, *Enzyclopädisches Wörterbuch der kritischen Philosophie*, 1: v. See also Mellin's letter to Kant of September 6, 1797: "I permit myself to send you the enclosed copy of [the first volume of] my *Encyclopedic Dictionary of Critical Philosophy*. . . . I flatter myself that I have seized the spirit of this philosophy through a continuous, twelve-year study of it and that I have understood your writings, at least for the most part, deeply esteemed professor" (12: 195–96; cf. 12: 234, 303–4).

9. Mellin, *Enzyclopädisches Wörterbuch*, 1: 277, 279.

10. Ibid., 1: 280.

11. Schmid, *Wörterbuch zum leichtern Gebrauch der kantischen Schriften*, 62–63. The first edition of this work appeared in 1788.

12. Willich, *Elements of the Critical Philosophy*, iii, 140. As noted previously (n. 1), Brandt and Stark assign a tentative date of 1781–1782 to the *Menschenkunde*. They also assign a date of 1777–1778 to the *Pillau* manuscript. So it is probable that Willich sat in on either or both of these versions of Kant's anthropology lectures.

13. Paton, *The Categorical Imperative*, 32.

14. Gregor, *Laws of Freedom*, 8. Gregor dedicated *Laws of Freedom* "to H. J. Paton" (v), and co-dedicated her translation of Kant's *Anthropology from a Pragmatic Point of View* to the memory of her "father and of Professor H. J. Paton" (v).

15. As one might expect, for the most part Kant does "focus on the negative" here—that is, he devotes far more discussion to species-wide hindrances to morality confronting human beings than he does to species-wide aids to morality. And while he generally succeeds in suppressing his

extraterrestrial enthusiasms in the anthropology lectures ("we have no knowledge of *non-terrestrial* rational beings"; *Anth* 7: 321, see also 7: 331; *Menschenkunde* 25: 859), it is important to remember that throughout Kant's life he maintained that human beings are only one subset of rational beings. This "human hindrances" aspect of practical anthropology does, I believe, make much more sense when placed alongside the assumption that there exists more than one species of rational moral agent. For instance, toward the end of his early work *Universal Natural History and Theory of the Heavens*, he speculates that the inhabitants of "Earth and perhaps Mars . . . would alone be in the dangerous middle road, where the temptations of sensual stimulations against the sovereignty of spirit have a strong capacity for seduction" (1: 366). The more intelligent inhabitants of Saturn, on the other hand, apparently aren't faced with such temptations. For discussion, see Larrimore, "Sublime Waste," 119–20. See also William Clark's discussion of "cosmo-anthropology" in "The Death of Metaphysics in Enlightened Prussia," 451–52.

16. But this is not exclusively the case. Statements concerning human hindrances to morality can also be found in the second main division of the lectures, "Characteristic." For example, toward the very end of the *Menschenkunde*, Kant stresses that "the human being has by nature a tendency to dissemble" (25: 1197; see also *Anth* 7: 332).

17. See also Allen Wood's important discussion of "the pluralism of reason" (*Kant's Ethical Thought*, 301–2), in which he forcefully argues against Habermas's charge that Kant's conception of philosophy is "monological" or "solipsistic." In the conclusion to his discussion of egoism in *Anthropology from a Pragmatic Point of View*, Kant states clearly that "the opposite of egoism can only be *pluralism*, i.e., the way of thinking of not being concerned with oneself as if one were the whole world, but of considering and conducting oneself as a citizen of the world. —This much belongs to anthropology" (7: 130).

18. Contra Max Weber's famous "requirement of 'value-freedom' in discussion of empirical matters" ("Value-Judgments in Social Science," 81).

19. In our own time, more and more social scientists have finally come around to the view that fiction also has truths to teach us about human nature. Moral theorists who are skeptical of the abstractions of theory frequently turn to fiction in hopes of finding a clearer illumination of the moral life. Kant's conviction that anthropology should enlist the aid of history, drama, fiction, travel books, and biography no longer sounds as strange as it once did. At the same time, in other lectures he is quite critical of novels. "Reading novels," he warns, "in addition to causing many other mental discords, also makes distraction habitual" (*Anth* 7: 208). And only adults should be allowed to read novels: "all novels should be taken out of the hands of children," on the ground that they "weaken the memory" (*Päd* 9: 473). (For related discussion, see "'Firm as a Rock in Her Own Principles'," Chapter 4 in this volume.)

20. Herman, *The Practice of Moral Judgment*, 77–78. For Kant though, *Weltkenntnis* is not typically "acquired in childhood as part of socialization." Its acquisition certainly *begins* in childhood, but, as we saw previously, what he has in mind is a more reflective knowledge of "the human being considered *cosmologically*" (*Geo* 9: 157)—a knowledge of what human beings share in common with one another and what they might be able to achieve in the future with one another. Such knowledge is not attainable by children.

21. Cf. Kaulbach, who characterizes Kant's philosophy of history as "an orientation for praxis." "Just as a traveler helps himself to a map, in order to identify the way and the destination," so, analogously, moral agents can also benefit from a map that describes the telos of their efforts ("Welche Nutzen gibt Kant der Geschichtsphilosophie?" 70, 78–79). Kant's anthropology and geography lectures also contribute to this map-making venture, Kaulbach

adds in another piece, insofar as they aim to provide the moral agent with "a plan, a map of the whole, within which one is able to determine one's own position and trace out for oneself the path by which one can reach one's chosen goals" ("Weltorientierung, Weltkenntnis und pragmatische Vernunft bei Kant," 61).

22. Mendelssohn, "Über die Frage: Was heißt aufklären?" 4.

23. Martha C. Nussbaum, "Patriotism and Cosmopolitanism," in Nussbaum with Respondents, *For Love of Country*, 7. See also her "Kant and Cosmopolitanism" (also published in German as "Kant und stoisches Weltbürgertum").

24. This passage also reflects the strong influence of Rousseau on Kant's thought. See especially part I of the *Discourse on the Sciences and the Arts* (1750), reprinted in *The Basic Writings of Jean-Jacques Rousseau*.

25. Rosen, *Kant's Theory of Justice*, 6n2. Rosen refers to KpV 5: 19 as one prominent text where this wider sense of "practical" is used: "Practical *principles* are propositions that contain a general determination of the will, having it under several practical rules" (see also *Gr* 4: 389, 400n, 420–21n).

26. See also Allen Wood's criticisms (*Kant's Ethical Thought*, 194–95) of Paton's and Gregor's rejection of Kant's claim that moral anthropology is a part of practical philosophy. I agree with Wood that the inclusion of moral anthropology as a part of practical philosophy is "both consistent with Kantian principles and quite illuminating as to the way Kant conceives of the [overall] system of moral philosophy" (195). However, our reasons for regarding moral anthropology as practical are somewhat different. Wood brings moral anthropology into practical philosophy by arguing that it concerns not just empirical information concerning the *means* to the fulfillment of our moral duties, but also, at least in some cases, a determination of "the *content* of . . . ethical duties" (ibid.). Assuming for the moment that this claim is true (it is not uncontroversial), I don't see how it meets the challenge of Kant's narrower sense of "practical"—viz., his claim that to count as practical, rather than theoretical, something must be based "entirely [*gänzlich*] on the concept of freedom" (*KU* 5: 173). I also think that Wood tends to underestimate the force of this challenge, in suggesting that we encounter it only in "the (unpublished) first introduction" to *KU* (194).

27. Kant, *Immanuel Kants Anweisung zur Menschen und Weltkenntnis*, ed. Friedrich Christian Starke, 124. ("Starke" was a pseudonym for Johann Adam Bergk. Bergk also edited the *Menschenkunde* version of Kant's anthropology lectures, reprinted in Academy vol. 25.)

CHAPTER 6

* This essay continues the main lines of investigation pursued in the previous chapter and deals with some of the same basic issues—viz., in what ways do Kant's views about human nature inform his ethical theory? What are the specifically *moral* aspects of his work on anthropology, and how do they differ from the better-known *pragmatic* aspects? The origins of the essay lie in an invitation that I received from Graham Bird to contribute to *A Companion to Kant*, which he was editing for the Blackwell Companions to Philosophy series. My basic assignment was to discuss the role of anthropology in Kant's applied ethics. Shortly after I began working on the essay, two generous invitations to present guest lectures on Kant arrived from England. The first was an invitation to present a keynote address at the Second UK Kant Society Graduate Conference on Kant, held at the University of Hertfordshire in March 2005. Graham Bird, who was then also president of the UK Kant Society, gave the second keynote address, and Isabell Ward, the conference organizer, was my host. The second invitation came from Alix Cohen, who at the time was still a graduate student in the Department of History

and Philosophy of Science at the University of Cambridge, but has since gone on to publish a number of important pieces on Kant's empirical studies of human nature, several of which are collected in her book *Kant and the Human Sciences*. Alix organized a one-day conference at Cambridge, Kant, Morality and the Sciences, in March 2005, for which Catherine Wilson and I were keynote speakers. An earlier version of this essay was presented at each of these conferences.

1. Hegel, *Elements of the Philosophy of Right*, § 135.
2. Williams, *Making Sense of Humanity*, 104.
3. Kitcher, "Kant," 250.
4. Kant, *Groundwork for the Metaphysics of Morals* (1785), ed. Hill and Zweig 180.
5. For discussion, see Kuehn, "Einleitung."
6. Cf. Wood, *Kant's Ethical Thought*, 193–96.
7. Stark, "Historical Notes and Interpretive Questions about Kant's Lectures on Anthropology," 23.
8. For further discussion, see Louden, *Kant's Impure Ethics*, 62–70; Wood, "Kant and the Problem of Human Nature," 40–42; and Frierson, *Freedom and Anthropology*, 53–56.
9. For further discussion, see Zammito, *Kant, Herder, and the Birth of Anthropology*, 221–53.
10. Scheler, *Die Stellung des Menschen im Kosmos* (1928), 51. See also Heidegger, *Kant and the Problem of Metaphysics*, iv, xxiii, 216.
11. For related discussion, see Kain, "Prudential Reason in Kant's Anthropology."
12. Brandt, "The Guiding Idea of Kant's Anthropology," 92.
13. Cf. Jacobs, "Kantian Character and the Problem of a Science of Humanity," 112–13.
14. See also Kant, *Vorlesung zur Moralphilosophie*, 4–5, 402–4.
15. See also ibid., 6.
16. See also Frierson's discussion of this topic in *Freedom and Anthropology*, 59–61.
17. For related discussion, see "Moral Strength: Virtue as a Duty to Oneself," chapter 2 in this volume.
18. Cf. Frierson, *Freedom and Anthropology*, 57–58.
19. For further discussion, see Louden, *Kant's Impure Ethics*, 144–52.
20. See also Louden, "The Second Part of Morals," chapter 5 in this volume.
21. For related discussion, see Louden, *Kant's Impure Ethics*, 33–61, 74–82; and Frierson, *Freedom and Anthropology*, 61–64.
22. For related discussion, see Louden, "The Second Part of Morals: Kant's Moral Anthropology and its Relationship to his Metaphysics of Morals.
23. Smith, *An Inquiry into the Nature and Causes of the Wealth of Nations* (1776), 456.
24. See Weber, "Value-Judgments in Social Science" (1917).
25. See Schleiermacher, "Review of Kant's *Anthropology from a Pragmatic Point of View*" (1799).
26. See Rorty, "Keeping Philosophy Pure: An Essay on Wittgenstein," esp. 19.

CHAPTER 7

* This essay was written soon after chapter 6 ("Applying Kant's Ethics") and is a continuation of some of the same themes. Alix Cohen, whom I first met when I presented an early version of chapter 6 at a small conference that she organized at Cambridge in March 2005, was later invited to serve as guest editor for a special issue of *Studies in the History and Philosophy of Science*, "Kantian Philosophy and the Human Sciences" (39.4 [December 2008]). She invited me to contribute a piece to this project, and I used the occasion as an opportunity to dig deeper into the particular understanding of human nature advocated in Kant's anthropology.

In this essay I argue for the central importance of a cosmopolitan conception of human nature for Kant's anthropology. Although deeply rooted in a variety of Kantian texts, the cosmopolitan conception also generates several tensions within Kant's anthropology. For instance, its emphasis on wide reflective knowledge of human nature does not sit well with claims Kant makes elsewhere concerning the empirical status of his anthropology. Similarly, its strong normative dimension seems to stand in conflict with his repeated assertions that anthropology is an observation-based discipline. After establishing the central importance of Kant's underexplored cosmopolitan conception of human nature for his anthropology, I try also to defend the overall coherence of his anthropology. An earlier version of this chapter was presented as a guest lecture to the Philosophy Department at Marquette University in February 2007.

1. Quite different, that is, from Ernst Platner's *Anthropologie für Ärzte und Weltweise*, which Herz had already reviewed in *Allgemeine Deutsche Bibliothek* 20 (1773): 25–51, and to which Kant refers earlier in this same letter. I discuss the key differences between Platner's and Kant's approaches to anthropology below.

2. Physical geography and anthropology, for Kant, comprise the two kinds of knowledge of the world, or "world cognitions" (*Welterkenntnisse*). For instance, in his *Lectures on Physical Geography*, he states: "Experiences [*Erfahrungen*] of nature and of the human being together constitute the world cognitions [*Welterkenntnisse*]. Knowledge [*Kenntniß*] of the human being teaches us *anthropology*, and to knowledge of nature we owe *physical geography*" (9: 157). Kant lectured on physical geography in the summer semesters, anthropology in the winter. For general discussion of Kant's university teaching, see Kuehn, *Kant: A Biography*.

3. For further discussion of Kant's physical geography and its relation to his anthropology, see Adickes, *Untersuchungen zu Kants physischer Geographie*; May, *Kant's Concept of Geography*; and Elden and Mendieta, *Reading Kant's Geography*.

4. For further discussion of Kant's empirical psychology and its relation to his anthropology, see Kim, *Die Entstehung der Kantischen Anthropologie*; Sturm, "Kant on Empirical Psychology"; and Makkreel, "Kant on the Scientific Status of Psychology, Anthropology, and History."

5. A new translation of this work, prepared by Paul Guyer, is included in Kant, *Anthropology, History, and Education*, ed. Zöller and Louden. In his "Translator's Introduction" to the text, Guyer notes that "the work contains little by way of detailed aesthetic theory. . . . Instead, the *Observations* is really a work in what Kant would later call 'anthropology from a pragmatic point of view'" (19).

6. For further discussion of the philosophical physicians, see Zammito, *Kant, Herder, and the Birth of Anthropology*, 221–53; and Cohen, "Physiological vs. Pragmatic Anthropology: A Response to Schleiermacher's Objection to Kant's Anthropology." For discussion of Herz and the vocation of medicine, see Davis, *Identity or History? Marcus Herz and the End of the Enlightenment*, 72–144.

7. I have prepared a new English translation of this text, which appears in both Kant, *Anthropology from a Pragmatic Point of View*, ed. and trans. Louden; and Kant, *Anthropology, History, and Education*, ed. Zöller and Louden.

8. I have translated some selections from this transcription, which are in Kant, *Lectures on Anthropology*, ed. Wood and Louden.

9. La Mettrie, *Man a Machine and Man a Plant*, 29. For further discussion, see Gay, "The Enlightenment as Medicine and as Cure"; and Schings, "Der philosophische Arzt."

10. An English translation of this text, prepared by Holly Wilson, is included in Kant, *Anthropology, History, and Education*.

11. An English translation of this text, prepared by Günter Zöller, appears in ibid.
12. English translations of these three texts are also available in ibid.
13. Scheler, *Die Stellung des Menschen im Kosmos*, 51. Heidegger's *Kant and the Problem of Metaphysics* is "dedicated to the memory of Max Scheler" (iv, see also xxiii, 216).
14. For discussion and references, see Louden, *Kant's Impure Ethics*, 68–69.
15. For discussion, see "Applying Kant's Ethics: The Role of Anthropology," chapter 6 in this volume.
16. A translation of part of this transcription, prepared by Allen Wood, is in Kant, *Lectures on Anthropology*.
17. A complete translation of this transcription, prepared by G. Felicitas Munzel, appears in ibid.
18. A translation of part of this transcription, prepared by Allen Wood, appears in ibid.
19. A translation of part of this transcription, prepared by Allen Wood, appears in ibid.
20. For related discussion, see Wood, "Kant and the Problem of Human Nature," esp. 39–41.
21. For discussion, see Thorndike, "Understanding Kant's Claim," who argues that Kant's claims regarding the connection between anthropology and morality are deeply influenced by the scholastic concept of practical philosophy that Kant encountered in Alexander Gottlieb Baumgarten's texts—texts which he used for his own ethics and metaphysics courses.
22. A translation of parts of the *Collins* transcription, prepared by Allen Wood, is in Kant, *Lectures on Anthropology*.
23. Again though, the scope of pragmatic anthropology is broader than that of practical anthropology. The former concerns *all* uses to which we may put our knowledge of human nature; the latter, only moral ones.
24. A translation of the *Mrongovius* transcription, prepared by Brian Jacobs, is included in Kant, *Lectures on Anthropology*.
25. For related discussion, see Louden, *Kant's Impure Ethics*, 16–19; and "The Second Part of Morals," chapter 5 in this volume.
26. See Louden, "The Second Part of Morals."
27. A translation of this essay, prepared by Holly Wilson and Günter Zöller, is included in Kant, *Anthropology, History, and Education*, ed. Zöller and Louden.
28. A new translation of this essay, prepared by Allen Wood, appears in ibid.
29. For a good analysis of Kant's position, see Kleingeld, "Kant's Theory of Peace." See also my "Peace through Federation," in Louden, *The World We Want*, 94–106.
30. Mary Gregor, for instance, toward the end of her "Translator's Introduction" to Kant, *Anthropology from a Pragmatic Point of View*, argues that Kant's pragmatic anthropology works under the guidance of the philosophy of history, and suggests that Kant views history "as the account of what nature does to prepare the human race for its final end" (xxii). But she also holds (following her teacher H. J. Paton) that Kant's moral anthropology is simply a misnomer—it is "not ethics but rather a sort of psychology" (*Laws of Freedom*, 8; see also "Translator's Introduction," xiii). Similarly, Reinhard Brandt, in his discussion of the vocation of the human being and its central role in Kant's anthropology, rightly stresses its strong species orientation, as I have also done in the present essay. But Brandt too denies that we find a moral anthropology in any of Kant's lectures on anthropology: "in none of its phases of development is pragmatic anthropology identical with the anthropology that Kant repeatedly envisions as the complement to his moral theory after 1770" ("Einleitung," xlvi; see also Brandt, "The Guiding Idea of Kant's Anthropology," 92). Both Gregor and Brandt deny that Kant's anthropology should be viewed as the second part of morals, the empirical counterpart to pure moral philosophy.

31. See Louden, *Kant's Impure Ethics*, "The Second Part of Morals," and "Applying Kant's Ethics" (chapters 5 and 6 in this volume).

32. This passage is one of many that appears in the margins of the *Handschrift* for *Anthropology from a Pragmatic Point of View*—Kant's handwritten manuscript that formed the basis for the book published in 1798. The *Handschrift* often differs from the two editions of the *Anthropology* that were printed during Kant's lifetime, and it is not known how many of the changes between the *Handschrift* and the printed editions were approved by Kant himself. Many scholars believe that the *Handschrift* gives us a closer indication of Kant's position. In my translation of Kant, *Anthropology from a Pragmatic Point of View*, supplementary texts from the *Handschrift* are printed as footnotes—e.g., the passage cited is n. 1 on 231. For further discussion, see the "Note on the Text and Translation," ibid., xxxvi–xxxix.

CHAPTER 8

* This essay's roots lie in an invitation that I received from Jens Timmermann to contribute to a volume that he was editing for Cambridge University Press called *Kant's Groundwork of the Metaphysics of Morals: A Critical Guide* (2009). Jens and I first met in Germany back in 1991, when he was an undergraduate at the University of Göttingen and I was visiting there as an Alexander von Humboldt research scholar. He has since gone on to publish a number of important works on Kant's moral philosophy—see, e.g., *Sittengesetz und Freiheit*; *Kant's Groundwork of the Metaphysics of Morals: A Commentary*; and his co-edited anthology with Reath, *Kant's Critique of Practical Reason: A Critical Guide*. My assignment for this project was to contribute a piece on the more applied side of Kant's *Groundwork*, with special reference to the famous passage near the beginning of section II, where Kant warns readers that one could not choose a worse method for ethical theory than "wanting to derive it from examples" (4: 408). The *Popularphilosophen* of Kant's day (Christian Garve is the most prominent example) advocated a morality based on examples, as do many neo-Aristotelian virtue ethicists at present. But this methodological strategy is diametrically opposed to Kant's. Kant's main aim in the *Groundwork* is to locate and justify a "*supreme principle of morality*" (4: 392) that holds with absolute necessity for all rational beings, and any specific examples or exemplars will be too weak to ground such a principle. However, once he turns to the more terrestrial task of applying this principle to the specific contingencies of human life—a task that he undertakes not primarily in the *Groundwork* but rather in other works such as his lectures on anthropology, education, and ethics—he speaks at length on the need for examples in human moral life. Kant was thus not oblivious to the power of examples after all. I have been interested in Kant's views about examples and their role in the application of his ethical theory to human life for many years. The present essay borrows some points from my earlier articles "Go-Carts of Judgment" and "Examples in Ethics." I thank Jens Timmermann, Andreas Vieth, Norbert Mertens, and an anonymous reviewer for helpful advice, and I thank the Alexander von Humboldt Foundation for its support of an enjoyable research visit to Münster, Germany, in June–July 2007, during which time a draft of this chapter was written.

1. *Entlehnen* also means "to borrow." In citing from Kant's *Groundwork*, I have made use of both Mary J. Gregor's translation, which is included in Kant, *Practical Philosophy*, trans. and ed. Mary J. Gregor (Cambridge: Cambridge University Press, 1996), and Allen W. Wood's more recent rendering in Kant, *Groundwork for the Metaphysics of Morals*.

2. Wilde, *The Portable Oscar Wilde*, 658.

3. For further discussion, see my "*Gemeine Menschenvernunft* and *Ta Endoxa*," in Louden, *Morality and Moral Theory*, 116–20.

4. "Is the pious [*to hosion*] loved by the gods because it is pious, or is it pious because it is loved by the gods?" (Plato, *Euthyphro* 10a). See also the preface to the first edition of Kant's *Religion within the Boundaries of Mere Reason*, where he proclaims that "on its own behalf morality in no way [*keineswegs*] needs religion, ... but is rather self-sufficient by virtue of pure practical reason" (6: 3).

5. In the following discussion, except where noted otherwise, I use the term "example" broadly to refer both to exemplars (morally exceptional individuals) and to specific instances of morally praiseworthy conduct.

6. "Is the pious not the same and alike in every action, and the impious the opposite of all that is pious and like itself, and everything that is to be impious presents us with one form [*idea*] or appearance insofar as it is impious?" (Plato, *Euthyphro* 5d).

7. The debate is not new, and goes back at least as far as Plato. For more recent contributions, see Hooker and Little, *Moral Particularism*; and Dancy, *Ethics without Principles*.

8. For instance, in the *Metaphysics of Morals* Kant refers to "the indescribable beauty of plants," arguing that a propensity to wantonly destroy what is beautiful in nature is a violation of moral duty (6: 443).

9. The most significant representative of this school of thought was Christian Garve (1742–1798), a prolific translator and author who was a major contributor to German Enlightenment culture. Garve's translations of Adam Ferguson (*Institutes of Moral Philosophy*), Edmund Burke (*A Philosophical Inquiry into the Origin of Our Ideas of the Sublime and Beautiful*), and Adam Smith (*The Wealth of Nations*) were instrumental in introducing German readers to British moral philosophy and aesthetics. He also produced translations and commentaries of Aristotle's *Politics* and (at the suggestion of Frederick the Great) Cicero's *De Officiis*. His own works (none of which, alas, has been translated into English) include *Über die Verbindung der Moral mit der Politik*, *Versuche über verschiedene Gegenstände aus der Moral, Literatur und dem gesellschaftlichen Leben*, *Über Gesellschaft und Einsamkeit*, *Einige Betrachtungen über die allgemeinen Grundsätze der Sittenlehre*, and *Übersicht der vornehmsten Principien der Sittenlehre, von dem Zeitalter des Aristoteles an bis auf unsre Zeiten*. (This last book is dedicated to Kant, and concludes with a forty-three-page discussion of the alleged inadequacies of his moral system.) Garve also published one of the first reviews of Kant's *Critique of Pure Reason*, complaining in his opening sentence that the *Critique* "often strains the attention of its readers to the point of exhaustion." An English translation is available in Sassen, *Kant's Early Critics*, 53–58. The review was first published anonymously in the *Zugabe zu den Göttingischen Anzeigen von gelehrten Sachen* 1 (1782). Stung by Garve's criticisms, Kant, according to Johann Georg Hamann, set out in 1784 to produce a "counter-critique [*Antikritik*]—though the title is not yet determined—against Garve's Cicero as an indirect answer to his review [of the first *Critique*]" (Hamann to Johann George Scheffner, February 18, 1784, in Hamann, *Briefwechsel*, 5: 129; see also Kuehn, *Kant: A Biography*, 278; Timmermann, *Kant's Groundwork of the Metaphysics of Morals: A Commentary*, xxvii). The result (though the final product does not match Hamann's description), published in 1785, was the *Groundwork of the Metaphysics of Morals*. For Garve, morality was not at all a matter of pure reason, and the concept of a specifically practical reason was foreign to him. For instance, in his concluding critique of Kant's ethics in *Übersicht der vornehmsten Principien der Sittenlehre*, he writes: "In the Kantian philosophy I hear talk for the first time of a *double* reason, a theoretical and a practical, and I experience neither the essence nor the ground of this distinction" (342). Garve's stance in ethics stressed common experience over abstract reasoning, historical examples over principles. In the last sentence of *Übersicht* he summarizes his criticisms of Kant's categorical imperative: "what I *ought to do*: this I am usually taught very accurately by consideration of my special circumstances and relationships, and it would

become difficult for me and by itself impossible to infer what I ought to do from the universal relations of human beings to one another" (383). For discussion of the *Popularphilosophen*, see Beck, *Early German Philosophy*, 319–24. For more information on Garve, see Fania Oz-Salzberger's entry on Garve in the *Encyclopedia of the Enlightenment*, 2: 101–2. See also part I (8: 278–89) of *Gemeinspruch*, where Kant responds to several of Garve's criticisms of his ethics.

10. "Beyond doubt" may seem too strong, given Kant's well-known insistence on the inscrutability of our moral status: we don't know with certainty who is morally good and who is not. At *Gr* 4: 407, for instance, he asserts: "In fact, it is absolutely impossible by means of experience to make out with complete certainty a single case in which the maxim of an action otherwise in conformity with duty rested simply on moral grounds and on the representation of one's duty" (see also *MdS* 6: 392; *Rel* 6: 51). But what is placed beyond doubt is the feasibility or possibility of virtue for human beings—not its certain attainment.

11. For discussion of this second part of Kant's ethics, see Louden, *Kant's Impure Ethics*; and "The Second Part of Morals," chapter 5 in this volume.

12. The examples from *MdS* come up in one of the many "Casuistical Questions" sections that Kant intentionally weaves into his presentation "in a *fragmentary* way, not systematically" (6: 411). His goal here is to engage readers with complex moral scenarios "that call upon judgment to decide how a maxim is to be applied in particular cases" (ibid.), and it is clear that he thinks adults as well as children will benefit from, and take enjoyment in, opportunities to exercise their practical judgment skills. At the same time, as I show later, Kant also warns that an overreliance on examples tends to weaken human beings' natural capacity for judgment.

13. I have prepared a new English translation of this text, which is included in Kant, *Anthropology, History, and Education*.

14. One reader has suggested that Kant's considered view is simply that while we cannot hope for a schematization of the moral law in which that law becomes an object of experience, we can still seek a sensible analogy for a pure concept of reason (in this case, the morally good will). Perhaps. But a neat interpretive solution to the puzzle is not necessary for my purposes.

15. Kant poses three questions in the *Critique of Pure Reason* (A 805/B 833) and in the *Menschenkunde* anthropology transcription (25: 1198): What can I know? What should I do? What may I hope? A fourth question (What is the human being?), to which the first three all relate, is added later in *Jäsche Logik* (9: 25), a letter to Stäudlin of May 4, 1793 (11: 429), and *Metaphysik-Pölitz* (28: 533–34). For further discussion of Kant's philosophy of hope, see my "Hope after Horror," in Louden, *The World We Want*, 213–23.

16. In Paul Menzer's important edition of Kant's lectures on ethics, *Eine Vorlesung Kants über Ethik*, which is based on the Brauer, Kutzner, and Mrongovius manuscripts, the word *Exempel* occurs here rather than *Beispiel* (138), while the rest of the quoted passage is virtually identical with the above passage from *Collins*. In a footnote in the *Metaphysics of Morals*, Kant tries to differentiate between *Beispiel* and *Exempel*. The two words, he asserts, "do not have the same meaning" (6: 479n). *Exempel*, he claims, is properly used in the sense of "taking something [or someone] as an *example* [*Exempel*]," whereas *Beispiel* is correctly used in the sense of "to bring forward an instance [*Beispiel*] to clarify an expression" (ibid.). Unfortunately, Kant rarely follows his own advice regarding how to use these two terms, even in *MdS*, where the advice is presented. For example, at *MdS* 6: 479 he refers to "*das gute Beispiel* of the teacher himself," whereas he should have referred to "*das gute Exempel* of the teacher himself."

17. For further discussion of this important point, see Wood, *Kant's Ethical Thought*, 133–37; and Grenberg, *Kant and the Ethics of Humility*. For an appreciative critique of Grenberg, see "Kantian Moral Humility: Between Aristotle and Paul," chapter 3 in this volume.

18. For example, toward the end of the first *Critique* Kant notes that he has "a strong belief (on the correctness of which I would wager many advantages in life) that there are also inhabitants of other worlds" (A 825/B 854). For additional references and further discussion, see Louden, *Kant's Impure Ethics*, 188n30, 212n89, 224nn10 and 13, 229n9.

19. "Émile shall have no head-pads, no go-carts, no leading-strings; or at least as soon as he can put one foot before another he shall only be supported along pavements, and he shall be taken quickly across them" (Rousseau, *Émile*, 42, cf. 11–12, 35–36).

CHAPTER 9

* This essay began as an invitation from Sharon Anderson-Gold and Pablo Muchnik to contribute to an anthology that they were co-editing called *Kant's Anatomy of Evil*. I had profited from Sharon's writings on Kant's philosophy of history in my earlier work (see, e.g., her *Unnecessary Evil*), and like her, I approach Kant's doctrine of radical evil from a multitextual perspective. Part I of *Religion within the Boundaries of Mere Reason* is of course the core text, but Kant's essays on the philosophy of history and his lectures on anthropology also make important contributions to the discussion. One particular connecting point between these different Kantian texts that I have wrestled with for some time, explored at length in the present piece, concerns Kant's frequent appeals to anthropology and empirical evidence within his discussion of the universality of evil in the *Religion*. Sharon, Pablo, and I have come to know each other better through our work with the North American Kant Society. Sharon was president of NAKS when she first spoke with me about contributing to the radical evil project. In 2009, I was elected president, and Pablo—who has also published a monograph on this topic, *Kant's Theory of Evil*—was elected vice president.

In preparing for this essay, I felt a need to better acquaint myself with the history of philosophical and theological discussion about evil. As a result, in the spring of 2007 I taught a new course for undergraduates at the University of Southern Maine called "Problems in Philosophy: Evil." One of the texts I read with students for this course was Richard J. Bernstein's *Radical Evil*. Bernstein's book opens with a critique of Kant ("Radical Evil: Kant at War with Himself"), and one goal of my essay is to defend Kant's position against several objections raised by Bernstein and other critics. The final arguments in the essay benefited from comments mailed in by Bernstein and from discussions with students in the class. When the essay was almost complete I received an exciting invitation from the Idealism Group and the Institute of Philosophy and the History of Ideas at Aarhus University, Denmark, to present a lecture on some of my recent work on Kant. A draft of the essay was presented in Aarhus in February 2008 and subsequently published in *Sats: Nordic Journal of Philosophy* 9 (2008): 7–27. Portions were written in Münster, Germany, in June–July 2007, made possible by financial support from the Alexander von Humboldt Foundation.

1. See, e.g., Bernstein, *Radical Evil*; Bernstein, *The Abuse of Evil*; Card, *The Atrocity Paradigm*; Grant, *Naming Evil, Judging Evil*; Lara, *Rethinking Evil*; Neiman, *Evil in Modern Thought*; Schrift, *Modernity and the Problem of Evil*. NB: I do not mean to imply that each of these books was directly inspired by 9/11: this is clearly not the case. But the twenty-first-century surge of philosophy books on evil is noteworthy, whatever the precise causes of the phenomenon might be.

2. Exceptions include Neiman, who assigns "a central place" to Kant in her narrative (*Evil in Modern Thought*, 61; see also her earlier book *The Unity of Reason*); Bernstein, who notes that it was Hannah Arendt's reference to Kant that initially aroused his interest and curiosity in the expression "radical evil" (*Radical Evil*, 3) and who opens his interrogation with a chapter devoted to Kant's account of radical evil ("Radical Evil: Kant at War with Himself," 11–45; an

earlier version of this chapter is included in Lara, *Rethinking Evil*, 55–85); and Card, who also includes a chapter on Kant ("Kant's Theory of Radical Evil," in *The Atrocity* Paradigm, 73–95). Part of my aim in this essay is to respond to several of Bernstein's criticisms of Kant's position on radical evil, criticisms which he often develops in the course of discussing appraisals that other commentators have offered of Kant's account.

3. McBride, "Liquidating the 'Nearly Just Society,'" 29, 36.

4. Cf. Dews, "Disenchantment and the Persistence of Evil," 52; Neiman, *Evil in Modern Thought*, 218.

5. Bernstein, *Radical Evil*, 4.

6. Michalson, *Fallen Freedom*, 61.

7. Bernstein, *Radical Evil*, 33.

8. Ibid., 35.

9. Kant's doctrine of the opacity of intentions is a major theme in Onora O'Neill's work. See, e.g., her *Constructions of Reason*, 7, 77, 85, 88, 98, 130, 14, 151–52.

10. Bernstein, *Radical Evil*, 235.

11. Ibid., 45.

12. For a defense of this position, see Strawson, "The Impossibility of Moral Responsibility."

13. As others have noted, here there appears to be a link to Hannah Arendt's later thesis concerning the banality of evil. In the epilogue to *Eichmann in Jerusalem*, she writes: "The trouble with Eichmann was precisely that so many were like him, and that the many were neither perverted nor sadistic, that they were, and still are, terribly and terrifyingly normal" (276). See also Anderson-Gold, "Kant's Rejection of Devilishness," esp. 48n30; and Allison, "Reflections on the Banality of (Radical) Evil: A Kantian Analysis," in *Idealism and Freedom*, 169–82. Allison's essay is also reprinted in Lara, *Rethinking Evil*, 86–100.

14. Augustine, *The City of God*, XII.7, 480. For a recent appreciation, see Hauerwas, "Seeing Darkness, Hearing Silence." Kant's inscrutability-of-freedom position has also received significant post-Kantian support. Schelling, for instance, in *Of Human Freedom* (1809), clearly endorses both Kant and Augustine when he states that "evil ever remains man's own choice . . . every creature falls through its own guilt. But just how the decision for good or evil comes to pass in the individual, that is still wrapped in total darkness" (59). See also Bernstein, *Radical Evil*, 93.

15. Arendt, *The Origins of Totalitarianism*, 459, see also viii–ix. Arendt briefly refers to Kant's concept of radical evil on this same page, but quickly dismisses it on the ground that Kant mistakenly thought that evil "could be explained by comprehensible motives." Kantian radical evil, as is well known, does not refer to an allegedly new type of evil never before witnessed by humanity, but rather to a universal propensity in the human species, one that is "in all cases somehow entwined with humanity and, as it were, rooted in it" (*Rel* 6: 32).

16. Arendt to Jaspers, March 4, 1951, in Arendt, *Hannah Arendt/Karl Jaspers Correspondence*, 166. See also Bernstein, *Radical Evil*, 207. Arendt includes a second anti-Kantian argument in this same letter to Jaspers, when she goes on to state that making people superfluous as human beings is different from using them "as a means to an end" (166). Here, the proper Kantian response, I believe, is to acknowledge that while not all cases of treating people as means to an end are also cases of making people superfluous, all cases of making people superfluous are cases of treating people as means to an end. Treating people as means to an end is a broader category than the category of making people superfluous, and the latter is simply the extreme limit of the former. A professor who requires that students read one of his new essays

is treating them as a means to his end, but in doing so he is not making his students superfluous. However, the Nazis' treatment of the Jews during World War II was clearly a case both of treating them as means to an end and of making them superfluous.

17. Bernstein, *Radical Evil*, 207, 208.

18. Ibid., 42. See also Allison, who (in commenting on an argument of John Silber), writes: "Great evil, it would seem, can involve as much self-sacrifice (at least as it is usually conceived) and intensification of personality as great virtue"; Allison, "Reflections on the Banality of (Radical) Evil," 176.

19. Louden, "On the Radical Evil in Human Nature," in Louden, *Kant's Impure Ethics*, 139. One passage from the *Religion* that I used to support my position was Kant's claim that "whenever incentives other than the law itself (e.g., ambition, self-love in general [*Selbstliebe überhaupt*], yes, even a kindly instinct such as sympathy)" (6: 30–31) determine our actions, such actions are evil. I took Kant here to be distinguishing self-love from other nonmoral incentives such as sympathy and ambition. But I think now that this interpretation is wrong, or rather (since the particular passage quoted still seems to me to support this interpretation), that the normal way of reading this passage does not in fact represent Kant's considered view.

20. Reath, "Kant's Theory of Moral Sensibility," in his *Agency and Autonomy in Kant's Moral Theory*, 16.

21. I have borrowed this contrast from Korsgaard, "Morality as Freedom," in her *Creating the Kingdom of Ends*, 165. See also Wood, *Kant's Moral Religion*, 213.

22. Nietzsche, *Beyond Good and Evil*, sec. 23.

23. Theodore M. Grene and Hoyt H. Hudson, in their English translation of Kant's *Religion*, render *teuflischer* as "devilish," and earlier discussions of this topic (e.g., Silber, "The Ethical Significance of Kant's *Religion*"; Anderson-Gold, "Kant's Rejection of Devilishness") follow their lead. However, partly because "devilish" is an ambiguous term, one of whose meanings is "mischievous, teasing, or annoying" (a meaning occasionally rendered in cartoons and Valentine's Day cards), I don't think it takes us very close to what Kant is talking about. "Diabolical" is a better translation for Kant's *teuflischer*. But even here, articulating what exactly *teuflischer*/diabolical in Kant's specific sense means is no easy matter.

24. Silber, "The Ethical Significance of Kant's *Religion*," cxxix.

25. Silber, "Kant at Auschwitz," 198, see also 194.

26. Bernstein, *Radical Evil*, 36, 41, 42.

27. Card, *The Atrocity Paradigm*, 91, 212. See also Martin Beck Matuštík, who complains that Kant "rejects without explanation" the possibility that human beings can be diabolical beings ("Violence and Secularization, Evil and Redemption," 41). Card goes on to develop and defend a non-Kantian conception of diabolical evil, which "focuses on the *harm* one is willing to inflict rather than on the reasons why" (211). She also holds that her "understanding of diabolical evil comes closer than Kant's does to the classic view of Satan as a corrupter, as one who tempts others to abandon morality or demote it to a low position on their scale of values" (212). However, as I argue below, this notion of "Satan as a corrupter" is not what Kant's argument against diabolical evil is about.

28. Silber, "The Ethical Significance of Kant's *Religion*," cxxix.

29. Bernstein, *Radical Evil*, 40.

30. I am indebted to Wood, *Kant's Moral Religion*, 212–14; and Allison, "Reflections on the Banality of (Radical) Evil," 174–77.

31. Allison, "Reflections on the Banality of (Radical) Evil," 176.

32. See Silber's discussion of Hitler, Napoleon, and Herman Melville's Ahab in "The Ethical Significance of Kant's *Religion*," cxxix.

33. Lotte Kohler and Hans Saner, the editors of *Hannah Arendt/Karl Jaspers Correspondence*, insert a note here that reads: "This passage may have influenced the subtitle of A.'s *Eichmann in Jerusalem: A Report on the Banality of Evil*" (702n6).

34. Arendt, *The Origins of Totalitarianism*, 459; Arendt to Jaspers, July 9, 1946, in Arendt, *Hannah Arendt/Karl Jaspers Correspondence*, 54; Jaspers to Arendt, October 19, 1946, ibid., 62. See also Bernstein, *Radical Evil*, 214–15.

35. A related potential problem: because evil is freely chosen, it is not a necessary feature of the human being; as Kant remarks, we can't infer evil "from the concept of a human being in general" (*Rel* 6: 32). But this additional claim seems to violate another key doctrine of the first *Critique*, viz., that universality and necessity "belong together inseparably" (*KrV* B 4, see also A 2). In the case of radical evil, Kant appears to be asserting that we encounter universality without necessity. However, as I argue below, the kind of universality relevant to Kant's discussion of radical evil is an empirical, species universality (one that applies to human beings, but not necessarily to other species of rational being). It is not the "strict" universality that we find in *a priori* judgments. And it is only the latter kind of universality that belongs inseparably with necessity.

36. Allison, *Kant's Theory of Freedom*, 154.

37. Michalson, *Fallen Freedom*, 46.

38. Bernstein, *Radical Evil*, 34–35.

39. Eberhard, "Ueber das Kantische radicale Böse in der menschlichen Natur," 41–42. (I thank the Universitäts- und Landesbibliothek at Westfälische Wilhelms-Universität in Münster, Germany, for providing me with a photocopy of this important essay.) See also Kosch, *Freedom and Reason in Kant, Schelling, and Kierkegaard*, 63n39.

40. Allison, *Kant's Theory of Freedom*, 155. See also Bernstein's criticisms of Allison's strategy in *Radical Evil*, 240–41n32.

41. Robert Merrihew Adams, "Introduction," in Kant, *Religion within the Boundaries of Mere Reason and Other Writings*, xiii.

42. Louden, *Kant's Impure Ethics*, 132. See *Rel* 6: 18, 26, 28, 32, 39.

43. Kosch, *Freedom and Reason in Kant, Schelling, and Kierkegaard*, 63. See also Louden, *Kant's Impure Ethics*, 132–33.

44. Bernstein holds that Kant's examples here are merely "evidence of his prejudices, based upon limited and highly selective anthropological sources" (*Radical Evil*, 240n31). That Kant harbored many prejudices, I do not deny. However, I think the main point of his brief litany of examples of evil found in "the so-called *state of nature*" is to signal disagreement with Rousseauian romantics who think that we somehow find innocent and uncorrupted human beings outside of Europe. Kant's point is that "they're people too." And because they are human beings, they too have a propensity to evil.

45. For further discussion, see my "Anthropology from a Kantian Point of View: Toward a Cosmopolitan Conception of Human Nature," chapter 7 in this volume.

46. A future orientation is nevertheless occasionally detectable in Kant's later discussion of grace, a concept that he regards as "very risky" and "hard to reconcile with reason" (*Rel* 6: 191), but which he is also willing to admit as something incomprehensible" (*Rel* 6: 53). See also part III of *Religion*—"The Victory of the Good Principle over the Evil Principle, and the Founding of a Kingdom of God on Earth" (6: 93–147). This part of *Religion* is closer to the teleological orientation of the later sections of the anthropology lectures and the philosophy of history essays.

CHAPTER 10

* This essay began as an invitation from Eduardo Mendieta and Stuart Elden to contribute a piece to an anthology they were co-editing called *Reading Kant's Geography*. Drafts of the essay were presented at an enjoyable interdisciplinary conference at Durham University, England, in January 2008, hosted by the Department of Geography. To a certain extent, Kant's lectures on geography represent the last frontier for Kant scholars. He began lecturing regularly on geography in 1756, and over the years various transcriptions of these popular classroom lectures have surfaced. But they have not been easily accessible for scholars, and have only recently begun to be published in the German Academy edition of Kant's works. (Volume 26.1, edited by Werner Stark, was published in 2009. An additional volume is forthcoming.) A poorly edited version of the lectures was published in 1800 by Kant's former student Friedrich Theodor Rink, and it was later included in Academy volume 9, first published in 1923 (9: 151–436). The first complete English translation, prepared by Olaf Reinhardt and David Oldroyd, is in Kant, *Natural Science*, ed. Watkins.

For Kant, geography and anthropology constitute the two parts of *Weltkenntnis*, or knowledge of the world—an empirically grounded pragmatic understanding of the world and its inhabitants. In this essay I focus on the conception of human beings that Kant employs in the geography lectures, arguing that it is not essentially different from what one finds in his anthropology lectures. Given that the geography lectures are one of the central background sources for the anthropology lectures (Kant began lecturing regularly on anthropology in 1772, treating the two as distinct disciplines only after this point), this claim concerning a shared conception of human beings should not be surprising. But it does challenge the views of many commentators, and it also raises a problem for Kant: just how does he distinguish geography from anthropology? Views about race also loom large in Kant's various discussions of human beings in the geography lectures, and in the concluding section of this chapter I argue that the geography texts offer us a means of testing the claims of commentators who hold that his views about race changed significantly in the 1790s. These claims, alas, are false.

1. Paul Gedan writes: "Kant in Königsberg and Gatterer in Göttingen were the first university lecturers who offered independent lectures in geography, thereby introducing what was until then an undervalued science in universities into the circle of academic disciplines" (Kant, *Physische Geographie*, ed. Gedan, vi). See also Adickes, *Kant als Naturforscher*, 2: 388; Bowen, *Empiricism and Geographical Thought*; Hartshorne, *The Nature of Geography*, 38; and May, *Kant's Concept of Geography*, 4, 51–52.

2. Withers, "Geography," 115. See also Livingstone and Withers, *Geography and the Enlightenment*.

3. As cited by Stark in "Immanuel Kants physische Geographie," 2. See also Vorländer, *Immanuel Kant*, 2: 56–57. Zedlitz wrote to Kant in February 1778, noting that he had enjoyed reading a rudimentary transcription of the geography lectures and requesting a better copy. See Stark, "Immanuel Kants physische Geographie," 2–3; May, *Kant's Concept of Geography*, 73.

4. Harvey, "Cosmopolitanism and the Banality of Geographical Evils," 532; and Droit, "Kant et les fourmis du Congo," as cited by Harvey, ibid.

5. Adickes, *Ein neu aufgefundenes Kollegheft nach Kants Vorlesung über physische Geographie*, 10. Adickes argues that the beginning part of Rink's text (9: 156–273) stemmed from Kant's 1775 lecture notes, while the later part (9: 273–436) stemmed from 1758–1759 lectures.

6. In the preface to *Anthropology from a Pragmatic Point of View*, Kant writes: "As for physical geography, it is scarcely possible at my age to produce a manuscript from my text, which is hardly legible to anyone but myself" (7: 122n).

7. Adickes, in *Ein neu aufgefundenes Kollegheft nach Kants Vorlesung über physische Geographie*, 43, suggests *pragmatische* rather than *praktische* here. See also Gedan's note at *Geo* 9: 515.

8. For related discussion, see Richards, "Kant's Geography and Mental Maps." Richards rightly draws attention to Kant's conviction that geographical space constitutes "a locational 'framework of knowledge'" (8), and he also draws some interesting parallels between Kant's conviction and more recent work on cognitive or mental maps. However, my own view is that he overtheorizes Kant's position. It is primarily a *pragmatic* and *practical* orientation that Kantian physical geography offers to students, a sense of what to expect once they leave their local communities—not an abstract "schema for co-ordinating with each other absolutely all things externally sensed" (7).

9. For related discussion, see my essay "Anthropology from a Kantian Point of View: Toward a Cosmopolitan Conception of Human Nature" (chapter 7 in this volume).

10. E.g., the geography entry in Johnston, Gregory, and Smith, *The Dictionary of Human Geography*, begins: "Geography can be formally defined as the study of the Earth's surface as the space within which the human population lives . . ., or simply as the study of the Earth as the home of people." And the first definition under "geography" in McKean, *The New Oxford American Dictionary*, reads: "the study of the physical features of the earth and its atmosphere, and of human activity as it affects and is affected by these, including the distribution of populations and resources, land use, and industries."

11. Arnoldt, *Kritische Excurse im Gebiete der Kant-Forschung*, 343.

12. Ibid.

13. May, *Kant's Concept of Geography*, 115, 70, 65.

14. Cohen, "Kant's Critique of the Human Sciences," 123.

15. May, *Kant's Concept of Geography*, 108, see also 72. See also the earlier citation from Arnoldt (n. 11).

16. Eze, "The Color of Reason," 106.

17. May, *Kant's Concept of Geography*, 113.

18. Eze, "The Color of Reason," 105.

19. May, *Kant's Concept of Geography*, 115.

20. Kant's extended discussion of China is in part a reflection of the strong Enlightenment interest in China initiated by Jesuit missionaries and intensified by Leibniz and Wolff. For discussion and references, see the section "German Philosophers and China" in my essay "'What Does Heaven Say?': Christian Wolff and Western Interpretations of Confucian Ethics."

21. See Hartshorne, *The Nature of Geography*, 39.

22. For discussion, see my "Peoples," in Louden, *Kant's Impure Ethics*, 87–93, and "National Character via the Beautiful and Sublime?" (chapter 12 in this volume).

23. Kames, *Sketches of the History of Man*, I: 39. After summarizing Montesquieu's position, Kames states: "It is my firm opinion that neither temper nor talents have much dependence on climate" (I: 40).

24. Montesquieu, *The Spirit of the Laws*, 221.

25. Buffon, *A Natural History, General and Particular*, 22, 27.

26. Translations of each of these essays are included in Kant, *Anthropology, History, and Education*.

27. E.g., the first statement on race cited earlier (9: 316) is missing entirely, but a version of the second statement (9: 317) is present. See *Holstein* 26: 96–97.

28. Kant is referring here to a draft of what eventually became his second race essay, "Bestimmung des Begriffs einer Menschenrace," first published in *Berlinische Monatsschrift* 11 (1785): 390–417.

29. In describing these three interpretive strategies, I have borrowed from Kleingeld, "Kant's Second Thoughts on Race." Advocates of the first strategy, Kleingeld notes, include Robert B. Louden, Thomas McCarthy, and Thomas E. Hill Jr. and Bernard Boxill.

30. Mills, "Kant's *Untermenschen*," 170. (Kleingeld also lists Emmanuel Eze and Robert Bernasconi as advocates of this second interpretive strategy.)

31. Muthu, *Enlightenment against Empire*, 183–84. See also Shell, *The Embodiment of Reason*, 387n23.

32. Kleingeld, "Kant's Second Thoughts on Race," 573, cf. 575, 586, 592. Contra Muthu and Shell, Kleingeld argues—as I have also done in the present essay—that in *On the Use of Teleological Principles* Kant continues to make assertions about "the preeminence of whites or Europeans over other human races."

33. Hume, "Of National Characters," 208n10.

34. Kleingeld, "Kant's Second Thoughts on Race," 575.

35. Ibid., 577n10, 575, 586 (my emphases in the last two quotations).

36. Jefferson, *Notes on the State of Virginia*, query XIV, 270.

37. I thank Eric Watkins for sharing a draft of Olaf Reinhardt and David Oldroyd's translation of Rink's edition of the *Physical Geography* (in Kant, *Natural Science*, ed. Watkins); Werner Stark for offering me access to electronic versions of the geography lectures that he is editing for publication in the German Academy edition; and Joseph S. Wood for giving me a crash course on geography. Finally, thanks also to Eduardo Mendieta and Stuart Elden for providing me with the opportunity to do some work on Kant's geography lectures.

CHAPTER 11

* This chapter began as an invitation from Steven M. Cahn to contribute an essay on Kant's philosophy of education for an anthology he was editing entitled *Philosophy of Education*. Over the years, Cahn has done a lot of important work not only in this area of philosophy but in others as well. See, e.g., *From Student to Scholar* and *Saints and Scamps*. His anthology contains substantial selections from central works in the philosophy of education, including an abridged version of my translation of Kant's *Lectures on Pedagogy* (first published in Kant, *Anthropology, History, and Education*). Each "essential text" is then followed by an "afterword" (the published title of the present essay) "in which a noted authority of our time highlights essential points from the readings and places them in a wider context." Kant's texts on education were among the very first that I turned to in my attempt to learn more about his theory of human nature. For instance, I began my translation of the *Lectures on Pedagogy* back in 1991. Cahn's invitation gave me a chance to revisit some of my earlier work in this area. In "Becoming Human" (which builds on my earlier analysis of Kant's philosophy of education in chapter 2 of *Kant's Impure Ethics*), I am particularly concerned to draw attention to some structural parallels between Kant's educational theory and his philosophy of history, as well as to show how his writings on education contribute to his theory of human nature. The present version of the essay restores a number of passages and notes that were deleted in the published text on the ground that they were "too scholarly and too sophisticated" for education students.

1. In this opening section I borrow from my "Translator's Introduction to *Lectures on Pedagogy*" in Kant, *Anthropology, History, and Education*, 434–36.

2. Kant, *Immanuel Kants sämmtliche Werke*, 9: xvi.

3. *Immanuel Kants physische Geographie*. These lectures are reprinted in volume 9 of the Academy edition (151–436). An English translation, prepared by Olaf Reinhardt and David

Oldroyd, is in Kant, *Natural Science*, ed. Watkins. For discussion, see Louden, "'The Play of Nature': Human Beings in Kant's Geography" (chapter 10 in this volume).

4. Rink, *Ansichten aus Immanuel Kants Leben*; Rink, *Sammlung einiger bisher unbekannt gebliebener kleiner Schriften von Immanuel Kant*; Rink, *Mancherley zur Geschichte der metacritischen Invasion*.

5. *Immanuel Kant über Pädagogik*. The *Lectures on Pedagogy* are reprinted in volume 9 of the Academy edition (437–99). My translation of the *Lectures* is included in Kant, *Anthropology, History, and Education*.

6. *Kant on Education* (*Ueber Pädagogik*), trans. Churton; *The Educational Theory of Immanuel Kant*, trans. and ed. Buchner. Buchner's edition also contains numerous translated selections on education from Kant's other writings and a detailed introduction. It remains today the best single source in English on Kant's educational theory.

7. See, e.g., Buchner, "The Division of Educational Activities," in *The Educational Theory of Immanuel Kant*, 73–80; Beck, "The Three Stages of Education," a section of "Kant on Education," 197–204; Frankena, "Dispositions to Be Fostered," in his *Three Historical Philosophies of Education*, 83–104; and Munzel, "Discipline, Cultivation, Formation," in Munzel, *Kant's Conception of Moral Character*, 279–88. See also my earlier discussion, "The Stages of Education," in Louden, *Kant's Impure Ethics*, 38–44.

8. John Locke expresses a similar conviction at the beginning of *Some Thoughts Concerning Education* (1693): "I think I may say that of all the men we meet with, nine parts of ten are what they are, good or evil, useful or not, by their education. 'Tis that which makes the great difference in mankind" (§ 1). Despite their strongly different philosophical orientations, Locke and Kant—indeed, Enlightenment intellectuals generally—stand united in their conviction that education is of supreme importance in human life.

9. E.g., at one point Kant advises parents not to employ any mechanical aids in helping young children to walk: "It is customary to employ leading-strings and go-carts in order to teach children how to walk. But it is striking that one should want to teach children how to walk, as if any human being could not have walked for lack of instruction. Leading-strings are particularly harmful" (9: 461). Similarly, Rousseau writes in *Émile*: "Émile shall have no head-pads, no go-carts, no leading-strings; or at least as soon as he can put one foot before another he shall only be supported along pavements, and he shall be taken quickly across them" (42, cf. 11–12, 35–36). Rousseau was a major influence on Kant's intellectual development. In a famous note that Kant wrote in the margins of his own copy of his 1764 book, *Observations on the Feeling of the Beautiful and Sublime*, he states:

> I am myself by inclination an investigator. I feel a complete thirst for knowledge and an eager unrest to go further in it as well as satisfaction at every acquisition. There was a time when I believed that this alone could constitute the honor of mankind, and I had contempt for the rabble who know nothing. *Rousseau* brought me around. This blinding superiority disappeared, I learned to honor human beings, and I would find myself far more useless than the common laborer if I did not believe that this consideration could impart to all others a value in establishing the rights of humanity.
>
> (20: 44)

Basedow was also strongly influenced by Rousseau. E.g., Part 4 of his *Methodenbuch* concludes with twenty pages of quotations from *Émile*.

10. E.g., at one point Kant stresses that children do not need to be kept as warm as adults, "for their blood is already much warmer than that of adults. The blood temperature in children is 110 degrees Fahrenheit and the blood temperature of adults only 96 degrees" (9: 458).

11. Jachmann, "Immanuel Kant geschildert in Briefen an einen Freund," 10. For further discussion of Kant's employment as a tutor, see Kuehn, *Kant: A Biography*, 95–99.

12. E.g., Buchner writes: "In his educational theory Kant despises the feelings.... The feelings of the individual are practically banished from any share in education, and the claims of aesthetics as making positive contribution to the realization of pedagogy's ideal are neglected" (*The Educational Theory of Immanuel Kant*, 89). In the *Lectures* Kant does refer to "the formation of the feeling of pleasure or displeasure" (9: 477), but—as is unfortunately often the case in Rink's text—the topic is not pursued in any detail. For discussion of Kant's views about the positive role of feeling in education outside of the *Lectures*, see Louden, *Kant's Impure Ethics*, 109–25.

13. Rousseau, *Émile*, 57–58. Rousseau's use of masculine pronouns is intentional, and here Kant also unfortunately follows him. Buchner points to "his complete omission of the education of girls" as constituting "perhaps the chief defect in Kant's treatment of educational theory" (*The Educational Theory of Immanuel Kant*, 84). Locke too reminds readers that "I have said *he* here because the principal aim of my discourse is how a young gentleman should be brought up from his infancy, which, in all things, will not so perfectly suit the education of *daughters*" (*Some Thoughts Concerning Education*, § 6). Condorcet, in *The Nature and Purpose of Public Instruction*, had the foresight to argue that public education "must be the same for women as it is for men" (134), but most Enlightenment educational theorists are not at their best when discussing gender. For discussion, see my "(Almost) Universal Education," in Louden, *The World We Want*, 28–33.

14. See, e.g., Willey, "Kant and the German Theory of Education"; Beiser, "A Romantic Education"; and Beiser, "Romanticism." Beiser argues that the early German Romantics developed *Bildung* in reaction against earlier Enlightenment educational reform efforts based on utility: "The educational reforms of the late eighteenth century might be summarized in a single word: *utility*.... Without a doubt, there was no aspect of the ideology of the *Aufklärung* the romantics despised more than its utilitarianism" ("Romanticism," 135, 137). Willey correctly points to Kant as the founder of "a rich, nuanced and essentially anti-utilitarian educational philosophy contained in the term *Bildung*" (543).

15. Humboldt, *The Limits of State Action*, 10 (translation altered slightly). John Stuart Mill would later use this passage as the epigraph for *On Liberty* (1859). The original title of Humboldt's book was *Ideen zu einem Versuch, die Grenzen der Wirksamkeit des Staats zu bestimmen*.

16. Herman, "Training to Autonomy: Kant and the Question of Moral Education," in her *Moral Literacy*, 131. See also Beck, "Kant on Education," 200–201.

17. In the following section, I borrow from my "Experimentation and Revolution," in Louden, *Kant's Impure Ethics*, 44–46.

18. My translations of these two short essays are included in Kant, *Anthropology, History, and Education*.

19. Raumer, *Geschichte der Pädagogik*, 2: 278. This passage from Raumer is cited by Quick, *Essays on Educational Reformers*, 274–75; and Painter, *A History of Education*, 274.

20. Goethe, "Dichtung und Wahrheit," in his *Gedenkenausgabe der Werke, Briefe und Gespräche*, 10: 673–74. Basedow, like many Enlightenment intellectuals (including both Goethe and Kant, albeit in different ways), was a deist.

21. Malaga is a sweet fortified wine originating in the southern Spanish port city of Málaga. Goethe and Kant's unflattering portraits contrast with Max Müller's entry on Basedow in the *Allgemeine Deutsche Biographie*. Here, Basedow is praised as "one whose true service as one of the boldest pioneers in the fight for human rights and human dignity, for fidelity to truth and intellectual freedom, has been confirmed both through the voices of the best of his time and

through the impartial judgment of posterity" (113). Müller (1823–1900) was a professor of modern European languages at Oxford University and Basedow's great-grandson. His entry is available online at http://de.wikisource.org/wiki/ADB:Basedow%2C_Johann_Bernhard. See also Giorgio Tonelli's entry on Basedow in *The Encyclopedia of Philosophy*.

22. Wood, *Kant*, 82.

23. As Frankena notes, in his advocacy of experimentalism in education Kant represents "a strong anticipation of Dewey" (*Three Historical Philosophies of Education*, 83, cf. 138–40).

24. Hume, *A Treatise of Human Nature*, III.I.ii. For related discussion, see Fink, "Three Sorts of Naturalism."

25. For related discussion, see "Making the Law Visible: The Role of Examples in Kant's Ethics" (chapter 8 in this volume).

26. Kant's references to casuistry in his discussions of moral education are uniformly positive—i.e., he does not follow contemporary dictionary definitions: "the use of clever but unsound reasoning, esp. in relation to moral questions, sophistry" (*The New Oxford American Dictionary*, s. v. "Casuistry").

27. For further discussion, see Louden, *The World We Want*.

28. "If we are willing to conceive education as the process of forming fundamental dispositions, intellectual and emotional, toward nature and freedom, philosophy may even be defined *as the general theory of education*" (Dewey, *Democracy and Education*, 328).

CHAPTER 12

* This last chapter began as an invitation from Richard L. Velkley and Susan Meld Shell to contribute a piece on the anthropological dimension of Kant's 1764 work, *Observations on the Feeling of the Beautiful and Sublime*, and his unpublished *Remarks* on this work for an anthology that they were co-editing, *Kant's "Observations" and "Remarks": A Critical Guide*. I first met Velkley in 2004 at the Beijing International Symposium on Kant's Moral Philosophy in Contemporary Perspectives (see the opening note to chapter 2). His earlier work *Freedom and the End of Reason*, as well as Shell's book *The Embodiment of Reason*, were both influences on my *Kant's Impure Ethics*. Over the years, each of us has worked to draw attention to the importance of cultural and historical factors in Kant's approach to practical philosophy. Traditionally—in large part due simply to its title—Kant's *Observations on the Feeling of the Beautiful and Sublime* has been treated as a work in aesthetics. I believe that its contribution to aesthetics is in fact rather minimal, but it does constitute (particularly in its final sections on gender and national character) an important source for Kant's later lectures on anthropology. A related topic explored in the present essay is whether the geography lectures (which, as I argue in chapter 10, are interconnected with the anthropology lectures) may in turn have been a source for some of the later anthropological material in the *Observations*. The publication in the German Academy edition of Kant's earliest geography lectures, which predate the *Observations*, enables us to explore (if not conclusively test) this hypothesis.

The specific area of anthropology examined in this essay is national character—a topic that has had a checkered career both within mainstream anthropology and in the reception of Kant's anthropology. In each case, the underlying cause is identical: attributing uniform personality traits to individuals living within the same national boundaries is held by many to be objectionable stereotyping. In Kant's case, there is the additional stain of race, which repeatedly manages to work its way into his discussion of national character in the *Observations*. In this essay I offer a qualified defense of Kant's emphasis on national character. To be sure, there are numerous inconsistencies and weaknesses in his account, and part of the aim of this chapter is to point them out. But national character is not a myth, and knowledge of it forms an integral dimension of Kant's pragmatic orientation toward the world and its inhabitants: without it, we cannot achieve *Weltkenntnis*.

Earlier versions of the paper were presented as a keynote address at the conference Kantian Ethics and Society, organized by Alix Cohen (see the opening notes to chapters 6 and 7), held at the University of Leeds in June 2009, and as an invited talk for a symposium on Kant's anthropology at the American Philosophical Association Central Division meeting in Chicago, February 2010.

1. Schiller to Goethe, February 19, 1795, in Staiger, *Der Briefwechsel zwischen Schiller und Goethe*, 87.

2. Guyer, "Translator's Introduction to *Observations on the Feeling of the Beautiful and Sublime*," 19. Similarly, Vorländer remarks that "the contents of the *Observations* are at bottom less aesthetic than moral-psychological" (*Immanuel Kant*, 158–59). On the other hand, John T. Goldthwait, in his "Translator's Introduction" to Kant's *Observations*, refers to it as "Kant's only aesthetic work besides the *Critique of Judgment*" (12).

3. See also Susan Meld Shell, who notes that in Kant's *Observations* the term "*Beobachtung* is used almost apologetically—in opposition to philosophy and in apparent disregard of method and thoroughness" ("Kant as Propagator," 456).

4. For further discussion of what exactly Kant means by "anthropology from a pragmatic point of view," see Louden, "Applying Kant's Ethics" and "Anthropology from a Kantian Point of View" (chapters 6 and 7 in this volume). On the other hand, Hume, in his essay "Of National Characters" (to which Kant owes a debt in his own discussions of national characters), *is* primarily concerned with the causal question. He holds that "the character of a nation will much depend on *moral* causes," and he is "inclined to doubt altogether" that national character depends on physical causes (Hume, "Of National Characters," 198, 200). Throughout his essay, Hume argues strongly against Montesquieu's environmentalism. Hume does not believe "that men owe any thing of their temper or genius to the air, food, or climate" (200–201).

5. Guyer, "Editorial Notes to *Observations*," 493n26, 495n39.

6. For further discussion, see Elden, "Reassessing Kant's Geography"; and Wilson, "The Physical Geography Lectures and the Origin of the Anthropology Lectures," in her *Kant's Pragmatic Anthropology*, 8–15.

7. Arnoldt, *Kritische Excurse im Gebiete der Kant-Forschung*, 343. See also May, *Kant's Concept of Geography*, 65, 70, 115; and Eze, "The Color of Reason," 106.

8. For further discussion, see "'The Play of Nature': Human Beings in Kant's Geography" (chapter 10 in this volume).

9. Kant, *Natural Science*, ed. Watkins. A competing early edition of the geography lectures—unauthorized by Kant and edited by Gottfried Vollmer—was published in four volumes in 1801. Kant repudiates the Vollmer edition in his *Nachricht, die den Vollmer erschienene unrechtmäßige Ausgabe der physische Geographie betreffend*, May 29, 1801 (12: 372). In a footnote at the end of the preface to *Anthropology from a Pragmatic Point of View* (1798), Kant writes: "As for *physical geography*, it is scarcely possible at my age to produce a manuscript from my text, which is hardly legible to anyone but myself" (7: 122).

10. For further details, see "Becoming Human" (chapter 11 in this volume). Rink also published one of the first biographies of Kant, *Ansichten aus Immanuel Kants Leben* (1805), and an edited anthology of some of Kant's essays, *Sammlung einiger bisher unbekannter gebliebener kleiner Schriften von Immanuel Kant* (1800).

11. Adickes, *Ein neu aufgefundenes Kolleghaft nach Kants Vorlesung über physische Geographie*, 10. Elden notes that Adickes "attempted to get the *Akademie Ausgabe* to produce a new version of the *Geography*, instead of relying on Rink's, but this was declined due to feasibility: the volume was already typeset" ("Reassessing Kant's Geography," 7).

12. The *Herder* lecture will be published in Academy volume 26.2 (forthcoming).

13. Guyer, "Translator's Introduction," 21; Kuehn, *Kant: A Biography*, 142.

14. Hume, "Of National Characters," 208n10. But see also Miller's remark about Hume's opposition to slavery at the end of this note, as well the variant reading of Hume's note on 629–30.

15. See, e.g., Larrimore, "Sublime Waste"; Louden, "Races," in Louden, *Kant's Impure Ethics*, 93–100; Hill and Boxill, "Kant and Race"; Mills, "Kant's *Untermenschen*"; and Kleingeld, "Kant's Second Thoughts on Race." The fourth section is reprinted in Eze's edited anthology, *Race and the Enlightenment*, 48–57, which may also have contributed to the shunning of this part of the *Observations*.

16. Cf. Caro Baroja, *El Mito del Caractér Nacional*.

17. Sartre, "Existentialism Is a Humanism," 291. At the same time, Kant's discussion of *moral* character does include a quasi-existentialist dimension. Essentially, he uses the term "character" in two senses—physical and moral. Physical character refers to what nature and the environment make of the human being; moral character refers to what "the human being as a rational being endowed with freedom . . . is prepared to make of himself" (*Anth* 7: 285, see also 119). National character is one aspect of physical character.

18. For further discussion, see Kra, "The Concept of National Character in 18th Century France." Kra explores the concept of national character in the works of D'Argens, Espiard de la Borde, Montesquieu, Helvétius, Diderot, Rousseau, and Condorcet. For a broader multinational survey, see Nathan Rotenstreich's entry "Volksgeist," in the *Dictionary of the History of Ideas*.

19. This dichotomy of political versus physical environmental causes of course does not exhaust the possibilities. National characteristics may also be inherited. But neither Montesquieu nor Hume seems to have entertained this possibility.

20. But not entirely. He assumes that there is a hereditary or innate component in national character that is further developed by cultural traditions such as language (see *Friedländer* 25: 654; *Anth* 7: 312, 319). In this respect, what Kant means by "national character" is similar to "ethnicity."

21. Terracciano et al., "National Character Does Not Reflect Mean Personality Trait Levels in 49 Cultures"; Caro Baroja, *El Mito del Caractér Nacional*. For a less dismissive approach, see Peabody, *National Characteristics*.

22. Herder, *Auch eine Philosophie der Geschichte zur Bildung der Menschheit* (1774), 28.

23. Cf. Rotenstreich, who notes that there is "no explanation as to . . . what makes these [viz., the manifestations of the beautiful and the sublime] the most appropriate expressions" of national character ("Races and Peoples," 105).

24. Burke, *A Philosophical Inquiry into the Origin of Our Ideas of the Sublime and Beautiful*. Guyer notes that Burke's work "had been made widely known in Germany by Moses Mendelssohn's review of the following year" ("Translator's Introduction," 19). For discussion of Burke and other eighteenth-century English writers on the beautiful and sublime, see Monk, *The Sublime: A Study of Critical Theories in XVIII-Century England*.

25. See, e.g., Hegel, *Vorlesungen über die Philosophie der Weltgeschichte* (1830), 1: 59 ("The *Geist* we are concerned with is the *Volksgeist*").

26. In Greek mythology, Proteus was a minor sea god who had the power of prophecy but who would assume different shapes in order to avoid answering questions. E.g., in Homer's *Odyssey*, he is described as one

> who will try you by taking the form of all creatures that come forth
> and move on the earth, he will be water and magical fire.
> You must hold stiffly onto him and squeeze him the harder.
> (4: 417–19)

27. Should we infer from this that ancient Greece and Rome surpass all modern European nations? For they each possessed a cast of mind in which "both feelings are united" (2: 211)—a feat that no modern European nation has managed.

28. Vorländer, *Immanuel Kant*, 160.

29. By "proper taste . . . for the noble [*das Edle*]," Kant means the second type of sublime. See also 2: 209, 243. But in his earlier survey of different European national characters, he seemed to rule out the possibility that any one European nationality exhibits both feelings. So here he must mean "in Western Europe as a whole, considered as one people."

30. As noted earlier, Kant's notorious comments about "the *Negroes* of Africa" (2: 253) are yet another example of his wandering tendency, for race is not the same as national character. The same is true of his remarks concerning "the *savages* . . . of *North America*" (ibid.). In his later essays on race Kant describes "the *copper-red* Americans" as one of the four races of the human species (*Menschenrace* 8: 93; see also *Racen* 2: 441, 432). But there are further complications surrounding the national character/race confusion: (1) Kant is following Hume's lead. Why do both authors, at least in some of their writings, conflate race with national character? (2) Most nations in the eighteenth century were more racially homogeneous than is the case today. But Kant does not normally identify a *Volk* or a *Nation* with a *Rasse*. E.g., he holds that there are four races (*Racen* 2: 432), but in his *Lectures on Physical Geography* he discusses approximately sixty different peoples (9: 377–436). (3) He also recognizes that not all peoples form sovereign states. E.g., some peoples remain in the state of nature and choose not to make the transition to statehood by means of a social contract. Such peoples, he asserts in the *Metaphysics of Morals*, "do not constitute states but only tribes [*Völkerschaften*]" (6: 343). In the *Observations*, Kant may be viewing both the "copper-red" Americans and "the Negroes of Africa" as stateless/nationless tribes and races. (4) Kant (and European Enlightenment geographers generally) lacked detailed information about the interior of both Africa and the Americas: "the interior of Africa is as unknown to us as the regions of the moon. . . . Another country very little known to us is America" (*Geo* 9: 229). Could he perhaps be treating the continents of Africa and North America as single nations in the *Observations*? (5) In 1764. when the *Observations* was first published, Kant did not yet have a clear and settled concept of "race." True, there is the important section of the *Lectures on Physical Geography* entitled "Concerning Human Beings" (9: 311-20), and, as noted earlier, Adickes argues that this part of Rink's text stems from 1758-59. However, in this text Kant still accepts a climatological account of race: "Because the color of human beings goes through all shades of yellow, brown, and dark brown, finally becoming black in the torrid zones, it is obvious [*wohl zu sehen*] that the heat of the climate [*die Hitze des Klimas*] is the cause [*Ursache*] of it" (9: 314). By 1775, when he publishes *Of the Different Races of Human Beings*, this climatological account has been replaced by one that puts much more weight on inherited factors, or what Kant calls "germs" (*Keime*) and "natural predispositions" (*natürliche Anlagen*) (*Racen* 2: 434).

31. Basedow, *Philanthropisches Archiv*, 1 (as cited by Niedermeyer in "Campe als Direktor des Dessauer Philanthropins," 46n7). For related discussion, see "Becoming Human: Kant and the Philosophy of Education" (chapter 11 in this volume).

32. Kant, *Bemerkungen in den "Beobachtungen über das Gefühl des Schönen und Erhabenen,"* 124, see also 27–28, 129. Translations of some of these *Notes*, including the passage cited above, are included in Kant, *Notes and Fragments*, 1–25.

33. Rousseau, *Considerations on the Government of Poland*, in *Rousseau on International Relations*, 172.

34. Rousseau, *First Version of the Social Contract* (1761), in *Rousseau on International Relations*, 109.

35. For related discussion, see Brandt, *Kommentar zu Kants Anthropologie in pragmatischer Hinsicht*, 465–66; Rotenstreich, "Races and Peoples," 109; and Louden, *The World We Want*.

BIBLIOGRAPHY

Adams, Robert Merrihew. "Introduction." In Kant, *Religion with the Boundaries of Mere Reason and Other Writings*, trans. and ed. Allen Wood and George di Giovanni, vii–xxxii. Cambridge: Cambridge University Press, 1998.
Adickes, Erich. *Kant als Naturforscher*. 2 vols. Berlin: de Gruyter, 1925.
———. *Ein neu aufgefundenes Kollegheft nach Kants Vorlesung über physische Geographie*. Tübingen: Mohr, 1913.
———. *Untersuchungen zu Kants physischer Geographie*. Tübingen: Mohr, 1911.
Allison, Henry E. *Idealism and Freedom: Essays on Kant's Theoretical and Practical Philosophy*. Cambridge: Cambridge University Press, 1996.
———. *Kant's Theory of Freedom*. Cambridge: Cambridge University Press, 1990.
Ameriks, Karl. "The Hegelian Critique of Kantian Morality." In *New Essays on Kant*, ed. Bernard den Ouden and Marcia Moen, 179–212. New York: Lang, 1987.
Anderson-Gold, Sharon. "Kant's Rejection of Devilishness: The Limits of Human Volition." *Idealistic Studies* 14 (1984): 35–48.
———. *Unnecessary Evil: History and Moral Progress in the Philosophy of Immanuel Kant*. Albany: State University of New York Press, 2001.
Anderson-Gold, Sharon, and Pablo Muchnik, eds. *Kant's Anatomy of Evil*. Cambridge: Cambridge University Press, 2010.
Anscombe, G. E. M. "Modern Moral Philosophy." *Philosophy* 33 (1958): 1–19.
Arendt, Hannah. *Eichmann in Jerusalem: A Report on the Banality of Evil*. Rev. ed. New York: Penguin, 1977.
———. *Hannah Arendt/Karl Jaspers Correspondence, 1926–1969*. Edited by Lotte Kohler and Hans Saner. Translated by Robert and Rita Kimber. New York: Harcourt Brace Jovanovich, 1992.
———. *The Origins of Totalitarianism*. San Diego, CA: Harcourt, 1994.
Aristotle. *Ethica Nicomachea*. Edited by I. Bywater. Oxford: Clarendon, 1890.

Arnoldt, Emil. *Kritische Excurse im Gebiete der Kant-Forschung*. Königsberg in Pr: Beyer, 1894.
Arntzen, Sven. "Kant on Duty to Oneself and Resistance to Political Authority." *Journal of the History of Philosophy* 34 (1996): 409–24.
Augustine. *The City of God*. Translated by Henry Bettenson. Harmondsworth, England: Penguin, 1977.
Austen, Jane. *Mansfield Park*. Edited by Kathryn Sutherland. London: Penguin, 1996.
Baier, Kurt. *The Moral Point of View: A Rational Basis of Ethics*. Ithaca, NY: Cornell University Press, 1958.
Baron, Marcia W. *Kantian Ethics Almost without Apology*. Ithaca, NY: Cornell University Press, 1995.
———. "Kantian Ethics and Virtue Ethics." In *Three Methods of Ethics*, ed. Marcia W. Baron, Philip Pettit, and Michael Slote, 32–64. Malden, MA: Blackwell, 1997.
Basedow, Johann Bernhard. *Philanthropisches Archiv*, 1. Stück (Dessau) (1776).
Beck, Lewis White. *Early German Philosophy: Kant and His Predecessors*. Cambridge, MA: Harvard University Press, 1969; reprint, Bristol: Thoemmes, 1996.
———. "Extraterrestrial Intelligent Life." In *Extraterrestrials: Science and Human Intelligence*, ed. Edward Regis Jr., 3–18. Cambridge: Cambridge University Press, 1985.
———. "Kant on Education." In Beck, *Essays on Kant and Hume*, 188–204. New Haven, CT: Yale University Press, 1978.
Becker, Wolfgang. "Einleitung: Kants pragmatische Anthropologie." In Kant, *Anthropologie in pragmatischer Hinsicht*, ed. Wolfgang Becker. Stuttgart: Reclam, 1983.
Beiser, Frederick. "A Romantic Education: The Concept of *Bildung* in Early German Romanticism." In *Philosophers on Education*, ed. Amélie Oksenberg Rorty, 284–99. London: Routledge, 1998.
———. "Romanticism." In *A Companion to the Philosophy of Education*, ed. Randall Curren, 130–42. Malden, MA: Blackwell, 2003.
———. *Schiller as Philosopher: A Re-Examination*. Oxford: Clarendon, 2005.
Bekoff, Marc, and Jessica Pierce. *Wild Justice: The Moral Lives of Animals*. Chicago: University of Chicago Press, 2009.
Bernstein, Richard J. *The Abuse of Evil: The Corruption of Politics and Religion since 9/11*. Cambridge: Polity, 2005.
———. *Radical Evil: A Philosophical Interrogation*. Cambridge: Polity, 2002.
Bird, Graham, ed. *A Companion to Kant*. Oxford: Blackwell, 2006.
Bledsoe, Robert. "Harnessing Autonomous Art: Enlightenment and Aesthetics Education in Johann Adam Bergk's *Die Kunst, Bücher zu Lesen*." *German Life and Letters* 53 (2000): 470–86.
Blum, Lawrence A. *Friendship, Altruism and Morality*. London: Routledge & Kegan Paul, 1980.
Borges, Maria. "What Can Kant Teach Us about Emotions?" *Journal of Philosophy* 101 (2004): 140–58.
Bowen, Margarita. *Empiricism and Geographical Thought: From Francis Bacon to Alexander von Humboldt*. Cambridge: Cambridge University Press, 1981.
Brandt, Reinhard. "Ausgewählte Probleme der Kantischen Anthropologie." In *Der ganze Mensch: Anthropologie und Literatur im 18. Jahrhundert*, ed. Hans-Jürgen Schings, 14–32. Stuttgart: Metzler, 1994.
———. "Einleitung." In Kant, *Vorlesungen über Anthropologie*, ed. Reinhard Brandt and Werner Stark, v–liv. Berlin: de Gruyter, 1997 (Academy vol. 25).
———. "The Guiding Idea of Kant's Anthropology and the Vocation of the Human Being." In *Essays on Kant's Anthropology*, ed. Brian Jacobs and Patrick Kain, 85–104. Cambridge: Cambridge University Press, 2003.

———. *Kommentar zu Kants Anthropologie in pragmatischer Hinsicht*. Hamburg: Felix Meiner, 1999.
Brooks, Rodney. *Flesh and Machines: How Robots Will Change Us*. New York: Vintage, 2002.
Buffon, Georges Louis Leclerc de. *A Natural History, General and Particular* (1748–1804). Selection reprinted in *Race and the Enlightenment*, ed. Emmanuel Chukwudi Eze, 15–28. Oxford: Blackwell, 1997.
Burke, Edmund. *A Philosophical Inquiry into the Origin of Our Ideas of the Sublime and Beautiful*. London: printed for R. and J. Dodsley, 1757.
Butler, Marilyn. *Jane Austen and the War of Ideas*. Oxford: Clarendon, 1975.
Cahn, Steven M. *From Student to Scholar: A Candid Guide to Becoming a Professor*. New York: Columbia University Press, 2008.
———. *Saints and Scamps: Ethics in Academia*. Totowa, NJ: Rowman & Littlefield, 1986.
Cahn, Steven M., ed. *Philosophy of Education: The Essential Texts*. New York: Routledge, 2009.
Card, Claudia. *The Atrocity Paradigm*. New York: Oxford University Press, 2002.
Caro Baroja, Julio. *El Mito del Caractér Nacional: Meditaciones a Contrapelo*. Madrid: Seminarios y Editiciones, 1970.
Cassirer, Ernst. *The Individual and the Cosmos in Renaissance Philosophy*. Translated by Mario Domandi. New York: Harper & Row, 1964.
Catchpole, C. K., and P. J. B. Slater. *Bird Song: Biological Themes and Variations*. 2nd ed. Cambridge: Cambridge University Press, 2008.
Cohen, Alix. *Kant and the Human Sciences: Biology, Anthropology and History*. Hampshire, England: Palgrave Macmillan, 2009.
———. "Kant's Critique of the Human Sciences." Ph.D. diss., Cambridge University, 2005.
———. "Physiological vs. Pragmatic Anthropology: A Response to Schleiermacher's Objection to Kant's Anthropology." In *Recht und Frieden: Akten des X. Internationalen Kant-Kongresses*, ed. Valério Rohden, vol. 5, 3–14. Berlin: de Gruyter, 2008.
Clark, William. "The Death of Metaphysics in Enlightened Prussia." In *The Sciences in Enlightened Europe*, ed. William Clark, Jan Golinski, and Simon Schaffer, 423–73. Chicago: University of Chicago Press, 1999.
Condorcet, Marie Jean Antoine Nicolas Caritat, Marquis de. *The Nature and Purpose of Public Instruction* (1791). In Condorcet, *Selected Writings*, ed. Keith Michael Baker. Indianapolis, IN: Bobbs-Merrill, 1976.
Cummiskey, David. *Kantian Consequentialism*. New York: Oxford University Press, 1996.
Dancy, Jonathan. *Ethics without Principles*. Oxford: Clarendon, 2004.
Darwall, Stephen, ed. *Deontology*. Malden, MA: Blackwell, 2003.
Darwin, Charles. *The Descent of Man, and Selection in Relation to Sex* (1871). Princeton, NJ: Princeton University Press, 1982.
Davies, Martin L. *Identity or History? Marcus Herz and the End of the Enlightenment*. Detroit, MI: Wayne State University Press, 1995.
Denis, Lara. *Moral Self-Regard: Duties to Oneself in Kant's Moral Theory*. New York: Garland, 2001.
De Waal, Frans. *The Ape and the Sushi Master: Cultural Reflections of a Primatologist*. New York: Basic, 2001.
———. *Primates and Philosophers: How Morality Evolved*. Edited by Stephen Macedo and Josiah Ober. Princeton, NJ: Princeton University Press, 2006.
Dewey, John. *Democracy and Education: An Introduction to the Philosophy of Education* (1916). New York: Macmillan, 1961.

Dews, Peter. "Disenchantment and the Persistence of Evil: Habermas, Jonas, Badiou." In *Modernity and the Problem of Evil*, ed. Alan D. Schrift, 51–65. Bloomington: Indiana University Press, 2002.
Droit, Roger-Pol. "Kant et les fourmis du Congo." *Le Monde*, February 5, 1999, "Les Livres," vi.
Eberhard, Johann August. "Ueber das Kantische radicale Böse in der menschlichen Natur." *Philosophisches Archiv* 2.2 (1794): 34–47.
Elden, Stuart. "Reassessing Kant's Geography," *Journal of Historical Geography* 35 (2009): 3–25.
Elden, Stuart, and Eduardo Mendieta, eds. *Reading Kant's Geography*. Albany: State University of New York Press, 2011.
Emsley, Sarah. *Jane Austen's Philosophy of the Virtues*. New York: Palgrave Macmillan, 2005.
Engstrom, Stephen. "The Inner Freedom of Virtue." In *Kant's Metaphysics of Morals: Interpretative Essays*, ed. Mark Timmons, 289–315. Oxford: Clarendon, 2002.
Erdmann, Benno. *Reflexionen Kants zur Anthropologie*. Leipzig: Fues, 1882.
Eze, Emmanuel Chukwudi. "The Color of Reason: The Idea of 'Race' in Kant's Anthropology." In *Postcolonial African Philosophy: A Critical Reader*, ed. Emmanuel Chukwudi Eze, 103–40. Cambridge: Blackwell, 1997.
Eze, Emmanuel Chukwudi, ed. *Race and the Enlightenment: A Reader*. Cambridge: Blackwell, 1997.
Fink, Hans. "Three Sorts of Naturalism." *European Journal of Philosophy* 14 (2006): 202–21.
Foot, Philippa. *Virtues and Vices and Other Essays in Moral Philosophy*. Berkeley: University of California Press, 1978.
Foucault, Michel. *Anthropologie d'un point de vue pragmatique: Introduction à l'Anthropologie*. Paris: Vrin, 2008.
———. *Introduction to Kant's Anthropology*. Edited by Roberto Nigro. Los Angeles, CA: Semiotext(e), 2009.
———. *Les Mots et les choses: Une archéologie des sciences humaines*. Paris: Gallimard, 1966.
———. *The Order of Things: An Archaeology of the Human Sciences*. Translated by Alan Sheridan. New York: Vintage, 1973.
Frankena, William K. *Three Historical Philosophies of Education: Aristotle, Kant, Dewey*. Glenview, IL: Scott, Foresman, 1965.
Frierson, Patrick R. *Freedom and Anthropology in Kant's Moral Philosophy*. New York: Cambridge University Press, 2003.
Garve, Christian. *Einige Betrachtungen über die allgemeinen Grundsätze der Sittenlehre*. Breslau: W. G. Korn, 1798.
———. Review of *Critik der reinen Vernunft*, by Immanuel Kant. *Zugabe zu den Göttingischen Anzeigen von gelehrten Sachen* 1 (1782): 40–48.
———. *Über Gesellschaft und Einsamkeit*. 2 vols. Breslau: W. G. Korn, 1797–1800.
———. *Über die Verbindung der Moral mit der Politik*. Breslau: W. G. Korn, 1788.
———. *Versuche über verschiedene Gegenstände aus der Moral, Literatur und dem gesellschaftlichen Leben*. 5 vols. Breslau: W. G. Korn, 1792.
———. *Übersicht der vornehmsten Principien der Sittenlehre, von dem Zeitalter des Aristoteles an bis auf unsre Zeiten*. Breslau: W. G. Korn, 1798.
Gay, Peter. "The Enlightenment as Medicine and as Cure." In *The Age of Enlightenment: Studies Presented to Theodore Besterman*, ed. W. H. Barber et al., 375–86. Edinburgh: Oliver and Boyd, 1967.
Geertz, Clifford. *Available Light: Anthropological Reflections on Philosophical Topics*. Princeton, NJ: Princeton University Press, 2000.
Goethe, Johann Wolfgang. *Gedenkausgabe der Werke, Briefe und Gespräche*. 27 vols. Edited by Ernst Beutler. Zurich: Artemis, 1950–1964.

Goldberg, Samuel Louis. *Agents and Lives: Moral Thinking in Literature*. Cambridge: Cambridge University Press, 1993.

Goldthwait, John T. "Translator's Introduction." In Kant, *Observations on the Feeling of the Beautiful and Sublime*. Berkeley: University of California Press, 1960.

Gould, Stephen Jay. "The Human Difference." *New York Times*, July 2, 1999, A17.

Grant, Ruth W., ed. *Naming Evil, Judging Evil*. Chicago: University of Chicago Press, 2006.

Gregor, Mary J. *Laws of Freedom: A Study of Kant's Method of Applying the Categorical Imperative in the "Metaphysik der Sitten."* Oxford: Basil Blackwell, 1963.

———. "Translator's Introduction." In Kant, *Anthropology from a Pragmatic Point of View*, ix–xxv. Translated by Mary J. Gregor. The Hague: Martinus Nijhoff, 1974.

Grenberg, Jeanine. "Courageous Humility in Jane Austen's *Mansfield Park*." *Social Theory and Practice* 33 (2007): 645–66.

———. *Kant and the Ethics of Humility: A Story of Dependence, Corruption, and Virtue*. Cambridge: Cambridge University Press, 2005.

Guyer, Paul. "Editorial Notes to *Observations on the Feeling of the Beautiful and Sublime*." In Kant, *Anthropology, History, and Education*, ed. Günter Zöller and Robert B. Louden, 490–96. Cambridge: Cambridge University Press, 2007.

———. "Kant's Morality of Law and Morality of Freedom." In Guyer, *Kant on Freedom, Law, and Happiness*, 129–71. New York: Cambridge University Press, 2000.

———. "Translator's Introduction to *Observations on the Feeling of the Beautiful and Sublime*." In Kant, *Anthropology, History, and Education*, ed. Günter Zöller and Robert B. Louden, 18–22. Cambridge: Cambridge University Press, 2007.

Hamann, Johann Georg. *Briefwechsel*. Edited by Arthur Henkel. Vol. 5. Frankfurt: Insel, 1965.

Haraway, Donna J. *When Species Meet*. Minneapolis: University of Minnesota Press, 2008.

Harbison, Warren G. "The Good Will." *Kant-Studien* 71 (1980): 47–59.

Hare, R. M. "Could Kant Have Been a Utilitarian?" In *Kant and Critique: New Essays in Honor of W. H. Werkmeister*, ed. R. M. Dancy, 91–113. Boston: Dordrecht, 1993.

Hartshorne, Richard. *The Nature of Geography*. Lancaster, PA: Association of American Geographers, 1939; reprint, 1961, with corrections by the author.

Harvey, David. "Cosmopolitanism and the Banality of Geographical Evils." *Public Culture* 12.2 (2000): 529–64.

Hauerwas, Stanley. "Seeing Darkness, Hearing Silence." In *Naming Evil, Judging Evil*, ed. Ruth W. Grant, 35–52. Chicago: University of Chicago Press, 2006.

Hegel, Georg Wilhelm Friedrich. *Elements of the Philosophy of Right*. Edited by Allen W. Wood. Translated by H. B. Nisbet. New York: Cambridge University Press, 1991.

———. *Vorlesungen über die Philosophie der Weltgeschichte*. Vol. 1: *Die Vernunft in der Geschichte*. Edited by Johannes Hoffmeister. Hamburg: Felix Meiner, 1955.

Heidegger, Martin. *Kant and the Problem of Metaphysics*. Translated by James Churchill. Bloomington: Indiana University Press, 1962.

Herder, Johann Gottfried. *Auch eine Philosophie der Geschichte zur Bildung der Menschheit*. Edited by Hans Dietrich Irmscher. Stuttgart: Reclam, 1990.

Herman, Barbara. *Moral Literacy*. Cambridge, MA: Harvard University Press, 2007.

———. *The Practice of Moral Judgment*. Cambridge, MA: Harvard University Press, 1993.

Herz, Marcus. "D. Ernst Platners, der Arzeneykunst Professors in Leipzig," *Anthropologie für Ärzte und Weltweise*. Erster Theil. Leipzig, in der Dyckischen Buchhandlung, 1772, 8. 292 Seiten. *Allgemeine Deutsche Bibliothek* 20 (1773): 25–51.

Hill, Thomas E., Jr. *Autonomy and Self-Respect*. New York: Cambridge University Press, 1991.

Hill, Thomas E., Jr., and Bernard Boxill. "Kant and Race." In *Race and Racism*, ed. Bernard Boxill, 448–71. Oxford: Oxford University Press, 2001.

Hinman, Lawrence M. "On the Purity of Our Motives: A Critique of Kant's Account of the Emotions and Acting for the Sake of Duty." *Monist* 66 (1983): 251–66.

Hinske, Norbert. "Kants Idee der Anthropologie." In *Der Frage nach dem Menschen*, ed. Heinrich Rombach, 410–27. Freiburg: Karl Alber, 1966.

Höffe, Otfried. "Kants kategorischer Imperative als Kriterium des Sittlichen." In *Ethik und Politik*, ed. Otfried Höffe, 84–119. Frankfurt: Suhrkamp, 1979.

Homer. *The Odyssey*. Translated by Richmond Lattimore. New York: Harper & Row, 1965.

Hooker, Brad, and Margaret Olivia Little, eds. *Moral Particularism*. Oxford: Clarendon, 2000.

Humboldt, Wilhelm von. *The Limits of State Action*. Edited by J. W. Burrow. New York: Cambridge University Press, 1969; reprint, Indianapolis, IN: Liberty Fund, 1993.

Hume, David. *Enquiries Concerning Human Understanding and Concerning the Principles of Morals*. 3rd ed. Edited by L. A. Selby-Bigge. Oxford: Clarendon, 2005.

———. "My Own Life." In Hume, *Essays Moral, Political, and Literary*, ed. Eugene F. Miller, xxxi–xli. Indianapolis, IN: Liberty Fund, 1985.

———. "Of National Characters." In Hume, *Essays Moral, Political, and Literary*, ed. Eugene F. Miller, 197–215. Indianapolis, IN: Liberty Fund, 1985.

———. *A Treatise of Human Nature*. Edited by L. A. Selby-Bigge. 2nd ed. Oxford: Clarendon, 1978.

Hursthouse, Rosalind. *On Virtue Ethics*. New York: Oxford University Press, 1999.

———. "Virtue Ethics and the Emotions." In *Virtue Ethics: A Critical Reader*, ed. Daniel Statman, 99–117. Edinburgh: Edinburgh University Press, 1997.

Hutcheson, Francis. *Philosophical Writings*. Edited by R. S. Downie. London: Dent, 1994.

Jachmann, Reinhold Bernhard. "Immanuel Kant geschildert in Briefen an einen Freund" (1804). In *Immanuel Kant: Ein Lebensbild nach Darstellungen der Zeitgenossen Jachmann, Borowski, Waisianski*, ed. Alfons Hoffmann. Halle: Hugo Peter, 1902.

Jacobs, Brian. "Kantian Character and the Problem of a Science of Humanity." In *Essays on Kant's Anthropology*, ed. Brian Jacobs and Patrick Kain, 105–34. Cambridge: Cambridge University Press, 2003.

Jefferson, Thomas. *Notes on the State of Virginia*. In Jefferson, *Writings*, ed. Merrill D. Peterson 123–325. New York: Library of America, 1984.

Johnston, R. J., Derek Gregory, and David M. Smith, eds. *The Dictionary of Human Geography*. 3rd ed. Oxford: Blackwell, 1994.

Johnson, Robert N. "Kant's Conception of Virtue." *Jahrbuch für Recht und Ethik* 5 (1997): 365–87.

Kagan, Shelley. "Kantianism for Consequentialists." In Kant, *Groundwork for the Metaphysics of Morals*, ed. and trans. Allen W. Wood, 111–56. New Haven, CT: Yale University Press, 2002.

Kain, Patrick. "Duties Regarding Animals." In *Kant's "Metaphysics of Morals": A Critical Guide*, ed. Lara Denis. Cambridge: Cambridge University Press, 2010.

———. "Prudential Reason in Kant's Anthropology. In *Essays on Kant's Anthropology*, ed. Brian Jacobs and Patrick Kain, 230–65. Cambridge: Cambridge University Press, 2003.

Kames, Lord (Henry Home). *Sketches of the History of Man*. 3rd ed. (1788). Edited by James A. Harris. Indianapolis, IN: Liberty Fund, 2007.

Kant, Immanuel. *Anthropologie du point de vue pragmatique*. Translated by Michel Foucault. Paris: Vrin, 1964.

———. *Anthropology from a Pragmatic Point of View*. Translated by Mary J. Gregor. The Hague: Martinus Nijhoff, 1974.

———. *Anthropology from a Pragmatic Point of View*. Edited and translated by Robert B. Louden. Cambridge: Cambridge University Press, 2006.

———. *Anthropology, History, and Education*. Edited by Günter Zöller and Robert B. Louden. Cambridge: Cambridge University Press, 2007.

———. *Bemerkungen in den "Beobachtungen über das Gefühl des Schönen und Erhabenen."* Edited by Marie Rischmüller. Hamburg: Felix Meiner, 1991.

———. "Bestimmung des Begriffs einer Menschenrace." *Berlinische Monatsschrift* 11 (1785): 390–417.

———. *The Cambridge Edition of the Works of Immanuel Kant*. 16 vols. Edited by Paul Guyer and Allen W. Wood. Cambridge: Cambridge University Press, 1992–.

———. *The Doctrine of Virtue*. Translated by Mary J. Gregor. Philadelphia: University of Pennsylvania Press, 1964.

———. *The Educational Theory of Immanuel Kant*. Translated and edited by Edward Franklin Buchner. Philadelphia: Lippincott, 1904; reprint, New York: AMS, 1971.

———. *Groundwork for the Metaphysics of Morals*. Edited and translated by Allen W. Wood. New Haven, CT: Yale University Press, 2002.

———. *Groundwork for the Metaphysics of Morals*. Translated by Arnulf Zweig. Edited by Thomas E. Hill Jr. and Arnulf Zweig. New York: Oxford University Press, 2002.

———. *Immanuel Kant über Pädagogik*. Edited by Friedrich Theodor Rink. Königsberg: Friedrich Nicolovius, 1803.

———. *Immanuel Kants Anweisung zur Menschen und Weltkenntnis: Nach dessen Vorlesungen im Winterhalbjahre von 1790–1791*. Edited by Friedrich Christian Starke. Leipzig: Expedition des europäischen Aufsehers, 1831; reprint, New York: Georg Olms, 1976.

———. *Immanuel Kants physische Geographie*. Edited by Friedrich Theodor Rink. Königsberg: Göbbels and Unzer, 1802.

———. *Immanuel Kants sämmtliche Werke*. Edited by Karl Rosenkranz and Friedrich Wilhelm Schubert. Leipzig: Leopold Voss, 1838–1839.

———. *Kant on Education* (*Ueber Pädagogik*). Translated by Annette Churton. London: Kegan Paul, Trench, Trubner, 1899; reprint, Bristol: Thoemmes, 1992.

———. *Kants gesammelte Schriften*. Edited by the Royal Prussian (later German, then Berlin-Brandenburg) Academy of Sciences. 29 vols. Berlin: Georg Reimer (later de Gruyter), 1900–.

———. *Lectures on Anthropology*. Edited by Allen W. Wood and Robert B. Louden. Cambridge: Cambridge University Press, forthcoming.

———. *The Metaphysical Principles of Virtue*. Translated by James Ellington. Indianapolis, IN: Bobbs-Merrill, 1964.

———. *Natural Science*. Edited by Eric Watkins. Cambridge: Cambridge University Press, forthcoming.

———. *Notes and Fragments*. Edited by Paul Guyer. Cambridge: Cambridge University Press, 2005.

———. *Physische Geographie*. Edited by Paul Gedan. 2nd ed. Leipzig: Verlag der Dürr'schen Buchhandlung, 1905.

———. *Religion within the Limits of Reason Alone*. Translated by Theodore M. Grene and Hoyt H. Hudson. 2nd ed. New York: Harper & Row, 1960.

———. *Vorlesungen über Anthropologie*. Edited by Reinhard Brandt and Werner Stark. Berlin: de Gruyter, 1997 (Academy vol. 25).

———. *Eine Vorlesung Kants über Ethik*. Edited by Paul Menzer. Berlin: Pan Verlag Rolf Heise, 1924.

———. *Vorlesung zur Moralphilosophie*. Edited by Werner Stark. Berlin: de Gruyter, 2004.

Kaulbach, Friedrich. "Welchen Nutzen gibt Kant der Geschichtsphilosophie?" *Kant-Studien* 66 (1975): 65–84.

———. "Weltorientierung, Weltkenntnis und pragmatische Vernunft bei Kant." In *Kritik und Metaphysik Studien: Heinz Heimsoeth zum achtzigsten Geburtstag*, ed. Friedrich Kaulbach and Joachim Ritter, 60–75. Berlin: de Gruyter, 1966.

Kim, Soo Bae. *Die Entstehung der Kantischen Anthropologie und ihre Beziehung zur empirischen Psychologie der Wolffschen Schule*. Frankfurt: Lang, 1994.

Kitcher, Patricia. "Kant." In *The Blackwell Guide to Modern Philosophers: From Descartes to Nietzsche*, ed. Steven M. Emmanuel, 223–58. Malden, MA: Blackwell, 2001.

Kleingeld, Pauline. "Kant's Second Thoughts on Race." *Philosophical Quarterly* 57 (2007): 573–92.

———. "Kant's Theory of Peace." In *The Cambridge Companion to Kant and Modern Philosophy*, ed. Paul Guyer, 477–504. Cambridge: Cambridge University Press, 2006.

Klemme, Heiner F., and Manfred Kuehn, eds. *Immanuel Kant II: Practical Philosophy*. Aldershot, England: Ashgate, 1999.

Knox-Shaw, Peter. "Philosophy." In *Jane Austen in Context*, ed. Janet Todd, 346–56. Cambridge: Cambridge University Press, 2005.

Korsgaard, Christine M. *Creating the Kingdom of Ends*. New York: Cambridge University Press, 1996.

———. "From Duty and for the Sake of the Noble: Kant and Aristotle on Morally Good Action." In *Aristotle, Kant, and the Stoics: Rethinking Happiness and Duty*, ed. Stephen Engstrom and Jennifer Whiting, 203–36. New York: Cambridge University Press, 1996.

———. "Morality and the Distinctiveness of Human Action." In *Primates and Philosophers: How Morality Evolved*, ed. Stephen Macedo and Josiah Ober, 98–119. Princeton, NJ: Princeton University Press, 2006.

Kosch, Michelle. *Freedom and Reason in Kant, Schelling, and Kierkegaard*. Oxford: Clarendon, 2003.

Kra, Pauline. "The Concept of National Character in 18th Century France." *Cromohs* 7 (2002): 1–6.

Kuehn, Manfred. "Einleitung." In Kant, *Vorlesung zur Moralphilosophie*, ed. Werner Stark, vii–xxxv. Berlin: de Gruyter, 2004.

———. *Kant: A Biography*. Cambridge: Cambridge University Press, 2001.

La Mettrie, Julien Offray de. *Man a Machine and Man a Plant*. Translated by Richard A. Watson and Maya Rybalka. Indianapolis, IN: Hackett, 1994.

Langton, Rae. *Kantian Humility: Our Ignorance of Things in Themselves*. Oxford: Clarendon, 1998.

Lara, María Pía, ed. *Rethinking Evil: Contemporary Perspectives*. Berkeley: University of California Press, 2001.

Larrimore, Mark. "Sublime Waste: Kant on the Destiny of the Races." *Canadian Journal of Philosophy*, suppl. 25 (1999): 99–125.

Linden, Mareta. *Untersuchungen zum Anthropologiebegriff des 18. Jahrhunderts*. Frankfurt: Lang, 1976.

Livingstone, David N., and Charles W. J. Withers, eds. *Geography and the Enlightenment*. Chicago: University of Chicago Press, 1999.

Locke, John. *An Essay Concerning Human Understanding*. Edited by Peter H. Nidditch. Oxford: Clarendon, 1975.

———. *Some Thoughts Concerning Education and Of the Conduct of the Understanding*. Edited by Ruth W. Grant and Nathan Tarcov. Indianapolis, IN: Hackett, 1996.

Louden, Robert B. "The Critique of the Morality System." In *Bernard Williams*, ed. Alan Thomas, 104–34. New York: Cambridge University Press, 2007.

———. "Examples in Ethics." In *Routledge Encyclopedia of Philosophy*, ed. Edward Craig, 3: 487–90. New York: Routledge, 1998.

———. "Go-Carts of Judgment: Exemplars in Kantian Moral Education." *Archiv für Geschichte der Philosophie* 74 (1992): 303–22.

———. *Kant's Impure Ethics: From Rational Beings to Human Beings*. New York: Oxford University Press, 2000.

———. *Morality and Moral Theory: A Reappraisal and Reaffirmation*. New York: Oxford University Press, 1992.

———. "On Some Vices of Virtue Ethics." *American Philosophical Quarterly* 21 (1984): 227–36.

———. "The Second Part of Morals: Kant's Moral Anthropology and Its Relationship to His Metaphysics of Morals." *Kant e-Prints* 1.2 (2002): 1–13; www.cle.unicamp.br/kant-e-prints.

———. "Translator's Introduction to *Essays Regarding the Philanthropinum*." In Kant, *Anthropology, History, and Education*, ed. Günter Zöller and Robert B. Louden, 98–99. Cambridge: Cambridge University Press, 2007.

———. "Translator's Introduction to *Lectures on Pedagogy*." In Kant, *Anthropology, History, and Education*, ed. Günter Zöller and Robert B. Louden, 434–36. Cambridge: Cambridge University Press, 2007.

———. "Virtue Ethics." In *Encyclopedia of Applied Ethics*, ed. Ruth Chadwick, 4: 491–98. San Diego, CA: Academic, 1998.

———. "Virtue Ethics and Anti-Theory." *Philosophia* 20 (1990): 93–114.

———. "'What Does Heaven Say?': Christian Wolff and Western Interpretations of Confucian Ethics." In *Confucius and the Analects*, ed. Bryan W. Van Norden, 73–93. New York: Oxford University Press, 2002.

———. *The World We Want: How and Why the Ideals of the Enlightenment Still Elude Us*. New York: Oxford University Press, 2007.

MacIntyre, Alasdair. *After Virtue: A Study in Moral Theory*. Notre Dame, IN: University of Notre Dame Press, 1981; 2nd ed., Notre Dame, IN: University of Notre Dame Press, 1984.

Makkreel, Rudolf A. "Kant on the Scientific Status of Psychology, Anthropology, and History." In *Kant and the Sciences*, ed. Eric Watkins, 185–203. New York: Oxford University Press, 2001.

Matuštík, Martin Beck. "Violence and Secularization, Evil and Redemption." In *Modernity and the Problem of Evil*, ed. Alan D. Schrift, 39–50. Bloomington: Indiana University Press, 2005.

May, J. A. *Kant's Concept of Geography and Its Relation to Recent Geographical Thought*. Toronto: University of Toronto Press, 1970.

McAleer, Sean. "Kant and Virtue Ethics." Ph.D. diss., Syracuse University, 2001.

McBride, William L. "Liquidating the 'Nearly Just Society': Radical Evil's Triumphant Return." In *Modernity and the Problem of Evil*, ed. Alan D. Schrift, 28–38. Bloomington: Indiana University Press, 2005.

McGrew, W. C. *The Cultured Chimpanzee: Reflections on Cultural Primatology*. Cambridge: Cambridge University Press, 2004.

McKean, Erin, ed. *The New Oxford American Dictionary*. 2nd ed. Oxford: Oxford University Press, 2005.

Mellin, Georg Samuel. *Enzyclopädisches Wörterbuch der kritischen Philosophie* (1797) reprint; Aalen: Scientia, 1970.

Mendelssohn, Moses. "Über die Frage: Was heißt aufklären?" *Berlinishe Monatsschrift* 4 (1784): 193–200; reprinted in *Was ist Aufklarung? Thesen und Definitionen*, ed. Ehrhard Bahr, 3–8. Stuttgart: Reclam, 1974.

Michalson, Gordon E., Jr. *Fallen Freedom: Kant on Radical Evil and Moral Regeneration*. Cambridge: Cambridge University Press, 1990.

Mill, John Stuart. *On Liberty*. Edited by Elizabeth Rapaport. Indianapolis, IN: Hackett, 1978.

Mills, Charles W. "Kant's *Untermenschen*." In *Race and Racism in Modern Philosophy*, ed. Andrew Valls, 169–93. Ithaca, NY: Cornell University Press, 2005.

Monk, Samuel H. *The Sublime: A Study of Critical Theories in XVIII-Century England*. New York: Modern Language Association of America, 1935.

Montesquieu, Charles-Louis de Secondat. *The Spirit of the Laws*. Translated by Thomas Nugent. New York: Hafner, 1949.

Muchnik, Pablo. *Kant's Theory of Evil: An Essay on the Dangers of Self-Love and the Aprioricity of History*. Lanham, MD: Lexington, 2009.

Müller, Max. "Basedow, Johann Bernhard." In *Allgemeine Deutsche Biographie*. 56 vols. Edited by the Historical Commission at the Bavarian Academy of Sciences, 2: 113–24. Leipzig: Duncker & Humblot, 1875–1912. http://de.wikisource.org/wiki/ADB:Basedow%2C_Johann_Bernhard.

Munzel, G. Felicitas. *Kant's Conception of Character: The "Critical" Link of Morality, Anthropology, and Reflective Judgment*. Chicago: University of Chicago Press, 1999.

Muthu, Sankar. *Enlightenment against Empire*. Princeton, NJ: Princeton University Press, 2003.

Neiman, Susan. *Evil in Modern Thought: An Alternative History of Philosophy*. Princeton, NJ: Princeton University Press, 2002.

———. *The Unity of Reason: Rereading Kant*. New York: Oxford University Press, 1994.

Niedermeyer, Michael. "Campe als Direktor des Dessauer Philanthropins." In *Visionäre Lebensklugheit: Joachim Heinrich Campe in seiner Zeit*, ed. Hanno Schmidt, 45–66. Wiesbaden: Harrassowitz, 1996.

Nietzsche, Friedrich. *Beyond Good and Evil: Prelude to a Philosophy of the Future*. Translated by Walter Kaufmann. New York: Vintage, 1966.

———. *On the Genealogy of Morality*. Translated by Maudmarie Clark and Alan J. Swensen. Indianapolis, IN: Hackett, 1998.

Nussbaum, Martha C. "Kant and Cosmopolitanism." In *Perpetual Peace: Essays on Kant's Cosmopolitan Ideal*, ed. James Bohman and Matthias Lutz-Bachmann, 25–57. Cambridge, MA: MIT Press, 1997.

———. "Kant und stoisches Weltbürgertum." In *Frieden durch Recht*, ed. Mattias Lutz-Bachmann and James Bohman, 45–75. Frankfurt: Suhrkamp, 1996.

———. *Upheavals of Thought: The Intelligence of Emotions*. New York: Cambridge University Press, 2001.

———. "Virtue Ethics: A Misleading Category?" *Journal of Ethics* 3 (1999): 163–201.

Nussbaum, Martha C., with Respondents. *For Love of Country: Debating the Limits of Patriotism*. Edited by Joshua Cohen. Boston: Beacon, 1996.

Oakley, Justin. "Varieties of Virtue Ethics." *Ratio* 9 (1996): 128–52.

O'Neill, Onora. "Consistency in Action." In *New Essays on Ethical Universalizability*, ed. Nelson Potter and Mark Timmons, 159–86. Dordrecht: Reidel, 1984.

———. *Constructions of Reason: Explorations of Kant's Practical Philosophy*. Cambridge: Cambridge University Press, 1989.

———. "Kant after Virtue." *Inquiry* 26 (1984): 387–405.

———. "Kant's Virtues." In *How Should One Live? Essays on the Virtues*, ed. Roger Crisp, 77–97. Oxford: Oxford University Press, 1996.
Oz-Salberger, Fania. "Garve, Christian." In *Encyclopedia of Enlightenment*, ed. Alan Charles Kors, 2: 101–2. Oxford: Oxford University Press, 2003.
Painter, F. V. N. *A History of Education*. Rev. ed. New York: Appleton, 1906.
Paton, H. J. *The Categorical Imperative: A Study in Kant's Moral Philosophy*. London: Hutchinson, 1947; reprint, Philadelphia: University of Pennsylvania Press, 1971.
Paton, Margaret. "A Reconsideration of Kant's Treatment of Duties to Oneself." *Philosophical Quarterly* 40 (1990): 222–33.
Peabody, Dean. *National Characteristics*. Cambridge: Cambridge University Press, 1985.
Pico della Mirandola, Giovanni. *Oration on the Dignity of Man*. Translated by A. Robert Caponigri. Washington, DC: Regnery Gateway, 1956.
Platner, Ernst. *Anthropologie für Ärzte und Weltweise*. Leipzig: Dyck, 1772; reprint, Hildesheim: Olms, 2000.
Potter, Nelson. "Duties to Oneself, Motivational Internalism, and Self-Deception in Kant's Ethics." In *Kant's Metaphysics of Morals: Interpretative Essays*, ed. Mark Timmons, 371–89. Oxford: Clarendon, 2002.
Putnam, Hilary. *Ethics without Ontology*. Cambridge, MA: Harvard University Press, 2004.
Quick, Robert Herbert. *Essays on Educational Reformers*. New York: Appleton, 1896.
Raumer, Karl von. *Geschichte der Pädagogik*. 4 vols. Stuttgart: Samuel Gottlieb Liesching, 1843.
Rawls, John. *Lectures on the History of Moral Philosophy*. Edited by Barbara Herman. Cambridge, MA: Harvard University Press, 2000.
———. *A Theory of Justice*. Cambridge, MA: Harvard University Press, 1971.
Reath, Andrews. *Agency and Autonomy in Kant's Moral Theory*. Oxford: Clarendon, 2006.
———. "Self-Legislation and Duties to Oneself." In *Kant's Metaphysics of Morals: Interpretative Essays*, ed. Mark Timmons, 349–70. Oxford: Clarendon, 2002.
Reath, Andrews, and Jens Timmermann, eds. *Kant's Critique of Practical Reason: A Critical Guide*. Cambridge: Cambridge University Press, 2010.
Richards, Paul. "Kant's Geography and Mental Maps." *Transactions of the Institute of British Geographers* 61 (1974): 1–16.
Rink, Friedrich Theodor. *Ansichten aus Immanuel Kants Leben*. Königsberg: Göbbels and Unzer, 1805.
Rink, Friedrich Theodor, ed. *Sammlung einiger bisher unbekannt gebliebener kleiner Schriften von Immanuel Kant*. Königsberg: Friedrich Nicolovius, 1800.
———. *Mancherley zur Geschichte der metacritischen Invasion: Nebst einem Fragment einer ältern Metacritik von Johann George Hamman, gennant der Magus im Norden; und einigen Aufsätzen, die Kantische Philosophie betreffend*. Königsberg: Friedrich Nicolovius, 1800.
Rippe, Klaus Peter, and Peter Schaber, eds. *Tugendethik*. Stuttgart: Reclam, 1998.
Rorty, Richard. "Keeping Philosophy Pure: An Essay on Wittgenstein." In Rorty, *Consequences of Pragmatism*, 19–36. Minnesota: University of Minnesota Press, 1982.
Rosen, Allen D. *Kant's Theory of Justice*. Ithaca, NY: Cornell University Press, 1993.
Rotenstreich, Nathan. "Races and Peoples." In Rotenstreich, *Practice and Realization: Studies in Kant's Moral Philosophy*, 100–110. The Hague: Martinus Nijhoff, 1979.
———. "Volksgeist." In *Dictionary of the History of Ideas*, ed. Philip P. Wiener, 4: 490–96. New York: Scribner's, 1968.
Rousseau, Jean-Jacques. *The Basic Writings of Jean-Jacques Rousseau*. Translated by Donald Cress. Indianapolis, IN: Hackett, 1987.

———. *Émile*. Translated by Barbara Foxley. London: Dent, 1911; reprint, New York: Dutton, 1974.
———. *Rousseau on International Relations*. Edited by Stanley Hoffmann and David P. Fidler. Oxford: Clarendon, 1991.
Ruderman, Anne Crippen. *The Pleasures of Virtue: Political Thought in the Novels of Jane Austen*. Lanham, MD: Rowman & Littlefield, 1995.
Ryle, Gilbert. "Jane Austen and the Moralists." In *Critical Essays on Jane Austen*, ed. B. C. Southam, 106–22. New York: Barnes and Noble, 1969.
Sartre, Jean-Paul. "Existentialism Is a Humanism." In *Existentialism from Dostoevsky to Sartre*, ed. Walter Kaufmann, 287–311.Cleveland, OH: Meridian, 1956.
Sassen, Birgitte, ed. *Kant's Early Critics: The Empiricist Critique of the Theoretical Philosophy*. Cambridge: Cambridge University Press, 2000.
Scheler, Max. *Die Stellung des Menschen im Kosmos*. Selection reprinted in *Philosophische Anthropologie*, ed. Hans Dierkes, 49–53. Stuttgart: Reclam, 1989.
Schelling, Friedrich Wilhelm Joseph von. *Of Human Freedom*. Translated by James Gutmann. Chicago: Open Court, 1936.
Schiller, Friedrich. *Sämtliche Werke*. Edited by Gerhard Fricke and Herbert G. Göpfert. Munich: Carl Hanser, 1965.
Schings, Han-Jürgen. "Der philosophische Arzt: Anthropologie, Melancholie und Literatur im 18. Jahrhundert." In Schings, *Melancholie und Aufklärung*, 11–40. Stuttgart: Metzler, 2001.
Schleiermacher, Friedrich. "Review of Kant's *Anthropology from a Pragmatic Point of View*". In *Schleiermacher on Workings of the Knowing Mind: New Translations, Resources, and Understandings*, ed. Ruth Drucilla Richardson, 15–19. Lewiston, NY: Mellen, 1998.
Schmid, Carl Christian Erhard. *Wörterbuch zum leichtern Gebrauch der kantischen Schriften*. Jena: Cröckerschen Buchhandlung, 4th ed.1798; reprint, Darmstadt: Wissenschaftliche Buchgesellschaft, 1976.
Schneewind, Jerome B. "The Misfortunes of Virtue." *Ethics* 101 (1990): 42–63.
Schopenhauer, Arthur. *On the Basis of Morality*. Translated by E. F. J. Payne. Indianapolis, IN: Bobbs-Merrill, 1965.
Schrift, Alan D., ed. *Modernity and the Problem of Evil*. Bloomington: Indiana University Press, 2005.
Shell, Susan Meld. *The Embodiment of Reason: Kant on Spirit, Generation, and Community*. Chicago: University of Chicago Press, 1996.
———. "Kant as Propagator: Reflections on *Observations on the Feeling of the Beautiful and the Sublime*." *Eighteenth-Century Studies* 35 (2002): 455–68.
Shell, Susan Meld, and Richard L. Velkley, eds. *Kant's "Observations" and "Remarks": A Critical Guide*. Cambridge: Cambridge University Press, 2012.
Sherman, Nancy. "Concrete Kantian Respect." In *Virtue and Vice*, ed. Ellen Frankel Paul, Fred D. Miller Jr., and Jeffrey Paul, 119–48. New York: Cambridge University Press, 1998.
———. "Kantian Virtue: Priggish or Passional?" In *Reclaiming the History of Ethics: Essays for John Rawls*, ed. Andrews Reath, Barbara Herman, and Christine M. Korsgaard, 270–96. New York: Cambridge University Press, 1997.
———. *Making a Necessity of Virtue: Aristotle and Kant on Virtue*. New York: Cambridge University Press, 1997.
Sidgwick, Henry. *The Methods of Ethics*. 7th ed. London: Macmillan, 1907; reprint, New York: Dover, 1966.
Silber, John R. "The Ethical Significance of Kant's *Religion*." In Kant, *Religion within the Limits of Reason Alone*, trans. Theodore M. Grene and Hoyt H. Hudson, lxxix–cxxxiv. New York: Harper & Row, 1960.

———. "Kant at Auschwitz." In *Proceedings of the Sixth International Kant Congress*, ed. Gerhard Funke and Thomas M. Seebohm, 177–211. Washington, DC: Center for Advanced Research in Phenomenology and University Press of America, 1991.
Singer, Marcus George. *Generalization in Ethics: An Essay in the Logic of Ethics, with the Rudiments of a System of Moral Philosophy*. New York: Knopf, 1961.
———. "On Duties to Oneself." *Ethics* 69 (1959): 202–5.
Slote, Michael. "Agent-Based Virtue Ethics." In *Virtue Ethics*, ed. Roger Crisp and Michael Slote, 239–62. New York: Oxford University Press, 1997.
Smith, Adam. *An Inquiry into the Nature and Causes of the Wealth of Nations*. 2 vols. Edited by R. H. Campbell and A. S. Skinner. Oxford: Clarendon, 1979.
Staiger, Emil, ed. *Der Briefwechsel zwischen Schiller und Goethe*. Frankfurt: Insel, 1977.
Stark, Werner. "Historical Notes and Interpretive Questions about Kant's Lectures on Anthropology." In *Essays on Kant's Anthropology*, ed. Brian Jacobs and Patrick Kain, 15–37. Cambridge: Cambridge University Press, 2003.
———. "Immanuel Kants physische Geographie—Eine Herausforderung?" http://staff-www.uni-marburg.de/∼stark/ws_lese4.htm.
———. "Kants Moralkolleg der 1770er Jahre: Die Relevanz der wiederentdeckten Nachschrift Kaehler." In *Aufklärung und Interpretation: Studien zu Kants Philosophie und ihrem Umkreis: Tagung aus Anlaß des 60. Geburtstags von Reinhard Brandt*, ed. Heiner F. Klemme, Bernd Ludwig, Michael Pauen, and Werner Stark, 73–103. Würzburg: Königshausen & Neumann, 1999.
Stohr, Karen E. "Virtue Ethics and Kant's Cold-Hearted Benefactor." *Journal of Value Inquiry* 36 (2002): 187–204.
Strawson, Galen. "The Impossibility of Moral Responsibility." *Philosophical Studies* 75 (1994): 5–24.
Sturm, Thomas. "Kant on Empirical Psychology: How Not to Investigate the Human Mind." In *Kant and the Sciences*, ed. Eric Watkins, 163–84. New York: Oxford University Press, 2001.
———. *Kant und die Wissenschaften vom Menschen*. Paderborn: Mentis, 2009.
Swanton, Christine. *Virtue Ethics: A Pluralistic View*. Oxford: Oxford University Press, 2003.
Tanner, Tony. *Jane Austen*. Cambridge, MA: Harvard University Press, 1986.
Terracciano, A., et al. "National Character Does Not Reflect Mean Personality Trait Levels in 49 Cultures." *Science* 310 (2005): 96–100.
Thorndike, Oliver. "Understanding Kant's Claim That 'Morality Cannot Be without Anthropology.'" In *Rethinking Kant*, ed. Pablo Muchnik, 1: 109–35. Newcastle upon Tyne, England: Cambridge Scholars, 2008.
Timmermann, Jens. *Kant's Groundwork of the Metaphysics of Morals: A Commentary*. Cambridge: Cambridge University Press, 2007.
Timmermann, Jens, ed. *Kant's Groundwork of the Metaphysics of Morals: A Critical Guide*. Cambridge: Cambridge University Press, 2009.
———. *Sittengesetz und Freiheit: Untersuchungen zu Immanuel Kants Theorie des freien Willens*. Berlin: de Gruyter, 2003.
Tomasello, Michael. *The Cultural Origins of Human Cognition*. Cambridge, MA: Harvard University Press, 1999.
Tomasello, Michael, C. Kruger, and H. H. Ratner. "Cultural Learning." *Behavioral and Brain Sciences* 16 (1993): 495–552.
Tonelli, Giorgio. "Basedow, Johann Bernhard." In *The Encyclopedia of Philosophy*, ed. Paul Edwards, 1: 251. New York: Macmillan, 1967.
Trilling, Lionel. *The Opposing Self: Nine Essays in Criticism*. New York: Viking, 1955.

Velkley, Richard L. *Freedom and the End of Reason: On the Moral Foundation of Kant's Critical Philosophy*. Chicago: University of Chicago Press, 1989.

Vollmer, Gottfried, ed. *Immanuel Kants physische Geographie*. 4 vols. Mainz and Hamburg: Gottfried Vollmer, 1801.

Vorländer, Karl. *Immanuel Kant: Der Mann und das Werk*. 3rd ed. Wiesbaden: Fourier, 2003.

Watson, Gary. "On the Primacy of Character." In *Identity, Character, and Morality: Essays in Moral Psychology*, ed. Owen Flanagan and Amélie Oksenberg Rorty, 449–69. Cambridge, MA: MIT Press, 1990.

Weber, Max. "Value-Judgments in Social Science." In *Max Weber: Selections in Translation*, ed. W. G. Runciman, 69–98. New York: Cambridge University Press, 1978.

Whiten, A., et al. "Cultures in Chimpanzees." *Nature* 399 (1999): 682–85.

Wick, Warner A. "Introduction: Kant's Moral Philosophy." In Kant, *Kant's Ethical Philosophy*, trans. James Ellington, xi–lxii. Indianapolis, IN: Hackett, 1983.

Wilde, Oscar. *The Portable Oscar Wilde*. Edited by Richard Arlington. New York: Viking, 1965.

Willey, Thomas E. "Kant and the German Theory of Education." *Studies on Voltaire and the Eighteenth Century* 167 (1977): 543–67.

Williams, Bernard. *Ethics and the Limits of Philosophy*. Cambridge, MA: Harvard University Press, 1985.

———. *Making Sense of Humanity and Other Philosophical Papers, 1982–1993*. New York: Cambridge University Press, 1995.

———. *Morality: An Introduction to Ethics*. New York: Harper & Row, 1972.

———. *Moral Luck: Philosophical Papers, 1973–1980*. Cambridge: Cambridge University Press, 1981.

Willich, A. F. M. *Elements of the Critical Philosophy*. London: Longman, 1798.

Wilson, E. O. *On Human Nature*. Cambridge, MA: Harvard University Press, 1978.

Wilson, Holly L. *Kant's Pragmatic Anthropology: Its Origin, Meaning, and Critical Significance*. Albany: State University of New York Press, 2006.

Withers, Charles W. J. "Geography." In *Encyclopedia of the Enlightenment*, ed. Alan Charles Kors, 2: 114–17. Oxford: Oxford University Press, 2003.

Wolff, Robert Paul. *The Autonomy of Reason*. New York: Harper & Row, 1973.

Wood, Allen W. *Kant*. Malden, MA: Blackwell, 2005.

———. "Kant and the Problem of Human Nature." In *Essays on Kant's Anthropology*, ed. Brian Jacobs and Patrick Kain, 38–59. Cambridge: Cambridge University Press, 2003.

———. *Kant's Ethical Thought*. Cambridge: Cambridge University Press, 1999.

———. *Kant's Moral Religion*. Ithaca, NY: Cornell University Press, 1970.

———. "Self-Love, Self-Benevolence, and Self-Conceit." In *Aristotle, Kant, and the Stoics: Rethinking Happiness and Duty*, ed. Stephen Engstrom and Jennifer Whiting, 141–61. New York: Cambridge University Press, 1996.

Zammito, John H. *Kant, Herder, and the Birth of Anthropology*. Chicago: University of Chicago Press, 2002.

INDEX

Adams, Robert Merrihew, 116
Adickes, Erich, 122, 132, 154
Affects and passions, 71
Allison, Henry, 114, 116
Ameriks, Karl, 13
Anderson-Gold, Sharon, 188
Anscombe, G. E. M., 23–24
Anthropology, and the question, "What is the human being?" xvii–xxviii
  development of Kant's views on, xvii
  empirical, 59, 76–77, 81, 86, 117–18
  empirical psychology and, 79, 124
  general versus local, xix, 68, 84–85
  theoretical versus practical, 53
  transcendental, 49, 59, 81, 118
  and the universality of evil, 115–19
  See also Moral anthropology, Pragmatic anthropology
Aquinas, St. Thomas, 26
Arendt, Hannah, 110–11, 115, 189nn13, 15, 16
Aristotle, xxv, 30–31, 41–42, 156
  on inclinations, 139
  on virtue, xxvii, 9, 13, 15, 20, 169n14
Arnoldt, Emil, 52, 126, 153
Augustine, St., 110
Austen, Jane, 39, 41–45, 174–75

Baier, Kurt, 17
Basedow, Johann Bernhard, 196–97n21
  and the Philanthropinum, 60, 74, 136, 142–44, 161–62
Becker, Wolfgang, 179n6
Beiser, Frederick, 196n14
Bernstein, Richard J., 108–09, 111–13, 116, 188, 191n44
Bestimmung, xviii, 76–77, 88–90, 138
Bird, Graham, 181
Bock, Friedrich Samuel, 136
Boleyn, Anne, 95
Borges, Maria, 178
Brandt, Reinhard, 51, 179n4, 184n30
Buchner, Edward Franklin, 137, 195n6, 196n12
Buffon, Georges-Louis Leclerc de, 80, 132
Burke, Edmund, 159
Butler, Marilyn, 41

Cahn, Steven M., 194
Campe, Joachim Heinrich, 143
Card, Claudia, 113, 190n27
Care, 138–39
  See also Education
Categorical imperative, 7, 63, 97, 112, 148–49
  Garve's criticism of, 186–87n9

Index

Character, the central concern of Kant's ethics, 24
   Moral education and, 73–75
   physical versus moral, 199n17
   See also National Character
Chimpanzees, xxii
Churton, Annette, 137
Civilization, xxii, 140–41
Cohen, Alix, 126, 181–82
Condorcet, Marie Jean Antoine Nicolas Caritat, marquis de, 196n13
Consequentialism, and Kantian ethics, 16
Corruption thesis, 32–34
   See also Grenberg, Jeanine; Radical evil
Courage, 12–13, 27–28, 39–41, 173
Crichton, Wilhelm, 143
Culture, xxii–xxiii, 75, 129–31, 140–41
Curtius, 95

Darwin, Charles, xxiv, 167n24
Dependency thesis, 32–34
   See also Grenberg, Jeanine; Radical evil
Descartes, René, xxi
de Waal, Frans, xxiv, 167nn14, 24
Dewey, John, 149
Dialectical illusion, 108–09
Discipline, 139–41
   See also Education
Duties to oneself, 11, 17–19, 36–37

Eberhard, Johann August, 116
Education, as a task of human reason, xxv
   and cosmopolitanism, 148, 161
   and morality, 94–96, 145–49
   negative, 139–40, 145
   positive, 140–41
   the need for experiments in, 143–44
   the need for naturalism in, 144–45
   the need for a revolution in, 142–43
   and the question, "What is the human being?" xvii
   three stages of, 138–41
   See also Pedagogy
Egoism, aesthetic, 55–56
   logical, 55
   moral, 56
   See also Moral anthropology: hindrances and helps

Elden, Stuart, 192
Engel, Johann Jakob, 133
Erdmann, Benno, 49
Examples, in pure moral philosophy, 91–94
   in the moral life of humans, 94–104, 185
Exemplars, moral, 34–37, 91–104, 185
Extraterrestrials, xix–xx, xxvii, 101, 180n15, 188n18
Eze, Emmanuel, 127–28

Fielding, Henry, 39
Foot, Philippa, 4, 12–13, 15
Formation, 140–41
   See also Culture, Education
Foucault, Michel, xix, 49, 166n6
Frederick II of Prussia (the Great), 95
Freedom, as a distinguishing characteristic of humans, xxii
   and cultural progress, xxiv
   growth of, 138
   and moral character, 141
   nature and, 145
   transcendental, 77, 109–10

Galileo, Galilei, 144
Garve, Christian, 186–87n9
Geertz, Clifford, 167n20
Goethe, Johann Wolfgang von, 143
Governance, as a task of human reason, xxv
Grace, 191n46
Gregor, Mary J., 54, 61–62, 168, 184n30
Grenberg, Jeanine, 26–28, 31–37, 39–42, 172–73, 177n34
Guyer, Paul, 151, 155

Habermas, Jürgen, 180n16
Hamann, Johann Georg, 137
Harbison, Warren G., 7
Hegel, Georg Wilhelm Friedrich, 31, 50, 65, 160
Heidegger, Martin, 67, 81
Herder, Johann Gottfried, 137, 157, 160–62
Herman, Barbara, 58
Herz, Marcus, 67, 78–79
History, and national character, 162–63
   Kant's philosophy of, xviii, 59, 119
   in the *Observations*, 160–61
   three stages of, 138–41

Höffe, Otfried, 7–8, 168–69
Human beings, and animals, xx–xxi
　and culture, xxii–xxiv
　in Kant's *Physical Geography* lectures,
　　124–35
　and morality, xxiv
　preservation, education, and governance
　　of, xxv
　technical, pragmatic, and moral
　　predispositions of, xxv–xxvi
　and the virtues, xxvii
　versus machines, xviii, xxi
Humboldt, Wilhelm von, 140
Hume, David, 26, 41–42, 145, 165n1
　and national character, 157, 160, 198n4
　and "Negroes," 134, 155, 200n30
Humility, as a virtue, 25–37
　Christian, 26, 28, 30
　false, 25, 40
　Kantian, 30, 39–41, 173
Hutcheson, Francis, 165n1

Jaspers, Karl, 111, 115
Jefferson, Thomas, 134
Jesus, as moral exemplar, 26, 30, 91, 96–97

Kant, Immanuel, and autonomy, 36, 74, 92,
　　102–03
　his commitment to free will, xix, xxii, 149
　on common human reason, 177n27
　on defining enlightenment, 91–92, 102
　and the divine command theory
　　of ethics, 91
　his doctrine of outer and inner sense,
　　127–28
　his doctrine of schematism, 97
　his experience as a tutor, 139
　and human exceptionalism, xx, xxvi, 90
　and the moralist's perspective, xxvii
　his *Observations* as a work in anthropology,
　　150–52
　his *Observations* as a work in geography,
　　152–55
　and the philosophy of hope, 98
　rudiments of his theory of human nature,
　　xix–xxvi
　and the question, "What is the human
　　being?" xvii–xix
　his writings on education, xvii
　his writings on the philosophy of history,
　　xviii
Kaulbach, Friedrich, 180–81n21
Kleingeld, Pauline, 134, 194n32
Klemme, Heiner F., 169–70
Kosch, Michelle, 117
Kuehn, Manfred, 155, 170

La Mettrie, Julien Offray de, 80
Langton, Rae, 26
Locke, John, 74, 175n1, 195n8, 196n13
Loparic, Zeljko, 178

MacIntyre, Alasdair, 3, 41–42, 50, 168
May, J. A., 126–28
McBride, William, 108
Mellin, Georg Samuel Albert,
　　52–54, 179n8
Mendelssohn, Moses, 58–59
Mendieta, Eduardo, 192
Michalson, Gordon E., Jr., 108, 116
Mill, John Stuart, 17, 26, 196n15
Mills, Charles, 133
Mohammed, 130
Montesquieu, Charles-Louis de Secondat, 132,
　　157, 160, 198n4
Moral anthropology, defining
　features of, 70–77
　and moral education, 73–75
　and moral *Weltkenntnis*, 72–73
　studies hindrances and helps to morality,
　　55–56, 70–72
　and the destiny of the human species,
　　58–61, 75–77
　See also Anthropology, Pragmatic
　　anthropology
Moral education, acroamatic, 146
　and ascetics, 147–48
　and casuistry, 148, 187n12, 197n26
　catechistic, 146–47
　dialogical, 146–47
　erotematic, 146–47
　and ethical didactics, 147–48
　goals of, 148–49
　methods of, 146–48
　should instill cosmopolitan
　　dispositions, 149
　and the grounding of character, 149
　See also Education

Morality, competing conceptions of, xxii, xxiv
    duties to oneself as foundation of, 11,
        17–19, 36–37
    human versus animal, xxiv
Moralization, 64, 141, 149
Muchnik, Pablo, 188
Müller, Max, 196–97n21
Muthu, Sankar, 134

National character, in Kant's geography
        lectures, 129–31, 197–98
    in the *Observations*, 150–63
    African, 129–30, 159
    Arabic, 130, 154, 159
    Brazilian, 129–30
    the causes of, 157
    of Ceylon, 129
    Chinese, 129–30, 159, 193n20
    Dutch, 159
    English, 151–52, 158
    French, 152, 158
    German, 151, 159
    Greek, 131, 161, 200n27
    Indian, 159
    Italian, 129, 131, 152, 158
    Japanese, 159
    Madagascan, 129–30
    Native American, 154, 159, 200n30
    the need for knowledge of, 156–57, 192
    Persian, 152, 159
    Roman, 161, 200n27
    Russian, 130
    Spanish, 151, 158
    via the beautiful and sublime, 158–63
    and what nature makes of humans, 153
Natorp, Paul, 137
Nietzsche, Friedrich, 22
Novels, Kant's opposition to the reading of,
        38, 71
    as sources of insight into human nature,
        38–39, 86, 174–75, 175n3, 180n19
Nussbaum, Martha, 60

O'Neill, Onora, 4, 7–9, 37, 168–69

Paton, H. J., 54, 61–62
Paul, St., 26, 30
Pedagogy, background of Kant's lectures on,
        136–37

Philanthropinum, 142–45, 148, 161–62
    See also Basedow, Johann Bernhard
Physical geography, Kant's lectures on,
        xvii–xviii, 79, 121–35
    compared to Kant's anthropology lectures,
        124–28
    cosmpolitan aim of, 124
    intentionally eclectic nature of, 122
    mathematical, moral, political,
        economic, and theological geographies,
        125, 129–30
    orientation aim of, 123–24
    as popular science, 122–23
    treatment of humans in, 124–35
    as useful and pragmatic, 123
    and *Weltkenntnis*, 123
Platner, Ernst, 67–68, 79–81, 117, 126
Politeness, 72
Pope, Alexander, 78, 166n1
Pragmatic anthropology, and a cosmopolitan
        conception of human nature, 83–90,
        118, 183
    as cosmological, 85–87
    different meanings of, 67–70, 81–83
    as empirical, 86–87
    and freedom, 81, 118
    and international law, 88–91
    as involving the use of others, 68, 82
    as normative, 87, 89–90, 118–19
    and political reform, 90–91
    pragmatic versus physiological, 67, 81,
        118, 126
    pragmatic versus scholastic, 67–68, 81
    as prudential, 68–69, 82–83
    and the philosophical physicians, 79–81
    and *Weltkenntnis*, 51, 56–58, 85, 152,
        180n20
Predispositions, xxi, 161
    cosmopolitical, 90
    to humanity, xxvi, 138–39
    to personality, xxvi
    and race, 200n30
    technical, pragmatic, and moral,
        xxvi–xxvi
Preservation, as a task of human
        reason, xxv
Price, Fanny, 39, 41
    and courageous humility, 42–43
    and Kantianism, 43–45, 174, 177n34

Pride, 26, 30
Race, competing accounts of Kant's views on, 133–35
 Kant's later views on, 134–35, 192
 in Kant's physical geography lectures, 131–35
 in the *Observations*, 155–56, 159, 197
 Kant's shift from climatological to biological accounts of, 132, 200n30
 physical versus moral accounts of, 133
 skin color and, 133
 versus national character, 156, 200n30
Radical evil, 24, 31–34, 60, 107–20, 189n16
 and anthropology, 115–19
 is both innate and freely chosen, 115–19, 191n35
 and human freedom, 109–10
 propensity to, xxvii, 168n29
 and the diabolical evil criticism, 113–15, 190n23
 and the explanatory impotence criticism, 108–10
 and the moral law, 112
 and the self-love criticism, 110–12, 175n10, 190n19
 three degrees of, 113–14
Rationality, human versus animal, xxi
 substantive versus instrumental, xxi
Rawls, John, 20–21
Reath, Andrews, 111–12
Republican regimes, 59, 72
Respect, 29–31
Richards, Paul, 193n8
Richardson, Samuel, 39
Rink, Friedrich Theodor, xvii–xviii, 136–37, 154, 175n2
Rousseau, Jean-Jacques, 72, 74, 80, 136, 196n13
 and negative education, 104, 140, 145
 his influence on Kant, 162, 195n9
Ryle, Gilbert, 41, 54

Sartre, Jean-Paul, xix, 156
Scheler, Max, 50, 67, 81
Schelling, Friedrich Wilhelm Joseph, 189n14
Schiller, Friedrich, 20, 40, 44, 150
Schleiermacher, Friedrich, 77
Schmid, Carl Christian Erhard, 53, 54
Schopenhauer, Arthur, 17

Schubert, Friedrich Wilhelm, 136
Self-conceit, 29, 31
Self-esteem, proper, 25–26
Seneca, 95
Shaftesbury, Anthony Ashley Cooper, 3rd Earl of, 41–42
Shell, Susan Meld, 197
Sidgwick, Henry, 17
Silber, John, 113
Singer, Marcus, 17
Smith, Adam, 75
Socrates, 43, 73, 91–92
Songbirds, xxiii
Stark, Werner, 130, 131, 171n8, 176n15
Stoicism, 20, 24, 28, 33
Sutherland, Kathryn, 41

Tanner, Tony, 41
Teleology, and living creatures, xviii
 in Kant's writings on education and history, 138, 145
Timmermann, Jens, 185
Tomasello, Michael, xxiii–xxiv
Trilling, Lionel, 41, 178n39
Typic, of pure practical judgment, 97

Unsociable sociability, xx, 75, 161

Velkley, Richard L., 197
Virtue, and emotion, 12–15, 19–22, 24, 44–45
 and habit, 9
 and human nature, xxvi–xxvii, 17, 23–24
 and inner freedom, 21, 23
 as moral strength, 22–24, 39–40
 as self-constraint, 19
 and the good will, 6–7
Virtue ethics, duties to oneself and, 11, 17–19, 36–37, 170
 maxims and, 7–9
 morally necessary ends and, 9–10
 the structure of, 4–6
 the elasticity of the concept of, 23
 See also Virtue
Vogt, Theodor, 137

Ward, Isabell, 181
Watson, Gary, 170n4
Weber, Max, 64, 77

Wick, Warner, 168, 170
Wilde, Oscar, 41
Williams, Bernard, 4, 17, 31–32, 50, 65
Willich, A. F. M., 53, 54
Wilson, E. O., xx–xxi, 166–67n13
Withers, Charles, 121

Wolff, Christian, 82
Wolff, Robert Paul, 6
Wolke, Christian Heinrich, 143
Wood, Allen W., xxi, 34, 180n17, 181n26

Zedlitz, Karl Abraham Freiherr von, 122

www.ingramcontent.com/pod-product-compliance
Ingram Content Group UK Ltd.
Pitfield, Milton Keynes, MK11 3LW, UK
UKHW041959230426
12048UKWH00008B/432